2004

Securing American Independence

Recent Titles in
Contributions to the Study of World History

Chinese Nationalism in Perspective: Historical and Recent Cases
C. X. George Wei and Xiaoyuan Liu, editors

By the Sword and the Cross: The Historical Revolution of the Catholic
World Monarchy in Spain and the New World, 1492–1825
Charles A. Truxillo

Passion, Politics, and Philosophie: Rediscovering J.-P. Brissot
Leonore Loft

Sanctions and Honorary Whites: Diplomatic Policies and Economic
Realities in Relations Between Japan and South Africa
Masako Osada

Personal Policy Making: Canada's Role in the Adoption of the
Palestine Partition Resolution
Eliezer Tauber

One King, One Law, Three Faiths: Religion and the Rise of Absolutism
in Seventeenth-Century Metz
Patricia Behre Miskimin

South Sea Maidens: Western Fantasy and Sexual Politics in the South
Pacific
Michael Sturma

A History of the French Anarchist Movement, 1917–1945
David Berry

Security and Progress: Lord Salisbury at the India Office
Paul R. Brumpton

Exploring Nationalisms of China: Themes and Conflicts
C. X. George Wei and Xiaoyuan Liu, editors

Tolerance, Suspicion, and Hostility: Changing U.S. Attitudes toward
the Japanese Communist Movement, 1944–1947
Henry Oinas-Kukkonen

Churchill's Guests: Britain and the Belgian Exiles during World War II
Robert W. Allen

Securing American Independence

John Jay and the French Alliance

Frank W. Brecher

Contributions to the Study of World History, Number 105

Westport, Connecticut
London

Library of Congress Cataloging-in-Publication Data

Brecher, Frank W.
    Securing American independence : John Jay and the French alliance / Frank W.
Brecher.
      p. cm.—(Contributions to the study of world history, ISSN 0885-9159 ; no. 105)
    Includes bibliographical references and index.
    ISBN 0-313-32591-X (alk. paper)
    1. Jay, John, 1745-1829. 2. Vergennes, Charles Gravier, comte de, 1719-1787.
3. Statesmen—United States—Biography. 4. Statesmen—France—Biography.
5. United States—Foreign relations—France. 6. France—Foreign relations—United
States. 7. United States—Foreign relations—1775-1783. 8. United States—History—
Revolution, 1775-1783—Peace. 9. United States—History—Revolution, 1775-1783—
Participation, French. I. Title. II. Series.
    E302.6.J4B74   2003
    973.3'24'0922—dc21   2002030749
    [B]

British Library Cataloguing in Publication Data is available.

Library of Congress Catalog Card Number: 2002030749
ISBN: 0-313-32591-X
ISSN: 0885-9159

First published in 2003

Praeger Publishers, 88 Post Road West, Westport, CT 06881
An imprint of Greenwood Publishing Group, Inc.
www.praeger.com

Printed in the United States of America

The paper used in this book complies with the
Permanent Paper Standard issued by the National
Information Standards Organization (Z39.48-1984).

10 9 8 7 6 5 4 3 2 1

Contents

Preface

> There are no contemporary, "formal histories. . . . Many of the
> Founding Fathers who thought about the matter concluded
> that the history of the Revolution could not be written until
> the documents had been all collected"—a hard requirement,
> and, even then, unlikely to "tell the truth."
>
> —H.S. Commager[1]

A unique document was found among the papers of William Livingston, governor of New Jersey, upon his death in 1792: "A History of the American Revolution Commencing with the Settlement
of the Colonies"—and down to the early months of 1776.[2] The
authorship is uncertain, although it is clear that at least two writers were involved and that they wrote from a postwar perspective.
Livingston's son-in-law, John Jay, then kept it in his possession
until his own death, in 1829, and no wonder, as it eloquently
breathed the life and work of that Founding Father and those of
his revolutionary colleagues who were of like mind. Moreover, it
met at least part of Jay's long-standing desire for someone inti-
mately familiar with the events to write such a history.

There can be no better way to set the stage for the following
study of Jay's diplomatic role in the Revolutionary War than to
summarize for the reader selected sections of that contemporary
history. Particular emphasis will be placed on those specific events
following the French and Indian War that convinced Jay, in 1774,

that the authorities in England were forcing such profound, undesirable changes on the North American colonies as to warrant resistance. It was from this perspective that Jay would always reject labeling the Americans as "revolutionaries," insisting instead that it was the London authorities who merited that designation for having unconstitutionally sought to alter the basic relationship between the mother country and the colonies.

Here is that summary.

Early Colonial Period

Except for the abortive charter given to Raleigh by Queen Elizabeth in 1584, and the very modern one given to Georgia in 1733, all the British colonies obtained their charters and their greatest number of European settlers between the years 1603 and 1688, that is, under four successive Stuarts during a period of struggle between prerogative and privilege, ending with a Revolution highly favorable to the rights of the people. In this entire period, which coincided with the development of British America, the latter was comprised entirely of people who were anti-prerogative.

At the time of the 1770's, the inhabitants of the British colonies were, for the most part, the second, third and some the fourth generation from the original immigrants. They were chiefly Protestants, a large percentage of whom were called "dissenters" in England, and all Protestantism is founded on a strong claim to natural liberty and the right of private judgment. They who belonged to the Church of England, mostly numerous in the southern states, were for the most part "Independents" as far as Church government and hierarchy were concerned. Thus, there were no Episcopalian bishops connecting the lowest curate with the Sovereign.

The slavery which was practiced in the southern colonies nurtured a spirit of liberty among the free inhabitants. It is in their opinion not only an enjoyment but a kind of rank and privilege. Therefore, they were both proud and jealous of their freedom, and they saw the increasing claims of Great Britain as having degraded them to a condition of dependence on British subjects equally humiliating with that which existed between their slaves and themselves.

Though slavery was not by law forbidden in any of the provinces to the northward of Maryland, yet it was in them but rarely practiced. The yeoman types who came to those northern provinces of America were uninterested in titles and didn't see their rights as coming from the manumission of princes but rather looked up to heaven as the source of those rights—claimed not from the promises of kings but from the parent of the universe. Unlike these yeomen, the residual beneficiaries of Europe's feudal system did not come to America as colonists.

The education of the settlers in like manner favored the cause of liberty. British America naturally abounded in the study of law, and lawyers naturally favor freedom. The enervating opulence of Europe had not yet reached the colonists, whose similar life styles promoted a sense of equality.[3]

The provincial constitutions of the British colonies nurtured a spirit of liberty. They had in effect the sole disposal of their internal government. Only the need to assure that no laws were repugnant to the laws of Great Britain marked their subordination. They also had to obey such restrictions as were laid on their trade by the British Parliament.

War with France and Its Aftermath

It is neither possible nor necessary to decide on the right of either nation to lands in contest, 1754 to 1763. As both of the contending powers considered the right of the native inhabitants as nothing, it is not wonderful that they differed in settling their own. Previous to a formal declaration of war, Great Britain, contrary to the usage of nations, seized on some hundreds of French merchant and fishing vessels and made some thousands of French sailors prisoners. This crippled the naval operations of France through the war, but inspired her with a desire to retaliate when a proper opportunity should present itself.

The Peace of Paris of 1763 gave Great Britain possession of an extent of country equal in dimensions to several of the kingdoms in Europe. The envy and fears of Europe were excited by this foundation for England's future greatness. The balance of power which European sovereigns have for a long time most studiously endeavored to preserve was now threatened. Kings are republicans with respect to each other and behold with democratic jealousy any one of their order towering above the rest. The wars of Europe versus Louis XIV are an example from the beginning of the present century of this mechanism at work.

As some men of reflection in England recognized after 1763, there is a limit for the size of empire as for all things human, and, as they foresaw, the seeds of discord were soon planted and speedily grew up to the rending of the empire. The removal of hostile neighbors increased the desire of the American colonists for independence. They felt now some confidence in their own military abilities as a result of the war's experience. They also gained confidence in their increasing numbers and their growing commerce.

While combustible materials were daily collecting in the new world, a spark to kindle the whole was produced in the old. Nor were there wanting those who, from a jealousy of Great Britain, wished to fan the flame[s]. In Great Britain, a tax was defined to be a tribute exacted by the supreme power of a nation. In America, it was said to be a free gift of the people to their rulers for protection and security, and, therefore, that taxation and representation were inseparable. The parent state appeared to the colonies to stand in the same relation to their local legislatures as the monarch of Great Britain to the British Parliament, i.e., both the legislatures and the Parliament have the right to raise funds independently of the King and the parent state, respectively. The monarch's prerogative is limited by that palladium of the people's liberty, the exclusive privilege of granting their own money.[4]

Great and flourishing colonies, planted at an immense distance with institutions resembling those of the parent state, were novelties in the history of the world. Where parliamentary supremacy ended, and at what point colonial independency began, were not ascertained. Happy would it have been had the question never been agitated, but much more so had it been compromised without the horrors of a civil war. The English colonies were originally established not for the sake of revenue, but on the principles of commercial monopoly. Only after 1763 did the parent state view them as instruments of taxation.

A perfect calm in the political world is not to be expected. The reciprocal happiness of the mother country and of the colonies was too great to be of long duration. The calamities incident to a state of war had scarcely ended by the Peace of Paris of 1763 when the germ of another war was planted which soon grew up and produced deadly fruit.

Grievances of the American Colonists, 1764–1774

In 1764, scarcely noticed trade regulations gave or granted colonial property to the King; and, in 1765, the ever-memorable Stamp Act was passed. The latter was too extensive a tax to pass unobserved by the unsuspecting colonists. It would have speedily drained the colonies of all their circulating specie; and, it was obstructive of all public and private business. Virginia's House of Burgess was the first to protest this tax, which kindled the latent sparks of nationalism. This was especially true of New England's inhabitants, who still felt the grievous sufferings to which their ancestors, the exiled and persecuted Puritans of the last century, by the rulers of England, had been subjected. Their descendants naturally opposed the Stamp Act with the same spirit which their forefathers had exhibited against the arbitrary impositions of the House of Stuart.

The American colonists also feared, if the Stamp Act was obeyed, that would lead to endless other Parliament-imposed taxes without end till their rapacity is satisfied or our abilities are exhausted.

The colonists also hated the misuse to which the revenue was put in England. For example, the British Treasury was well-known to be a fund for corruption. Even with regard to Britain's protecting them from their enemies, the colonists' perspective was that, when France had made war upon them, it was not on their own account but as appendages to Great Britain; and, that England, in fact, rendered little or no help versus the numerous savages of the wilderness.[5]

The anti–Stamp Act protests of 1765 were not the exhibitions of a thoughtless mob, but for the most part planned by leading men of character and influence who were friends of peace and order. They well knew that the bulk of mankind is more led by their senses than by their reason. If only England had approached the colonies in a more cooperative manner after the Seven Years' War, these leaders surely would have secured the necessary local support for voluntarily raising the funds sought by the motherland.

This Stamp Act episode was the first direct step to American independency, and it ended with the claims of the two countries not only left undecided, but a foundation was laid at a future period for their extending to the impossibility of a compromise. From that day forward, the colonists, instead of feeling themselves dependent on Great Britain, conceived that, in respect to commerce, she was dependent on them. For her part, Great Britain's "Declaratory Act," while abolishing the Stamp Act, asserted that Parliament had the right "to bind the colonies in all cases whatsoever." In that one comprehensive sentence, the Americans not only were deprived of liberty and property, but of every right incident to humanity—although, at first, it was the subject of but few comments.[6]

When England, in 1767, introduced small duties on tea, the ingenious

Mr. Dickinson of Pennsylvania on this occasion presented to the public
a series of letters, signed "a farmer," opposing Parliamentary taxation as
potentially ruinous, because it could serve as a precedent for major taxes.
It is now that the Declaratory Act comes to the fore of American political
debate, being seen as a foundation for every species of oppression.
Therefore, a repeat of America's actions versus the Stamp Act now took
place, and Americans now saw England as determined to exercise its
government with greater strictness than heretofore. For example, with
the granting to commanders of warships new powers of custom house
officers, there was foreseen the barring of American trade with the Spanish and French West Indies—a trade which was a great source of specie
with which the colonies were able to pay for England's manufactured
goods. Those naval commanders were ignorant regarding trade matters
and, therefore, commerce in fact was soon damaged even far beyond
what the strict letter of the law required.

Another example of new strictness by the London authorities was that
judges' salaries were now paid by the Crown, with their attendant loss
of independent allegiance to local justice.

From 1768 onward, letters from American-based officials to the Government of England urged coercive measures. These letters were acci-
dentally discovered and made public.

In this setting, the *Gaspie* incident occurred in Providence, Rhode Island: a customs boat was dragged out to the Commons and there reduced to ashes. This led to the King's deciding to send two regiments
from Ireland to support civil government in Massachusetts, a measure
which sparked an uproar in the colonies. No threat of invasion from a
formidable enemy could have excited a greater alarm than this intelligence.

Next came the King's parliamentary speech condemning Boston and
its alleged threat to break from England. Parliament's two Houses duly
followed up this speech by asserting its supreme authority in every part
of the British Empire. In this state of mutual distrust, every incident,
however trifling, contributed to widen the breach. Parliament then authorized the King, on February 13, 1769, to take "further measures . . . to
maintain a due execution of the law in Massachusetts," especially to
bring the "chief authors" of the "late disorder" to justice; and, to bring
them to Great Britain, in accordance with a Henry VIII statute.

The Americans saw this authorization as contrary to the spirit of the

Constitution in England, and their steady opposition helped assure that Parliament's perseverance was of but short duration. But, its policy of taking a middle course was a bad one, because it lacked the advantages of either opposite extreme and meant acting without a decision. In line with this policy, Parliament now repealed the previous revenue law regarding America, excepting that part of it which imposed a duty of three pence per pound on tea.

Commercial, financial, revenue and trade matters alone would never have led to the Revolution. Other matters arose in which every individual was interested. One was the Non-Import Association adopted by the colonies. It was as much a matter of retaliation as it was a denial of revenue to England and, for American merchants, a matter of revenue protection and even increase.

Another matter was the tea tax and its consequences. While the English government's respect for law blocked her punishing the colonies for their Association, the Tea Party was different, because it did overleap the bounds of constitutional resistance and insured the sanction of penal laws. The Tea Party was decided upon at a public meeting and, therefore, was, in a qualified sense, the act of the town. Those who consult on public matters should act coolly; otherwise, decisions will be poor ones. In a reversal of roles with the Americans, the post–Tea Party actions by Parliament and King were disproportionate and based on rage, and they predictably led to a worsening of the situation.

The policy-makers who insisted upon Parliamentary supremacy deeply regretted the old colonial charters, which were seen as having given too many powers of government, and liberties, to them, and as now being constantly used by them to oppose England with a view to laying the foundation of future States.

Of course, it was in fact only now that England began to care what happened in those colonies, and it consequently used the Tea Party as a tolerable pretense to revoke the charters. That attempt helped spread the problem into all thirteen colonies: when the human mind is agitated with passion, it rarely discerns its true interests and but faintly foresees consequences. Thus, the Parliamentary manner of presenting to the inflamed Americans all three of the retaliatory Acts at the same time produced effects on their minds infinitely greater than could have been expected from any single one, or especially from the Boston Port Act alone. That Act led to a fire, which in turn was given added fuel from the combination of Acts, allowing the fire to flame out with increasing vehemence. As was said in America at the time, "property, liberty, and life are all sacrificed on the altar of ministerial arrogance."

Now, with the convening in 1774 of the first Continental Congress, all thirteen colonies formed a firm union, because the only favor the least culpable could expect was to be the last that would be devoured. The events of this time may be transmitted to posterity, but the agitation of the public mind can never be fully comprehended but by those who were eye witnesses.

CHAPTER 1

Two Determined Diplomats

May 1774 witnessed two separate historical events an ocean apart. They would force immediate changes in the careers of a middle-aged French diplomat, Count de Vergennes, and a young New York attorney, John Jay. While for the one, Vergennes, appointment as Minister of Foreign Affairs marked the natural culmination of an ambassador's ambition, for the other, Jay, assuming a political role meant an abrupt ending to a budding law practice. What was common to both men was the unexpected nature of the turns in their respective lives.

King Louis XV died on May 10, 1774, and was succeeded by his grandson, nineteen-year-old Duc de Berry, now Louis XVI and totally unprepared for his role. He had been but indifferently educated and largely kept out of state affairs by the old king. The new monarch recognized his need for guidance and lifted seventy-four-year-old Count de Maurepas out of twenty-five years' exile to be his adviser, more precisely, his Mentor, as the count would soon be universally called. In choosing a government, the two were attracted to Vergennes by his established skills as a diplomat and, importantly, by his total lack of personal involvement in court intrigues. In fact, Vergennes himself had been called back to service only a few years earlier, in 1771, after a three-year exile. He was then sent to Sweden, where he had the good fortune to be the ambassador of King Gustavus III's most important foreign ally just a few months before that king competently executed a coup d'état that strengthened his throne at the expense of political enemies at home and diplomatic ones abroad.

While Vergennes from the start was skeptical of Gustave's chances of success in his planned coup, and played only a reluctant part in its successful operation, his stock inevitably rose at Versailles for having been associated with the Swedish king's welcome victory. Vergennes's experience in Stockholm was in sharp contrast with that at Constantinople, his only other ambassadorial post (1756–68). There he was faulted by Foreign Minister Choiseul in the late 1760s for not having energetically pursued his instructions to encourage the Turks to declare war on Russia. Choiseul sought this action as a way to divert Empress Catherine II's Russia from being overly aggressive in Central Europe, notably Poland, which was long seen by both France and the Ottoman Empire as a key bulwark against Russian expansionism. Poland, even then, was in clear danger of being partitioned, as would be the case beginning in 1772. The irony was that just as Vergennes was being recalled and barred from further governmental service, the Turks, in fact, took the very step desired by Choiseul (although admittedly Vergennes had never agreed with the policy, believing it to be against the interests of his host country, presumably a French ally).[7]

There was another, more personal factor in Vergennes's *disgrace*, as the French call a peremptory dismissal: He had offended court sensibilities—even the court of the notoriously immoral Louis XV and his equally scandalous chief minister, Choiseul—by having lived with, fathered two children by, and then married the French-born widow of a Turkish medical doctor. Moreover, it was only after having done all that, that Vergennes informed Versailles of his actions. Even then, he neglected to give the basic biographical details on his wife and had to be coaxed by Choiseul to do so. Not surprisingly, those details were not the kind the court of Louis XV expected of a French ambassador's wife. If Vergennes's own roots in the nobility were provincial, recent and lowly, his wife's family background was even lower, as well as murky, rural, and certainly not noble. When Vergennes was recalled to service with the dismissal of Choiseul, the king insisted that he go to Stockholm alone and leave his wife and children in France. Vergennes, torn between his desire to resume his lifelong work and his deep love for his family, accepted the condition, although he would remain in Sweden only with a heavy heart, as reflected in his repeatedly expressed desire for a transfer closer to home, specifically to Switzerland (which offered the further attraction of not having a stuffy royal court from which his wife might be banned).

In this light, one can well imagine both the utter surprise and utter joy with which he received the news from Versailles in July 1774 that he was appointed as Louis XVI's foreign minister, and with only the moderate, quite tolerable restriction that his wife, although allowed to reside in Versailles, was not to appear at court. As he explained to Beaumarchais in 1776 in appropriately theatrical terms, "[F]or a long time I was in the *parterre* [stalls] before arriving on stage."[8] Vergennes hastened back to France and was already at his new post by September 1774, at which time he drafted a *tour d'horizon* of France's international situation for the benefit of his new master, whom he would faithfully serve with ever-increasing rewards and responsibilities until his death early in 1788.[9] In that world survey of 1774, Vergennes only incidentally identified the long-simmering turmoil between France's traditional adversary, England, and its restless, rapidly growing colonies in North America as a prospective avenue for weakening English power. But he did see it as a subject to be followed closely by France, whose interest it clearly was to keep that turmoil going. This policy approach was not new to the French government, which had been tracking the American issue from its start. For example, Ambassador Givern reported from London in 1766 that the Stamp Act had led to an American revolution and that Lords Chatham (William Pitt) and Shelburne were unsuccessfully working against the view of the government that parliamentary authority extended beyond the borders of Great Britain itself into the colonies. Still, at this period, no one in France, certainly not Vergennes, foresaw the need or desirability of France's risking an open confrontation, let alone a war, with England over a North America that, only a few years earlier, had been the conflagration point for a Seven Years' War so devastatingly costly to France.

And yet within three years of that *tour d'horizon*, that is exactly the situation in which France found itself. Step by step, in a classic example of "in for a penny, in for a pound," Vergennes led his king and government into activities whose only possible outcome could be open, direct warfare between France and England, once again, as twenty years earlier, initially over North America. Whereas Versailles' policy in the 1750s led to its losing that continent, the results of this later American conflict would be liberation of most of that valuable territory from London's control. There can be no comparison between English losses worldwide in this war and French losses in the previous Seven Years' War, if only because the earlier conflict, unlike the later one, included the murderous theater of operations on the European continent itself. Nevertheless, those English losses were sufficient to force it to recognize America's independence and also to solicit a general peace with the three European powers who had joined in the war as co-belligerents of the U.S. Those three were France, Spain and the Netherlands, only one of which, France, would even recognize American independence before 1782, let alone become a formal ally of the U.S. That general peace of 1783 cost England a retrocession to Spain of Minorca and the Floridas, the latter having been won by it in the previous war. However, despite every diplomatic and military effort by Spain, England did manage to retain what many in that island nation (though not King George himself) considered its most valuable European possession, Gibraltar, which it had been occupying since the War of the Spanish Succession at the start of the century. In contrast to Spain, neither France nor the Netherlands had significant territorial ambitions at English expense, the former fighting mainly to weaken English power by depriving it of the thirteen rebelling colonies, and the latter fighting mainly as a result of an English declaration of war over a Dutch insistence on broader maritime rights than England was prepared to allow. Thus, the secondary focus of Vergennes's 1774 world survey would prove to be the great cause of his ad-

ministration and the vehicle that would elevate him to the very
pinnacle of broad ministerial power by a grateful Louis XVI.[10]

There were few leading personalities in the diplomatic and governmental world of 1774 who were not known to Vergennes, if
only by reputation. Benjamin Franklin, who transcended that
world by his scientific and literary achievements, was certainly
one of them and would become Vergennes's major, and most welcome, American counterpart at Versailles during the war. But the
name of John Jay, who, to Vergennes's great regret, would prove
to be the dominant American figure at the Paris peace negotiations
of 1782, was totally new to him until well into the war, and understandably so. Even Jay, as late as 1781, would have been aston-
ished at the central role he would come to play at Paris. After all,
he was to be but one of five Americans elected by the Continental
Congress that June to serve as a team of peace commissioners.
However, a series of coincidences would progressively reduce that
number to one, Jay himself, during the crucial weeks leading to
the basic U.S.-English agreement of November 30, 1782. That
agreement contained "provisional articles" of the peace—and
those articles would prove to remain fully intact to form the heart
of the subsequent definitive peace treaty of September 3, 1783.

Thomas Jefferson was one of those five commissioners, but he
declined to leave Virginia. Henry Laurens of South Carolina was
another, but he was already a prisoner of war in London's Tower,
having been captured at sea by England and, though later released
on parole, did not make himself available for the Paris talks until
days before 30 November. John Adams of Massachusetts was a
third, after having been Congress' only designated peace commissioner from 1779 to 1781, but he chose to remain at his post
in the Netherlands following that country's belated diplomatic
recognition of the U.S. in May 1782 in order to negotiate a loan
and also a treaty of commerce and friendship. Adams did not
arrive in Paris until 26 October, by which time the essentials of
the U.S.-English treaty had been decided. That left only Franklin and Jay, whom Franklin in April 1782 had urgently called to
Paris from his thankless and fruitless post of the past two years

at Madrid in order to help him carry out what was clearly shaping up to be serious, burdensome and complex peace negotiations with the English.[11]

Soon after arrival at Paris in June, Jay and Franklin took turns being sick and unavailable for duty—but Jay's absence came first and at a less critical negotiating period than during Franklin's absence.[12] Accordingly, it was only Jay who was "on seat" to represent the U.S. at the peak of the talks, in late summer. Moreover, Jay did not fall ill until after he had ample opportunity to consult with Franklin for several days regarding the state of play in the negotiations. Those consultations with Jay helped Franklin to shape the fundamental document that would eventually provide the basis for the core of the 30 November written agreement with England.[13] Franklin's document actually was in the form of an informal note of 10 July given to England's still-unofficial negotiator with the Americans in Paris, Richard Oswald.[14] It outlined the "necessaries" as well as the "advisables" that Franklin saw as the American conditions for a peace agreement.

While this series of negotiating events gave great satisfaction to the Americans, whose key concern was obtaining English recognition of the independence of the entire thirteen United States, and to the English, whose major opening concern was to separate the U.S. from its French ally, it was far from a happy sequence for Vergennes, because the Americans not only virtually ignored him and his government during their negotiations but also had not even informed him of the 30 November treaty until its signature. This procedure was contrary to Vergennes's long-standing agreement with the Congress (which openly and proudly proclaimed it as an example of its close alliance with the French) that the American commissioners would only work in tandem with, and indeed under the guidance of, Versailles during the peace talks, so that while each set of negotiations would be conducted on a separate track, the U.S.-English one and the European-English one, they would end only with simultaneously signed agreements. In this way, so Vergennes thought, neither of the two allies would be left on its own to fight the English without the other, as that would have been contrary to the solemn provision of their 1778

Treaty of Alliance banning a separate peace unless with the consent of the other party. Now this was exactly the unhappy, greatly feared situation in which France believed it found itself that 30 November.

Of course, the Americans in Paris had good reasons for their conduct, most notably an unwillingness to risk, by delay, securing the highly favorable terms for the U.S. that the English clearly were ready to accept. Placing the U.S. national interest into the hands of France, especially tied as that ally had become to fellow Bourbon Spain's particular war aims, would have both dangerously delayed a U.S.-English accord that was within reach and also jeopardized its liberal terms. Moreover, it might have required the U.S. to remain in a war, not for its own goals, which were now assured, but for those of the two Bourbon powers. These latter goals were far from compatible with those of the U.S. In fact, some were, or at least seemed very much to be, in direct conflict with American interests, especially: (1) France's presumed interest in having restrictive fishing rights in both Canadian and Newfoundland waters and (2) Spain's dual ambition of preventing the U.S. boundary from reaching the Mississippi River and denying the U.S. an equal right with it to navigate that river down to its mouth for commercial purposes. Still another reason for the Americans' conduct was their conviction, Jay's much more than Franklin's or that of the Congress itself, that it was intolerable for their new nation to be seen to be under the policy direction of France.[15]

Given these considerations, coupled with the painful lessons learned during his failed Spanish mission, Jay at Paris rapidly convinced himself that the French, in their negotiations with the English, were actively placing a high priority on undermining America's own negotiating stance so as better to achieve the military and diplomatic aims of the two Bourbon powers.[16] Therefore, he decided to disregard congressional instructions and negotiate without either consulting or taking guidance from Versailles; he also orchestrated a campaign of disinformation at French expense. His success produced a certain ambivalence in the Congress when news arrived there of the isolated 30 November treaty and the manner in which it was achieved. The predominant feeling was one of immense joy over the provisional articles themselves, but a joy alloyed with deep concern among many, including Robert Livingston, the U.S. Secretary for Foreign Affairs (and Jay's most intimate friend and former law partner), at the appearance of a betrayal of U.S. treaty commitments to France. That appearance had moral as well as practical implications for the fledgling nation, whose alliance with France was seen as remaining vital to its military and financial security even in the postwar period. In fact, to this day, the events of 1782 have played an aggravating role in U.S.-French relations. In France's standard historical memory, the U.S. commissioners at Paris not only violated their instructions, which were based on an express understanding between the two countries as to how to proceed at the negotiations, but also, more seriously, the provisions of the 1778 Alliance Treaty itself. Fortunately for Vergennes's France and the U.S.-French relationship, the immediate, practical costs to France of this basically separate peace by the Americans proved to be limited, because the European negotiators were able, quite unexpectedly, as we shall see, to bring even their war with England to a close a few short weeks after the 30 November U.S.-English treaty.

This culmination to the wartime U.S.-French alliance was also remarkable in the way it bears on Jay's personal odyssey, 1774–82. Summarized briefly: From Jay's first political involvement in 1774 until the Declaration of Independence, his goal, as a member of the first and second Continental Congresses, had been the relatively conservative one of achieving America's demands without breaking from the motherland; once that goal became obsolete, he decided to give his all, at whatever personal price to himself and his beloved family, for the cause of independence, first as a senior official in New York State, 1776–78, and then as a member, and quickly president, of the Continental Congress, December 1778–September 1779; finally, from 1780 to 1782, he served in Spain as the (unaccredited) U.S. minister plenipotentiary and, from June 1782 to his return to America in mid-1784, in France as a peace commissioner.[17] In all his roles as a U.S. official and supporter of the alliance with France, Jay, prior to coming to Paris, had earned the plaudits, although increasingly tentative and conditional ones as time went on, from his immediate French colleagues—whether Gérard, France's minister plenipotentiary to the U.S. in 1778–79, or Montmorin, France's ambassador to Spain—and even at times in messages from Vergennes himself. Given this record, it is a measure of how profoundly Jay changed course, once he put on his peace commissioner hat in Paris, that Vergennes would write of him and John Adams in 1783 that "they are too cosmopolitan to take us into their calculations if they can catch a glimpse of the advantages they could have from the side of the Court of London."[18]

There is no question but that Jay's family background, coupled with his unhappy experience in Spain, contributed to the dramatic events of late 1782. He had inherited a strong dislike and distrust of France for its treatment of his paternal ancestors, who were Huguenots (Calvinists) and had fled France after Louis XIV's Revocation (1685) of Henry IV's Nantes Edict of Tolerance (1598).[19] Jay's antagonism extended to Roman Catholicism itself, as would become evident in his drafting of a 1774 appeal issued by the Continental Congress to the people of Great Britain (and also, later in life, in his efforts to place Catholic-specific political curbs in the Constitution of New York State). Moreover, the converse of this cultural inheritance was Jay's strong sense of loyalty to England for having offered a refuge to the fleeing Huguenots. This attitude also manifested itself religiously in the deep devotion of Jay's family to the Church of England.

Alongside these social traits and political loyalties, and reinforcing them, was the great commercial success of the Jays in their new homeland. This success was complemented by marriages to members of the most prestigious families in New York, including John's own to a Livingston. Not surprisingly, by the revolutionary period of the 1770s, the Jays, now in their third generation in America, were profoundly sensible and protective of their high status in society. It would be fair to say that, minus the trappings of nobility, the family was as elitist and class conscious as the aristocracies in Europe.[20] As a family whose house servants included slaves, although always only referred to as "servants," the

Jays were quite visibly wedded to a form of aristocracy that was more rigidly class oriented than was typical of wealthy families in the more northern sections of British America. As we shall see, even after the Declaration of Independence, Jay would add to his slaveholdings with a personal purchase of a fifteen-year-old boy in Martinique while en route in December 1779 to his post in Europe. However, Jay by then also had begun to advocate a gradual form of compensated emancipation, and he developed into a lifelong, active leader in the American movement to end the system of slavery.[21]

Clearly, there were important shared values between the French count, Vergennes, himself only two generations removed from a purely Huguenot family background, and the aristocratic American, Jay, and these could have helped cement their common political goals.[22] Both were totally devoted to family and country, and each overcame a visceral dislike of the other's society to support the French-American alliance. For his part, Jay went so far as to acknowledge, while in Spain, that he not only had changed his attitude toward France once it became an ally of the U.S. but also now felt a positive love for the country and the way it was living up to its commitments to America. Nevertheless, all this would not prove enough to ward off Jay's deeply embedded suspicions about European diplomacy and its diplomats. Those suspicions were exacerbated to such an extent by his calvary in Spain that, once in France and able to act from a position of strength and with a sense of independence from the detested European court system, all his lawyerly instincts would come to the fore and would steel his nationalistic resolve not to be a mere subordinate of Vergennes. The government of England, too, and not for the first time, would come to feel the force of his personality as it sought to satisfy his pre-conditions for opening formal negotiations in the summer of 1782.[23]

At that time, Jay rejected Vergennes's advice not to lose valuable time by demanding that London revise its wording of Oswald's "full powers," a standard diplomatic commission that one negotiator shows to his opposite number to document that he has his government's authorization to speak for it on a specific subject.

Jay's problem with Oswald's was twofold: first, that he could not accept its existing language referring not to the "United States" but to "colonies and plantations"; second, that it failed to be, in and of itself, the vehicle for England's formal recognition of the independence of the U.S. Jay considered solving the latter problem a prerequisite for the negotiations to proceed, not on the basis of subordination by one side to the other, as would, in his view, be the case given the existing language in Oswald's commission, but on the basis, as he often put it, of each side negotiating "on an equal footing" with the other. Jay did not want to see America wait for the signing of the treaty itself before achieving that acknowledged equality with England, nor did he want the latter's recognition of independence to be dependent on fulfillment of the various other provisions that the prospective treaty necessarily would also contain. Rather, Jay saw the role of the treaty itself as merely to close the war, independence having already been separately recognized by England.

Vergennes tried unsuccessfully to convince Jay of the insignificance of this issue, suggesting that the American wanted to start the negotiations at a point where they were to end up. The French minister jocularly went on to note that France itself regularly negotiated and signed treaties with England that cited as one of the king of England's titles that of "King of France." More substantively, perhaps, Vergennes urged Jay to rely less on a purely unilateral, and therefore readily revocable, legal document, such as Oswald's commission, and more on the clear *political* fact that the Parliament, government and king of England were all firmly committed to recognizing U.S. independence in a formal treaty. Nevertheless, Jay persisted in his position that the language of Oswald's powers had to be changed as a condition precedent to any negotiations on peace terms. In doing so, Jay was on firmer ground regarding his first problem with that language than his second one. That is because it had long been congressional policy, at least prior to the great Yorktown victory of October 1781 and the subsequent momentous political changes in England, not to negotiate with any English official whose powers described the Americans as British subjects; therefore, Jay was acting quite consistently with that policy, although not obligatorily, given that the new climate in London created diplomatic openings that Benjamin Franklin, for one, believed should and could be seized upon without risking congressional ire.

As for Jay's second goal in seeking a change in Oswald's powers, that of having it be the vehicle, under the Great Seal of King George, for explicit recognition of U.S. independence, even he had to backtrack in view of the impractability of that demand due to legal and political obstacles in England.[24] Nevertheless, he would later claim that his success in having Oswald's commission revised to refer to the "U.S." and not to "colonies," and the like, in and of itself represented the sought-after recognition of American independence at the very outset of substantive, official peace talks.

Assessing this matter within the context of Jay's overall negotiating strategy will help lay the basis for determining the impact and appropriateness of that strategy as it affected the wartime alliance between the U.S. and France. In order to achieve that purpose, this study will (1) trace the full course of that alliance, *with an emphasis on the particular experiences and viewpoints of Jay and Vergennes*, and (2) examine whether the Jay-dominated negotiating strategy and tactics were merely, as he freely acknowledged and sought to justify, a violation of congressional instructions or, more significantly for the history of the two nations, a major violation as well of U.S. treaty commitments to France.

CHAPTER 2

The Pre-Independence Outlook, 1774–76

THE VIEW FROM VERSAILLES AT THE DAWN OF LOUIS XVI'S REIGN

The focus of French policy, as Vergennes assumed his new role that late summer of 1774, was on the need for reform, both domestic and in the military. The premise was that France would remain at peace while the government devoted its policies and resources to rehabilitating the nation, internally, from its clear political, economic and social stagnation and, internationally, from its fall in status as a major world power following its humiliating defeat by the English in the Seven Years' War, 1756–63. The cost to France of that diminished international stature had been painfully demonstrated as recently as 1772, when it was virtually ignored by Russia, Prussia and Austria, as they proceeded to partition part of Poland, which was a traditional ally and defensive bulwark for France in Eastern Europe against a penetration toward France by the mercurial and ever-dangerous Russians.

The goal under Louis XVI was to establish the public sector on a sound footing and to rebuild the army and navy on a more modern basis. Time would be needed as well as financial resources. Accordingly, an expensive war was to be avoided. France was to use its diplomatic skills to maintain its existing set of alliances with Spain and Austria and to create firm friendships with others, notably Russia and Prussia. An aspect of this strategy was to adjust and reinforce its traditional alignment with the barrier-type, less powerful states of Sweden, the Ottoman Empire, and even rump-Poland. As always, France's major preoccupation was England (as we shall refer to Great Britain in keeping with the dominant practice of the day outside the British sphere). That island nation's naval power and overseas possessions were the basis for its military and commercial strength, its hegemony on the high seas, and its ability to tilt the balance of power on the European continent according to its needs of the moment by allying with any one group of land powers or another. However, one encouraging factor for the French strategists of the 1770s was that the English victory of 1763 over the two Bourbon powers, France and Spain, had now created a general wariness toward the English in almost all of the European capitals and not merely Versailles. As we shall see, given that new situation, England in the upcoming American War would prove to be unsuccessful in its search for major allies to help it fight its several enemies.

This point touches upon a key strategic consideration for France as it contemplated the possible implications of the budding conflict between England and its American colonies: If there was one predictable feature of any future French-English war sparked by events in North America, it was that France would not be fighting a land war in the Western Hemisphere, while, in sharp contrast, England most certainly would, as it confronted a challenge from the Americans. However, far less certain for France was whether, in that next conflict, it could avoid the disastrous situation of the Seven Years' War, when it had to support a major overseas naval and colonial war against England, while simultaneously fighting a full-scale land war on its home continent. Thus, an ever-present Vergennes preoccupation would be, in the event of a new war, the need to avoid a repetition of that experience (an avoidance that many American leaders, including John Adams, had failed to recognize as also being in the interest of their own country's cause). Accordingly, any account of his policies during the American War of Independence must include his management of French relations with the ever-volatile European powers. This entails an understanding not only of the short-run French goal of keeping the continent peaceful during the course of the war itself but also of their longer-run one of assuring that postwar European conditions would be conducive to a stable peace in which France played a controlling role. As a step toward that longer-term goal, Vergennes preferred that any war with England be a limited one that would leave England weakened and defeated but not so devastated or conquered that it could not play a new, more constructive role, hopefully in a junior partnership with a now-revitalized France, in maintaining that peace.

To summarize, Vergennes in 1774 saw as France's first and foremost priority the strengthening of its military power as a precondition to reestablishing the nation as a full participant in any European event affecting the balance of power. Another priority was to work with the European powers with a view to diminishing England's domination of the world's oceans and its attendant ability to damage the colonial and commercial interests of those powers. In this context, France needed (1) to deepen the existing friendly relations that it was already maintaining with all its continental neighbors, including Prussia as well as Russia, and (2) to keep a watchful eye on the nascent clash between the English colonies in North America and their motherland as the most promising avenue for achieving the weakening of that traditional French nemesis without having to confront it directly.

The French believed that the commercial and financial implications for England, if it were to lose North America, were enormous. English trade with its colonies was valued at over £5 million pounds a year, employing 800 to 900 sails of ships.[25] This meant that tension between those two entities could possibly open the door for Bourbon interests to displace British ones in this commerce, which, in standard French thinking during the interwar period of the 1760s and 1770s, could now, with all its future increases, be gained by France and Spain, if they would protect the American shipments. But it must be said that, alongside the lucrative prospect before them, the French authorities constantly maintained a cautious skepticism that it would ever actually come to fruition. For example, on January 1, 1768, the embassy in London opined to Versailles that if Holland had been as disunited and leaderless as British America is today, it would "never have broken away from Spain" and that British America is able to act to shake things up but not "to follow with wisdom a plan for a revolt."[26] The embassy believed that only outside help could enable the colonists to achieve that. In any event, the French diplomatic staff in that year disappointingly witnessed what they described as Lord Chatham's self-promoting pressure on the king to win the repeal of the Stamp Act before the colonies were forced either to rise up violently or to bend to the will of London.

The bleak embassy assessment of immediate prospects for a colonial revolt against England coincided with that of one of Versailles' earliest secret agents sent to British America, Johann de Kalb, who wrote Choiseul on January 13, 1768, from Philadelphia, that the colonies see their commercial, not military, power as too great for England seriously to limit their liberty, real or imagined.[27] By July 31, 1769, Choiseul regretfully would endorse this analysis when he wrote his ambassador in London that the government of England seems to have "renounced its initial resolutions for forcing the colonies to submit unconditionally to English will, and to substitute for them more moderate ones," although he soon thereafter more optimistically would add (8 September) that the colonies, unlike the joy that they displayed in 1766 merely at the revocation of the tax acts, now were steadily increasing their demands with each new English revocation.[28]

It was often said of Choiseul that "activity took the place of principles," but he was restrained by the advice given him in a dispatch of November 18, 1768, by Ambassador Chatelet in London along the following lines: It is a shame that France and Spain have to remain passive, given English-American problems, but "precipitate demarches" would only lead to their rapprochement and to their joining "immediately" in an attack on French possessions; England is headed toward permanent downfall, given its problems with America, and France should wait and give the process "the final blow"; the time to act is when France can attack; the time to prepare is when France must be on the defensive; so France must work discreetly right now in close cooperation with

Spain to develop plans and preparations that would be right for any and all circumstances.[29] Choiseul, in fully concurring with the ambassador, answered on 22 November in substance as follows: even if an English-American understanding is reached, sooner or later the Americans will create a "major fire"; after religious fanaticism, that of "liberty" is the most ardent cause at the implementation stage of a rebellion and the most dangerous in its consequences; if there is an English-American war, France and Spain infallibly will become the target, and so, even though desiring peace, they must act as though they will certainly be dragged into trouble by England.

These are words that Vergennes himself might have written a few years later, just as, in fact, he did repeat Chatelet's subsequent observation, in late 1768, that war in America would offer France and Spain an "opportunity perhaps never to be repeated."[30] That ambassador insightfully further observed that, three years earlier, the American situation was seen as leading to French action only in the next generation, but now it was seen as requiring France to move in a few years, if not months—and that will have the greatest of consequences for the European political system.

By the time Vergennes came into power, the North American situation had, of course, evolved considerably. This naturally excited his aspiration, as outlined above, to see England both weakened in a colonial war and then ready to cooperate with France in a combined role as arbiters of intra-European affairs.[31] A precedent of sorts existed for such a cooperative relationship, France and England having played something like that role episodically in the aftermath of the War of the Spanish Succession—especially during the administrations of Fleury at Versailles and Walpole at London.[32] But, at that time, it was usually England that was the dominant power and France the deferential one; moreover, Vergennes's ideas for that partnership incorporated recent intellectual concepts, including those growing out of the works of the Enlightenment with their emphasis on more open international trade and less dependence on the mercantile system of monopoly control by the metropole over colonial economies. There were political figures in England who shared aspects of Vergennes's vision, and they would come to assume leading governmental roles in the 1780s in a timely development helpful to the peace process ending the American War and to the partial fulfillment of that Frenchman's postwar plans, notably the conclusion of a commercial treaty between the two in 1786 (which was much more profitable to England's advanced economy than to France's still relatively backward one).[33]

But a ten-year crucible would be facing Vergennes before he could even be within reach of that desired diplomatic situation. In the interim, France would have to deal with:

1. Catherine II (the Great) of Russia and her forced confrontations with the Ottoman Empire, among other worrisome initiatives.

2. Frederic II (the Great) of Prussia and his constant diplomatic maneuvers, so hard to read and so often disruptive of stable relations within Europe.[34]

3. The mother-son Austrian team of Maria-Theresa and Joseph II, and especially the son's energetic determination to strengthen the Habsburg's hold over the so-called Holy Roman Empire (of which he was the "emperor"), while also expanding Austrian-controlled territory to the east and south—Joseph's pursuit of these diplomatic goals was in the clear knowledge that he was destabilizing a post-1756 French-Austrian alliance that had been cemented by the Choiseul-arranged 1771 marriage of his sister, Marie-Antoinette, to the future Louis XVI.[35]

4. Charles III of fellow Bourbon Spain and his still-simmering grievances against both France and England, each of whom had at one time or another in that aged monarch's life humiliated him and cost him part of his territorial possessions, in France's case allegedly by having forced upon him a premature peace with England in 1762–63.[36]

And then, of course, there was the perennial core issue of the French-English relationship. This was the key to French rehabilitation as a great power, one that, if properly managed, could regain for France its true stature as the dominant actor on the European continent. As during much of France's two previous reigns, Louis XVI's Versailles viewed post-Tudor England as its principal and "natural" enemy. Thus, the new king and his government readily absorbed the lessons of the recent past and closely studied the course of action of that period's leading French statesman, Choiseul. Accordingly, it would be useful to review the highlights of those brief years between France's war against England in the previous generation and the advent of Louis XVI.

In a dispatch of March 14, 1769, to his London embassy, Choiseul expressed the fear that England's "odious" 1755 act on the high seas against France at a time of peace "could be repeated" and so the ambassador should seek to identify England's "true" motives behind its current friendly demeanor—England always carries within it "a spirit of hatred and jealousy towards France."[37] As early as August 1764, Choiseul was writing that embassy: France would love to see the government there continue in confusion; only Grenville understands English finances, and so his return to power would be harmful to French interests, because he'll be pro-peace but will put England in excellent shape to fight France in ten years; therefore, France would be better off fighting the war three years from now instead of ten.[38]

These messages reflected the underlying French assumption that England's very existence as a dominant naval power was a threat and an obstacle to enhancement of French military and commercial influence and strength. War with it was, as always, a question not of if but of when. This attitude was especially deeply rooted in periods, such as the late 1760s, when France felt at too great a disadvantage in its competition with the "Anglo-Saxons," a grasping, perfidious and commercially insatiable people, according to standard French thinking. Wherever it turned, France saw itself as confronted by an adversarial England—whether overseas, increasingly including portions of India, or in the North Atlantic fishing grounds where it had treaty rights on and off the coast of Newfoundland, or even in its own homeland, where England, based on the Treaty of Utrecht ending the War of the Spanish Succession, 1712–13, was posting a commissioner at Dunkirk to ensure French adherence to the severe limitations placed on their developing that channel port as a potential jumping-off point for an invasion of the British Isles, which were so close by that their white cliffs were visible on a clear day.[39]

Still another important French grievance against England in those years, one that would prove to be relevant as the France of Vergennes's period sought to justify its aid to the American rebels, was that England was giving material and political support "to the Corsicans at a time when we were fighting them" over the incorporation of their island into metropolitan France pursuant to a treaty with Genoa, Corsica's former owner. France argued that its absorption of Corsica was "totally without threat to English interests."[40] As Choiseul had earlier put it: "Since 1763, we have always been acting in full keeping with all that England could desire of us," and, maybe, France cannot say the same regarding England's policy toward it.[41]

Typically for all French leaders who followed him, Choiseul then referred back to the naval actions of 1755 to show that England did not need a pretext to start a war: Its unwarranted actions at that time have forced France now, he wrote, to have a policy of "repairing the losses of the last war" by reestablishing its army and navy, taking precautions to protect its colonies and having international allies—if England sees this as a basis for its "lack of confidence in us, I can only say that France, by this policy, will be more stable and less fearful of any English misbehavior," because only when two powers are self-confident can they have a true basis for confident relations.

Disregarding clear evidence that the new reign of English-born George III represented a departure from his two Hanoverian-born predecessors' often aggressive maritime and especially continental policies, the Choiseul-led government of Louis XV, throughout the postwar years of the 1760s, actively prepared France to resume its armed conflict with England by implementing a series of military reform programs designed to raise the nation's fighting capabilities on land and at sea. Choiseul's message of October 12, 1768, to the embassy in London spelled out his philosophy: There are two kinds of basis for confidence between powers, a sense of honor and justice or, treaties and allies; the Fleury-Walpole relationship was a condition precedent for an alliance based on mutual confidence; "I lack Fleury's talent for persuasion," and, moreover, Walpole is not the head of the government of England, "which is too erratic for me to establish a relationship of personal confidence, one that is necessarily based on a sense of honor and justice." Choiseul would add the next year: If Lord Chatham (William Pitt) returns to power, that could lead to an English declaration of war on Spain, and "maybe" France, which would be the same thing; though France is unprepared for war, if it is inevitable, it would be best for it to begin it than be at the receiving end (a sentiment fully shared by Choiseul's political enemy, Vergennes).[42]

Given this outlook, it will be no surprise that Choiseul's government, as noted above, sought to obtain essential intelligence regarding the situation in British America. Illustratively, he instructed the London embassy in 1768 to collect economic information, colony by colony, because, "in the event my dream can come true," France must be ready to offer immediate advantages to them at a rupture, which is inevitable "sooner or later"—"my strategy is to accelerate the process."[43] Furthermore, the very first French concert with Spain on the subject of aiding British America in its efforts at independence came at the end of 1768, when Choiseul sent a memorandum, actually drafted by Ambassador Chatelet in London, to both kings setting forth the view that:

1. The two powers should bend their established commercial policies and work more closely with the Americans, because that would have long-term political benefits by leading to an increased desire on their part for independence and by increasing their means for achieving it; moreover, France and Spain would also benefit economically from such a flexible new policy.

2. Unless the two powers intervened, they will eventually lose the entire New World. Even if that intervention was successful, and the Bourbons thereby risked losing their own possessions to the Americans, that still would be worth it, because English power would have been destroyed.

3. France's seizing the British American colonies cannot be a war goal.

The only foreseeable goals for France are their independence from England, their having commerce with France, their supplying the West Indies (which France can hardly do from Europe), and, finally, France's having an implied contract with them for mutual military and political support (to be enforced and guaranteed by their own needs).[44]

It is remarkable how close Vergennes's own analysis and policy would be to those of his nemesis and predecessor, Choiseul.

Louis XV's final, post-Choiseul years were marked by a sharp swerve toward pacifism and a correspondingly strong desire for a rapprochement with England, but the new government at Versailles was under the ineffective direction of d'Aiguillon, a creature of Louis's latest and last influential "Favorite," Madame du Barry. The change in policy can be vividly seen in the sharp contrast of tone regarding England in the correspondence between d'Aiguillon and the French embassy in London. For example, while Choiseul had described England's Secretary of State Rochford as a "threat to the peace" who wanted to play the "Mr. Pitt" of Seven Years' War fame, and not the later, more harmless "Mylord Chatham," d'Aiguillon's ambassador, Guines, in June 1772, would say of Rochford and his senior minister, Lord North, that they "really want peace" and have proved it in all circumstances, including "most ably seconding the intentions of the King."[45]

The contrast in portrayals of King George is similarly striking, the d'Aiguillon government more accurately reading that monarch's intentions as based on a "political strategy . . . of peace."[46] Unlike Choiseul's government, which took but slight account of, or interest in, the possibilities of developing a rapprochement with the still-youthful English king, d'Aiguillon's recognized that George, aside from his welcome personal hatred of France's own *bête noire*, Lord Chatham, was demonstrably rejecting inherited Hanoverian policies that overly involved England in continental affairs and was favoring instead those that gave priority to cultivating England's overseas and maritime assets (an emphasis that helps explain his dogged determination to keep a tight rein over his American colonies).[47] George III's new approach also accepted the premise that it would be in England's interest to conduct itself overseas in a less belligerent manner than in the past as a way to temper the historical enmity of the European powers toward any English hegemonic tendencies.[48] Moreover, during the crisis between England and the two Bourbon powers in the late 1760s over possession of the Falkland Islands, the king favored peace, while the Parliament was for war.[49]

In 1772–73, George also approved entering into a negotiation for a friendship and commercial treaty with France. This was in partial response to the post-Choiseul change in Versailles' policies, which had included such bold Choiseul brinkmanship over the recent contest between fellow Bourbon Spain and England for possession of the Falklands that a rather frightened Louis finally became convinced he had to replace his senior minister. Louis would soon openly rue this decision when Austria ignored France, its ostensible ally, as it joined in the power grab of Polish land—he was certain that such a humiliation would never have occurred under a Choiseul government.

Versailles in Louis XV's final three years went so far as to sympathize with the London authorities in their struggle with the Americans, d'Aiguillon in 1774 welcoming their apparent decision to adopt "a more vigorous policy . . . to bring the colonies back to obedience. It could have been that this was the only decision available to His Britannic Majesty. He has for too long a time been needlessly wearing himself out by seeking to use means of sweetness and reconciliation."[50] Given such a perspective, it is no wonder that this period witnessed that stab at a friendship and commercial treaty between the two traditional enemies—in the event, a major war would intervene before such an agreement could be achieved in the final stage of d'Aiguillon's successor government, now more than ever under Vergennes's control, that minister having added financial affairs to his portfolio.

If there was one shared assessment of England's leaders between d'Aiguillon and his predecessor as well as successor, it unsurprisingly was regarding Chatham, who even the d'Aiguillon government saw as "the greatest man of his century" but feared as "the one man in England who could be dangerous to France," because he had the people's confidence.[51] In Versailles' consistent estimation, so long as he was around, he would be "by acclamation prime minister of an England which is being threatened." Fortunately for France, by now Chatham was too old and ill to take on this role. However, despite this last, rather obvious truth, even Vergennes, until Chatham's death in May 1778, would remain wary of a return to power by that statesman; for example, on December 10, 1775, he advised the London embassy that "the threat to France will come if present English policy fails and a less peaceful Chatham government takes the existing force in America to French and Spanish possessions in America to compensate for its losses in British America."[52]

The 1771–74 peace-oriented interregnum at Versailles was more of a royal aberration than an integral part of the nation's political culture, whose basic, deeply institutionalized policy drive was toward reestablishing France's status as a recognized great power and an arbiter of European diplomatic life. To achieve this goal, the opinion of the new government of Louis XVI held that it would be necessary, once again, to prepare for a military confrontation with the traditional enemy, England; such a confrontation was inevitable and, at the right moment, desirable. As put by the French ambassador to England, Noailles, on January 9, 1778: England is France's only adversary to be feared. Similarly, Vergennes wrote on 17 January: "England is our primary enemy—our others only take force and energy from it."[53]

Certainly, this last was typical of Vergennes's entrenched mindset. His long diplomatic career back to the 1740s was shaped by the dogma of the Anglo-Saxons as France's "natural enemy." Moreover, that Frenchman, alongside his overt role as a diplomat, from his earliest assignments had also been a member of Louis XV's Secret du Roi, the special unit composed of a select few foreign service officers who were privately given policy directives by the king that often were inconsistent with France's official, overt foreign policy.[54] Those directives were not made known even to the Minister of Foreign Affairs of the moment (a fact that upset Choiseul endlessly), nor to the concerned ambassador, unless he himself was a member of the Secret. Rather bizarrely, the directives of that elite organization for its last decade were drafted and transmitted to the field by the channel of Louis's special adviser, Count de Broglio, despite his having been exiled to his estates along with his older brother, the heroic but politically abrasive Marshal de Broglio, toward the end of the Seven Years' War.[55]

The world outlook of this invisible royal service by far exceeded, in its international ambitions for France, and in its estimate of the nation's true potential as a military and economic power, the more cautious, less imaginative one of officialdom. Vergennes, even with his conservative political style, fully shared this nationalistic, aggressive outlook and, while clearly emotionally driven by a thirst for revenge against England and the detested Treaty of 1763, coolly applied all his diplomatic expertise in pursuit of the Secret's constant goal of giving France the status of a major power commensurate with its high evaluation of the nation's actual and potential strength. In this spirit, he successfully worked to dilute Louis XVI's early instruction not only that the Secret be disbanded, as it immediately and permanently was, but also that its records and reports be destroyed, which the more important largely were not. Vergennes also managed to assure that his old boss, Count de Broglio, would be allowed to retain his access to the throne in the form of written, unofficial policy memoranda (which would soon include a heavy focus on North America), although this time they would not be bypassing the foreign minister.

Incredible as it may seem, Broglio actually worked in the early years of France's participation in the American War to establish himself as commander in chief of the American army, replacing Washington. That Frenchman based his proposal to Versailles on reports from his associates in the U.S., notably the de Kalb who had first gone to North America for Choiseul and who now was commissioned in the Continental Army as a general, that Washington was a mediocre military man as well as one unsuitably burdened still with "his old prejudice against the French," a reference to his historically important role in France as the "murderer" of a Canadian military officer in the Ohio region in 1754 at a time of peace between France and England.[56] (Of course, by 1782, attitudes would change, and even Broglio's nephew, the marshal's son, would come to America asking to serve under that American commander.)

Other examples of Vergennes's facilitating the extension into the new reign of vestiges of Louis XV's Secret include: (1) urging the London embassy, in June 1775, to employ, as an intelligence source for reporting on policy debates within the English government, a local expatriate, the famous and controversial transvestic Secret agent Chevalier d'Eon, on grounds that despite his having been dismissed from the service by Louis XV, "his Court is still that of France" and (2) hiring Broglio's former senior adviser and secretary, Hennin, in 1778, as one of his principal deputies, replacing Gérard, who that year was sent as France's first minister to the U.S.[57]

Another important dimension in Vergennes's approach to fulfilling his bold, long-term goals for France was the rather courageous personal political backing he gave, upon assuming office, to those of his co-ministers who were in the vanguard of enlightened policy makers. Although, once his diplomatic career began, he had spent only the years 1749–50 and 1769–71 in France itself, he realized that if France was to develop its power potential, implementing a major reform program was clearly the route to follow domestically. At its start, then, far from any inherent conflict within Louis XVI's government over priorities and resource allocations, as between domestic and foreign security demands, there was a congruence of interest. All recognized that basic changes were needed to promote domestic production and internal trade, and to rationalize revenue raising, if France was truly to develop a modern economy capable of supporting a military apparatus in the service of France as a world power.

The principal reforming figures in the government's initial management of domestic affairs were Anne-Robert Turgot, on the financial side, and Chrétien Guillaume de Malesherbes, on legal and social matters, including responsibility for the all-important relationship with the dozen regional courts, or "parliaments," spread across the country.[58] But even before France's entrance into the American War, affairs would not go well for these two inevitably controversial ministers, whose tenure would last only two short years, and the advent of French military involvement would create even deeper fissures within the government's new leadership. The most dominant figure in the remodeled government of 1777 was Jacques Necker, Turgot's powerful and influential successor. That Swiss-born Protestant banker would play an often antagonistic role, not excluding diplomatic meddling, as he sought to block Vergennes's politically and financially expensive war policies.

That Vergennes, as early as April 12, 1777, foresaw the unavoidability of this political conflict, given his own already explicit militaristic intentions for France, is clear from the burden of his message to Ambassador Ossun in Madrid:

Louis XV left France in a terrible financial situation, and it worsened under Turgot; but Necker was now in his place and has a more realistic approach. That should enable France to borrow on better terms than it did for its old debts as well as to increase revenue to appropriate levels; therefore, 1778's revenue should exceed expenditures *unless war intervened*; the structure of France's debt should soon be as solid as England's. All this argued for a *continuation of peace*.[59]

Contrary to Vergennes's expectations, the tension between him and the resolutely anti-war Necker would help force a temporarily panicky and insecure Foreign Minister, behind America's back, to dilute his support for the French-U.S. alliance during a stressful period of the war, 1780–81, when prospects seemed dim for an early achievement of the goals France set out for itself in the Treaty of February 6, 1778.

NORTH AMERICA ON THE EVE OF REVOLUTION

The elimination of the century-old French Canadian menace as a result of the French and Indian War freed the British American colonists from having to look to the mother country for their security and, in John Adams's view, marked the start of the process of revolution and union that led to their Declaration of Independence in 1776. Thus the end of that war marked the beginning of the history of the United States. While the opening military battles would not take place until 1775, it was in September of the previous year that a landmark event occurred in that process of revolution and union: The first Continental Congress met with the participation of all the colonies (initially except Georgia). At that session, to draw on the words of the previously cited contemporary History found in William Livingston's papers, the Congress quickly agreed on a detailed course of action given the "universal view" of the colonists; local attachments or particularities were forgotten, or rather sacrificed, on the "altar of patriotism."

Vergennes's ministry followed these events in America closely and perhaps more astutely than the related ones in England itself. In January 1775, the embassy in London reported that the Americans were no longer acting on the basis of separate provinces; England could not any longer just go and punish one colony; the Americans were organizing for war; George evidently saw it preferable to take forceful action on his own than to lose his authority to Chatham; if George succeeded, he would be more powerful than ever and "freed forever from the fears caused him by Chatham," while, if he lost, he at least would have deferred for a time the return to power of this "imperious minister."[60] (On March 9, 1775, Vergennes himself opined to that embassy that North's policies were too contradictory to work and would lead to a Chatham government, which, in turn, would create a "new order of things, and we have solid reason to fear that that would be at the expense of the tranquility of Europe.")[61]

It was the unifying event of the 1774 Continental Congress and its immediate antecedents at the local level that first brought John Jay to political life and notice. Dropping his law practice in the spring of 1774 in favor of full-time involvement in the cause of American liberties, the twenty-nine-year-old would never return to it. Instead, his talents and indefatigable energy would be immediately recognized and utilized by his fellow-activists in both New York and Philadelphia. With his powerful pen, forceful personality and brilliant legal mind, Jay quickly and permanently assumed a large role as a propagandist and legislator for colonial America; as a political and quasi-military leader of his native colony, New York, and then as chief justice of the State of New York, whose freshly drafted constitution was in important part a Jay product; and, finally, back to the national level in late 1778, as described earlier. Following the conclusion of the Peace Treaty of 1783 in Paris, Jay returned to the U.S. (July 1784) and, as desired by the Congress, became the nation's second Secretary for Foreign Affairs, 1784–89; he wrote all the five essays in the Federalist Papers that dealt entirely and specifically with genuine foreign affairs, a subject considered important enough to have been placed among the very first of the Papers (numbers 2, 3, 4, 5, and 64) and then was "appointed," in the language of the Constitution, by President Washington, with Senate consent, as the first chief justice of the Supreme Court, 1789–95, ending that service with a special diplomatic assignment in 1794 that led to the so-called "Jay's Treaty" with England controversially settling some of the outstanding issues remaining from the peace treaty between the two countries on terms many saw as too liberal in favor of England and as a "repudiation" of the American alliance with France.[62]

Returning to New York State as governor, Jay served two terms before retiring after the start of the new century to his farm, a bereaved recent widower who had long looked forward to a quiet life dwelling "securely and happily under the shade of my vine and fig tree."[63] It is worth noting, in summary, that among Jay's distinctive features as a Founding Father is that no other senior American leader can match his unique combination of continuity and variety of service, unbroken from 1774 down to 1801, at both the national and state levels and within every branch of government. Another distinction, one that clearly had direct practical bearing on his performance, is that, unlike the overwhelming majority of America's revolutionary leadership, Jay's family background was non-English, five of his eight great-grandparents being of Dutch origin and the other three of French.

In his long line of positions, none has been more heralded than his role as peace commissioner in Paris; nor has any been more controversial for Jay both in his own lifetime and in the writing of American history down to the present day. To understand properly both the substance of Jay's actions in that role and their diplomatic and military import, we need to examine in some depth the man's personality and political outlook, as well as the larger world in which he worked—for our purposes, the Bourbon world of France and Spain. A good starting point would be to picture the circumstances in the New York of 1774 that might help explain why a heretofore rather apolitical, wealthy, newly married man would depart from his life's pattern and progressively risk his all in a political and military confrontation with a motherland toward whom he felt great love and profound appreciation.

Explanations run from the frivolous to the more credible: that he acted in this way in order to spite a profoundly loyalist family, the De Lanceys, after he had been rejected in consecutive marriage proposals by two De Lancey daughters; that his subsequent marriage to a Livingston brought him into a circle of active American patriots; that he had seen how the parliamentary laws had negatively and unfairly affected American economic life, very much including his own; that he sincerely believed America, even more than England, was the country to which he owed his primary political allegiance and whose prosperity depended on a greater degree of autonomy from the metropole than had earlier been the case; and that to stand by inactively while the more radical, "lower-class" elements in New York took over the leadership of the protest movement and pursued a misconceived policy of total independence from England would be to abdicate a defense of his family's and America's true interests.

Jay's own, consistently applied view of who among the Americans were for, and who opposed, the Revolution provides insight into his motives, and it was succinctly stated to Spain's foreign minister, Floridablanca, in an April 28, 1780, memorandum submitted in response to a long list of written questions presented to him upon his arrival at Madrid: Only officers of government, officials of the Church of England and "foreign adventurers, buyers and sellers" were pro-England; the bulk of the population was with the Revolution; some are neutrals; and finally there are "persons who, in every revolution, like floating weeds in every storm, obey the strongest wind and pass from side to side . . . a pusillanimous race," one that is "much less dangerous, though far more contemptible" than Loyalists or Tories, because when with the English side, they do all but fight against the rebels, and when with the revolutionary side, do all but fight against the English.

Thus, it was in late May of 1774 that Jay embarked on his life's new direction by agreeing to become a member of an extralegal committee of New Yorkers who were organizing to support Boston in its appeal for help to counter the recent London edict totally closing its port in punishment for the Boston Tea Party of 1773 and related resistance to English taxation and pricing policies. Similar committees were being organized in each of the other colonies. The main expedient these colonial committees adopted to pressure London to change those policies was to institute and enforce a trade ban against England. Another feature of the protest movement, and one that would have great consequences for both the American people and Jay personally, was the calling of the very first continentwide congress, which began meeting in September 1774 at Philadelphia. Jay was one of the delegates chosen by his provincial committee to represent New York, and he dutifully left Sarah, his bride of four months, and his many family and business commitments, to attend that congress without any fixed date set for his return to New York.

Summarizing what the History found in Livingston's papers has to say about these matters:

The first congress limited itself to rights infringed since 1763. Still, its approbation given to the resolutions entered into by the inhabitants of Massachusetts' Suffolk Country extinguished the hopes of those who wished for peace at all events. The latter hoped the Congress would only offer financial aid to Bostonians, pay for the tea, and also pay compensation for damages in Boston with a view to encourage England to reopen the port. Instead, they saw it pass a resolution assuring Massachusetts of its backing in case of extremities, which they interpreted as equivalent to a declaration of war against England.

Yet others hoped that the Congress' measures would encourage England to relax its unconstitutional policies and go back to a policy which had led to the repeal of the Stamp Act. But the opposite occurred, proving that in government, as well as in religion, there are mysteries from the close investigation of which little advantage can be expected. The hinge of the problem here was: where the supremacy of the empire ended and the independency of the local colonies began was to the best informed a puzzling question; happy would it have been for both countries had the clarification of this doubtful point never been attempted.

The congress did not content itself with a bare statement of its rights but enforced its claims by creating an Association to suspend all imports and exports from Great Britain, Ireland and the West Indies (except rice exports). The congress had derived encouragement by the two earlier successes of import bans. But it also indulged in extravagant opinions of the importance and even of the necessity of the colonies' trade to Great Britain. It was *export* suspension that was the new, unprecedented step regarding which the congress foresaw even greater successes than the import suspensions had—the goals were "bankrupt" English merchants and a "starved" West Indies. Events proved that young nations, like young people, are prone to overrate their own importance.

In addition to all these incitements, the congress tried the force of eloquence in a well-conceived petition to the people of Great Britain; also, a memorial to the inhabitants of the British colonies and an address to the inhabitants of Canada. These were all written with a high degree of animation. Coming from the heart, they were calculated to move the heart.

The congress did all this in less than eight weeks and dissolved itself by its own act on October 26, 1774, but planned a next meeting on May 5, 1775, unless England gave redress to its grievances. The publication of the congress' proceedings obtained that direction which the people wished for, and had patiently waited for, in their zealous desire to do something for their country.

One third of the forty plus members of congress at Philadelphia were lawyers who had earned the peoples' confidence by having worked in the common cause at the provincial level, where measures required both their expertise and talent to address large bodies and their knowledge of rightful liberties and how to defend them.

The Assembly of New York was the only constitutional legislature which refused its approbation of the congress' determinations. New York City had long been the headquarters of the British army in the colonies, and many of its families were connected with people of influence in Great Britain. As for the colony of New York as a whole, the unequal distribution of land fostered an aristocratic spirit. New York's party for the royal government was both more numerous and respectable than in the other colonies. Still, only a single vote won it for the anti-congressional decision.

It was at this opening, unification phase in the struggle between America and England that Jay, who until July 1776 would not fully accept the view that only independence and "the sword" could settle the controversy, made his national mark by drafting that congressional "Address to the People of Great Britain" just referred to. Jefferson, while still uninformed of who the drafter was, not having joined the Congress until 1775, described that document as "a production certainly of the finest pen in America."[64] It also was produced by a man whose intellect harnessed and articulated a personal set of social and political values that are worth summarily noting at this stage in his career:

1. Great Britain particularly deserved the allegiance and regard of the Jays, who found refuge and prosperity under its sovereignty after having fled religious persecution in France. In a letter of June 11, 1783, to the president of the Continental Congress, Elias Boudinot, a fellow descendant of Huguenots who had asked his help in obtaining a consular appointment for a nephew, Jay showed that his sentiments regarding his family's past were still very much alive.

2. Both France and Roman Catholicism were anathema, and British America needed to keep both away from its frontiers if it was to be secure from unwanted political and religious encroachments.[65]

3. In internal American affairs, the Jays' privileged socioeconomic status was to be tightly safeguarded from usurpation by violence-prone, "lower-class" Americans. In a letter of April 27, 1776, Jay wrote to console a friend, Alexander McDougall, whose military performance was being severely criticized: There is an "instability which from various causes often strongly marks popular opinion of men and measures in times like these. . . . Posterity you know always does justice." In a letter of December 11, 1777, to Philip Schuyler, he would explain the unfortunate delay in obstructing the Hudson River as follows:

"The people begin to grow sensible of it. They must feel it, it seems, before they can perceive." But his attitude would evolve, and by September 1780, he was more positive about the possibilities of drawing upon all classes of people for leadership roles: "Knowledge is essential to the duration of liberty. . . . We must take care of young Americans—much depends on the rising generation."[66] Still, Jay would never lose his sensitivity to class standards, as when he wrote on March 1, 1783, to John Adams: "I must postpone our meeting with the Count [Vergennes], because my man, Manuel, went to the Fair and therefore my hair can't be combed."[67]

4. Present difficulties between the colonies and London were due to ministerial misbehavior and not to any inherent conflict of interest between the Americans and their king or their fellow subjects in Great Britain, who surely will ultimately prevail and bring the government and Parliament back to proper colonial policies. (A French analysis of this period was closer to the mark, as would be corroborated by the language of the Declaration of Independence itself: "George is the most obstinate prince in the world," and England's ministers are only thinking of how "to save their heads . . . , and they will never take those decisions so necessary in great crises"; meanwhile, "the Americans, to an unprecedented extent, are brought to a degree of furor and enthusiasm," and "the Opposition in Parliament throws oil on the fire," so "how could it possibly be put out?")[68]

Perhaps a concise summary of many of the above points, as well as a harbinger of Jay's philosophy as a diplomat in France, can be extracted from a letter he wrote from Albany on April 29, 1778, to his closest friend after Robert R. Livingston, Jr., Gouverneur Morris, who at that time was serving as a member of New York's delegation to the Continental Congress, then based at York, Pennsylvania:

The influence of Lord North's conciliatory plan is happily counterbalanced by the intelligence from France [that a treaty had been signed with the U.S.]. There was danger of its creating division. A desire for peace is natural to an harassed people, and the mass of mankind prefer present ease to the arduous exertions often necessary to ensure permanent tranquility.

What the French treaty may be I know not. If Britain would acknowledge our independence and enter into a liberal alliance with us, I should prefer a connection with her, to a league with any power on Earth. Whether those objects be attainable, experience only can determine. I hope the present favorable aspect of our affairs [post-Saratoga] will neither make us arrogant or careless—moderation in prosperity marks great minds and denotes a generous people. Your game is now in a delicate situation and the least bad play may ruin it [the reference is to the arrival from England of peace commissioners hoping to win acceptance of North's conciliatory plan]. I view a return to the domination of Britain with horror, and would risk all for independence, but, that point ceded, I would give them advantageous commercial terms. The destruction of old England would hurt me. I wish it well. It afforded my ancestors an asylum from persecution.

It is obvious that Jay also felt a strong devotion to his family and, most strikingly, a deep love for, and profound loyalty to, his aging father, Peter.[69] Although there were older brothers, only John showed the personal character, and had the physical well-being, to take on the role as his father's main emotional and practical support and as the near-universally accepted head of family. It is no small matter, therefore, to note that even as Jay gave his all in the service of the American cause, he was constantly weighed down by a regretted inability to be present and to provide the attention his family needed. (His wife was often ill and both his parents would, in his absence, die during the revolutionary period, leaving no full-time presence of a family member to care for John's older siblings: two blinded early in life by smallpox and a third retarded.)[70] Moreover, Jay's one able-bodied, highly competent older brother, "Sir James" (knighted in 1763 for his fund-raising service to King's College and another college in Philadelphia, a service that paradoxically turned into a scandal and an embarrassment to the Jay family when he disputed his financial share in the collection, to which the king had personally contributed), would spend much of the war as a shadowy figure suspected of being a Loyalist and of seeking to play each side off the other in the hope of personal monetary gain by the sale, as he described it in a letter to Vergennes, of "plans of maritime warfare" that he had developed and was ready also to propose to the English government.[71] Interestingly, at war's end, this brother along with one of Henry Laurens's sons and also Franklin's son, William, the ex-governor of New Jersey, were all in England and considered Loyalists, leaving John Adams as the only U.S. peace negotiator without that family encumbrance. Well before then, Jay's relations with Sir James had become strained and distant, and they would remain so.[72]

Despite John's family devotion, he consciously accepted the risk of disaster for himself and his entire family as the price he had to pay to act on his convictions regarding the justice of his country's demands on England. As he wrote to James De Lancey on January 28, 1778:

Notwithstanding the opposition of our sentiments and conduct relative to the present contest, the friendship which subsisted between us is not forgotten, nor will the good offices done me by yourself and family cease to excite my gratitude.

How far your situation may be comfortable and easy I know not [the friend was a prisoner of war of the Americans at Hartford]. It is my wish and shall be my endeavor that it be as much so as may be consistent with the interest of *that great cause to which I have devoted everything I hold dear in this world* [emphasis supplied]. I have taken the liberty of . . . immediately to advance you $100 on my account.

In his rather stoical stance, Jay was comforted by an unshakably profound religious belief (his "philosophy" expressly was his "Christianity") that would remain an important part of his life to its end.[73] Jay, on January 6, 1776, wrote Robert Livingston regarding the latter's loss, all in 1775, of his father, grandfather, and hero brother-in-law, General Montgomery, who had fallen at the foot of Quebec (see Appendix A): "Consolation in seasons of poignant distress" can be found in a "resignation to the dispensations of a benevolent as well as omnipresent being. . . . But remember, my friend, that your country bleeds; it calls for your exertions."[74]

It should be added, however, that this was far from the full extent of Jay's method of handling adversity, because he also placed great stress on "amusement and exercise," on being of a joyful frame of mind, all of which he would regularly include in his exhortations to himself and to his loved ones in distress— "despondency ill-becomes a man."[75]

Educationally, Jay was carefully schooled in the classic tradition, culminating in his attendance at the elite, still-minuscule King's (now Columbia) College, from which he graduated in 1764 with the goal of joining a law firm as a clerk paying for the privilege of being trained for eventual admittance to the bar. Luckily, just at this time Parliament lifted the Stamp Act, which had stultified legal practice in America. The profession now opened up new business opportunities, and this facilitated Jay's acceptance into a well-established firm. By 1768, after having worked hard and well for that firm's head, Benjamin Kissam, who came to like and admire him, and also after having taken the rather *pro forma* master's degree from King's College, Jay was licensed by New York Governor Tryon to practice as an attorney-at-law.[76] He then joined with his dear friend, Robert Livingston, a fellow graduate of King's College (1768), to establish their own firm, which was dissolved within two years, when Jay began his own practice.[77] In a letter of April 2, 1765, Jay displayed the rather strong and eloquent mix of emotional, social and purely cerebral factors that would always be associated with their friendship and that perhaps help explain its ultimate demise shortly after the end of the Revolutionary War. Here are excerpts from that self-revealing document, whose sentiments surely neither man ever lost sight of in their personally painful struggle to iron out policy differences as key officials involved in the negotiations for American independence:

After we parted last Saturday evening I retired to my room, and spent the remaining part of it in reflecting upon the transactions of the day, particularly of such of them as immediately related to our present and future connection. I always find myself greatly embarrassed when I attempt to speak my sentiments on a subject that very nearly concerns me. Your proposal was made with remarkable delicacy. Convinced that friendship was one of the greatest blessings as well as advantages this

life can boast, I have long since thought seriously of engaging a connection of this kind with one whom I might have reason to think qualified
for such an intimacy by being not only of similar professions and circumstances with myself, but one whose disposition would concur with
his fidelity and good sense [to assure that, once the connection is entered
into, it] ought ever to be preserved inviolable. I was so happy to have
had your proposal and *your kindly offer to point out every rock that may
endanger my safety in our voyage to eternity* [emphasis supplied].

We have now entered into a connection of the most delicate nature, a
connection replete with happiness and productive of very extensive advantages; it will heighten the joys of each by adding to the felicity of
both, and the misfortunes of either will by being divided become more
tolerable. Let our kindred spirits then unite in nourishing the increasing
flame, let the interest of one be the interest of both, and let us constantly
disdain every malignant insinuation of insidious or malevolent hearts—
in a word, let us maintain a virtuous friendship while here below, and
in the world to come we shall not be divided.

Worth adding at this point is a comment in Jay's letter to Livingston of January 6, 1776: "Let us unite in proving by our example, that the rule, which declares juvenile friendships like
vernal plants, to be of short continuance, is not without exceptions
even in our degenerate days."[78] The two would succeed in maintaining their friendship just long enough to exchange godfather
roles in the early 1780s.

As we see, none of Jay's formal higher education or practical
experience can be said to have had direct relevance to a career in
international affairs or diplomacy; nor had his personal interests
inclined in that direction, despite having spent a few early childhood years at a French Huguenot–run school in New Rochelle,
New York. One is tempted to apply to him what Robert Livingston said of himself, upon assuming the position of Secretary for
Foreign Affairs—that he was totally unprepared by education or
experience for such a post.[79] Jay never traveled much beyond his
beloved region of birth until his departure for Europe; nor did
even the French language take hold in his adult years, although
he did improve especially his reading skills in it while in Europe.[80]

One clue as to his lifelong attitude regarding contemporary foreign cultures can be derived from a letter he wrote on October 13, 1782, to his friend and, since 1781, the U.S. Superintendent of Finance, Robert Morris, whose two sons were being educated in Europe. Jay argued there against "our young people leaving their own country to be educated abroad," particularly on the subjects of "religion, morality, virtue and prudence. . . . I fear that the ideas which my countrymen in general conceive of Europe are in many respects rather too high. If we should ever meet again, you shall know my sentiments very fully on this head."

Jay was a most sociable person, if rather stiff and formal except with his most intimate of friends, when, in fact, he could even turn racy (to Gouverneur Morris on November 5, 1780, regarding Morris's loss of a leg in a road accident: "A gentleman in France wrote me that Mrs. Plate[r] after having much use of your legs had occasioned your losing one of them.") and jauntily humorous (to William Livingston on July 14, 1780, regarding the birth of a daughter: "[A]s the Saints are at war with the heretics," we won't follow local tradition and give her the name of the ninth's Saint and instead will "name it after some sinner that will probably have more affection for it.").[81]

Prewar, Jay spent the bulk of his limited spare time attending, and often helping to manage, debating and dancing societies, in addition to his family activities. A perhaps telling episode indicative of his lifelong propensity to make unnecessarily hasty, unilateral decisions, often poorly communicated to affected persons, with consequent hotheaded exchanges or cooled friendships, can be gleaned from an incident in early February 1773, when, as one of three "managers" of a dancing society, he found himself ready to fight a duel with Robert Randall, a candidate he had rejected for admission into the society: "[Y]ou did not appear to me to be connected with the people who frequent the assembly. . . . [M]y objection arose from my ignorance of your acquaintance with the subscribers. . . . [I]f any reasonable person will say I have injured you or that you have a right to satisfaction, I will ask your pardon or fight you." While the issue predictably was resolved by an installation rather than a duel, it probably helps explain Jay's 1781 view on the practice of dueling, that "pride will in general be too strong for reason."[82]

THE IMPLICATIONS FOR FRANCE OF THE AMERICAN REVOLUTION'S BECOMING A MILITARY CONFLICT, 1775–76

The American Colonies' Move toward Independence

The political consequences of the battles of Lexington and Concord in April 1775 were enormous, not least of which was the transformation of the Continental Congress into a quasi-government organizing a "Continental Army," issuing its own form of currency, dispatching representatives abroad, resolving on policy matters for the consideration of each of the thirteen rebelling colonies and, finally, declaring those colonies as united and independent of England.

The following is a summary of what the contemporary History found in William Livingston's papers says about this period:

The unexpected acts of the first Continental Congress disappointed and mortified the British government, which had flattered itself that the Boston malcontents were but a small party headed by a few factious men and that the rest of the colonists would be pro-government once they saw its firmness. Even if the colony of Massachusetts sided with Boston, England believed no other colony would; anyway, the Association surely would fail, or be short-lived, given its cost to individual welfare and especially the history of competition and differences among the colonies. England also remembered the obstacles which prevented the colonies from acting together in the execution of schemes planned for their own defense in the late war against the French and Indians.[83]

Now, however, colonists perhaps felt greater danger from the English threat to their liberties than from French encroachments on Indian territories in their neighborhood; or perhaps, the time to part being come, the colonies were now disposed to union—it seemed as though one mighty mind inspired the whole. All classes and all colonies sacrificed, not from the pressure of present distress but on the generous principle of sympathy with an invaded sister colony and the prudent policy of guarding against the precedent that might in a future day operate against their liberties.

A great and powerful diffusion of public enthusiasm took place. The animation of the times and the enthusiasm of the day raised the actors in these scenes above themselves and excited them to deeds of self-denial that the interested prudence of calmer seasons can scarcely credit.

Following the closure of the first Continental Congress, the Parliament of Great Britain was suddenly dissolved. Americans saw that act as due to the desire to have a new Parliament returned before the proceedings of their Congress could be known in Great Britain and, therefore, to have a more submissive Parliament than if elected after the British people knew that all thirteen colonies were opposing the current policy of Parliament.

The scheme had that desired result for the king and the government, whatever their true motives. The king's speech of November 30, 1774, reflected a continuation of the coercive policy; it also reported that criminal resistance was present now in all thirteen colonies and in the form of the Association. News of the speech and Parliament's endorsements arrived in America in February 1775, when the Association's bans were in effect, and those were now executed with more vehemence than before.

England next banned the export of arms, and the like, into America, and this incited the Americans to make them themselves, leading in turn, to their fear that England would soon coerce them physically. Accordingly, there followed a large increase in the number of militia troops. It took until February 1775 for the king and the government to present to Parliament plans of coercion, at which the British nation would have previously shuddered. The delay in presenting those plans perhaps was due to the need for London to get more information from America or to the need to better prepare government agencies. The information it did get was from slanted sources, for example, governors who exaggerated American opposition to parliamentary acts and to colonial subordination to England and who claimed that America was openly aiming at independence.

In fact, neither Massachusetts nor the other American colonies planned to go farther than to obtain a redress of grievances. Nevertheless, all pro-American petitions were sent to a special parliamentary committee, which buried them—hence, its nickname was "The Committee of Oblivion." Benjamin Franklin and Arthur Lee were refused the opportunity

to be heard at the bar of the House of Commons in support of the Petition of the Continental Congress. Here was a truly critical moment for
the union of the empire, given that the new Parliament, with good grace,
could have changed the old one's policies. But the Minister for American
Affairs ran the show with a view to getting approval for harsh means.
For example, he said: "We have lately saved them from conquest and
slavery, and they now repay us with a false accusation of designs on
their liberty"; and, "The Americans are now incessantly laboring to abol-
ish the sovereignty of Britain over them."

Although, even in 1774–75, America was willing to drop its resistance
if Britain would repeal the controversial acts, the latter received the matter in a different light: To recede at this time would be to acknowledge
that the ministry had hitherto been in the wrong—a concession rarely
made by private persons but much more rarely by men in public stations.
In the government's opinion, to retract was to relinquish all authority
over the colonies. But this was to confuse the opposition of freemen to
what they deemed unconstitutional innovations with the turbulence of
licentious mobs breaking over the bounds of law and constitution. American opinion and British opinion were opposed. The former saw Britain
as wishing to deprive them of liberty, while the latter believed the Americans were seeking redress only as a specious pretext for a policy of
independence. Therefore, jealousies of each other were reciprocally indulged to the destruction of all confidence and to the final dismemberment of the empire.

Both Houses of Parliament demanded, in an Address to the King, to
declare Massachusetts in a state of rebellion, and they assured him that
it was their fixed resolution, at the hazard of their lives and properties,
to stand by His Majesty. Here is where Parliament passed the Rubicon.
It was a virtual declaration of war. Remarkably, the Address was made
known in some colonies on the exact same day—and, in the rest, near
that day—of the commencement of hostilities between the British troops
and the people of Massachusetts.

Britain's military and naval buildup, along with its other measures and
schemes, was undertaken in the expectation that the inhabitants, to obtain a riddance of this heavy pressure, would generally interest themselves in procuring obedience and submission to the late acts of
Parliament. It was in this spirit that a parliamentary act restrained the
trade of Massachusetts and also that of Connecticut, Rhode Island and
New Hampshire; moreover, a ban was placed on fishing on the banks
of Newfoundland or other places cited by the legislation. Parliamentary

vengeance was clearly being leveled particularly at the New England provinces on the premise that an unemployed population would clamor in favor of reconciliation. But that policy operated against itself: Fishermen were now reduced to the necessity of turning soldiers; and the parliamentary acts themselves aroused increased fear and indignation regarding English intentions and presumed power, threatening to make of Americans slaves the most wretched.

Earlier acts were only against Massachusetts; now these were more comprehensive, on grounds, according to Lord North, that the other cited colonies had aided and abetted their invaded sister, and therefore, Britain, by this new penal statute, had to curb their close ability further to aid Massachusetts. All this only (1) helped to solidify the unity of all thirteen colonies, including those of the most moderate in popular attitude, and (2) hurt the British economy, notably its fishing sector, which depended heavily on American sources of supply, and its merchants, because a large debt was at that time due to them from the New England provinces.

Britain forgot that the two preceding concessions on the part of Parliament in the years 1766 and 1770 were followed with peace and tranquillity in the colonies and a recommencement of the commercial intercourse between the two countries. Instead, solid revenue was their object, and therefore Britain needed to break the spirits of the colonies. It ignored Congress' Petition and also that of British merchants. Parliament determined that it had no time to waste with enquiries regarding its policy of coercing the colonies into submission. The consequence of all this was that there was an increasing colonial disposition to add to their claims, leading, in turn, to a British disposition to coerce them still more: From the colonies' only demanding exemption from internal taxation came the British scheme for a tea tax, which led the colonies to deny Britain's right of taxing them in any form for a supply [i.e., revenue], which led to London's deprivation of Massachusetts' charter and right to local trials, and so on, which led to a colonial denial of Parliament's claim of internal legislation (although still admitting a parliamentary right to bind their trade), which led to Britain's stretching that acknowledgment by America into a ban on foreign trade and on fishing on their own coasts, presumably to be lifted once the colonies submitted to Britain's power to tax—all this, finally, led to the fast opening in America for a total renunciation of Britain's sovereignty over the thirteen colonies.

In sum, there was a fatal progression from small to greater breaches;

from a three-pence tea tax to 340 chests being sent into the sea; and from
the closing of a port and the establishment of a new model charter to
twelve colonies uniting as an Association. The situation was one of reciprocal cause and effect between liberty for America and supremacy for
Britain. Then came the restraining acts, including adding five more colonies to the trade ban between British America and the entire world
(with the purposeful exception of those parts—Great Britain, Ireland and
the British West Indies—that the colonies themselves had targeted for a
ban by their Association). The five were New Jersey, Pennsylvania, Maryland, Virginia and South Carolina; the rationale was the same as stated
earlier regarding the four New England colonies—that is, they had
adopted the continental Association. It is remarkable that the remaining
three of the Associated colonies—New York, Delaware and North Carolina—were omitted in this legislation. In America, this was seen as a
device calculated to promote disunion. But the three renounced immediate advantage and shared the fate of the others by continuing to adhere
to the Association. The indulgence granted by London to New York in
being kept out of this restraining legislation was considered by some as
a premium for her superior loyalty: New York's legal, constitutional Assembly, unlike her unofficial one, had refused to approve the proceedings of the Congress. Accordingly, in Britain, much was expected from
New York's moderation. But just as Parliament was framing the Restraining Acts, this very Assembly petitioned it for a redress of the colony's grievances. It was disappointing to Britain that even the loyal New
York leadership was claiming exclusive rights regarding taxation, self-
government, the justice system, and so on. This, in London's view, was
inconsistent with the legislative authority of Parliament as contained in
its Declaratory Act and could only mean that even the legal and loyal
colonial constitutional assemblies would be unable to serve as mediators
looking toward a reconciliation. It also now became clear to Britain that
all thirteen colonies were united on the fundamental principle of exemption from parliamentary taxation. The inevitable conclusion, in this manner of thinking, was that either eternal variance must subsist without
end or arms must decide the controversy. Therefore, the king's final act
in that session of Parliament, on May 26, 1775, which was to thank it for
its support, actually was an act to usher in the horrors of war and eventual dismemberment of his empire. Up until that time, as far as Britain
was aware, no substantial blood had been shed; that completion of the
miseries of civil war would now speedily follow.

The French Reaction

The repercussions of all these and related subsequent developments in North America and England were strongly felt in France. One was the direct clash of interest at sea between it and England as a consequence of the latter's declaring the colonies as "rebels" on August 29, 1775, and then imposing a total trade embargo on them in December 1775. This entailed seizures by English warships (and, starting in 1777, private "vessels of force") of French and all other neutral shipping whenever there was even the slightest suspicion that such shipping was in violation of the embargo and its extremely broad definition of contraband and rights of inspection.[84] Also by 1777, England was seizing French sailors aboard merchantmen for impressment into its naval service or placement under its custody. Rarely were seized ships, or their cargoes, quickly returned or equitably compensated, England claiming that only its (slow-moving) Admiralty Courts had jurisdiction over disputes with neutrals regarding justification for those seizures. This situation had been anticipated by Vergennes, who wrote the embassy in Madrid on August 7, 1775, that England is likely to "cease to be pacific and try to regain popularity" with the Americans by attacking France and Spain; if so, it will "begin by acts of piracy."[85]

During that same period, he began to receive and rebut, increasingly coldly, British Ambassador Stormont's complaints about American ships in French ports. Vergennes's position was that, unlike England's changing policies regarding freedom of the seas, from the narrow definition of Cromwell to the more liberal one of 1727, when a rapprochement prevailed between Walpole and Fleury, and now back to Cromwell's, that England is master of all commercial regulations at sea, France consistently has supported that maritime freedom, although subject to circumstances and conditions.[86] The Frenchman asserted to Stormont that none of the latter gave basis for England to treat "all American products aboard French ships as contraband." Vergennes also maintained to the ambassador that (1) it was only English domestic law that justified their policy of "merchandise changing hands, changed possessor"; (2) only French ships found close to the American colonies, or to England, should be liable to visits; and (3) any ships entering French ports under the English flag had a right to hospitality, as in previous years—France was a trading nation and not in a position to investigate the background of each of those ships.[87]

Additional difficult issues for the two nations were in sight: for example, how to deal with the predictable consequences of the resolution passed by the Continental Congress on April 16, 1776, authorizing privateers to seize English ships worldwide. One such consequence, as Vergennes fully realized well in advance, would come to the fore as soon as those privateers began bringing their English prizes into French ports for disposition, because that in turn would bring Stormont rushing back into his office with fresher, and more justified, complaints than ever before.[88]

Another repercussion for France of American developments was the raising of diplomatic and military tensions with England. The latter naturally assumed, from the start, that the French could not humanly resist the temptation to dip into troubled waters and take advantage of England's difficulties by giving material support to the rebels. As reported by the French embassy in January 1775, Chatham told the House of Lords that the French are like "vultures, cruising over the British Empire and devouring with their eyes the prey they will grab at the first opportunity."[89] On December 6, 1776, a London dispatch to its ambassador in Madrid justified England's own naval buildup in American waters in part on its view that "a fleet was preparing to sail from France, and its destination probably for the West Indies, where it could not fail of giving seeming encouragement to the colonies in rebellion," thereby making it "highly expedient [for England] to be in a proper state of defense."[90]

And, indeed, France *was* "dipping in troubled waters," although at this stage only in a sporadic and cautious way, even as it was reassuring the English that "we don't want to profit in any way from the problem of our neighbors."[91] But France also was making it crystal clear that "it is important for us to be on the alert to prevent those problems from flowing back on us"—as, for example, with regard to England's maritime policies and actions. Vergennes, in this ambivalent vein, spelled out for the guidance and use of his London embassy (June 23, 1775): "The spirit of revolt, wherever it breaks out, is always an upsetting example. There are moral sicknesses like physical ones; the ones and the others could become contagious. This condition must lead us to a policy of *preventing the spirit of independence from spreading to the areas which are of interest to us in this [American] hemisphere*" (emphasis supplied). The Frenchman characteristically then added the caveat, which also served as a basic rationale for his early diplomacy regarding the American War: "[T]he English will feel their hurt less, if they could make us share it or at least compensate for it."[92] Fully aware of this French security concern, Lord North in April 1776 evidently sought to build on it for his own purposes (i.e., that of discouraging France from entering the war) by indirectly warning that "if France should lift a finger against England, it would be necessary to give *carte blanche* to the Americans"— that is, to grant them enough to win their military cooperation against France.[93]

At this early period, each of Versailles' Vergennes-orchestrated moves toward involvement in the war was as much an ad hoc response to the initiatives of those outside government as a product of any plan within it. For example, in the summer of 1775, it accepted the offer of a private individual, Bonvouloir, made through the embassy in London, to go as a secret agent to Philadelphia, first, to assess the strength and political determination of the rebels; and, second, if appropriate, to encourage them in the belief that the French government would be receptive to discreetly providing them with war materiel and financial assistance.[94] It is startling how significant this agent's obscurely begun mission proved to be in the history of the French-American alliance. His reporting was upbeat regarding America's prospects and helped convince Vergennes in 1776 to aid them more actively in three major categories: maritime connections, war materiel and hard cash. Bonvouloir's meetings in December 1775 with members of

Congress, including Jay and Franklin, also were most important, because they reassured the Americans that their hopes for French support were not pie-in-the-sky, as England was asserting.[95]

The official rationale for Versailles' positive follow-up to Bonvouloir's assurances in Philadelphia of French interest in the American cause was explained by Vergennes months later, after he had a chance to study all of Bonvouloir's reports and had learned of the Declaration of Independence: "I am not surprised that the members of the Congress are men of quality, truly heroic and seek independence"; while existing circumstances make it unlikely "that any power could wish to form political ties with them, at least in the near future," it does make sense to trade with them under the guise of their "continuing to use the safeguard of the English flag, which allows others to accept them without having to examine the device"; "for political and commercial reasons, France has decided to grant maximum facilities to American ships, whose exports to it being only their own agricultural products, can do no harm; therefore France has also decided to go so far as to give those American exports duty free status"; and all the above measures were to be kept from the knowledge of England, whose prospects of success in America could not be very good.[96] (By then, of course, both the French and Spanish governments also were on the verge of secretly financing the purchase and shipment of arms to the Americans, as will be discussed below in connection with another of those privately suggested and implemented contacts between the Americans and the Bourbons, that by Beaumarchais.)

But throughout this early period in the American War, France concentrated its efforts on domestic reforms and the continuing rehabilitation of its military and naval forces. War was to be avoided with any power whatsoever, a rule that particularly annoyed its Bourbon ally, Spain, which, by 1776, was in the midst of a confrontation in South America with Portugal. The latter was pressing into disputed territory even though it was particularly weak and exposed during this period due to the preoccupation of its protective ally, England, with its North American problem. The confrontation between the two Iberian powers predictably soon led to armed conflict off the shores of Brazil and in present-day Uruguay. France rejected Spanish pleas that winter to make at least a show of joining forces with it in American waters. Interestingly, the English themselves were close and well-informed observers of this intra-Bourbon disagreement. Secretary of State Weymouth reported to Ambassador Grantham on April 18 and 29, 1777, that Foreign Minister Floridablanca was claiming to France that it should send an expedition force to the West Indies to counter a prospective English threat. According to Weymouth's sources, Floridablanca was alleging that the reality of that perceived English threat would become clear under the following circumstances: "in the case of submission [to Britain] on the part of America, when conquests in the House of Bourbon should be a compensation for the expense the rebellion had occasioned; or, in the case of the Americans' establishing their independency, these projected conquests were to be the atonement to the [British] nation for the loss sustained." Weymouth added that the Spanish knew their claim about English intentions was "wrong" but were using it anyway in order "to conceal" their real desire, which was "to engage the House of Bourbon into a war."[97]

Floridablanca was indeed making this argument to France. This was to turn Versailles' standard line to Spain against itself. For example, on August 7, 1775, in assessing the implications of the now-violent American uprising, the French had made the case to Madrid that Spain, like France, should militarily prepare for a looming war with England: "Although we would seem to be the ones who are most immediately threatened, it would not be surprising if the storm hit Spain before us. The English could expect as great advantages, and even more considerable ones, against Spain than against us. Also, England could find a pretext for war easier versus Spain than France; e.g., over Spanish-Portuguese issues."[98] However, once the Spanish-Portuguese clash occurred, France felt it had to pull Madrid back from too-precipitate a step that might draw the Bourbons prematurely into war with England. Thus, on May 14, 1776, it was commending its ambassador to Spain, Ossun, for having fended off Spanish demands that

France send 12,000 troops to St. Domingo, because Versailles saw that island's climate as a "cemetery" and also because that troop movement, accompanied by the necessary naval force, would provoke England at a time when France and Spain still lacked an interest in starting a war with it, one that could not be "legitimate."[99] By that time, the French view regarding the situation in North America was a gloating one, as is clear from its rhetorically asking Madrid: "What could we better desire than England's present war versus itself?"

Vergennes months later buttressed this view by telling the Spanish ambassador, Count Pedro de Aranda, on April 26, 1777: England lacks a major naval force in American waters, so it would be a provocation for France to send one; England also is "emptying its home island of troops," so it is showing no plan to be hostile against the two Bourbon powers; and if France were to send a fleet to American waters, and England did, too, then the "sea captains" would be the ones to hold the key to peace or war—"one knows well how to start a war, but can't know where, how and when to end it."[100] This French unwillingness to take even the risk of war with England would be used by Madrid from late 1777 into 1779 as a bitterly expressed reason for *Spain's* now rejecting French pleas that it join with it in the American War against England.

Other factors were at play in this reversal of French-Spanish war policies:

1. Spain not only had quickly achieved its basic military goal in South America of defending its territorial claims versus Portugal but was the beneficiary of a change in Portuguese policy following the death of the king, Joseph I, and the dismissal in March 1777 of the strongly anti-Spanish prime minister, Pombal. That change allowed the now-powerful queen, Marie I, who had family ties to the Spanish Bourbons, to make "an overture for conciliation" to Spain.[101] This led to a treaty of friendship between the two Iberian powers, signed in September 1777, curbing Spanish ambitions to absorb Portugal itself.

2. Spain's Charles III, following the military episode with Portugal, was increasingly reluctant to risk repeating his misfortunes of 1762–63 at

England's hands; moreover, his grudge against France for having coerced Spain into what he considered a premature peace at that time
would soon become deeper than ever in the face of France's unilaterally entering into open military alliance with the Americans in February 1778. In addition, Charles was in his final years and did not
wish to risk undermining his important achievements, and likely historical fame, as a domestic reformer; he wanted to have peace until
the end of his reign and, in 1777, felt that he had nothing to gain now
in a war with England. France feared he was slipping into a Ferdinand
VI–type "inertia."[102] (However, when the true dimensions of the cost
to English power of the American War became clear, Charles, who
never stopped hoping to see England "humiliated," would become
open to seizing the opportunity of reaping (a) great additional "glory"
by striking England and forcing it to return lost Spanish territory,
most importantly Gibraltar, but also Minorca and the Floridas, and
(b) greater security for Spanish America, which, or at least he so convinced himself by then, would be less threatened by a divided Anglo-
Saxon presence in North America.)[103]

3. The replacement, announced in November 1776, of Grimaldi by Floridablanca would immediately usher in a fresh approach to Spain's
policy toward the American War. Where the Genoan was widely perceived to have "a blind deference towards France," as in Spain's
having agreed in 1776 to match France's 1 million livres secret contribution to the Americans, and to channel those funds entirely
through Versailles, now there not only would no longer be such indirect channeling, but sizable financial aid itself would also be ter-
minated.[104] This change was but a harbinger of a fierce, new Spanish
determination no longer to shadow French policy toward the U.S.,
most certainly not when it came to giving diplomatic recognition or
openly allying with it militarily. This barring of any kind of official
recognition of the Americans would continue even as Spain became
a co-belligerent of France against England, much to the shock and
surprise of the Continental Congress and its unaccredited minister in
Madrid, John Jay.

4. Coupling these Spanish developments was an evolution in French policy that would lead France into war with England in formal—but
entirely separate—alliances with the U.S. and Spain. These two alliances were based on treaties that were possibly contradictory, cer-

tainly overlapping and mutually complicating. They were signed in
1778 and 1779, respectively. While December 1780 would see the entrance into the war against England of a fourth power, the Netherlands, the latter would never become a formal ally of any of the other
three, somewhat simplifying Vergennes's diplomatic task. In this
tangle of de facto allies and co-belligerents (only one of whom, France,
would even recognize the U.S. prior to the great victory of Yorktown
in October 1781), there was the germ of the friction between the Americans and the French that would reach its crisis point at the Paris peace
negotiations of 1782.

The question naturally arises as to how and why France entered
into such a wide range of commitments that required it to juggle
several balls in the air at once, militarily and diplomatically. The
basic answer is, France believed, and would till the very end of
the war, that it needed Spanish naval help if it was to defeat the
English in what was looming to be a worldwide maritime war.
Without the Spanish fleet, France's navy, even though revitalized
and expanded, would lack that increment of numerical strength
it needed, especially in ships-of-the-line, in order to have a good
prospect of success against the vaunted English prowess at sea.
Vergennes did not see Spain as able to help France confront England in a land war, but that it could truly do so at sea. By extension, Vergennes also sought to encourage tension, if not actual
armed conflict, between England and all other powers having a
maritime presence—the Netherlands being the most significant of
this group, which was composed mainly of three other "northern
powers" of Russia, Sweden and Denmark.

Although historically and most naturally a land power, France
recognized that to capitalize on England's current embarrassment
it had to take advantage of a relatively calm European continent
by concentrating entirely on its potential, especially when in combination with others, as a sea power on a par with England. As
Vergennes put it: "It is important to assure that a naval war not
spread into a European conflict, and so, it is best if we receive
war instead of making it"; still, if war comes, "our purport is not
to prepare for defense, but for offense as well as defense. Other-

wise, England would cut us up at its pleasure."[105] Of course, when Vergennes says that France should "receive war instead of making it," he obviously really means that the other European powers should be given a basis for interpreting any start of a French-English war as having been due to English, not French, aggression; in this way, England's chances for gaining continental support and allies, as it did in previous wars, would be substantially lessened. Thus, he told Aranda on April 26, 1777, that "if I could be sure of its not spreading into Europe, I would approve starting the war with England right now"; but it was essential that England be seen as the initiator, because while Spain was "protected from European continental issues, France bears all of their weight, a possible ruinous situation."[106]

In the view of the foreign minister, if France were to succeed in completing the naval buildup begun by Choiseul following the 1763 peace, but then halted during the d'Aiguillon interregnum of 1771–74, and if it were to get Spain to join with it in a future war, France then would be in the happy position of reversing the unfavorable military outcome of the Seven Years' War. In that last conflict, as noted, England had the advantage of superior land forces in North America along with a dominant navy, while France was bogged down in both a maritime-cum-colonial war *and* a major land one in Europe, where England needed send but a minor part of its troops. Now, in the mid-1770s, there was a serious prospect of fighting England strictly in a maritime war at a time when that enemy was itself bogged down in a land war on the North American continent, where the Americans, at least theoretically, had numerical and certain key geopolitical and logistical advantages over it.[107]

As Vergennes wrote his ambassador in London on August 7, 1775: "The last war is not a precedent for the next one"; the French and Spanish navies were now stronger, and North America was no longer pro-English; the government of England "gravely errs if, as you report, it believes that we ardently regret the loss of Canada. It could well repent having itself made such an acquisition. Despite the Spanish retreat from Algiers [a recently failed

Grimaldi-sponsored military expedition that would contribute to his dismissal and that would be so costly as to put a crimp in Spain's ability to help the Americans], the Spanish navy is still intact."[108] Garnering ever more ambitious strategies with each passing year, Vergennes by 1776 envisaged that if Spain were to join with France, England's strategic concerns would be so widespread, not excluding having to assure land and sea protection of its home islands and its European possessions of Gibraltar and Minorca, that Bourbon sea power, when supplemented by a wise use of the abundant numbers of French and even Spanish troops, could well carry the day against overstretched, undermanned English fleets and armies.

The above-outlined strategic outlook began to take shape at Versailles even prior to news of America's Declaration of Independence, which was heralded as early as March 1776 in a dispatch to Vergennes from the French embassy in London. Vergennes's various messages and memoranda of this period reflect a growing conviction, sincere or not, that willy-nilly France could not avoid a confrontation with England in consequence of events in North America and at sea. At least starting in August 1775, Vergennes regularly expressed the fear that a surprise English attack was a constant and distinct possibility, given that "in the war of 1755, it had been assuring our ambassador in London of its most pacific assurances even as it was already attacking us by land and sea"; therefore, France should prepare for it—"If we cannot ward off the blow, at least let us try to foresee the approximate period when it might be struck."[109] On April 6, 1776, that Frenchman interpreted a reported departure for the West Indies of an English naval squadron, even though the modest Bourbon presence in those waters could not be "giving concern to the English," as part of a plan by Secretary of State Germain to initiate a war with France and Spain so as "to replace the American War with a foreign war" while entering into a fifteen-year truce with the colonies.[110] By July and August 1777, he was advising that if England, as in its last campaign, cannot beat America in its present one, it could be so hard pressed by the situation as to see only a "foreign war" as the way out: "The crisis is approaching rapidly."[111] Finally, on

January 25, 1778, in the last of the series of major memoranda serving as key links in the development of French policy up to the treaties with the U.S. of 6 February, Vergennes urged the need to act immediately, or else, with 30,000 French sailors on merchantmen and fishing boats due to leave France within the next three weeks, France would be encouraging England to repeat "the outrages of 1756 [1755?]."[112]

Alongside this sense of inevitability of still another war against the "natural enemy" was a growing sense of excitement, based partly on a massive exaggeration of American military strength, that France, as put by Vergennes at the start of 1778, actually was facing an "opportunity that may not repeat itself for centuries" to take revenge for the Treaty of 1763 and, by doing so, to reduce England to a more moderate and hopefully constructive role in maintaining a French-arbitrated European balance of power; egged on by his pro-war ambassadors in London and the Hague, the foreign minister similarly was advising Spain at that time that present circumstances "perhaps may never again give us this precious moment."[113]

In summary, the considerations moving France in this militaristic direction between 1775 and 1777 included the following:

1. Huge stakes were involved. An England deprived of the thirteen rebelling colonies, aside from suffering the loss of naval manpower, as noted above, would be denied monopolistic access to a wide range of natural resources as well as to a steadily growing, wealthy market for its own, mainly manufactured products. Similarly, England—even if ultimately victorious militarily after having had to fight over a long period to control a discreetly French-sustained rebellion in North America—would then have to keep a tight lid on that permanently restless land, thereby distracting it from its perennial meddling in European continental affairs and in the maritime commerce of others.

2. There was a possibility, even perhaps a probability, of an English attack on Bourbon possessions in the Western Hemisphere. This was true *whatever the final result of the English-American contest.*[114] Those possessions would be at risk due to English aggression, either solely on their own, with the goal of compensating the motherland for the

loss of the rebellious colonies, or in combination with the Americans after a reconciliation based in part on mutual agreement to use their still-primed military power at the expense of their temptingly closeby, underprotected and resource-rich neighbors. Given that bleak and broadly feared prospect, strained as it seemed to some even at that time (Floridablanca was one such skeptic) and certainly seems now to us, Vergennes's France could rather plausibly proclaim to itself and the world at large that entering the war was fundamentally an act of *prudent self-defense.*

It was with this line of argument that Vergennes gradually maneuvered Louis XVI and his government into a course of action that could have but one outcome: full-scale war with England. However, not all at Versailles at the time, perhaps not even Vergennes, recognized that the policy would require France to eat humble pie for years in its effort, first, to convince Spain to join it in war and, second, after that was achieved, to reach agreement on a military and diplomatic strategy compatible with France's own wartime and postwar goals.

FROM REBELLIOUS COLONIES TO AN INDEPENDENT STATE

France would not have had to face such a stark policy choice between war and peace in 1777–78 had it not been for its having chosen to become progressively more involved from 1775 onward in the ballooning rebellion in North America. No other issue on the horizon in the years 1774–76 posed such a serious international issue for it; moreover, even with that rebellion and attendant English military operations, there was absolutely no threat, immediate or long term, of an attack on France proper, and only a rather theoretical one on French overseas possessions. Therefore, it was basically only due to the largely voluntary, if understandably irresistible, French interest in promoting that rebellion that Versailles found itself in 1775–77 focusing the closest attention on its details and nuances. In such a situation, the decisions made at Versailles regarding the nature and extent of its involvement on the rebel side, 1775–77, ineluctably were based in the first instance on an assessment of America's prospects for success. From the French point of view, as from that of the Americans themselves, the definition of "success" was a complex matter. Did it mean forcing England merely to back down from its insistence on Parliament's right to tax or otherwise interfere with colonial life? Could the issue be resolved, even after Lexington and Concord, by peaceful negotiations, or must it be by the sword? If the latter, would it even then be sufficient for "success" to see the reestablishment of the pre-1763 relationship, or would it be necessary to go all the way and create an entirely separate, independent nation?

The answers to these questions could only come from North America itself. If Vergennes had looked only to John Jay and his like-minded group of influential, conservative members of the Continental Congress for those answers, he would have been totally discouraged through the early months of 1776 from any meaningful planning for direct assistance to the American cause. That is because Jay's position on all these questions, until the very advent of the Declaration of Independence, was one of relative moderation:

1. At first, try to limit the conflict with England to a purely political one of negotiations between it and the Continental Congress, buttressed by American economic pressure on the motherland.

2. Later, when force had been resorted to in 1775 with the Massachusetts battles, the appointment of General Washington to head a Continental Army, and the invasion of Canada, consider military means as an additional instrument of pressure in the contest with London and not as a vehicle for a definitive break with it.[115]

3. Even into June 1776, reject the passage of a declaration of independence as neither authorized by the people of New York nor desirable as a way to solve the crisis.[116] (With respect to this last point, Jay, at the time the Continental Congress was preparing for the passage of the Declaration of Independence, was in his native province focusing on the establishment of a new "mode of government" pending "a peace with Great Britain."[117] Even Robert Livingston, although a member of the congressional committee in Philadelphia charged with draft-

ing the declaration, was a principled proponent of delaying its passage, and he, along with his fellow New York delegates, honored their instructions not to sign the document.)

To the extent this set of Jay's positions reflected overall American policy, any French initiative in open favor of the rebellion obviously would have been foolhardy in the extreme. And, in fact, those positions did seem to be carrying the day in America: Despite every effort of the more radical party led by John Adams ("My talent, if I have one, lies in making war"), even the Continental Congress through 1775 and into the first months of 1776 had been adhering to a middle course of action that was designed, at least ostensibly, to leave the door open to reconciliation with England.[118] Thus, it followed up its 1774, Jay-drafted "Address to the People of Great Britain" with still another appeal, this one to the king on July 5, 1775—the "Olive Branch Petition."[119] When the news spread in America in early 1776 that George III, in his speech to Parliament of 26 October, had firmly rejected the Congress' appeal, it was accompanied by the powerful pamphlet just published by Thomas Paine as *Common Sense*.[120] The two overlapping events generated an enthusiasm for full independence that was so broadly shared as to be politically irresistible notwithstanding continuing efforts by the Jay-type moderates to prevent a formal declaration.

Jay himself, in the three months preceding the adoption of the Declaration, was away from Philadelphia and heavily engaged as a leading member of the New York provincial assembly.[121] In that role, he helped establish smooth cooperation between that body and General Washington, whose Continental Army, as it was known in contradistinction to the various state militia, was now concentrated in the area in anticipation of an English attack on New York City. It was during this very period that Jay, who never actively wore a military uniform but had solicited a commission as colonel of the second regiment of the New York militia (issued on November 3, 1775), greatly added to his luster by playing a key role in a successful operation, carried out by the special New York security committee he headed, that famously broke up a

Loyalist military and political conspiracy to aid the enemy and assassinate Washington himself (the identified agent for the intended latter act was a soldier in Washington's army named Thomas Hickey, who was duly hung toward the end of June 1776).

Jay, that spring and summer, used this heavy involvement in New York affairs as a reason—some say, excuse[122]—to resist the urgent appeals of his fellow moderates serving in the Congress at Philadelphia to return to that city and help them try to stem the tide favoring the adoption of three fateful steps: a declaration of independence, a standard framework for commercial and friendship treaties with foreign powers and a plan for a confederation of the thirteen colonies, once independent. Jay's absence from the Congress during the crucial week of 1 July did not in and of itself cost him the glory of being a signatory of the Declaration, given that, as noted, the New York delegation there was under explicit instructions from the assembly not to approve such an act; moreover, that absence saved him from having actively to oppose the Declaration in the face of majority opinion. However, once Jay in New York learned of the Declaration's passage, he made a remarkable, immediate change, *not in his actions*, for he had been a "militant patriot" almost from the beginning of his political career, but in his policies and goals, no longer adhering to the cautious view that it would be best for the colonies to remain under English rule, if the terms were right. Now, he would risk his all for a complete break, just as the signers of the Declaration were doing. The first manifestation of this change was his drafting of a resolution adopted by the New York assembly in White Plains as early as 9 July concurring in the Continental Congress' Declaration: The Rubicon was crossed.

CHAPTER 3

From the Declaration of Independence to the Battle of Saratoga

FALL 1776–WINTER 1777–78

The die would also be cast for France by that Declaration, which set off another in Vergennes's series of major policy analyses for the king and his Council, this one of August 1776, called *Considerations*, a vital link in the major phases of France's progressively more bellicose reaction to events in North America under Louis XVI.[123] This particular analysis, which followed a policy exercise of March–April 1776 leading to the initiation of secret and indirect Bourbon financial aid to the Americans through Beaumarchais, still did not urge immediate French recognition of the U.S. but it did conclude that reconciliation between England and the Americans was now unlikely, and it did successfully recommend (1) that France help keep the English struggle with its rebellious colonies alive pending the predictable English war on France—as Vergennes would put it in his next major policy paper, *Reflections*, January 5, 1777, "Our very defensive moves will lead to a war with England"; and (2) that France act on the premise that it would be better off having such a war than having to live with an unavoidably "precarious peace," because the advantages of war would by far outweigh its inconveniences (such as avoiding uselessly heavy financial costs merely to keep on ready alert an inactive military and naval establishment while waiting for the

English to choose the right moment to commence hostilities) and because a winning war would "efface the shame of 1755 and subsequent disasters."[124]

This last policy exercise, basically stretching from August 1776 to January 1777, cemented the course of action Versailles had initiated that late spring of 1776 for the surreptitious provision of a modest level of aid to the Americans. The French would now begin to move more boldly and, within eighteen months, actually enter into a formal treaty relationship with the U.S. (February 6, 1778). This last step was the functional equivalent of a declaration of war on England, with whom diplomatic relations would be broken in March 1778 upon official notification by France to it that a treaty of friendship and commerce had been signed with the Americans the previous month. (A second treaty, one laying down the provisions for a contingency military alliance with the U.S., temporarily remained unacknowledged publicly by France.) Versailles proceeded in this manner despite the abstention of Spain, whose government, as noted, had moved away from undue French influence under the strong nationalistic direction of the new foreign minister, Floridablanca, Grimaldi having been exiled back to his native Italy, as ambassador to Rome, in early 1777.[125]

As in the period 1775-76, the French authorities would take these later, fateful steps toward direct participation in the American War, not by purposefully adopting a preconceived action plan but by reacting to external pressures and proposals tending toward such participation. The two most notable examples of this ad hoc approach are those initiated by Beaumarchais and Lafayette.

The former had achieved national fame as a playwright only in 1775 with his *Barber of Seville*, but this was not the original basis of his influence at Versailles. There, he had spent years as a watchmaker and musician who parlayed his popularity with Louis XV's daughters into a modest fortune by using his influence with them, and through them the king, to obtain certain decisions desired by the likes of the principal court bankers, the Paris brothers, Joseph and Montmarte, who dutifully and generously rewarded him financially. More recently, he had done yeoman service for

Louis XVI and his queen, Marie-Antoinette, by going to London and successfully squelching the publication of scandal-mongering pamphlets against that royal couple.

It was while performing that personal service that Beaumarchais met Arthur Lee, a Virginian, who had shared the Massachusetts agency with Franklin prior to the latter's flight back to America in 1775, and became enthusiastic over the prospective usefulness to France of the cause of the rebellion in America. During the course of the winter and spring of 1775–76, he convinced a receptive but still procrastinating Versailles, including at a personal meeting with the king in late September 1775 arranged by Vergennes and Navy Minister Antoine Sartine, to finance secretly a front company that he would establish to carry out a surreptitious arms trade for the benefit of the Americans.[126] His specific proposal was to establish with secret French government funds a private trading firm that would fill in the time gap pending completion of the government's war preparations.[127] As he was wont to say, supplies don't talk.[128]

Still, that proposal remained on the drawing board through May 1776, although Vergennes kept assuring him that his "foresight" was appreciated and that "I am closer to you than you think."[129] Finally, by June 1776, Beaumarchais received his funds (including a matching 1 million livres from Grimaldi's Spain, per above), and he was in business as Hortalez & Company.[130] This operation, together with self-financed European purchases by the Continental Congress itself (initially under the coordination and leadership of Silas Deane, who arrived in France in early July 1776 as America's first "deputy" in Europe), accounted for nearly all the weaponry and ammunition available to the U.S. military at its victorious battle of Saratoga, September–October 1777.[131]

Lafayette was all of nineteen years of age when, as a junior army officer, he risked his life and reputation by undertaking the apparently foolhardy act of defying official (if less than sincere) orders and slipping off to the U.S. in early 1777 with several fellow officers in a ship he himself had chartered and loaded with war materiel.[132] Upon arrival that July in Philadelphia after a difficult trek up the coast from the Carolinas, he offered the Congress his volunteer military services along with a free grant of the arms. The American leaders were alert enough to recognize that, in him, they would possibly have a prestigious link to Versailles and, therefore, an additional weight as they sought the leverage to sway France toward joining with the newly independent nation against a shared enemy, England. Accordingly, Lafayette was commissioned a major general in the Continental Army—without pay and initially without command.[133] He would retain this commission even after France in 1780 sent its own army to fight as a discrete unit alongside, and under the strategic command of, Washington; thus, in the long months of battles in Virginia in 1781 leading up to, and including that of Yorktown, Lafayette would serve as a key field general in the American army.

In Beaumarchais and Lafayette, the U.S. gained more than an arms supplier and a wealthy military officer of the upper nobility. Both were activists in France for the American War, influencing governmental, military and popular opinion (although far themselves from sharing in Versailles' confidential political and military strategies). That this broad support made it all the easier for the government to continue and deepen its participation in the war is clear from Vergennes's late December 1777 dispatch to Montmorin in Spain: "Our public, which sees the need for this [upcoming treaty with the U.S.], believes it already done and applauds it strongly."[134] Moreover, once France was in the war as a full-fledged belligerent, both those men, especially Lafayette, remained as direct channels for the U.S. to the highest authorities at Versailles. For example, that young but capable and articulate general used winter stays in France during the conflict to emphasize America's needs, which included the permanent presence in that theater of a major French army and a naval squadron; these were reluctantly agreed to by the government in early 1780.[135]

For its part, the Congress, soon after issuing the Declaration of Independence, wisely decided to send to France its most famous member, Franklin, who left the U.S. on 26 October and arrived at Nantes in December, his American ship having en route taken and brought in an English prize. At least as early as 1767, French diplomatic correspondence cited, and favorably, the political work of

Franklin as a defender of British America and as an insightful analyst of the commercial issues between the colonies and the mother country. The French embassy in London consulted him regularly and, for example, wrote on August 12, 1768: "Benjamin Franklin is Pennsylvania's agent, a very bright man, very well intentioned toward us, and happily very rarely consulted by the English government. Events have justified his predictions. Colonial resistance has only steadily increased."[136] Choiseul, having read some of Franklin's analyses, agreed (21 August): "It's a good thing that the English fail to consult the author" of those papers.

Franklin maintained regular contact with that embassy up to the time of his flight from England.[137] For example, in November 1774, he spoke to embassy officers of the high quality and seriousness of the members of the Continental Congress and gave them a report on that body's secret resolutions. At the time of his "sudden departure," the embassy reported on March 20, 1775, that it had observed to him that America lacks the means for an effective break from England and can only on its own find them using its own resources, because right now "the Americans have neither a navy, nor allies, nor a Prince d'Orleans [meaning that, unlike a seventeenth-century effort led by that prince to replace his brother as king of France, America lacked someone ready to lead the country in replacement of King George]."[138] On 2 April, Vergennes wrote back: "Benjamin Franklin's return to Philadelphia is of great interest here. He enjoys the confidence of the colonies, and therefore his views and counsels will powerfully influence their resolutions. The English government must now be feeling its error in having maltreated him."

On July 7, 1775, the French ambassador advised that Franklin "is the man heaven has made as the one most suitable to create a free nation." Of course, the English, and most notably Ambassador Stormont, the future Foreign Secretary under North, had a different view of Franklin, whose arrival at Nantes that December 1776 prompted him to write London on 20 December: Franklin had fooled so many "sagacious" Englishmen, they should, for their "own honor," acknowledge that he was a "master of trickery"; he had already tricked those in Nantes of the colonies' "flourishing situation and England's desperate one."[139] (Franklin, as noted, had left the U.S. on 26 October, the same day three years later when the Jays would "lose sight of land" on their way to Europe.[140] Franklin's trip proved so arduous as to lead him to rule out a return to America except in peacetime, even were he to resign from his diplomatic post before then.)

Despite his age, Franklin was physically and mentally adequate to the task, as his long tenure at Paris attests.[141] While he later became the sole U.S. minister at the French court, he initially was but one of three "commissioners" there, or "deputies," as the Europeans commonly called them in this prerecognition period. Congress, by 1778, would rue its decision to have such a clumsy triumvirate. The other two were Deane and Arthur Lee, who came to his new post in early 1777 from England. It was first with Lee in England, as noted, and then with Deane in France that Beaumarchais cooperated the closest in conceiving and implementing the secret arms supply program.[142]

That program, including the de facto granting of most favored nation (MFN) status to U.S. ships, quickly became the focus of a cat-and-mouse game between the French court and the able, energetic and well-informed Stormont.[143] Neither side was fooling the other in this game, which almost daily was becoming increasingly complex, but neither was willing to force a confrontation over the program prior to 1778. The sources of friction were multiplying: For example, from the French viewpoint, to seizures of their ships at sea there now was added "a new type of irritation"—the English were "intolerably" making seizures in the Bay of Biscay, "where they are cruising so far from American shores"; and from the English viewpoint, access to French ports was being authorized now both to American merchant ships and to their privateers—and not only for replenishment and repairs but also for armaments and for disposition of prizes under the flimsiest of excuses and pretenses.[144]

It is useful to examine the internal French reaction to this last-cited English grievance: Versailles decided it could not return to their English owners the prizes being brought in by U.S. ships because then "the Americans would hate us for centuries, as we'd

be calling them pirates. . . . Still, even a precarious peace for now
would be better than war, so we will renew explicitly our port
orders barring entry of privateers and prizes, and we will give a
copy of them to England [meaning: reject England's demand that
Versailles take what would have been the unprecedented step of
publishing those orders] with a request that, on its part, it should
give us liberty and immunity of our flag and Spain's, too."[145] Naturally, this was mere gamesmanship.

Obviously, this situation could not continue for very long without major deterioration in bilateral relations between France and
England. The Versailles posture of denying to the English what
everyone knew it actually was doing, and of withholding formal
acknowledgment of the political quality of the American presence
in the country even as Vergennes and his staff were surrepti-
tiously maintaining direct, personal (but, from its side, strictly
oral) contact with Franklin and his fellow commissioners, starting
as early as a meeting involving Vergennes himself on December
28, 1776, was farcical and served merely as a temporary expedient
pending French completion of its naval buildup, American demonstration of its staying power versus England and, hopefully,
Spanish agreement to join with France in the war that was increasingly coming into view. (As late as October 31, 1777, Vergennes, evidently set back by recent American military defeats
and by Floridablanca's having thrown cold water in August on
his proposal to commence war early in 1778, was writing to Ossun
that France's navy needed one more year "to be at the point it
should be.")[146]

It was in this context that the French foreign minister reacted
so interestingly on October 3, 1777, to news of the American loss
of Ticonderoga in July to Burgoyne. Vergennes understandably
saw that defeat as a "major event," but he also believed that the
Americans were now so tired of their defeats and their personal
deprivations that, as he had been arguing at least since his memorandum of July 27, 1777, *it behooved France to do more to keep them
fighting* and to preclude their joining with England in a compen-
satory attack on French and Spanish possessions.[147] While he rejected as of "doubtful reality" most of the aid demands he had

received from the deputies in Paris, such as for eight large warships, he did now assure them of an (undefined) increase in financial assistance, which, for the first time, would be given in cash directly by the government. But two conditions were attached *and obtained* by Vergennes to that aid: (1) Congress must assure that no peace negotiations would be entered into with England without French knowledge and concurrence, and (2) "all that is conspicuous must be avoided" in their aid relationship. While Vergennes himself was thinking of a grant of 6 million livres for 1778, the king soon thereafter approved only half that amount, to be given quarterly.[148] Of course, upon the news in early December of the American victory at Saratoga in October, these aid amounts would be regularly, if modestly, increased in association with the creation in February 1778 of the French-American military alliance.[149]

It should be noted that by October 1777 the French government was already so committed to participating in the war that, for all practical purposes, it had no choice but to do what it prudently could to keep America fighting despite the Ticonderoga defeat. For example, even prior to taking the just-described direct financial aid measures in late fall, it decided in August to send troops and a small-sized, but provocative, fleet to the West Indies, where all French forces were put on alert; moreover, it ordered its cruising warships back to port, embargoed its merchantmen from leaving Brittany ports and called back the Newfoundland fishermen. Obviously, Vergennes had won Versailles to the view that the French-English relationship was getting out of control and war was unavoidable whatever course of action was chosen, and that, therefore, France must prepare for it *irrespective* of Spanish policy.[150]

That the government of England in 1777 not only was well aware of Versailles' true intentions but also at times was willing frankly to reveal that fact is clear from its having told the French embassy that, despite France's protests of its peacefulness, it is "ruining itself in preparing for war."[151] This candor was designed to warn France of the dangers of its current policies toward rebellious America; therefore, it was in keeping with London's strong desire to avoid an immediate conflict, contrary to Vergennes's charge that its policies at sea were specifically designed to draw France and Spain into declaring war.[152] In support of that desire to maintain the existing peace with the Bourbons, England was being forced to balance, on the one hand, having to take essential naval measures designed to deprive the rebels of outside materiel and financial support with, on the other hand, also having to exercise purposeful restraint in its diplomatic relations with France and Spain—at least until after putting down the rebellion. Certainly, England was sincere when, in August 1780, it acknowledged to the Spanish government that the distinct war between the two was "so manifestly disadvantageous to the interests of Spain as well as to those of this Kingdom."[153] It seems true that London felt the same about the war with France. Unfortunately for it, the spectacle of being bogged down and humiliated in North America proved too enticing to those traditional enemies to resist coming in for the spoils, whereas, had the English been militarily—or politically—more successful against the Americans at an early stage in the uprising, or had they succeeded in their sustained effort to obtain allies on the European continent, such as Russia or Austria, surely the Bourbons, ever wary of their enemy's naval prowess, would have swallowed their grievances against English actions on the high seas and remained out of the war. As it was, the spoils won by France and Spain in 1783 proved to be neither as extensive nor as easily obtained as they had hoped and expected in 1778–79.

Vergennes was encouraged in his moves toward war by the relative calm that was reigning in Europe, where the outlook was for a reasonable period of general peace on the continent itself; as he wrote in July 1777, no European power was likely to become involved in a maritime war. More specifically, the three other major continental powers were still digesting their territorial gains of the early 1770s in Poland. The perennial Russian-Turkish conflict also was quiescent following the latest armistice between the two, and, in any event, the consensus of both France and Spain was that Russia had too many domestic problems to get involved in

England's, freeing the two Bourbon powers of any fear that Catherine would help that island nation at their expense. Additionally, it was believed likely that Russia would even "see with a kind of pleasure" a successful American break from England.[154]

This was clearly an opportune time for France to take on a relatively isolated England without the risk of also having to fight a land war in Europe. As assessed by Vergennes at various periods beginning with January 1777 and up to France's signature of its fateful treaties with the U.S. in February 1778: Austria would not join the English side against its own formal ally since 1756, France, whose queen was a Habsburg;[155] that alliance with Vienna also served to protect France against Prussia, which, moreover, was likely to recognize the U.S. out of hatred of England, even though it was not a trading nation; only a Russian-Swedish war could possibly engage France, which could limit its help to financial aid, because Sweden would be able to hold out for a long time, especially given that Frederick's poor health would block Prussia from giving military assistance to the Russians against it; France's upcoming war with England would remain a naval one, would be less expensive than its present open-ended situation of having to stay at a high level of alert, and would be able to stay focused on England as the power that alone was responsible, for nearly a century, for all the great wars; even a Russian-Turkish war would not distract France from its "true object"; the recent Austrian-Palatine understanding dividing the Bavarian succession apparently had ended that potential threat to the peace; there was no other power able to war on France on the continent; and, finally, Holland was moving toward France and against England.

While this assessment proved erroneous regarding the Bavarian problem and also Prussia's policy toward the U.S., the rest was quite accurate. However, contrary to Vergennes's expectations and hopes, Spain now became a question mark as a fighting partner for France: the replacement by Floridablanca of Grimaldi, coupled with the rapprochement between Spain and Portugal, cooled Madrid's war ardor. Thus, Spain's above-noted August 8, 1777, response to France's July proposal, that the two decide at that time to embark on war by January or February 1778, was an important indicator and forecaster of the affront Spain would feel at the unilateral French signature of its treaties with the Americans and of the hesitancy with which Spain would belatedly enter the American War. The essence of the Spanish position consisted of the following:

—It would not agree to "fix the epoch" now for entering the war;

—The two powers should avoid actions which would tempt England to attack;

—France had failed "to prove" that there could be no English reconciliation with the colonies, or that England was definitely planning to war on the House of Bourbon whatever France and Spain chose to do— to the contrary, England could use the Bourbon powers' own aggressive actions against it as a motive to solicit, for the sake of its own security, American cooperation, a cooperation that the Americans would likely agree to on the basis of English recognition of their independence;

—Many in England would see any aggressive Bourbon action as "perfidy";

—"If we accelerate war, we would be advancing the very evils we fear," e.g., a reconciliation between England and the colonies, European enmity, etc.;

—Given England's immunity from any interference the Bourbons might try to introduce in its movement of ships and troops to the American theater, coupled with the fact that North America's coastline of over 3,000 miles lacked a safe harbor for Bourbon ships let alone a single French or Spanish port, even a strictly maritime war on the part of France and Spain could not put a dent into the situation in America, where, moreover, a landing of Bourbon "auxiliary troops" would be harder to execute effectively than the French scheme of a purely naval strategy;

—Experience argued against an invasion of England, if it was to serve merely as a diversion, and that, therefore, France and Spain might at best merely threaten it as a way to limit the number of German mercenaries being sent to America;

—The Americans would not be helped by Bourbon attack on Gibraltar or Minorca, where England, in any event, already was concerned over their security and was taking precautionary measures, *which the Americans would surely fail to see as helping them by forcing England to allocate resources in Europe vice America—actually, the present situation is best for the colonies, too, because, in an open war, "our own needs and difficulties would be too great to help America" as compared to the present fact that the existing help to the Americans was not at all "modest" but rather "enormous and effective"* [emphasis added];[156]

—The Bourbons' own goals should be to prevent any war with England, and to convince the Americans to see a need both for a joint guarantee from France and Spain, and for their avoiding the "trap" England might be laying for them of offering an English-American war on the Bourbon powers. Such a war would only end in depriving them of the latter's "shelter and protection," and in allowing the English to subject them more easily, because London would always prefer to reconquer the colonies than to continue in a war against a France and Spain ready to drop the American cause;

—France and Spain should tell England that *they want to mediate and not to fight.* If England declined, the colonies would then see that there was no hope of their reconciliation with it; and,

—France and Spain should not use the American Deputies in Europe as the channel for any Bourbon offer of an alliance, which could only be "indecent, unjust and useless," *the Americans never having offered France or Spain anything of "interest," and such an alliance likely only to "scare them into fearing a new war without any end in sight."*

The comment put on this message on 9 August by Ambassador Ossun was apt: Spain here shows its desire "to set back or even avoid war."[157] But this would not deter Vergennes, whose next moves, as we have seen, went in a direction contrary to Floridablanca's advice. Furthermore, while he advised Spain through Ossun on 20 and 22 August that France consented to the delay in reaching a decision on a time frame for entering the war, he added the skeptical observation that it remained to be seen if England would allow the Spanish-prescribed course of action to take place and that Madrid's proposals could only lead to French "humiliation," by having to accept England's "so revolting and imperious" conditions—a great power is able to withstand "losses," never "humiliation." Not coincidentally, it was during this period, as noted, that Versailles decided to send troops and frigates (but expressly no ships-of-the-line in the hope of curbing any English counteraction) to the West Indies and also to replace its longtime ambassador to Spain with one more energetically in tune with the fresh wind blowing in France following the death of Louis XV, in effect replacing an ambassador who was close to the Spanish king with one close to the French king—Montmorin, although a few years older, having been a childhood companion to Louis XVI.

Vergennes believed that Spain was in the same situation as France: between peace and war, but France was closer to war. That Spain itself recognized the truth of at least the first part of this view is evident from the sharp exchange in late September of 1777 between Floridablanca and Grantham, who had complained about the openness of Spanish ports to American "corsairs." The Spaniard's martial response to a shocked Grantham was that Spain had issued the same port orders as France's and that while Spain didn't wish to "antagonize the American Anglo-Saxons," it will always honor its treaty commitments with England, with which, however, it has "unsatisfied grievances, so that, if England meets our demands, we will do the same regarding England's. . . . Spain desires peace . . . but does not fear war."[158]

On the very eve of the opening of Franco-American negotiations leading to the treaties of February 6, 1778, Floridablanca was warning France through Aranda that Spain "does not want to be confronted belatedly by a French declaration [of war] which would be a disastrous commitment and oblige us to have recourse to violent and extraordinary actions."[159] Nevertheless, Spain was tied to France formally by their Family Compact of 1761, and though undesirable, because it would elicit only a minimum and unenthusiastic Spanish contribution (e.g., twelve ships-of-the-line), that treaty could be activated unilaterally by either side, if absolutely necessary.[160] That there was tension underlying the Family Pact, making it a weak reed for France to resort to by purely legalistic means, was made clear on April 12, 1777, when Vergennes complained to Floridablanca that his "boast" to Grantham of Spain's having refused to receive American deputies, in express contrast with France's policy toward them, was raising undesirable doubts in England regarding the unity of the two Bourbon powers and that the English were gaining the impression that Spain was too fearful of them to admit giving hospitality to an American rebel, even though the English themselves were in regular contact with them.[161]

Vergennes further noted that Grimaldi, too, had made such a boast, even as Spain and France were cooperating in aiding the Americans, but France at that time did not complain, given Grimaldi's having that "Italian touch"—France expected more from Floridablanca, who, Vergennes additionally observed, should have known that all France was doing was listening to the Americans at Versailles, willy-nilly. Spain, in fact, should be "more interested in the shape of future American events" than France was. Vergennes's final point was that Spain should also understand that the deputies were fanatics trying to promote morale in America by sending out "self-serving" letters claiming that France was about to sign an agreement with them; in this regard, Vergennes concluded, Maurepas personally had asked that he, Floridablanca, be informed that France would only do so the minute England recognized the U.S.

Of course, Vergennes was not being frank with the Spaniard. Moreover, by putting this last point in the mouth of Maurepas, who was not a forceful or consistent actor in this process and basically went along with all Vergennes's recommendations from beginning to end, he was giving future protection to the integrity of his own word. However, the contrast between this message and the actions of France less than a year later surely further exacerbated the tensions between France and Spain regarding policy toward the American War. Fortunately for France, Spain, too, had many grievances against England that only a war could ultimately satisfy—notably England's occupation of Spanish territories, outworn trading and wood-cutting privileges (usually abused by the English) in Central America and interference with Spain's civilian shipping. Indeed, it was the very realization of this fundamental Spanish interest on Floridablanca's part that helps explain his own diplomatic ambivalence and frequent resort to shifting positions as, like Vergennes at Versailles, he worked to align the Spanish king and government in favor of a policy that would put Spain in an optimum condition to strike, but only at the right moment and only pursuant to explicit advance understandings with its French ally regarding military strategy and peace terms—Spain was not once again to be ignored and then left in the lurch, as it had been in 1761–62. In this sense, Vergennes was paying the price for his old tormentor Choiseul's high-handed treatment of Spain, and specifically Charles III, during the Seven Years' War.[162]

Among Vergennes's range of arguments as he struggled to convince Spain of the justice of his policies was one that needs to be spotlighted because, while apparently sincere, at least at this stage, it was equally clearly wrong, with attendant negative implications for U.S.-French relations. That erroneous argument was: "No conflict of interest exists between America and Spain."[163] Versailles acted on this stated position throughout the war and into the peace negotiations, insufficiently appreciating the depth of American feeling regarding their right to have the Mississippi River for a western border and as an unhampered trade route down to the Gulf of Mexico, and the corresponding depth of Spanish resistance to granting this claimed right. French interventions at Philadelphia and later at Versailles were counterproductive, antagonized the U.S. uselessly and would give ammunition to those Americans who favored a postwar tilt toward England and not France.[164]

This clear error was not a result of lack of attention to the issue. As early as October 17, 1778, a French strategy document, noting that the Spaniards were intent on keeping America away from the Mississippi, raised the question: "Should we try to convert Spain with regard to the Americans?"[165] On this question, Montmorin wrote on 19 October that he feared a Canada and Acadia remaining with England, as was Versailles' stated goal, would lead to friction with the Americans and, therefore, would create the threat of still another war between France and England, in which event Spain was not likely to fight alongside France, because Franco-American relations were already a source of much of Spain's irritation at France; moreover, the ambassador continued, in such a war, circumstances would not be so favorable to France as they were now, partly because the U.S. is not likely to be a strong power even in the medium term.[166] It is obvious from subsequent French behavior with regard to this issue that Versailles did not heed Montmorin's advice and opted to back England's retention of Canada and, much to Jay's dismay, to work harder on the U.S. than on Spain regarding the Mississippi issue, Vergennes at one point (and Gerard frequently) candidly explaining to the U.S. that in any situation requiring a choice between supporting one or the other France must always choose Spain.

The more France became enmeshed in the American War as 1777 progressed, the more the deputies there took full advantage of the openings afforded them by this fact to drag Versailles into open disagreements with England[167]—for example, by the above-mentioned, well-publicized letters to the U.S. prematurely claiming that an alliance was in negotiation, and by encouraging American ships to make less-than-discreet use of their access to French ports. This latter practice, at one stage, became so blatant that France, to keep the peace with an irate England, felt it had to clamp down on the freedoms it had been giving to American privateers almost openly to enter with their prizes, sell them, arm themselves, and so on. This, in turn, led to the unusual situation of the deputies, in October, now being the ones to complain to Versailles regarding what they considered its overly vigorous campaign of curbing the Americans in order to appease England— they used such terms as "contradictions and restrictions" in their criticism of recent French actions. Vergennes read into these American moves the design to draw a rejection from France that would allow them to reconcile with England, which the deputies were expressly threatening to do in their memoranda to him— even as they were pleading for financial aid.[168]

The deputies also included Spain in their complaining memoranda to Vergennes.[169] That country was now clamping down on American privateers in Spanish waters and ports and even more severely so than was France. The Spanish response to these reported complaints, which, as in France, were also accompanied by indirect requests for additional financial aid, was clearly that of irritation. Charles himself was reported to have been upset at what was considered the excesses of American corsairs in both his as well as French ports. Moreover, Spain took the view, in opposition to Vergennes's following the American loss of Ticonderoga, that not only were the colonists far from ready to give up the fight but surely they understood that even more valuable to their cause than additional financial aid was the military value of cargo reaching them aboard merchantmen regularly leaving Bilbao, and especially of the "diverse military preparations" by Spain and France that inherently were helping to prevent England from "descending on the colonies with all its strength."

Vergennes specifically rejected this last claim on the grounds that "our passive arms" do not curb England's ability to fight the colonies and that all Spain's policy amounts to is to depend on "simple persuasion" to keep America in the war.[170] There is solid reason to suspect that an unstated Vergennes incentive for seeing France actively participate in the war was a premise implicit in all his analyses, that is, that an American victory while France was seen only to have stood passively by would not meet the nation's purposes: Only a France that itself stood over a defeated England could regain for it the international stature it truly deserved and once had.

Despite this move toward a more unilateral policy on the part of post-Grimaldi Spain, momentum toward an English-Bourbon confrontation was mounting, as also reflected in Versailles' intensified competition with London for influence in the royal courts of Europe. As Versailles would put it once in the war: "It is in increasing England's problems in Europe that we will foil it in America."[171] Russia was the centerpiece of this diplomatic contest because it was capable of providing twelve ships-of-the-line and also the manpower desperately being sought by England to supplement the relatively limited number—and quality—of troops it could ship on its own to the American theater either from the British Isles or by means of mercenaries supplied by cash-hungry German princes.[172] Russia also had great leverage over the policy direction of Prussia and Austria, each of which sought its backing in their political struggle for control over the Germanic center of Europe, a struggle so intense that it would nearly lead to a major war between the two in 1778–79, just when France, which surely would have been drawn into that conflict, was itself entering into the American War. Still another factor underlining the need for France to maintain influence with Russia was its traditional role as a defender of the Ottoman Empire's status in Europe, where Turkish territory was being constantly nibbled at by the Russian and Austrian Empires, threatening, in turn, so Vergennes feared, the present satisfactory status of the Italian peninsula. As noted earlier, France at this time was in a favorable, although far from intimate, relationship with Russia, having successfully helped broker an agreement between St. Petersburg and Constantinople temporarily settling their latest conflict over border lands, notably in Crimea. In addition, Prussian interests favored moving Russia more toward French than English positions, and Frederick accordingly was using his significant, if exaggerated, personal influence with Catherine in ways helpful to Versailles.[173]

These favorable diplomatic circumstances reinforced a more general basis for Franco-Russian cooperation, that is, their partially shared dislike of England's maritime dominance and its increasing interference in commercial shipping. This factor would become even more significant and helpful to France once the present war expanded and England began to take even harsher measures at sea, and closer to European shores, against neutral shipping, particularly that of the previously cited "northern powers," whose self-designated diplomatic leader was Catherine the Great. Ever alert to opportunities to enhance her personal glory, she took on this role even though Russia in the early 1770s had benefited from English naval support in its war against the Turks and despite the fact that, in its own right, Russia was scarcely as important a seagoing trading nation as were Sweden, Denmark and especially the Netherlands. (Catherine had high hopes that Russia would develop relatively soon into just such a nation.)

Vergennes early recognized this common interest with Russia (one that would be marred for a period by a temporarily overexuberant Spanish policy of seizing Russian and other neutral shipping that had ventured into the Straits close to Spain's blockade of Gibraltar starting in 1779), and he steadily encouraged a budding movement there and in the other northern powers to pressure England into adopting less strident policies regarding their commerce, including their commerce with belligerents, so long as no contraband was involved. Of course, it was precisely over these two points—trading with the "enemy" and the definition of "contraband"—that separated England from other maritime nations. England naturally wished to use its near-hegemony over the sea lanes to block any commerce with its enemies; and it insisted on a much broader definition of what constituted contraband than any of the others saw fit to adopt. In sum, given all the above considerations, and happily for French fortunes, Russia would decline tempting English financial and territorial incentives (e.g., Minorca) to ally with them militarily, or at least to employ its warships in ways supportive of England's maritime activities; nor would Russia provide England with troops for its American war; moreover, Russia would organize in 1780 an armed Neutrality League, which, though it eventually fell far short of its threat to use military means to protect members' merchant shipping, did further hamper the English war effort and did help assure the entrance of the Netherlands into the war against England with consequent further strain on the English navy.[174] Also recall that Portugal, much to London's dismay and anger, would join the Russian-led League before the war ended, although it would not do so until after having followed a pro-English policy for most of that war. The most notable feature of that policy was Portugal's "receiving even armed vessels" into its ports (read: English ones only, given the military realities in those waters).[175]

FRANCE'S REACTION TO AMERICA'S VICTORY AT SARATOGA, NEW YORK, OCTOBER 1777

Versailles first caught wind of this major, even "miraculous," event as early as 23 November, and it "decides the King," because, as Vergennes would subsequently observe, it made him "feel the necessity of finally taking a definitive decision."[176] Louis personally signed off on a 6 December handwritten note from Vergennes to the American deputies inviting their "proposals" on a most confidential basis and requesting that reports on their future negotiations only be shared with the president and selected members of the Continental Congress.[177] Thus, the foreign minister had succeeded in obtaining royal agreement that now was the time to move quickly and reach firm agreements with the U.S., in part because that very victory reportedly was generating increasing political support in England's Parliament for a fresh, conciliatory approach to the Congress.[178] Vergennes was warning that this new approach might be put in the hands of Chatham and be so liberal in its terms as to be irresistible to a nation that still retained strong residual ties to the motherland, and especially to Chatham, a possible successor to North in the ever-fearful view of the French government.[179] Such a scenario could well overcome American enthusiasm for the kind of total separation envisaged in the Declaration of Independence. Adding to the plausibility of all the above was that, even prior to news of Saratoga, King George, in a parliamentary speech on 21 November, had used, for the first time, the word "peace" in discussing relations with the colonies. Vergennes was further advising that such a reconciliation, were it to occur, would mean that France had lost its great opportunity to deflate English power; more than that, it then would have to face a totally new, dangerous threat to its own colonial and maritime interests. As he put it in a dispatch to Montmorin on 11 December, in mimicry of a point made to him by Beaumarchais in a note of that same date, "The power which first recognizes American independence will be the one who will collect all the fruits of this war."[180]

In a word, Saratoga paradoxically brought both the convincing evidence of American fighting and staying power that France had been seeking and also the distinct possibility, or at least so Vergennes and his ambassador in London, Duc de Noailles, were successfully arguing in support of their policy of active participation in the American War, that the rebellion might now convert itself from a positive event enhancing French interests to a sharply negative one, in which the primed armed forces of England and the U.S. would combine to rid Anglo-Saxon America of its hated Bourbon neighbors.[181] To buttress their case, Vergennes and Noailles warned that now that the Americans have earned a major victory even without visible Bourbon aid, the Congress, as Chatham himself was telling the Parliament, had an honorable basis for negotiating an agreement with England.[182] From the perspective of those two Frenchmen, now endorsed by the king in Council (although with the innocuous caveat that no major commitments were to be made to the Americans pending receipt of Spanish views): "The time for reflection is passed," and treaties between France and the U.S. were the only way to block such undesirable developments; furthermore, those treaties had to be negotiated and signed before any English negotiating team could arrive in America with blandishments.[183]

This was true even if Madrid could not immediately be brought on board—and even if France's own military and naval preparations were not as yet fully ready for the inevitable consequences of such a French recognition of U.S. independence. Accordingly, Versailles, that same month of December, sent an urgent message to the Congress, through the deputies and delivered by one of its own frigates directly to the U.S., assuring it of France's "protection and support."[184] Of course, it did so in an effort to blunt the anticipated English initiative for a reconciliation with America.[185] That initiative had been foreshadowed by the above-cited parliamentary speech from the throne; Versailles, egged on by Franklin, willingly believed, as Vergennes wrote Montmorin on 13 December, that this speech gave the English a "twenty-day head start on us in letting its reconciliation policy out."[186] The French message to Philadelphia also urged the Congress not to entertain the expected English proposals, given the promising role of France— and, rather brashly and misleadingly, of Spain![187]

Starting on December 12, 1777, Vergennes and his staff conducted intense negotiations with the three American commissioners (actually, with Franklin and Deane, Lee already unwarrantedly looked on by the French as of doubtful loyalties to them), successfully culminating in the signature on 6 February of a pair of treaties, one for a prospective (*eventuelle*) military alliance and the other governing commercial relations.[188] While only the latter treaty had been spelled out by the Congress in its detailed instructions and authorizations to its commissioners, Franklin and his colleagues well knew that a military alliance would also be enthusiastically welcomed by that body.[189] Accordingly, they boldly worked out with the French a treaty text largely on their own initiative and, in doing so, played the kind of creative, rather independent negotiating role that a new team of colleagues assigned to Franklin four years later would duplicate in peace talks with England, this time with Franklin only reluctantly participating, because the negotiating strategy adopted by that new team risked undoing the very alliance treaty that he had helped put together in 1778.

The major points of that alliance treaty with France included these: Hostilities, even if only de facto, between France and England, would definitively activate the alliance;[190] no peace would be agreed to by the signatories without English recognition, tacit or explicit, of U.S. independence; neither party was to end its participation in the war separately from the other, unless with its prior concurrence; each guarantees the other's postwar security in the possession of their respective American territories, as defined at the time of the peace treaty ending the war; and, in a secret article, Spain was to be invited to become a signatory.[191] When coupled with the provisions of the second, "friendship and commercial treaty," France at this time clearly was giving full and generally welcome assurances to the Americans that

1. it expected no special postwar commercial favors from the U.S., only being desirous of having the same privileges as those that America may accord to any other nation. Here Vergennes clearly was recognizing that France's "acquiring a new commercial opening ... can only have a very secondary importance"; an England "monopolizing American commerce certainly gained greatly, but an American commerce open to the world" perhaps would be the only realistic, albeit minimum, goal for France, whose "major goal" was that of "greatly weakening England by means of subtracting one-third of its empire from it";[192]

2. it sought no territorial gains or retrocessions of lost colonies on mainland North America, although it did intend to clarify and better pro-

tect its existing fishing rights in the North Atlantic waters off Canada (leaving the door open to a possible conquest and retention there of Ile Royale [Cape Breton Island] and Newfoundland).[193]

A fair summation of French policy toward the Americans regarding future political and commercial relations between the two was contained in the king's instructions for the opening meeting of 12 December with the deputies: "Were we to negotiate with the Americans, we would have nothing to demand of them for ourselves that would be a problem for them: the guarantee of our islands and of our possessions in Western America, and the reciprocal liberty of commerce conforming to the laws where it will be carried out."[194] Well into 1778, Vergennes saw no problem in the U.S. having a legal right to Mississippi navigation down to the Gulf of Mexico, given his stated assumption in a dispatch to Gérard of 26 October that the Americans at a minimum would have postwar control of the "Ohio valley," which he recognized was an integral part of the Mississippi network.[195]

However, as specifically regards territorial issues, a harbinger of future problems that would plague U.S.-Bourbon relations, especially once Spain entered the conflict, can be detected in Vergennes's May 1, 1778, reaction to a proposal privately given Franklin by an English member of Parliament who was seeking to promote reconciliation with the Americans.[196] That proposal included:

1. giving the Floridas to the U.S. The foreign minister believed that such an act would serve the English goal of using that territory as an "apple of discord" between the Americans and Spain. On 29 March, he had already included in his instructions to the departing minister to the U.S., Gérard, the point that, unlike fishing and drying in and off Newfoundland, the U.S. did have an interest in the Floridas and also a "plan of conquest" there; consequently, he should prepare the Congress for "an eventual withdrawal" in favor of Spain, at least regarding Pensacola and those parts of the coast on the Gulf of Mexico that were so strategically important to Spain.

2. allowing England to retain Canada. This the foreign minister very

Securing American Independence

much favored, because it would "perpetuate mistrust" between the
Americans and the English and would "get the Americans to have to
stick closer to us." (Worth noting is that this French policy regarding
Canada was considered so sensitive for their relations with the U.S.
that it was to be treated as among France's tightest held secrets
throughout the war.)

3. also allowing England to retain Nova Scotia. Vergennes opposed this
   because that peninsula's port of Halifax could be used as a safe
   support base for naval forces attacking French and Spanish possessions; instead, the foreign minister favored France's (or perhaps
   America's) obtaining Nova Scotia either by force or treaty negotiations.

On fishing issues, France, at this early negotiating stage—a period during which it foresaw the possibility of a U.S. conquest of
Newfoundland, casting doubt on the validity of France's existing
treaty-based fishing rights on that island's coastline—was more
concerned with obtaining *American* assurances that *it* would continue to have access to those fishing grounds without the Americans claiming exclusive rights there. According to an internal
French note of January 27, 1778, cited above, the deputies, when
asked, readily gave Versailles such assurances, as follows: "If the
U.S. wins, it would be prepared to guarantee us a share in the
fisheries." By October 26, 1778, Vergennes's position regarding the
permissible reach of American rights to fisheries in Newfoundland waters had become more precise now that it was increasingly
clear there was no prospect of an American conquest of Newfoundland: "I don't know if we could commit the English to admit
the Americans there, as they have sufficient coastal territory without extending it so far to the north."[197] Perhaps here is the origin
of the fishing issue as a major bone of contention between the two
allies. France now would begin to be aware of the dangers—both
to its treaty-based fishing and drying rights in Newfoundland waters and to its policy of limiting American war goals to the minimum possible—stemming from what it considered as the
"laughable" claim of New England that France should support
the alleged continuing rights of Americans to fish in all prewar
waters just as they had as subjects of King George.[198]

Gérard in Philadelphia would counter that claim by arguing to members of the Congress that "were England to accord the Americans the fisheries on the basis of the same rights that they had earlier possessed as subjects of the British crown, then the Americans wouldn't need French help in making that arrangement."[199] Gérard further advised his counterparts that France might well back U.S. fishing demands off Nova Scotia and nearby coastal waters, but only to the extent that it didn't prove to be an obstacle for peace, because "France would be in the right to reject it as being outside its commitments." That French diplomat took these positions in keeping with his instructions, which declared that, regarding Newfoundland fishing, "there is nothing for us to negotiate with the Congress" because that is a matter only regarding France's need to protect the fishing and drying rights it gained by its treaties with England.

A year later, on September 25, 1779, Luzerne, Gérard's successor, was instructed that, regarding the peace-deferring fishing demands of the so-called anti-Gallican party in Congress headed by Sam Adams and the Virginian Richard H. Lee (Arthur Lee's brother),

"we distinguish between two types of fishing": high seas versus coastal, including islands; the U.S. has no "rights" off Newfoundland, Nova Scotia, or Canada, while France's are based on treaties with England, the "proprietor"; France's treaty commitment to the U.S. to guarantee its territory is only on a contingency basis and to be defined only at war's end; the Americans are committed by treaty with France to respect France's legally established exclusive fishing zones, present or future, and "it is possible that France will conquer" Newfoundland and Cape Breton Island, in which event the U.S. would then not have any automatic right to fish off the coast of those two islands; reciprocally, a U.S.-owned Acadia [the traditional French name for modern day Nova Scotia and the adjacent mainland territory, now called New Brunswick] or Canada would be authorized to bar France, although guarantor, from fishing along those coasts; France has "generously" renounced taking Canada or Acadia strictly out of consideration for the U.S.; in war, "all property is considered as non-existent," and, therefore, an American conquest of those two lands would give them in the first instance only *jus ad rem*, in contrast to the *jus in re* France has by treaty rights in Newfoundland; the U.S. should not begrudge France's being able to "obtain the slight advantage of extending its fisheries at Great Britain's expense"; right now, the U.S. "has no rights at all to the fisheries."[200]

Spain soon made clear to France its unwillingness to accede to the alliance treaty and angrily rejected French suggestions that it contemplate joining in the prospective war against England even if only as an ally of France. Floridablanca, typically raking over old coals, charged France with having let Spain down by declining earlier to help it defeat Portugal and, so he argued to the open astonishment of Vergennes, who correctly claimed that Madrid in that period never mentioned this prospect, possibly England, too, if that power had decided to go to the defense of its client state against the Bourbons.[201] The Spanish foreign minister also labeled as "Quixotic" France's decision to help America openly versus England because such a war was strategically unnecessary for French purposes, given England's clear inability to defeat the rebels even without French participation; the many points reported to be in North's peace plan remained contrary to the independence the Americans were insisting upon and without which there could never be a reconciliation with the metropole; and, that decision might well lead to France's own exhaustion, as well as England's. Finally, Floridablanca asserted that, precisely in line with France's own arguments, it was because Spanish possessions were more at risk than French ones that Spain had to be even more cautious and prudent than France, especially given that Madrid's financial and naval situation was too unsatisfactory for it to consider taking on the English. To underline his hardened antiwar policy following the signature of the Franco-American accords, the Spaniard announced that the additional financial aid his government in December had said it was considering would now be withdrawn because those accords surely meant it would be France that henceforth would be the source for meeting all of America's needs.[202]

However, Vergennes would refuse to take the Spanish no for an answer. Late in 1778 he wrote Floridablanca to argue that the rupture that had occurred in the diplomatic relations between France and England was forced by the latter's actions of March and gave France no alternative but (1) to enter into a war that was one of "legitimate self-defense" and not "at our own initiative" and, (2) to activate its "contingency commitment of support to the Americans."[203] Vergennes, as noted, had already sent an energetic young ambassador, Montmorin, to Madrid to replace the elderly Ossun, who in August 1777 had badly misread Spanish intentions, wrongly forecasting that they would concur in the French proposal that the two enter into the war by January or February 1778. The foreign minister instructed Montmorin, who had his first, and chilling, meeting with Floridablanca on 23 December, to keep the pressure up for a Spanish entrance into the fray. While Spain, indeed, would do just that a year after the U.S.-French treaties, it never would follow France's lead regarding the U.S. This policy mystified even Montmorin, who wrote as early as January 28, 1778: Given Floridablanca's acknowledgment that Spain eventually will have to enter the war, if France is in it, "it is hard for me to understand why Spain won't get the U.S. on its side." A month earlier, on 23 December, that ambassador reported that Charles's "resolution" was not in line with Louis's and that, therefore, Vergennes should not "judge my zeal by its results."[204] John Jay, as the uninvited American presence in Spain, would reap the full sour harvest of that intra-Bourbon discord, drawing conclusions from it that bear on his later conduct as a peace commissioner in Paris.

These international developments were occurring even as France was undergoing serious change in domestic policy. Turgot initiated his reform program with great fanfare and overly didactic royal decrees. Some of the reforms in marketing procedures were so sharply introduced as to produce street and communal violence in protest of the higher prices and the disruptions of established food supply lines. This violence was on such a large scale in 1775 as to be called "The Flour War"—urban dwellers believed that food shortages were due to speculators, including royal and ministerial ones, cashing in on the lifting of domestic and international trade restrictions. Some at the time argued that these tensions at home should be taken as a warning sign against France's voluntarily accepting the burdens of a war it had the option to avoid.

This domestic turmoil, in fact, paradoxically would work in favor of U.S. interests because the two key reformers (Turgot and Malesherbes) left office just as the American War was reaching the point of no return in 1776. With their departure, Vergennes's influence with the king and his Mentor, Maurepas, was temporarily strengthened at a key period, and there now was less resistance in the Council to the steps the foreign minister was proposing to assure that the Americans would have the wherewithal to continue their struggle against England.[205]

The predictable consequence of these and related developments was the decision to recognize the independence of the U.S. and to align with it formally by treaty. The final spur toward that decision, as we have seen, was the American victory of October 1777 at Saratoga, which is located along the "moving highway," or "path of nations," as the classic water-based invasion route between Canada and New York City was known by European settlers and native Indians alike.

SARATOGA'S IMPACT ON THE POLICIES OF THE UNITED STATES

John Jay's New York had been the major focus of military strategy on the part of both the U.S. and England ever since the latter's evacuation of Boston in March 1776, when it was clear to all that England would have to regroup in Canadian territory and ports, particularly Halifax in the first instance, and quickly return to the rebellious colonies in great military force but not to outlying Boston.[206] The colony of New York was the obvious target because of its major city's vulnerability to attack from the open seas and its inland territory's openness to invasion from the north; moreover, its population was considered as much less prone than that in most of the other rebelling colonies to a complete break with England. Accordingly, this is where Washington brought the bulk of his army by summer 1776 and where Jay, as a member of the New

York provincial assembly and many of its key committees, played a very active role in assuring effective cooperation between that general and New York's political and military leadership.[207]

From April 1776 on, Jay would be absent from Philadelphia and helping in New York's effort to establish a brand-new governmental structure even as it struggled to ward off a total occupation of the state by England.[208] That enemy was now close to executing its plan to occupy the city and port area of New York as its base of operations for a military operation, whose goal would be to split the thirteen rebellious colonies by having an invasion force come down from Canada by way of Lakes Champlain and George to link up with one coming up the Hudson River from that city. By fall 1776, New York City indeed would fall to the Howe brothers—General William and his elder, Admiral Richard. However, thanks in important part to the ubiquitous General Benedict Arnold, this time serving as commander of the first, if most modest, U.S. naval force in history, on Lake Champlain, England's opening attempt at invasion from Canada was thwarted on that lake that same year.

By early 1777, Jay and his fellow members of what had now been designated as New York's "Convention" were busy drafting and, in April, approving a constitution for the state. In this task, they were helped by the advice of Washington's freshly appointed aide-de-camp, now Lieutenant-Colonel Alexander Hamilton, in a remarkable correspondence that dealt with the imminent combined military threat from Canada to the north and New York City to the south even as it addressed the pros and cons of various constitutional issues. Following the constitution's adoption, but especially after the October victory at Saratoga, Jay, as the state's first chief justice, spent the bulk of his time in that capacity, including delivering a broadly disseminated pronouncement to New York's first grand jury emphasizing the positive features of that document.[209] By this period, of course, he was well known continentally as a talented propagandist, most recently demonstrated by his having drafted the appeal of December 1776 from the Convention to the state's residents urging them not to lose heart despite England's recent military gains at New York City.

That appeal was then picked up by the Continental Congress, which distributed it to key groups around the country, most notably in German translation for the benefit of a large, and politically doubtful, element in the population of Pennsylvania and nearby states.[210]

Mid-1777 brought a second, more threatening English invasion from Canada.[211] By August, Burgoyne had reached the Hudson River itself, having forced an American evacuation of Fort Ticonderoga, whose garrison failed to fire even a shot before fleeing southward.[212] That ignominious defeat naturally brought the wrath of many in the military and political leadership on the commander of the northern department of Washington's army, General Schuyler, who would be defended by his fellow New Yorker Jay in what soon took on the coloring of a regionally based political issue, because the "Eastern" states of New England were now saying they would not send their militia to serve under him.[213] Thus, on 11 July, Jay wrote to Schuyler in the standard way he always wrote in support of those of his close friends who might be under what he considered unjustified attack (e.g., Deane): "Let not the insinuations of the wicked discompose you. The best and greatest of men in all ages have met with the like hate, and gloriously risen superior to calumny."[214]

The end result was that both the Congress and Washington soon recognized the need to placate Schuyler's critics as essential to defeating Burgoyne, and they replaced him with his predecessor and New England favorite, Horatio Gates, a Virginian many in New England preferred even over Washington, who was deemed to be too cautious a leader and perhaps too personally ambitious as well.[215] This action displeased Jay, as is evident from his 12 September letter to Schuyler: Washington and Congress "were assured that, unless another general presided in the northern department, the militia of New England would not be brought into the field. The Congress, under this apprehension, exchanged their general for this militia—a bargain which can receive no justification but from the supposed necessity of the times." That Jay himself, however, clearly recognized that New York *needed* New England's military help at this "critical and interesting conjuncture" is seen in his having joined with other New York leaders in recommending to Washington that he appeal to Massachusetts and New Hampshire, in the name of America's "general interest" and also that of New England's own "preservation," to send troops to the aid of the New Yorkers opposing Burgoyne. Washington acted on that recommendation, thus setting the stage for Schuyler's replacement.[216]

All this was in the midst of the military crisis created by the combination of Burgoyne's movements toward Albany and the Howe brothers' maneuvering their large forces on land and sea in a manner that ultimately proved threatening to America's political center at Philadelphia (an apparent change from the original plan for a link-up of forces, as described above).[217] Jay, in his one major mission directly related to the Burgoyne invasion, was sent in late July with his close friend and colleague in the state government, Gouverneur Morris, to serve briefly as New York's Safety Council emissaries to Washington's New Jersey headquarters. Their mission was "to confer with his Excellency on the state of the northern department of the army, the means of reinforcing it, etc."[218] The general, forced to keep his focus on the Howes, was unable to do more than to send two continental regiments stationed at Peekskill to Schuyler, plus Daniel Morgan's sharpshooting corps of riflemen stationed at Trenton, and also Benedict Arnold, Washington explaining that he had "prevailed" on the latter "to repair to the northern department to assist in the opposition" and that Arnold was a general of "judgment, bravery and enterprise" and also is "well acquainted with the country."[219]

A word needs to be said here as to just how desperate a situation the New Yorkers really were in as they faced Burgoyne's army descending down the Hudson following its seizure of Ticonderoga, and we can best offer that word in all its drama by summarizing the analyses Hamilton periodically made for the benefit of Jay and company, at their request, in the weeks leading up to Saratoga (Hamilton having become the New York Convention's semiofficial correspondent at Washington's headquarters in New Jersey):[220]

7 *May*: There is now doubt here that Howe's plan is to cross the Delaware River and go to Philadelphia. Rather, he apparently plans to go

somewhere by water, either Philadelphia or up the Hudson River; or perhaps all this is English deception. All reports are that the English army is in too poor a shape to carry out any material operations by land; your job is to keep supplies out of its reach. [A few days later, Hamilton advised that] it seemed fully the opinion of our generals that the last year's project for uniting the two enemy armies by the conquest of your state, will be prosecuted in the current campaign.

28 June: It is clear that some people will attribute the Fabian conduct of our army either to cowardice or to weakness. As you observe, England's conduct is so eccentric as to leave no certain grounds on which to form a judgment of their intentions. Our conduct is based on the fact that the liberties of America are an infinite stake, and we should not play a desperate game for it, or put it upon the issue of a single cast of the dice, unless our strength was so great as to give certainty of success. [On 6 July, Hamilton added:] Another possible scenario for a major battle was one where the enemy forces it on Washington by Howe's gathering all his forces on Staten Island, including those that could be spared from Canada, and all that are now at Rhode Island, etc., and then making a point of coercing us by some means or other to an action. [Hamilton further commented that] Howe, if he was a man of sense, would do just that, because, were he to go northward or southward, every new post he took would weaken his main body and make it the more liable to be ruined by the collective strength of the American forces; but, as it was, Howe was not such a man but rather an unintelligible gentleman, one who makes it difficult to risk a conjecture as to what he might do. [In contrast, Hamilton believed Burgoyne to be a brilliant officer.]

6 July: Reports are that English ships are preparing for a two-month voyage. Washington is covering Philadelphia and also the Hudson River route just in case reports are correct that Howe will go up there in connection with England's serious move from Canada. We're not certain whether the northern alarm is but a diversion designed to facilitate a move by Howe on Philadelphia.

29 July: Robert Livingston's estimates of Burgoyne's numerical strength should be reduced to not much more than 8,000 enemy troops on or approaching the Hudson, of whom perhaps one sixth was unfit with disease, mostly smallpox caught at Isle St. Noix; keep in mind that Burgoyne had to leave a certain number of troops to garrison Ticonderoga. Washington agrees with my analysis of these numbers; has written to the Eastern states' assemblies, as you suggested, appealing for militia to help Schuyler; but cannot accept your idea of stripping the ships to the eastward of your State of their canon for your forts and ships—and I doubt the utility of your going to the Continental Congress or the Board of War on this issue. [Hamilton made the following additional observations in this message:] The Indians and Canadians with Burgoyne were not by any accounts numerous; Schuyler's 5,000 continental troops and the Eastern states' militia represent a grand total of 8–10,000, and these men cannot sleep so soundly when the danger is so imminent—therefore, if Burgoyne is not stopped, it would have been for reasons other than the want of men; Washington had the same number of troops as these 8–10,000 and was able last year to keep Howe's 16–17,000 at bay with them; and, Burgoyne cannot advance all that rapidly as to preclude our getting all our forces together. On the whole, I am clearly of the opinion that, unless Howe cooperates with Burgoyne against your state, it has very little to fear.

10 August: I sympathize with you in this critical period and concur that Burgoyne's successes involve the most important consequences to America, and that the loss of New York State would be more damaging than any that could be struck by Mr. Howe to the southward. Washington concurs with us on all this, but already has helped you to the extent his circumstances allow. The unpardonable backwardness of your Eastern neighbors leaves you with everything to fear. If Howe operates so far to the southward as every appearance seems to indicate, Charleston is now thought to be the place of his destination, but this defies common sense. Northward [i.e., up the Hudson] seems to be out of the question, given his great, costly move so far south. If it is Charleston that is his destination, there is no way we can get there. If Burgoyne keeps moving southward, we must find the means to stop him. It may not be bad if our armies join against him. The Indians, after a few drubbings, should revert to character and go home; but, I know a panic dread of Indians is an important factor in our misfortune. Morgan's corps should be a good way to curb the Indians—it would do no harm for you to exaggerate the number of his troops.[221]

In the event, and helped by Burgoyne's having dispatched some 800 men in a doomed expedition in July to Bennington, east of the Hudson River, for needed supplies, Gates presided over the strategically important surrender at Saratoga of the entire English army on 17 October.[222] Also contributing to that happy result for the Americans was their August success in blocking a separate English force of 1,700 men, half composed of Indians, and under the command of Barry St. Leger, from moving down the Lake Ontario–Mohawk valley route toward Albany, where, as a second prong in England's invasion plan, it was to link up with Burgoyne's main army. St. Leger's force was stopped at Fort Stanwix when its siege there was broken following a victory at Oriskany by a New York militia unit of 900 men, commanded by General Nicholas Herkimer, which was coming to the relief of the fort. At Oriskany, the New Yorkers had been intercepted by a detachment from St. Leger's force and, after one of the bloodiest battles of the war, in which "the greatest part of the militia left [Herkimer] on the first onset," the enemy was defeated by "the remainder," which "kept the field," leaving "fifty dead Indians on the ground."[223] Some of those Indians were chiefs, whose deaths, when reported at the siege site, disheartened the bulk of St. Leger's Indian units, which deserted him. That development, coupled with the even earlier news that, yes, Benedict Arnold had been detached from the Saratoga area and was leading a relief force that was now headed for the fort, gave that English commander no choice but to retreat back to Canada. Hamilton, writing to his New York friends from Wilmington on 1 September, considered the "relieving of Fort Schuyler [as Stanwix had been renamed by the Americans] . . . a very happy and important event, and will concur with the two happy strokes given by Harkness and Stark [at Bennington] to reverse the face of affairs and turn the scale against Mr. Burgoyne."

The capitulation terms agreed to by Gates and Burgoyne would create a major, running problem between France and the U.S. once they entered into their 1778 alliance, because they provided for the return of the surrendered army to Great Britain. Vergennes on November 18, 1778, would instruct Gérard to assure that the Congress kept that army in America notwithstanding the Gates-Burgoyne agreement.[224] Congress *did* in fact, even prior to French intervention on the matter, use whatever expedients it found necessary, in Vergennes's November words, "to keep it in America: it is clear that, if it returns to Europe, the English King would be free to use it against us." Among those expedients was the charge, as the deputies put it in a letter to Vergennes on April 10, 1778, that certain of the behavior of the English soldiers was in "breach of capitulation" terms—thus, over 8,000 prisoners of war would be detained by the U.S. for the duration.[225]

As would be the case at Yorktown, Virginia, almost exactly to the day four years later, this victory came totally unexpectedly, almost as a miracle, to most Americans and to the French at Versailles. After all, the disarray in the American camp was notorious, and pessimism reigned following the near-simultaneous capture of Philadelphia by the Howes, a loss that had forced the Congress to move to the inland town of York, Pennsylvania, and the army under Washington to spend a miserable winter at Valley Forge a few miles upriver on the Schuylkill from Philadelphia.

The English success at Philadelphia, fortunately for the U.S., came at the expense of their strategically more threatening master plan for subduing the rebels. Burgoyne had been counting on the implementation of that plan's core feature, a move upriver to Albany by the bulk of Howe's (after July, General Henry Clinton's) New York army, almost to the moment of his capitulation.[226] Splitting the Americans into two geographically separated areas would have represented a much graver plight for them than did the mere occupation of their political capital, whose loss, despite the early spin on it by Stormont at Versailles, did not seriously dent any military or even political cohesiveness among them.[227] Even till today, the behavior of the Howes in opting for this operation, as well as regarding their other, earlier moves, notably during the battle of Long Island, seems inexplicable, *unless* one accepts the plausible theory that, having only under duress accepted their respective American commands, they never truly sought a purely military victory over the enemy.[228]

With the victory at Saratoga, Jay, as noted, would now largely settle down to his apolitical role as New York's chief justice, a role that, while appropriate and acceptable, did not arouse his enthusiasm and, in fact, eventually put him in a glum and restless mood. Moreover, he was ill at ease regarding the major military problem of direct concern to him—the urgent need to strengthen the forts along the Hudson River and to install obstacles across it. He worked on this problem with Robert Livingston and other New York officials. Writing to Gouverneur Morris, now a member of Congress at York, Livingston on January 29, 1778, complained that while the Congress' resolutions on this subject were entrusted for execution to Gates, "in the same breath" that body correctly recalled that general, whose "every fidelity is suspected, whose ignorance is notorious, and whose negligence has already endangered the State. . . . [He is] unfit to command a division of the Grand Army." (Gates was a former career British Army officer.) Livingston then went on to propose that "Jay and myself will make a board of correspondence here, and you and Duer there," where, as representatives of "the country" of New York, their task was to prod the Congress to "take steps for our defense."

If there was a bright side to Jay's situation in 1778 it was the respite it gave him and his family from their hectic pre-Saratoga months of separation and from their fear of physical harm, not only at the hands of the ever-threatening, ever-so-close enemy forces but also at the hands of those forces' militant local, Loyalist supporters, some of whom, more accurately, were straightforward criminals. Even as Jay was thus largely withdrawing of his own volition from the center of the national, and even provincial, political and military scene, so the U.S. as a whole would now begin to take on a low-key posture versus the English presence on its soil.[229] Washington's unstable army, struggling at Valley Forge (notwithstanding the substantial material help it could and should have gotten from the various states), would in the main avoid large, existence-threatening battles, while the Congress would increasingly focus on seeking international—mainly French—support for its cause. For example, G. Morris would write his New York friends via Livingston on May 3, 1778, that, with the arrival of Silas Deane's brother carrying the texts of the two treaties of 6 February, the Congress sees Spain, Austria and Prussia as following suit.[230] That body was further encouraged in its tendency to look increasingly abroad for the key means of defeating the English by the benefits that so immediately came to the U.S. from its treaties with the French, benefits that can be described as follows: Without the treaties, Washington at Valley Forge, as he himself anticipated, almost certainly would have had to face a spring offensive by Howe, whereas, with France now entering the war, Washington instead saw that English general prematurely returned to England and his successor, Henry Clinton, come down from New York to organize a London-ordered hasty retreat back to New York to join the bulk of his land and sea forces, the feeling being that the army in Philadelphia would be too exposed to a French naval attack in combination with one by the American army.[231] That retreat, in turn, opened a fresh opportunity for the American army itself to take the offensive and harass the suddenly vulnerable enemy as it crossed New Jersey; moreover, the English move completely undercut any leverage an arriving London peace commission may have had to achieve reconciliation with the colonists. (That "Carlisle" commission had been purposefully kept ignorant of London's order for the Philadelphia retreat prior to its departure for America.)

The Congress after Saratoga also would be preoccupied by its task of organizing a political framework for the disparate thirteen states, one that could serve as a suitable partner for the kind of mutually supportive relationships and alliances with other powers that it now saw as the most effective and expeditious route to final victory. At that time, the consensus of the American leadership was that, despite the great recent victory, only such external help could bail the financially desperate, regionally divided United States out of its quandary of how to evict from its soil a rejected metropole having the military and naval strength, and manifest political determination, to remain as long as necessary to bring the rebels back into the fold.[232] It was as though the Congress, and the individual states, now were looking to France to complete the task so well advanced by the U.S. victory over Burgoyne.[233] By March 18, 1779, Vergennes was complaining to Montmorin that France was trying hard to get the U.S. "to undertake some kind of enterprise."[234] As late as March 14, 1781, Luzerne was reporting on the Congress' lack of energy and loss of prestige since Saratoga.[235]

CHAPTER 4

From the French-U.S. Alliance to Spain's Entrance into the War, February 1778–April 1779

FRANCE'S MILITARY AND DIPLOMATIC STRATEGY AND ACTIVITIES

At first blush, one might have expected that such a long-anticipated war between France and England would have been ushered in by a series of major battles, at least at sea, in the first year of its outbreak. But this was not the case. Instead, 1778 witnessed only minor naval skirmishes on the fringes of merely posturing maneuvers by the two sides' main fleets. Many at the time—and since—viewed this record as a major strategic error by Vergennes's France on the grounds that it cost it a chance to end the war quickly by virtue of a decisive blow, such as a secure landing on the underdefended British coast following a victorious sea battle for domination of the Channel. After all, France was the power that forced the confrontation and determined its timing, presumably in the belief that it had the military and naval capability to defeat a nation already taxed severely by its struggle across the Atlantic.[236] As the French embassy in London wrote Vergennes, following its March 14, 1778, delivery to the English government of France's 10 March "Declaration" announcing the signing on 6 February of a friendship and commercial treaty with the U.S.: that action has assured France of "a century of peace by a year of war."[237] Certainly, this was the general view of the American people, who anticipated that a French intervention would guarantee within a few short months an English recognition of U.S. independence and, therefore, an end to the war, or at least the particular war between the U.S. and England. Alas, the problem was not to be solved so simply!

Given this key issue for France's war strategy, a general understanding of that nation's diplomatic and military circumstances in 1778 becomes vital for our purposes:

1. Did France miscalculate its relative strength in deciding to participate in the American War? Note that, by 6 February, Versailles had already lost hope of Spain's joining in its alliance with the U.S., at least in the *near term*, and yet felt too committed by then not to proceed on its own in signing the treaties of that date.

2. Did the French government sincerely intend to strike a major blow against England in the enemy's home waters and territory during that very first year of alliance with America, if ever? Note that (a) the French military planning document of January 27, 1778, expressly stated that France would not be able to undertake any major expedition that year; and (b) on March 27, 1777, Vergennes had written to Ossun that France cannot afford to "crush" England, as that would lead to a general war by upsetting the European balance of power—"Let's let England itself work towards its own destruction." Vergennes further observed, "In my forty years' experience, I've seen alliances try to wipe out a power, and I never saw any do so. . . . Nor should we be silent regarding our impossibility to sustain simultaneously a maritime war and a land war." The minister confirmed this modest view of the means and goals of France's participation in the American War when, on June 20, 1778, he made clear that the nation was not considering England's physical destruction, or reduction to a province, but rather its decrease in power so that it could not continue to be the consistent, major instigator against French interests.[238]

3. If France, contrary to the above viewpoints, nevertheless did sincerely intend to fight a major naval battle in the Channel as a preliminary to a landing on the English coast, did failure to do so result from incompetence or merely bad luck in the execution of the strategy's purely military and naval aspects? Note that France, in spring 1778, notwithstanding the uncertainties of the outcome of the looming naval

battles in the Channel, was clearly taking a positive approach and preparing at great financial expense to land large numbers of troops on the English coast in the event of a major Channel victory giving France control over those waters. For example, the French ambassador to The Hague, just returned from lengthy consultations at Versailles, wrote on 25 April recommending that the government meet with an English naval officer who was offering his services to either France or Spain and who may have "some useful ideas and helpful intelligence for our planned attack on the English coast."[239]

4. On the other hand, and contrary to the above premises, did France in fact never plan to take on the English in a major operation, either at sea or on land, until it had Spain at its side as a co-belligerent? After all, as late as October 31, 1777, Vergennes was reporting to Ossun that the French navy needed one more year "to be at the point it should be"; even on February 12, 1779, he would be writing to Montmorin that no "unilateral" invasion was feasible.[240] Moreover, he would re-gretfully say, in postwar comments to a colleague in his ministry, that Ossun, having become a member of the king's Council following his return from Spain, unfortunately had succeeded in convincing that group in 1778 that France "must await the decision of Spain" before undertaking any major attack on England. Vergennes then continued: "Never had a Council seat been more poorly occupied than by the one which Ossun occupies, and never has a Council seat been more disastrous for France."[241]

Typically, the reality of Vergennes's policies was more ambiv-alent than the seemingly straightforward statements outlined above. Moreover, even those statements tended to be vitiated by others he would make for different audiences. For example, that minister's views, as expressed soon after the diplomatic break with England in March 1778, were more bellicose toward England than were those of 1777. Thus, in that April, he wrote that France could not plan definitively, because it was still uncertain whether Spain would come in with it or not. "Without Spain," Vergennes continued, "it would be prudent for it to risk all to crush England right then, when its power was not yet at full strength; but, if Spain would come in with France, then it would be best 'to give a hand to luck' and abide our time, because our combined strength would overcome England's in the longer run without our having to take that risk."[242] By June 20, 1778, in his continuing effort to convince Spain to join in, Vergennes sought to correct Madrid's stated belief (which it would assert throughout the conflict) that France was interested in fighting "only weakly" in a limited war against England, by now assuring Floridablanca that all that was required of Spain was "to advise us what to do, and we'll do it, if we could have joining us 12–15 of your ships-of-the-line in a combined, not separate, operation designed to deliver a decisive blow." Finally, by the end of 1778, Vergennes was lamenting to his Spanish counterpart that whereas six months earlier France and Spain together could have brought England to its knees, now the situation had changed, with England strengthened everywhere, "and only God knows what will be possible."[243]

In attempting to answer the above-listed questions, and to work through the labyrinth of Vergennes's verbiage, most notably concerning whether his postwar goal of establishing a diplomatic partnership with the English in and of itself had a dampening effect on any all-out French military effort against that island nation, a review is necessary of the military and political steps actually undertaken by France in that initial period of its participation in the American War. Among those steps was the quick dispatch (13 April) to North American waters of a modest naval squadron from the Mediterranean port of Toulon; it was under the command of a very senior military officer serving as admiral—Lieutenant General Charles d'Estaing. This operation, at the least, met a need to show the French flag in the theater of operations of most concern to their new American ally. Even though d'Estaing in a later phase would add to his original complement of troops several thousand from West Indies–based regiments, his North American mission, in the context of France's overall strategy focus on European waters, was designed only as a "diversion," although one that possibly could help "shorten the war" and also open the way to tempt Spain to initiate attacks of their choice on England's American possessions and assets.[244] Moreover, d'Estaing was instructed to limit his activities to purely coastal operations in support of whatever military tactics the U.S.

chose to carry out on its own part against the common enemy. This restriction was in line with France's initial vision of its role in North America, that of merely serving as an offshore "auxiliary" to the main, entirely American military force confronting the enemy army. Another key limitation imposed on the mission was that, under no circumstances, was it to give encouragement to— and only under the extreme duress of having to prevent a breakdown in the cooperative relationship between the two allies to provide assistance for—any American plan to invade and conquer inland Canada.[245]

Not surprisingly, the end result of d'Estaing's year and a half stay in American waters fell well short of American needs and expectations, although, as we have seen, its very prospect did contribute to London's decision to evacuate Philadelphia.[246] Moreover, what few specific operations against the enemy d'Estaing did undertake in direct cooperation with the Americans were so ineffective and so marred by poor implementation as to have worsened rather than improved mutual confidence between the two allies. Vergennes, who a month earlier had already exhibited a concern over possible negative fallout from d'Estaing's unhappy operations in America, by November 1778 was rejecting harsh criticisms being leveled against that French officer by "trouble-makers both in America and in Europe."[247] He did, however, have to acknowledge that d'Estaing's mission thus far had been a disappointment, even as he argued that it "shouldn't be seen as a total failure," having contained enemy forces and destroyed "large numbers of English warships"; and that his setbacks were due to circumstances beyond anyone's ability to "anticipate and prevent."[248] It is noteworthy that all this controversy occurred even prior to the failure of the one major military operation conducted jointly by d'Estaing and the American army: the attempt to conquer Savannah in September–October 1779.

In summary form, the experience of d'Estaing's mission accounting for Vergennes's defensiveness was as follows:

During its initial stay in North American waters, July–November 1778, it failed to bottle up, or seriously attack, the large English fleet in New York harbor in accordance with his assigned part of a hopelessly overambitious plan coordinated with an admittedly skeptical Washington to seize that place by land and sea; and it then failed, partly due to stormy conditions at sea, to wage a serious battle off his next coastal stop, the strategically less important enemy garrison at Newport, on Rhode Island, where the English now had also sent part of its fleet to counter d'Estaing's moves.

It was especially this last episode that produced "troublemakers" in America: General Sullivan, commander of American forces cooperating with the French in that area, subsequently charged d'Estaing with having prematurely left the scene, thereby forcing his army, which was still on that island, to undertake a risky evacuation back to the mainland.[249] D'Estaing acted as he did despite personal, shipboard entreaties from Sullivan and Lafayette "to stay, with assurances that, if he would land his troops, the British force would be subdued."[250] That admiral, however, "remained inflexible" for two days on grounds that his orders were to go to Boston in the event of "any disaster." Even though he then did take his squadron to that safe port, Sullivan managed, by the night of 30–31 August, to evacuate the island, just in advance of the arrival from New York of additional enemy ships and men.[251] By January 1779, Sullivan's public criticisms of d'Estaing's performance at Rhode Island had succeeded in exciting much of the local population, with attendant repercussions in Europe, where the English were given an opening for a propaganda campaign seeking to undermine the Franco-American alliance.[252] By 16 May, however, Gérard would be able to report that, upon his informing the Congress that d'Estaing would again become available from the West Indies for combined operations with American forces, most of that body's membership—but not the "opposition leaders" of New England and their supporters, the Lees of Virginia, who all remained silent—showed due appreciation to France, with some, notably those from Pennsylvania and South Carolina, going on to denounce those members who were belittling that U.S. ally.

In the meanwhile, d'Estaing's post-Newport moves were, first, as noted, to Boston, where the time for refitting and replenishment took longer than he thought necessary, keeping him there until 4 November, when he left for the West Indies behind schedule— only just before year's end did he arrive at Martinique. There, his squadron joined with other French naval and military units in their fundamental duty of protecting the French islands in the Caribbean and taking the offensive when possible against English targets of opportunity in that theater. Even in those waters, d'Estaing's operations would prove less than fully satisfying to his superiors. As President Jay described them on January 31, 1779, in a letter to New York's Governor George Clinton: d'Estaing reportedly tried to "retake" St. Lucie from the English, who had recently landed there "without opposition" and quickly conquered it; but that admiral could not get to the smaller enemy squadron in the harbor; therefore, he landed "a considerable body of troops and attempted to carry the fort by assault"; he was repulsed and forced to leave the island; however, other than this failure, d'Estaing's ships had succeeded in taking many "prizes and prisoners of war (filling Martinique's jails and public buildings)."[253]

It was only on his squadron's way back to France in the late summer of 1779 that d'Estaing would revisit U.S. shores, where he experienced another failed land and sea attack on English-held territory; this time at Savannah. That defeat was attributed by him to the poor performance of his American partners. As Vergennes would describe the event based on d'Estaing's own report to him when he returned to France in December 1779:

The final attack on 9 October "failed due to the feeble and careless American role under General Lincoln, who did not block the English troop reinforcements from entering Savannah from the north in full force, requiring a wounded d'Estaing (in the arm and knee) to withdraw";[254] still, there were two good results, one being that General Henry Clinton had to cancel an expedition to the West Indies [Vergennes clearly was in error on this point, as that New York–based enemy commander was not at all in a position to undertake such an operation], and the other that the Americans had so devastated Georgia "as to render it useless to England"; finally, Savannah had been only an operation of last resort, because d'Estaing could not get to Newfoundland due to storm damage to his squadron and to lack of time, and it cost him "dearly": 168 killed in action and 400 wounded in action, the latter being left with the Americans by de Grasse at Chesapeake Bay, where he had gone for food supplies prepared for him by the Americans to take back to the West Indies.[255] [Actually, as Gérard had explained in a May 6, 1779, message to Versailles, de Grasse's original mission was to obtain a four-month food supply for d'Estaing's squadron as it moved northward with a view to capturing Halifax and Newfoundland prior to returning to France.][256]

The perceived strategic value to the two allies in their revised plan to seize Savannah was that it would facilitate a "planned U.S.-Spanish expedition to capture West Florida" by way of Georgia, given that U.S. troops had no alternate route to that target and that it was "impracticable" for Spanish ships to carry them there.[257] In the event, Spain itself over a year later would capture Pensacola, west Florida's capital, without significant U.S. participation—the leadership of that successful expedition, which drew on Havana-based forces, was in the hands of the competent and aggressive New Orleans–based governor of Louisiana, Bernardo de Galvez, a nephew of Spain's minister for the Indies, José de Galvez. Ironically, Vergennes, unaware of the September 1779 Savannah attack, had written a few weeks later to Montmorin that it was a shame Spain had not told d'Estaing of this joint west Florida plan with the Americans, because then "he could have, in passing, attacked Savannah . . . *en route* to Halifax and Newfoundland."[258]

There was no lack of reciprocal recriminations from the American side against the performance of d'Estaing, despite the courage he had displayed in personally leading his troops ashore.[259] Nevertheless, it is clear that John Jay, at least at Madrid, took a more appreciative view of that officer's contribution to the U.S. war effort, as he wrote to Montmorin at San Ildefonso on August 1, 1780: "We are told that Count d'Estaing is to be with you tomorrow. . . . Although curiosity is not among my dominant passions, I confess I have always a desire of seeing and conversing with those who have either done things worthy to be written, or written things worthy to be read." Jay went on to say that he would also like to pay d'Estaing "that tribute of gratitude and respect which every American owes to his generous efforts in our cause," and, if the admiral did not plan to pass through Madrid, he'd like himself to go immediately to San Ildefonso.

While the death of the Jays' infant daughter blocked that trip, they would meet d'Estaing later that month in Madrid and would become friends, including exchanging home visits in Paris. William Carmichael, Jay's secretary of legation in Spain, also had a friendly relationship with that Frenchman, whom he had known from his earlier assignment as secretary to the U.S. deputies in Paris.[260] Jay, in that early August 1780 opening contact, had sent Carmichael to express his "regret" at being unable to come to San Ildefonso, and this resulted in the following report to him from Carmichael: "I waited on the Count d'Estaing, who received me as an old acquaintance. . . . I dined with him this day [7 August], when he mentioned his concern that his endeavors to serve America had not been attended with the success he wished; you may easily conceive my answer. . . . He showed great regret and no dissatisfaction with respect to the U.S."

Alongside the d'Estaing mission of 1778 was the more ambitious and sizable one given by Versailles to Admiral Louis d'Orvilliers as commander of the main French fleet in the Atlantic based at Brest, where France had over thirty-six ships-of-the-line armed and ready to sail.[261] Following a standoff naval skirmish between frigates off the French coast on 17 June, the very first exchange of fire between the two enemies in the formally undeclared war, orders were issued to that admiral to take his entire fleet out of Brest and seek out the English one under Admiral August Keppel, "avoiding however to enter the Channel."[262] The ostensible goal was to create the conditions at sea suitable for a major invasion of England by the French troops ostentatiously gathering along the opposite coast under the command of the rehabilitated Marshal de Broglio.[263] Not surprisingly, given similar overly grandiose French invasion threats in past wars (not to mention a later one, by Napoleon), this scenario never took place:

D'Orvilliers proved unable, or unwilling, actually both, to risk such a naval battle without clear numerical superiority, which he thought he lacked; and on the English side, Keppel, too, seemed less than anxious for such a battle—as Weymouth advised Grantham for Spanish consumption on 30 June: Keppel's not having taken "several merchant ships bound to the ports of France . . . even after" he had "detained" the French frigates [a reference to the 17 June skirmish], "proves evidently that he had no orders" for the purpose of committing "hostilities in the European seas." (Weymouth might also have mentioned, this time for his ambassador's private information, that Keppel, like d'Orvilliers, felt the numerical situation did not adequately favor his fleet over that of his counterpart, a key factor explaining the inconclusiveness of the subsequent encounters between the two fleets that summer.)[264]

The net result of all the above was that the entire naval fighting season in the waters separating France and England ended without any serious action whatsoever, rather conveniently precluding a risky French attempt to invade the enemy's homeland. Even the Spanish were relieved at this result. Floridablanca in June, and again on 11 August, had urged the French to keep their Brest fleet in the harbor and not risk a defeat that could decide the whole war. As Montmorin commented in June, this was a clear hint of Spain's continuing interest in joining the war, but only if and when it felt the time was right.[265] That Floridablanca's warning had fallen on receptive ears is evident from Versailles' prudent orders of 17 August to d'Orvilliers, following that equally prudent earlier order to stay out of the narrow waters of the Channel, to avoid a "second battle," the first one having occurred in July without major damage to either side.[266]

What was keenly missed by French military and political leaders was the presence of Spain as a fighting ally. That, at least on paper, would have given them the superior force they felt they needed if they were even to attempt to defeat the historically awesome English navy, which since 1692 had been cowing its French counterpart. Thus, Versailles in August 1778 decided that England's now having succeeded in deploying forty-five ships-of-the-line in the Channel imposed a requirement on France to have sixty there—a figure attainable in the near term only with Spain as partner.[267] Failure to bring the latter into the war at this early stage was not for lack of trying. Vergennes, from 1776 on, never stopped pressing Madrid to be active in the American War.[268] For a while, he was succeeding, as seen in Spain's matching France's secretly delivered financial contribution to the rebels to help cover the cost of war material being shipped to them from Europe. But that Spanish official aid was sharply curtailed with the termination of Grimaldi's tenure in early 1777 and would not be resumed in any meaningful way under Floridablanca, not even after Spain's secret agreement with France of April 12, 1779, bringing it into the war against England.[269]

A flavor of Floridablanca's jaundiced view of the Americans, and of the new French alliance with them, may be gleaned from his April 1778 description of the U.S. deputies in Paris as "Roman Consuls to whom oriental kings came to beg for support"; and, as noted, of the alliance itself: pure "Quixotism."[270] Moreover, he described Franklin as lacking in "talent" and dismissed the value of Gérard's having been instructed to facilitate U.S.-Spanish relations by claiming that Spain "has nothing to untangle with the Americans." It is unimaginable for Grimaldi to have taken this line as consistently as Floridablanca would.

It would not be an exaggeration to say that there was little France would not have done to obtain Spanish participation in the war.[271] Accordingly, Montmorin was given carte blanche to agree in writing to any demands Madrid might make as a condition precedent to a military alliance with France, whether regarding overall war strategy or terms of peace.[272] Moreover, in this court-ship, the ambassador, and through him the court at Versailles itself, submitted to an incessant stream of verbal and diplomatic abuse from Floridablanca that, in Vergennes's own words, "scandalized" them and that would have been intolerable for the proud French in any other circumstance.[273] As Montmorin complained in February 1778, "One has to tremble upon undertaking a war together with Spain." That ambassador went on: Floridablanca's "character and the circumstances" made his own "task hard to handle." The ambassador defined the problem in several ways:

that Floridablanca felt his advice had been ignored by France since his coming into power, and his pride was hurt; that, by basic character, he is distrustful of others; and that "the Spanish are a bit like children," who need to be excited by brilliant things and to see close at hand the advantages "of the wise and moderate views adopted by the King." On the positive side, Montmorin underlined that the minister does believe in maintaining close ties among the Bourbons, and he has become "my friend, despite heated arguments"; he added that a Chatham entering the English government would give Spain the shudders. The following month, March, that ambassador would supplement his assessment of Floridablanca's personality in these terms: He sees himself, and correctly, as, by nature, "either too extreme in all, or too moderate, or overly excited."[274]

Aside from constantly insulting the fighting abilities of the French navy and rehashing all past grievances of Charles III against the French, starting with the Seven Year' War, when he made "sacrifices" for the losing French cause, and then going through to the recently concluded war with Portugal, in which France had declined to participate, and on to France's next having put in jeopardy, through its recent treaties with the American colonies, the safe arrival of Spain's treasury ships from America, Floridablanca now initiated an unwelcome, unhelpful, foredoomed, yearlong mediation effort to end the French-English war on amicable terms.[275] This move had followed what Vergennes on 3 April had described as a "glacial" response from Charles to Louis's personal appeal for Spanish participation with France in the American War. While Versailles "without restriction" publicly endorsed Spain's mediation initiative, which it officially accepted in May even before London conditionally did, its private criticisms of this Spanish policy of procrastination included that it weakens the Bourbon Family Compact of 1761 and displays that even the most foolproof treaty commitments can be avoided and that it shows Spain as wanting "to reap without having to sow," meaning that Spain was trying to extract gains for itself from the American War without risking a belligerency.[276] France believed that all this was not a result of any conscious goal of Floridablanca but that it was due to "his fiscal spirit, which was the essence of his initial profession . . . nothing is gratis on Spain's part."[277]

In line with his private assessments for Vergennes's benefit, Montmorin regularly and astutely pointed out to him in this period, 1778–79, that a failed mediation and resultant entry of Spain into the war would profoundly raise Spanish ambitions well beyond the currently modest and manageable ones associated with the mediation effort, such as being rewarded by a grateful England with the return of west Florida. Moreover, were Spain to become a belligerent, France would then necessarily have to endorse its new ally's heightened ambitions, most importantly for the return of Gibraltar, and even make them its own, and that would "render the war's duration uncertain" and would make Spain more of a burden than a help to France.[278] For its part, Spain felt that once France achieved *its* war goals, "peace negotiations would not be pleasant for Spain."[279]

Spain's mediation effort of 1778–79 could only have been successful if it was based, as in its final stages it in fact would be, much to an unconsulted Versailles' temporary discomfort, on France's disavowing some of its most basic commitments to the U.S. in their alliance treaty of February 1778.[280] Not until Spain in early spring 1779, one full year after its opening move in April 1778, finally acknowledged to France that London would certainly reject its proposals, such as allowing English forces during a lengthy truce period to remain in a quasi-independent U.S., could France finally breathe a sigh of relief and enthusiastically sign with Spain on 12 April the alliance agreement it had long sought. It felt that way even though Madrid had wrung from it a commitment to remain in the war until Spain recovered its territories lost to England, with Gibraltar at the top of the list, a most dubious goal and one that clearly would complicate France's ties to the Americans.[281] In return, Spain committed itself, among other, relatively insubstantial quid pro quos, to back France until it honorably met its own treaty obligations to the U.S. This overall result, successful for France even if belated and at a predictably high cost, bore out Vergennes's tolerance of Floridablanca's behavior and his desire that the Spaniard not be replaced. As he wrote at one point prior to the April agreement: "I hope Floridablanca's health does not lead to his resignation; overall, he is a good man for the job, although [Minister of the Indies Galvez] would be a good successor." By October 1778, Montmorin, too, was expressing a strong preference for Floridablanca to remain in office, because that minister did believe in the Bourbon alliance and was "open to Spain's entering the war as the only way to retrieve Spanish territory in English hands."[282]

There was a major additional source of international tension for France during this interim between the signing of its alliance treaties with the U.S. and Spain, respectively: Austria's power grab of Bavaria. Basing his military move on the fiction of a legal claim to that electorate, Emperor Joseph II brought the continent to a war-fever pitch, with Prussia in the vanguard, because Austria was threatening to upset the balance between those two Germanic powers in their competition for control over Central Europe's so-called Holy Roman Empire. France was "necessarily involved," if only due to its Treaty of Westphalia role there as a "guarantor of the peace," not to speak of its continuing ties with Austria by virtue of the 1756 treaty between the two for a defensive alliance.[283] Moreover, this crisis was complicating Vergennes's strategy for the French role in the American War just as that role was about to become one of open belligerency.[284]

This last point is clear from his having sent in his own hand the following message to Montmorin on March 10, 1778:

"Despite Austria's threatening, I'd say nearly hostile, act against France by occupying the major part of Bavaria," France is not acceding to Prussia's request that it join in against Austria, and France is even keeping Berlin in the dark regarding the possibility of activating the French-Austrian alliance, although not Austria, whom France is explicitly telling that it will not join it against Prussia but rather, at best, will stay neutral. But [the message continued] Spain should see that, in America, France must act in its own interest and even before the U.S. has ratified the treaty with it of 6 February, because England will soon learn of it, ratified or not, and France must show confidence in that agreement and not give the slightest hint it doubts America's good faith—in fact, France does have that confidence in the U.S.

Neither France nor Russia, which for its part was tied to Prussia by a 1764 treaty of defensive alliance, wished to see an armed conflict between those two bitter rivals, and to complete our story, they combined to intimidate Austria into a less ambitious frame of mind and to convince Prussia, by the autumn of 1778, to withdraw the troops it had sent early that summer into Austria's Bohemia (the same province Prussia had invaded in 1756 at the start of the Seven Years' War, but this time neither Prussia nor Austria was interested in fighting a determined war, so the two armies had remained largely inactive after that August action).[285] The two outside powers also obtained the belligerents' agreement to a mediation, which was successful and led to a "treaty of peace" signed in May 1779 at Teschen.[286] That fully settled the issue by virtue of an Austrian withdrawal from most of Bavaria. Happily for France, this experience assured it of a calm, even friendly, situation on its land borders, allowing Vergennes, whose diplomacy in the affair was generally recognized as masterly, to boast with reason that "Europe today, to England's disappointment, is for our side."[287] It also helped further France's goal of enhancing its influence over Russian policies regarding England and the Ottoman Empire, as outlined earlier. Furthermore, it calmed Charles III's fears of a French land war, thus easing Spain's way into the war against England.[288]

As for the reaction of the U.S. to the Teschen treaty and related European events in general, we have President Jay's letter of August 24, 1779, to Washington: "The conduct of France in establishing peace between Russia and the Porte has won the heart of the Empress [Catherine]. . . . [289] The Emperor and Prussia are under similar obligations. The latter wishes us well," and Austria is too financially strapped "to support the expenses of war without subsidies from Britain who at present cannot afford them." Portugal and "the Dutch" will not help a Britain "who, like a tower in an earthquake sliding from its base, will crush every slender prop that may be raised to prevent its fall." But this "fine sky" for the

U.S. may soon change—in all determinations, "the mutability of human affairs should have a certain degree of influence."

This jibes well with Vergennes's analysis a few months earlier that despite France's now having Catherine's goodwill, "earned by our having saved Russia from a war" with the Ottoman Empire, and by France's having now made Russia a "compass" for Germany, that gain was to be less counted on than Prussia's great influence in St. Petersburg to counter England's blandishments: Frederick would "never agree to see Catherine put herself in England's hands."[290] Similarly, Montmorin believed that Russia's backing of France's mediation efforts over Bavaria helped to repair past Russian-French relationship problems (which, of course, were due importantly to their opposing policies regarding Sweden, Poland and the Ottoman Empire, not to speak of Russia's problem with the Franco-Austrian alliance as a possible threat to its security in Europe).

THE NORTH AMERICAN THEATER OF OPERATIONS

France in winter 1778–79, as we have seen, had definitely lost valuable time in seeking to gain the upper hand militarily over an England notorious for beginning wars unimpressively, if at times treacherously, but ending them with flourish. France's threat to England's home fleet, its menace of a massive invasion of England itself, its effort to gain Spain as a military ally and its tokenism in sending d'Estaing to North American waters all went by the wayside in terms of decisive results.[291] Furthermore, the U.S., aside from its seemingly never-ending demands on limited French funds, was not behaving as aggressively or effectively versus the common enemy as Versailles had been led to expect following the victory at Saratoga. For example, at Monmouth, New Jersey, where Washington's army in late June 1778 had caught up with a desperately retreating English army trying to get from an evacuated Philadelphia to the safety of New York City, the American field commander, General Charles Lee, allegedly performed so poorly, turning a seemingly certain victory into a near-defeat prevented only at the last minute by Washington himself, that he would be court-martialed and punished. Bitterness against Lee was particularly strong because many Americans believed that the Monmouth battle had the potential of giving the U.S. "a gloriously finishing of the war."[292]

Similarly, after much planning and military preparations in the winter of 1778–79 for another U.S. attempt at conquering Canada, that of 1775–76 having been a failure after a promising start with the capture of Montreal (Appendix A), realities finally intervened during the course of the following years to convince both Washington and the Congress that the operation was not feasible.[293] Among the reasons for this last political and military change in strategy by the Americans were these: (1) France's clear, open policy that, at best, it would only help the U.S. carry out coastal attacks on the enemy;[294] (2) even without the burden of mounting an invasion to the north, the patent inability of Washington's army, unless it had the help of French "supremacy at sea" in North American waters, to evict an English army and supporting fleet based in the U.S. and capable of sending expeditions up and down the coast to occupy other parts of American home territory;[295] (3) the enemy had failed to evacuate the U.S. by the end of 1778, as had been the assumption, or better, the hope of the Americans; and (4) the war materiel needed to open another front was obviously lacking—by now, Congress' financial credit was weakening along with the value of its paper money, and enemy ships were most effectively blocking supply routes between America and sources of supply in the West Indies and Europe.[296]

The French view of this abortive Canadian expedition was a mixed one. On the one hand, Versailles, at this stage in the war, was so anxious to see the U.S. military "reinvigorated" and used to keep the English busy as a useful diversion to help its own upcoming campaign outside North America, which hopefully would be carried out jointly with Spain, that it encouraged the Congress to authorize that expedition rather than see Washington's army and the various state militias stand by idly, leaving France "to bear the full burden" of the war. On the other hand, the French at this same period were highly doubtful that such an expedition would actually be executed, given Washington's known skepticism about it and also the congressional doubts that *either* its enemy, England, or its ally, France, would allow the U.S. to retain "Quebec and Halifax" at the peace.[297] In point of fact, France by now had reluctantly acknowledged to itself that in the unlikely event the Americans did manage to conquer that Canadian heartland, "it would be quite necessary to let them keep it, were the peace to depend on it." This reluctance to see the U.S. absorb Canada was part and parcel of Gérard's instructions of October 26, 1778, to forward France's overall postwar goals of limiting the geographical reach of the U.S. to the extent practical by discouraging it from "demanding the navigation of the Mississippi" and by encouraging it to cede the Floridas to Spain in the event the Americans conquered them from England. As regards the western boundary of the U.S., France assumed the Americans would be kept from the left bank of the Mississippi above west Florida by some combination of English and Spanish sovereignty there, perhaps along with protectorates over Indian territory.

Not surprisingly, given the centrality of France in the strategic thinking, militarily and diplomatically, of the Congress regarding Canada, that body designated Lafayette as the (unfortunate) commander of a prospective 1778 expedition, whose departure point was to be Albany, New York. The hope obviously was that the appointment would help win over the French to a more receptive policy of military cooperation in that venture. Another consideration underlying the appointment of Lafayette was that the Congress, as was true even of Versailles itself (as we have seen by its having d'Estaing at Boston issue that naive call on the French Canadians to fight as "nephews" of Montcalm), was under the illusion that the bulk of those people still felt a deep loyalty to France and would therefore respond more positively to a U.S. invasion if it was led by a Frenchman and Catholic rather than by an Anglo-Saxon. Suggestive of the American reasoning is Ambassador Aranda's 1778 report to Madrid that John Adams told him that Lafayette's appointment was made in the hope of winning over the Canadians.[298]

Lafayette himself, even after the cancellation of the Canadian expedition he was to have conducted, shared the American view, although not for the same reasons, that absorption by the U.S. of Canada was a desirable objective. This is made clear from his letter to Vergennes of July 18, 1779, from Le Havre, France, his departure point back to America after having spent some months at Paris and Versailles.[299] In it, he recognized that the two men had "differing views" regarding Canada, notably over the minister's judgment that even though "the idea of a revolution in Canada would be charming for all good Frenchmen," who would like to see that country returned to the motherland, a Canada within the U.S. rather than retained by England would be against France's national interest. Lafayette, in contrast, saw "room for serious debate" on this, arguing the desirability of delivering "our oppressed tbrothers" from English rule and making Canada a "pro-French, fourteenth State," one that, moreover, would likely to be the "preponderant power in the conflicts that surely will one day divide America." That general saw this as a prospect "worth thinking about" but, knowing of Vergennes's opposing position, assured him he would "not act on my ideas."

Gérard, for his part, adhered to his March 1778 instructions, which were along the lines of those given to d'Estaing—that is, if pressed by the Congress to render French help to a U.S. invasion of Canada, to respond "with the reserve prescribed by the King." Still, he advised Versailles, in dispatches of September 20 and 24, 1778, that "the best way" of reinvigorating the American military effort was to encourage the Canadian expedition by complementing it with a French expedition to attack Newfoundland and the islands in the Gulf of St. Lawrence and by the French fleet's blocking England from sending reinforcements to North America. Barring such an operation, Gérard foresaw the Continental Army dwindling down to 8,000 troops by 1779. Moreover, he reassured Versailles that the U.S. had no ambitions to retain Newfoundland, even if it were to help France conquer it, although the Americans would prefer that the French do that on their own. In contrast, the U.S. did fear, so Gérard advised, that, were England to be allowed at the peace to retain Canada and both Floridas, that would put it in "too-formidable a position."[300] (As to be discussed, Jay in 1782 at Paris clearly had a different view and favored precisely an English possession of the Floridas even though they also were retaining Canada.)

Of course, it was precisely this latter fear that Versailles wanted to see, at least regarding Canada, because, as stated in those March instructions, "the possession of these three lands, or at least of Canada, by the English would be a useful way to get the Americans to be concerned and vigilant, and, therefore, to have them feel the full advantage and need for the alliance and friendship of the King, and consequently that it is not in their interest to destroy those ties." Accordingly, the instructions continued, "If pressed and Gérard had to commit French help rather than risk a strain in the alliance, he should make clear, but delicately, that the intended conquests should not be made an essential condition to the future peace." (By October 1780, French policy on the Canadian–Nova Scotia issue would become even more refined, as follows: Only after the English were expelled from all thirteen states should anyone "concern himself with these two targets"; however, specifically regarding Halifax, "it would be infinitely desirable for us *or the Americans* to control" that base permanently.)[301]

Accordingly, the battle lines in North America remained largely stationary during the fifteen-month period between France's signing its alliance with the U.S. in February 1778 and then with Spain in April 1779.[302] This was especially true after the English army fled Philadelphia in favor of concentrating nearly all its strength at New York. This meant that the region surrounding that city would remain as focal point of military action, just when Jay and colleagues upstate were creating and giving life to a postindependence governmental structure. In this situation, with Washington and his army based in the vicinity, Jay, as a senior member of the state government, inevitably also would assume military responsibilities of a sort along with his basic function as chief justice. Thus, for example, he would seek sources of military supplies and equipment, particularly heavy artillery being manufactured in Connecticut, even as he found time to conduct trials and root out Loyalist spies. Among Jay's principal colleagues in these endeavors, as noted, was his closest friend, Robert Livingston, now the "second officer of the state" as chancellor and also fellow member of the Council of Revision, the very active, limited body that ruled on the constitutionality of legislative acts.[303] Little did either of the two realize that, well before war's end, both would be serving in senior, foreign policy positions for the U.S. government, Jay overseas and Livingston, his supervisor, at least theoretically, as the nation's first, if extremely circumscribed, Secretary for Foreign Affairs (and predecessor to Jay in that very same position); even more astonishing, and personally distressing for the two of them, would have been the knowledge that the clashing responsibilities of those positions would largely cost them their close friendship over issues of war and peace.

But between 1778 and that later period, both men's attention was concentrated on: New York's precarious security situation in the face of the enemy in its midst; discharging the duties of their respective offices, such as Jay's road trips as touring chief justice conducting his trials; and making the case for New York in its difficult, high-profile political contest with New Hampshire and Massachusetts for possession of "Vermont," most of whose own inhabitants, since their proclamation as a republic in 1777, were demanding recognition by the Continental Congress as a state separate and independent of the three established ones claiming in one form or another sovereign jurisdiction there. Jay and associates, who typically were landowners in that region, saw this demand as nothing less than an intolerable "rebellion" against New York that might require suppression by force.[304] It would be this issue that would provide the occasion for the New York authorities in late 1778 to send Jay back to the Congress in Philadelphia as their most effective spokesman in the intensifying legal and political fight for control of Vermont.

As the French assessment of the Vermont problem is of interest to this study, following is a recapitulation. On August 20, 1781, Luzerne put it this way in a dispatch to Versailles:[305] "The Congress could well vote Vermont into the union, especially after captured enemy correspondence now proves that the English are active there, seeking to win that population to England's side;

New York's delegates are trying to block Vermont from having representatives here on grounds that any congressional invitation for it to do so would only be motivated by a fear that otherwise it would go over to the enemy";[306] and the southern states backed New York, given their fear that a successful Vermont secession could become a precedent for their own "districts" in the west. The issue, Luzerne continued, also was over maintaining the north-south political balance in the Congress and all this could pose a problem for France, especially if Vermont's boundaries are set in a way that "they fall within the French-U.S. treaty terms of the mutual guarantee of territories"; if so, we would have a problem of recognizing Vermont as a state, unless we could avoid also having to recognize expanded U.S. limits, because, unlike New York's, Vermont's territorial claims "are very unreasonable" and affect Canada, and consequently could become a negotiating problem at the peace, given that "circumstances might force us to leave to England a part of the territory of which Vermont is composed." [Luzerne ended the message with a request for instructions.]

During Jay's New York–based period, May 1776–November 1778, he was able to spend precious time with his full family, including a son born in January 1776.[307] While he periodically had the help in running family affairs of two able brothers, they, too, would largely, and later even permanently, be absent in pursuit of personal interests, leaving a frail, recently widowered father to do his best in managing a large household and caring for his two blind children. Nevertheless, consistent with his long-established determination to give priority to the needs of his country over those of his family, Jay accepted the assignment to Philadelphia, where he would be joined only by his wife, in March, and from which place the two, now and forever inseparable, would depart in October 1779 with heavy hearts on that dangerous and trying assignment to the Old World that would have such a large consequence for the future of the new one.

It is only now, with his arrival at Philadelphia in early December, that the paths of Vergennes and Jay begin more directly to cross.[308] Despite an absence of two and a half years, Jay was immediately elected by the Congress as its president.[309] That office was just being vacated by South Carolina's Henry Laurens, who had been caught up in the throes of a personal-cum-political feud in which two of the Congress' three commissioners in France, Silas Deane, of Connecticut, and Arthur Lee, of Virginia, were accusing each other of malfeasance and worse (Franklin himself would not escape unscathed from this feud, in which he strongly defended Deane against Lee). The feud had boiled into a full-fledged, regionally tinged battle in the Congress itself, actively involving Gérard, too. Deane, who had been recalled from France with John Adams taking his place, was in Philadelphia and publishing newspaper articles (5 December) harshly condemnatory of his accusers and of the way Congress was treating him. When Laurens, a strong defender of Lee and closely associated in the Congress with Lee's brother, Richard, proved unable to obtain that body's approval of his proposal to chastise Deane for those publications, he chose to resign his office without further ado. Since Lee's congressional supporters tended to be from the New England states and from elements within the delegations of Virginia and South Carolina, a successor to Laurens was sought from a more neutral region—hence, attention was turned to the New York delegation and, by process of elimination, to the readily available, newly arrived, highly regarded John Jay. The latter was also acceptable for a separate reason: Some members, especially those from New England, desired to neutralize him in this manner so as to keep him from participating in committee and floor debates on issues of interest to them, notably that of Vermont. (However, being president did not deprive Jay of the right to vote on each and every resolution, nor to participate in his state delegation's private deliberations—rights Jay fully utilized.)[310]

In any event, Jay was now suddenly no longer a senior official in one of thirteen states but titular head of the entire country. Consequently, especially in the continuing absence of a congressional decision to establish executive agencies of government (the Articles of Confederation would not be ratified by all the states and put into operation until 1781),[311] Jay served as well as the primary channel for all correspondence between the Congress and other bodies, such as the state governments and foreign powers. In that capacity, he would develop a close working relationship with the representatives in Philadelphia of the only two foreign powers maintaining direct, open contact with the Congress—France's fully accredited minister plenipotentiary, Gérard, and Spain's quite unofficial "observer," Juan Miralles, whose discreet presence since his landing at Charleston in January 1778 was designed by Floridablanca in a way not to provoke the English.[312] The dispatches of these two men helped make the name and person of John Jay familiar to the courts of Europe. In turn, Jay would now begin to have his very first practical experience with the great powers of the world, whose diplomatic and even commercial practices had remained outside his range of personal, educational and professional interests until now. It would be a mutual learning experience: Those powers will have rarely met a diplomat of Jay's ilk! Moreover, not even the Continental Congress would be exempt from having to contend with Jay's strength of views as its representative abroad.

In 1779, two of the main international and security issues of concern to the Congress were the following: (1) maximizing the value of the alliance with France by eliciting substantial financial and material contributions from that great, and presumably wealthy, power and (2) working with France to fulfill the expectations embodied in the secret article of their alliance treaty that provided for Spanish accession.

As to the first issue, there already was broad disappointment in the U.S. regarding the results of the first year of the alliance. Some of the reasons for this were touched upon earlier, especially American uneasiness at France's weak military performance in the Channel. There now arose a doubt about the political will of France to wage an all-out war. That doubt was deepened by Vergennes's initiative, in the context of the Spanish mediation of 1778–79, by which he proposed to them the possibility of entering into a truce with England—an admittedly "imperfect recognition" of their independence. In support of the proposal, which included a provision for the "total evacuation of enemy troops," Vergennes drew on the precedent of the Netherlands' break from Spain two centuries earlier.[313] As an alternative to a direct, separate U.S.-English truce, that Frenchman offered the possibility of a peace treaty between France and England that would incorporate into it such a truce between the U.S. and England, including a guarantee of it by France. In December 1778, Franklin told Vergennes that he anticipated an affirmative American response, given the French offer of a guarantee, and that such an arrangement would offer the U.S. "the time and means to solidify and perfect its domestic institutions." But Gérard, in May 1779, reported that George Washington rejected this "new idea of a truce" and that the Congress and American people would likely agree with their general. Of course, by then, events in Europe had made the entire subject obsolete with the assured entrance of Spain into the war as France's ally. That development led to a switch in the French line at Philadelphia: Whereas, before news of it, Gérard was trying to convince the Congress, as he told Jay in July, to look on a truce as merely a "masked" peace and a de facto recognition of U.S. independence, after it, and in line with new instructions from a Versailles now totally focused on seeking a "decisive" military victory against England, he was urging that body to drop the idea of a truce and hold out only for a definitive peace treaty dictated to a crushed enemy.[314]

This episode was the first in a pattern that subjected the U.S. throughout the war to the whipsaw effect of changing French needs elsewhere. Thus, when Versailles was insecure about its war with England, as in the period just reviewed, the Americans were pressured by it to be flexible about peace terms; but when prospects were better for a military victory, as when Spain entered the war, the policy was to harden the U.S. into a fighting machine holding out for what amounted to a dictated peace. As we shall see, once that optimistic period ended and Vergennes's France was seeking an honorable but quick way out of the war, as in the period following the failure of the Bourbons' 1779 and 1780 campaigns, it would try to use proxies, notably a Russia interested in mediating, as a discreet way to obtain American agreement to peace terms that fell far short of its original treaty and related commitments to them.[315] Even after the great, unexpected change in fortune deriving from the Yorktown victory of October 1781 (a victory that itself was the consequence of a 1780 decision by France, desperate to find a new military theater of operations after its second straight inconclusive European campaign, to base a small-sized army and accompanying naval squadron directly on U.S. territory), Versailles would struggle to keep the U.S. military active against England. It did so, not because it itself wished for further victories but because the war perforce was continuing—and even intensifying—outside North America due to the determination of its ally, Spain, to hold France to its promise of April 1779 to fight until Gibraltar was recovered; moreover, France was still facing an England apparently determined for its part to continue the war and compensate for its North American losses at Bourbon expense.

Of course, there also were attendant diplomatic complications for France arising from these changing strategies at the military level. For example: (1) Even as it was periodically encouraging the U.S. to be militarily aggressive, it sought to rein in what it considered to be America's overambitious, therefore theoretically peace-delaying, territorial and other postwar goals, such as New England's demand that the U.S. retain the identical fishing rights its population had when under English rule;[316] (2) notwithstanding Spain's unforthcoming policies toward the U.S., based on its concerns for the future of its empire in the Americas, the French, for their own immediate military needs and not for any postwar goals and interests in North America, which were largely nonexistent, never stopped trying to reconcile their two separate allies, even at the risk of antagonizing the Americans by tilting toward Madrid's position on western boundaries, Mississippi navigation and the retrocession to Spain of both Floridas;[317] and (3) at the peace negotiations of 1782, Vergennes was caught between having to keep up America's fighting spirit while also facilitating the diplomatic side of U.S.-English relations so that, once all the other belligerents were ready for peace, the negotiating track between the two Anglo-Saxon nations would not delay a final, universal settlement of the war—a balancing act he failed to perform, although events following the separate and premature peace agreement between the U.S. and England of 30 November happily relieved France of having to continue fighting into 1783 without its original ally.

As to the second diplomatic issue preoccupying the Congress during Jay's tenure as its president, that body was encouraged by Gérard to continue to expect that a Spanish belligerency would also bring that nation into alliance with the U.S., or at least would convince it to provide substantial material and financial help to the U.S. This optimism naturally became even more pronounced later in 1779, when definitive news arrived of Spain's entry into the war.[318] Surely, that act would lead to a formal connection between the Americans and Madrid, or so assumed the Congress and its president. Perhaps a letter of 30 May to Livingston in New York from Gouverneur Morris, still a member of Congress, usefully captures the context of that Spanish issue, including the mood in Philadelphia, just prior to news of that nation's belligerency:

The Congress is a "scene of politics high and low. I may add it is the scene of faction, anarchy, and detraction." Never were the affairs of any country in a better and a worse situation than those of America at this moment. The American people aren't contented just with being "free, . . . other luxuries" entice them and there is too much paper money seducing them. That money has "impaired the national industry to a degree truly alarming. . . . [A]fter foiling the giant [at Saratoga], we shrink at the touch of a child." England is likely soon to take Charleston, South Carolina, and then "collect their Tories and endeavor to weary us into a submission by harassing our coasts and frontiers and striking at our money [by counterfeiting]." England will then control Halifax, Rhode Island, New York, Portsmouth [Virginia], and Charleston; meanwhile, we will be depleting "our little remaining resources" by having "with little armies" to keep an eye on the enemy's "motions" and preventing "their ravages."
    On the other hand, there is hope, "like the bottom of Pandora's Box." Spain is likely to join the war, and, therefore, "while France keeps Great Britain at bay, Gibraltar and Jamaica will call for protection, which they

may not perhaps obtain." If d'Estaing can keep England's St. Lucie squadron checked, "five ships of the line would cleanse the continent of [America's] foes." Or, a French naval victory in Europe or America "would turn the balance so powerfully in our favor as to cover our enemies with confusion." The likely result of all this is the usual continuing war until each side is too "exhausted" to continue.

Alongside these two international issues, the Congress struggled to give energy to the upcoming military campaign of 1779. President Jay, in a 19 February letter to New York Governor Clinton, reflected just how uphill that task was at a time when the enemy had taken all of Georgia:

It is doubtful our having ordered reinforcements for General Lincoln will be able to change the fact that Georgia is now under the English; "Besides, you know militia cannot be kept long in the field"; South Carolina is not under immediate threat, but "several circumstances render it vulnerable"; all the Departments "are placed under the immediate direction of General Washington," including, therefore, "the security of the frontiers. . . . The coast from Delaware to Chesapeake is extremely infested by privateers from the City of New York"; Pennsylvania is "immersed in politics and perplexity"—the scarcity of bread in its east and south is become a serious subject, and the opposition to its Constitution is "respectable and formidable. . . . Arnold [based at the time at Philadelphia] is run hard by them."

The Congress felt frustrated in its powerlessness to marshal on its own authority the domestic resources it knew the nation as a whole had at its command in order to meet the needs of the war effort, most important, those of Washington's army. Jay, commiserating with Washington, who had sent him a "long and friendly letter" on 14 April, one that convinced him that he had the general's full confidence, wrote back on 21 April that those members of the Congress who were criticizing his performance as commander in chief instead of being full of "gratitude" are examples of a situation to be seen often in "the history of mankind" to the "dishonor of human nature," and those examples "will multiply in the course of the Revolution. . . . Envy delights to walk in the shade of merit and, like the serpent of old, to bite its heel." Jay continued: In this work of bringing "form" and "order and harmony" to the present "political chaos" caused by "the dissolution of our [colonial] government," the general was, "in the style of one of your professions, a master builder, and God grant that you may ever continue a free and accepted mason."

Also worth excerpting is this letter's broader assessment of the general situation in the U.S.:

New modes of government not widely understood, nor in certain instances approved, . . . a wide field open for the operations of ambition— man raised from low degrees to high stations and rendered giddy by elevation, . . . latitude in principles as well as commerce, . . . suspension of education, . . . fluctuation in manners and public counsels and moral obligations, . . . indifference to religion, . . . [all these] are circumstances that invite evil. . . . It gives me pleasure, however, to reflect that the period is approaching when we shall become citizens of a better State, and the spending of a few troublesome years of our eternity in doing good to this and future generations is not to be avoided or regretted.

Of course, on top of these leadership and social problems, the Congress and country were striving to create a new governmental structure for the nation. The Articles of Confederation were being stalemated at the state level and, as noted, would not come into force until 1781; meanwhile, the Congress was reduced to making mere appeals to the states for contributions of money and manpower in support of the national cause. In this regard, one of Jay's last acts as president would be to circulate over his name a long and detailed congressional appeal, drafted by a special ways and means committee, urging the several states to remain optimistic over the chances for success of the American cause and to honor the Congress' request to them that they contribute $15 million to it through taxation, so as to avoid the need for it once again to resort to the printing presses to finance the war; accordingly, the appeal included an impressive array of specific economic facts to buttress its case that the nation could afford that tax, which, as always, was a most sensitive subject in America, even when it came to its own government.[319] (A struggling Superintendent of Finance Robert Morris would lament, upon assuming office in 1781, that the states as a whole had failed to make more than a token contribution towards that goal of $15 million.)

It was in this bleak national setting that Jay accepted the results of the congressional election choosing him as minister plenipotentiary to Spain. That appointment, with one qualification (that Jay should have been given the role Congress at this time gave to John Adams, that of peace negotiator with England), delighted Gérard and also the newly arrived Luzerne.[320] They were happy with President Jay's support down the line of essentially all of the positions that Gérard had taken in defense of France's image as America's stalwart ally. Did not Jay join him in defending the Deane-Franklin side, so favored by Vergennes, against Lee and his congressional backers, led by the delegations of New England? Were not those New Englanders, so unlike Jay, "anti-gallicans" who preferred England to France as America's ultimate partners? Did not Jay go even beyond a congressional resolution, which had dismissed Thomas Paine as secretary to its Committee on Foreign Affairs for having published pro-Lee articles containing privileged information embarrassing to France and the alliance, by expressing in his publicly released notification letter to Gérard his personal pleasure at that congressional action? Did not Jay assure Gérard that he strongly agreed with France that the U.S. should and will stay within the boundaries of the thirteen rebelling colonies "at the time of the Revolution," except possibly for making Canada the fourteenth state?[321]

It is a measure of Jay's performance as president that he left the Congress with the explicit goodwill of the great majority of the members and also of the leadership of the nation as a whole, whether in the Continental Army or at the state level. This reflects both the respect those individuals naturally felt for a man of outstanding personal qualities, whether in intellectual or moral terms, and the effort Jay himself made to work fairly and cooperatively with the various regional interests in the country. For example, he managed to steer a middle course on the fishing issue, which was

the key litmus test New Englanders applied to members in determining their acceptability as voting partners in balancing regional
interests. Specifically, the question was whether the U.S. should
include its claims to prewar fishing rights in Canadian and Newfoundland waters as part of its irreducible (in Franklin's termi-
nology, "necessary") war aims, failing which no peace was to be
made. Jay's posture was supportive, but not to the extent of the
most extreme form of those claims by which some New Englanders were actually demanding, as a condition precedent to a
peace, recognition of American rights to the same degree they had
them while still subjects of the English Crown.[322] An important
Jay motive for not alienating the New Englanders was his need
for at least some understanding on their part regarding New
York's position on Vermont.[323]

The manner in which Jay was elected to be minister to Spain
reflected his solid, but not dominant, standing in Congress. Voting
was in sequence, because other overseas positions were also to be
filled. The most important contest (Franklin already having long
been confirmed as sole representative to France) was that for appointment as commissioner to negotiate a peace with England. Jay
and John Adams were the major candidates for this, the most-
sought-after and prestigious of the open posts, although it was the
one that had least basis in reality in view of current diplomatic
conditions. Jay lost to Adams, who had remained in Massachusetts following his recent return from France and would leave directly from Boston for his new post in Europe without visiting the
Congress for consultations.[324] But Jay did receive the next-most-
sought-after posting, given the possibility—indeed, the generally
assumed likelihood during this period of great congressional optimism regarding the prospects of European support—that Spain
would soon become America's second formal ally now that it, too,
was at war with England.

A word should be offered here regarding Henry Laurens's appointment at this time as minister to negotiate a loan from the
Netherlands, a country that Laurens had visited several times in
his business life. Given that the Congress was unsure of Dutch
policy, it instructed Laurens (as it also had Jay and Adams) to go

first to France in order to obtain guidance from Vergennes. It was while at sea in September 1780 that he would be captured by the English as a "prisoner of war"; they also managed to salvage from the waters confidential papers that he, suspiciously in the eyes of Luzerne and some members of Congress, had failed to sink prior to capture. In the meanwhile, John Adams, in need of a role once he understood at Versailles that his commission was a dead letter for the foreseeable future, had gone at his own initiative from Paris to Amsterdam, where he soon received a congressional commission as Laurens's successor, while Laurens himself would become a prisoner of war in the Tower of London, where his apologetic behavior would fall short of that of a strong, consistent American patriot. Even though Laurens would be released on parole at the end of 1781, and conditionally allowed to travel to the continent, he took the position at that time that his status as a parolee precluded acting on his "surprising" appointment (June 1781) as one of the five U.S. peace commissioners.[325] Pleading that his poor health necessitated rehabilitation in southern France with French relatives (Laurens was of pure Huguenot stock) or at provincial spas, he avoided going to Paris until just days prior to the signing of the peace agreement between the U.S. and England on November 30, 1782. By then, he had been released from parole. Thus, while he became a signatory of that treaty, and was duly included soon thereafter in Benjamin West's famous painting of the American signatories, Laurens played no role in the negotiations themselves—except to succeed in having inserted into the treaty a provision favoring the return to their owners of slaves who were in English hands at the end of the conflict.

As for John Adams's efforts in the Netherlands, it would not be until 1782, by which time Yorktown had made clear to the Dutch and all the world that American independence was assured, that he would succeed in obtaining, successively, accreditation for himself as minister plenipotentiary, diplomatic recognition of the U.S., a modest cash flow from loans provided by Amsterdam's banking community and, finally, on 6 October, a treaty of friendship and commerce. Prior to these successes, he had his "constitution wrecked" by the Dutch as he made strenuous public efforts, undertaken contrary to the good advice of the competent French ambassador to the Netherlands, to win each of these things, all to no avail and to the despair of Secretary Livingston in Philadelphia and Vergennes at Versailles, each of whom urged, as Vergennes put it, that he not thus expose his country as well as France to needless and predictable diplomatic embarrassments.[326] Adams, following the Netherlands' recognition of the U.S. in the spring, chose to stay in that country until he completed the loan and treaty negotiations. Only then did he agree to put on his hat as peace commissioner and go on to Paris, where he had the previous year all but destroyed his personal relations with both Franklin and Vergennes. Adams finally arrived in the French capital on 29 October, after an unhurried three-week trip from the Netherlands. Thus, his active role in the negotiations with England was a relatively limited one, the basic terms of the peace agreement having been largely settled by the early part of that month. His main contribution was to strengthen Jay's hand on the U.S. team and to help win minor and ambivalent additional advantages for New England fishing privileges in English-held waters off Canada and Newfoundland.

CHAPTER 5

From the French-Spanish Alliance of April 1779 versus England to the Militarily Victorious Year of 1781

THE VIEW FROM FRANCE

There was a celebratory mood at the court of Versailles upon news of the signing in Madrid on April 12, 1779, of a secret agreement with Spain committing the latter to joining the war against England. This came after years of France's having to swallow its pride as Charles and his volatile foreign minister, Floridablanca, regularly castigated it for past betrayals and failures to live up to the spirit of the Family Compact of 1761. As we have seen, more than mere castigation, Spain also was until this very moment putting France through a crisis by virtue of its mediation proposals so contrary to France's commitments to the U.S. Fortunately, and as Spain itself recognized by signing this April agreement with France, that mediation effort was in its last gasps, England, much to France's relief, clearly about to reject the Spanish proposals. There now was left only the formality of Spain's breaking off the mediation, rupturing diplomatic relations with England, then issuing its declaration of war (within the framework of a suitable document justifying that act). The fact that Spain signed the agreement with France even prior to the break with England was advantageous to France, according to Montmorin's 13 April dispatch, because it meant Spain was entering the war of its own volition, giving France more leverage over it.

At last, Versailles had that naval superiority allowing it to take to the seas in an offensive mode. But was that superiority merely a numerical one? This was not a theoretical or rhetorical question in either Bourbon capital, where a century-old experience of disastrous maritime woes at England's hands cast its shadow on strategic thinking. Moreover, and aside from respect for the proven fighting qualities of that Anglo-Saxon navy, there were valid doubts by Versailles about the seaworthiness of either the French or the Spanish navy and about the capability of the two to cooperate efficiently and smoothly—experience here, too, was not reassuring for the French side.

In sum, while having more ships-of-the-line than the enemy in a given theater of operations was a legitimate and essential consideration in determining whether one had a prospect of victory, it was not a sufficient assurance of that victory. Other factors also at play left open an entire series of basic strategic and operational questions, such as: How best to use the two allies' offensive capabilities, in a massive invasion of the enemy's homeland or in attacks on its overseas assets? and, How to work together, as combined units under a single command or as separate but coordinated ones in designated battle zones? These issues subsumed other important questions intrinsic to developing a common strategy in an era when so much depended on the whims of nature and when timely intelligence sharing over long distances was all but impossible.

These purely military considerations were additional to, even shaped by, political ones that further complicated the efforts of the two Bourbon allies to develop an appropriate set of strategies for their first joint campaign of the war:

1. If the main French goal in the war was the uncomplicated and seemingly unselfish one of reducing England's oversized power by assuring America's independence, Spain's, as the 12 April agreement clearly showed, was the more narrow, more openly nationalistic one of regaining territories lost to England since the days of Cromwell in the mid-seventeenth century.

2. If the French were in the war opportunistically to enhance their role relative to that of the English in the European balance of power, the

more insular Spanish were in it with relatively little concern for their particular role in that continental arena, but with a major concern for their ability to maintain control over their widespread empire in Asia and the Americas, where a major rebellion was breaking out under the leadership of the Indian leader in Peru, Tupac Amaru.

3. If France's economic and commercial goals in the war were primarily focused on assuring that an independent U.S. established a truly open trading system in which the French enjoyed the same access to its markets as anyone else, Spain's corresponding goals were more focused on freeing itself from the unequal commercial treaties, the illegal trading practices and the outright infringements of Spanish sovereignty in Central America that England had been enjoying at its expense for decades. Still deeply mercantalistic and colonialist, Spain did not share at all France's interest in promoting trade with the U.S. In fact, the last thing Spain wanted to see was an independent U.S. prosperous enough to be a valuable commercial partner for anyone. Rather, Spain's hope was that this potentially dangerous new Anglo-Saxon neighbor would remain a weak, internally divided nation unable to pose a threat to the nearby Spanish possessions.

It is this last point that provides an important key to the tensions that would underlie relations between the U.S. and Spain, and also between the U.S. and France as the war drew to a close. Versailles, in trying to reconcile its two separate and distinct alliances, fruitlessly sought throughout the war to reassure Spain that the Americans, *especially* if they became independent of England, were perhaps centuries away from having the power to threaten the Spanish Empire; and while doing so, it also sought to promote U.S.-Spanish wartime cooperation by urging the Americans, as outlined earlier, to ease their positions on the reach of their western boundary and the extent of their questioned— and very questionable—"rights" to navigate the Mississippi River down to its mouth on the same basis as those secured by England in the peace treaty of 1763. This approach revealed to the Americans a distinct tilt in French policy in favor of Spanish over U.S. interests, and their suspicions would be aroused even further as France, whose policy expressly was to "keep Spain happy," and to give priority support to Spain's war aims over those of all others, became increasingly enmeshed both militarily and diplomatically in Spanish-specific aspects of the war against England.[327]

Therefore, by 1782, America's leaders would have to face the hard question as to whether this by now clear French bias favoring Madrid had gone so far as to violate the terms and purposes of the U.S.-French treaty of alliance, thereby freeing the way for the Americans to end the war on the liberal terms England was offering them even as its war against the Bourbon powers was continuing full blast. Jay's firm answer to this most basic of questions was in the affirmative, and with Adams's moral, if mostly distant, support, he overrode the strongly pro-France Franklin's ineffective remonstrations by overseeing the negotiation and execution of what could only be considered a de facto separate peace. Jay's moves manifestly went beyond the intentions of Congress and its Secretary for Foreign Affairs, but their qualms were overwhelmed by the preliminary peace agreement that was soon reached (January 20, 1783) between England and its European enemies and by Vergennes's policy of sweeping the issue under the rug. Nevertheless, as impressive as it was as a diplomatic achievement for a fledgling nation, the U.S.-English peace treaty of November 30, 1782, which was given the fig-leaf title of "Provisional Articles" for a definitive peace treaty, did come at the cost of American honor, at least in the eyes of the French as well as many others even in America and England, and this historical fact needs better to be recognized as we look back at that period.

Consistent with the priority importance it attached to obtaining Spanish participation in the war, Versailles, in line with that April 1779 agreement, deferred to Madrid's strong preference regarding strategy for their opening military campaign. That preference was, in Floridablanca's enthusiastic words (hiding a true, additional motivation, revealed later in the war, which was to force a Spanish navy he himself mistrusted to perform well in at least one single operation), to deal England a decisive blow that would end the war right at its start, the blow being a massive invasion of England itself.[328] Of course, this strategy did not really match the views of Versailles—and for two major reasons:

1. Militarily, it envisaged the rather unrealistic scenario of a joint French-Spanish fleet arriving at, and dominating, the English Channel precisely in that brief midyear season when the winds were right for such an invasion. Also, the entire makeup of the invading land forces, including 10,000 cavalry, was to be French—an overly expensive and risky undertaking for Versailles to have endorsed sincerely.[329]

2. Politically, such a strategy was out of proportion to the relatively limited kind of war Versailles had in mind: France "has no intention to humiliate England" or to "crush" it.[330] Far from destroying English power at its base, as Madrid desired, the French wanted a more modest victory, one that would leave England as a significant player in the European balance of power, but this time, as noted, with reduced ability to harm French interests, and with a willingness to cooperate with France in a post-Utrecht-type relationship whereby the two would be the "arbiters" guaranteeing continental stability, France playing the role of senior partner.[331] Additionally, the French feared that even a successful invasion and occupation of parts of Great Britain would boomerang, at least diplomatically, because the European powers would then tend to switch their wariness from a present, comforting focus on England to one on the two Bourbon Houses, revitalized and combining preponderant land and sea power in Europe's own backyard, as Vergennes phrased it.

Nevertheless, the momentum of French-Spanish pre-1779 military planning, coupled with perceived advantages attached to a policy of at least giving Spain's all-out strategy an opportunity to prove its value, led Versailles to agree to the plan—in fact, that French agreement had been nothing less than a precondition imposed by Spain for the military alliance that was finally entered into on 12 April.[332] For the next few months, France dutifully went through the motions of preparing with Spain for an authentic invasion of underdefended England, or possibly of a restless Ireland, whose internal politics were being investigated by secret agents of France, focusing on what Vergennes considered the more potentially rebellious Protestant north, and of Spain, which saw the Catholic south as the more promising area.[333] Large numbers of troops remained massed near the logical jumping-off points along the French Atlantic coast; and warships and trans-

ports were visibly being armed, supplied and collected—all at
enormous financial cost, only a derisory part of which Spain offered to cover. At a minimum, these tactics, from the perspective
of Versailles, would have the advantage of forcing the enemy to
be on the defensive at home rather than on the attack against
Bourbon overseas assets (and incidentally U.S. ones); opening up
the possibility of victorious sea battles against an outnumbered,
hopefully discouraged enemy fleet; allowing, if events at sea
matched expectations, the actual crossing of French troops to attack selected enemy coastal positions with a reasonable prospect
of seizing them for the duration, at great cost to the body politic
of the English nation; and facilitating the continuing mission of
d'Estaing in American waters by the diversionary events in and
near the Channel, perhaps even, according to an overexuberant
Vergennes in June, damaging English interests in North America
to such an extent during the course of that admiral's return trip
to France that they would be forced to recognize the independence
of the U.S. All in all, then, the French were reasonably content to
go along with Madrid's strategy, especially knowing that, in the
final analysis, they maintained control over the extent of their military and political risks, which were to be minimized by prudently
avoiding the uncertainties of a massive invasion from France
across waters not clearly under the assured control of Bourbon
fleets. As reasonable as this French approach was, by year's end
it opened Versailles to serious criticism at home and from its allies.
This was due to the fact that, by fall 1779, it was evident that, as
in 1778, France's prudent course of action, even as it guaranteed
against a major disaster, also had failed to do serious damage to
an England whose relative weakness was probably but temporary.
Both Bourbon powers were being broadly perceived as lacking in
the political will needed to employ to maximum effect their superior military and naval strength. Particularly the Americans,
once again, felt let down by the lackluster performance in European waters, where the French and Spanish fleets were so slow in
getting their act together, and "the elements of nature" were so
uncooperative with the Bourbons, that no major, let alone decisive,
battles were fought;[334] by the slight attention paid by the two to

the North American theater of operations; and by an increasing conviction that France will be unable to deliver on its implicit promise to bring Spain into the war as an ally not only of France but also of the U.S. This American view would generate such a fear in Versailles of a U.S. defection to England that it would help determine France early in 1780, as noted, to decide to send to North America that same year a French army and naval squadron to serve permanently there as a separate force, but one under the general direction of General Washington.[335]

Vergennes very personally shared the disappointment in the Bourbon performance of 1779, recognizing that his country, despite the great financial cost of its operations, was wasting its window of opportunity militarily and also on the diplomatic front.[336] The European continent was politically quiescent for the moment, but how long could that last?[337] How long could France have that tranquillity along its borders it needed in order, unlike its situation during the preceding war, to marshal all its strength against England's maritime power? How long before the enemy would rescue itself from its present diplomatic isolation and once again begin to garner military allies on the continent to threaten essential French interests there? How long before the restless land powers of Austria, Prussia and Russia complete their present phase of recovering from that devastating Seven Years' War, and of digesting the spoils of recent territorial gains in Poland and the Ottoman Empire, and once again act aggressively to satisfy their ever-expanding appetite for a larger share in the balance of power?

Undoubtedly, the European diplomatic scene at the moment was auspiciously favorable to Bourbon interests. Austria's brash co-monarch, Joseph II, was still being somewhat restrained by Maria-Theresa and by having been thwarted in his recent power grab of Bavaria. Successful French-Russian mediation of that Bavaria problem, and France's appreciated complementary role of curbing Turkish war fever over increasing Russian influence in the Crimea, tended to reinforce the reasonably smooth relationship between Versailles and St. Petersburg; furthermore, Frederick the Great's influence with Catherine the Great was giving a boost to that warming trend. Finally, England's major effort to win Russian naval and other military and diplomatic cooperation by now had clearly failed, and Russia in 1779–80 was gradually moving in quite another direction, one that would culminate in the establishment of an association of neutral powers to protect their shipping from undue interference on the high seas—England, of course, was the major source of that interference, while France was a major beneficiary of that neutral shipping, which most importantly included naval stores from the northern powers.

Prussia's policy at this time, consistent with its post-1762 antagonism toward George III's England, was to encourage Russia in this initiative, which took the form of a Neutrality Association, also referred to as the "Armed Neutrality," based on a written code of conduct governing maritime commerce, including a definition of contraband that was much narrower than English practice would allow. The League's code was to be enforced by armed warships of signatory nations, essentially the northern ones of Russia, Sweden, Denmark and the Netherlands, patrolling in designated waters around the European continent. (By late summer 1781, it was so clear that the enforcement part of the Neutrality League had become a dead letter that John Adams quite justifiably could refer to "armed neutrality" as merely a "sublime bubble," while others, not excluding Empress Catherine herself, ridiculed it as the "armed nullity."[338] Similarly, England's ambassador to Russia joked at the expense of the minuscule Russian merchant fleet that it enjoyed a ratio of 3:1 as between warships and the merchantmen they were supposed to be protecting.)

Frederick the Great was also useful to France regarding Austria, an ally of France in name, but exaggeratedly suspected by Versailles of harboring pre-1756 ambitions to align with England in support of a policy of expanding Vienna's sphere of influence in the empire at Prussia's expense. As demonstrated during the course of the Bavarian crisis, Prussia provided a third-party check for France on these unwelcome Austrian ambitions (which also threatened the Turkish presence in Europe, a French interest). Pursuit of those ambitions could only damage France's standard policy of isolating England, restraining Russia's move westward and southward and keeping as many of the German principalities as possible independent of either Austria or Prussia.

Vergennes, by end 1779, began to fear that his military-diplomatic strategy was unraveling. The complex features of having an unprecedentedly close coordination of French-Spanish naval operations proved to be an insuperable obstacle. Almost miraculously, the two fleets did manage to rendezvous successfully off Spain's northern coast and did head for, and reach, the Channel—but they did so only under separate commands (Madrid would not concur in the appointment of a single commander for a combined fleet until near the war's end—d'Estaing was its choice, to Versailles' amazement) and only after operational delays had cost them the loss of an important segment of the fighting season. Moreover, once in the Channel, they failed to operate together aggressively or efficiently, and they and the equally timid English fleet mostly just shadowed each other rather than doing battle. The net result was the absence of any strategic changes in the European theater of operations during 1779, with an attendant increase in tensions between the two frustrated allies.[339] Factors accounting for this result include mutual distrust and lack of confidence between the naval officers of France and Spain; sheer technical difficulties of having to adapt to shifting weather conditions even as two distinct navies had to learn to operate together on the basis of common signaling, and so on; the underlying French skepticism about the chances for success of a major cross-Channel invasion (historically considered as a counsel of despair for France at the losing end of a war); and the equally ambivalent Spanish attitude, split as it was between deploying the bulk of its naval forces relatively far from home shores for any length of time or using those forces primarily for a blockade of Gibraltar. In sum, by September 1779, after but a few short weeks of cruising in and near the Channel, all fleets were back in port and ministries were back to planning for still another campaign—that of 1780.

And yet the war was now worldwide and all belligerents had year-round military concerns requiring constant attention, especially regarding fleet assignments. For example, Spain's focus that winter of 1779–80 was on defensive measures abroad and on Gibraltar, where it hoped against hope to force an English surrender merely by a blockade-supported siege preventing that place from receiving replenishment of men and supplies from an England equally determined to force major armed convoys through that blockade. Therefore, Spain was now pressing a bemoaning France to assign a substantial part of its Brest fleet to patrol the waters between England and Spain as a supplement to the blockading efforts of the Cadiz fleet—efforts that created a problem for French policy toward Russia, which was upset at Spain's having seized two Russian merchantmen off Gibraltar (but which happily then turned the incident to advantage when it used those temporary seizures not as a reason to take action against the Bourbons but as a diplomatic cover for its February 1780 announcement of the establishment of a maritime association that was "neutral" and not specifically anti-England in design).[340] Before the year was out, that Spanish appeal proved fruitless in that a major English armed convoy under Admiral George Rodney arrived at the Straits of Gibraltar unmolested by any French fleet; moreover, not even the Spanish managed to put up any significant resistance once Rodney approached the fortress. That admiral was able to bring his largely unscathed convoy into the harbor and then escort it out without incident, following which he took a large part of his squadron on to American waters.

Faced with back-to-back failures of its opening war strategy, 1778–79, Versailles in early 1780 took the above-mentioned fateful and difficult decision to land a French army on U.S. territory, where it would fight as a discrete unit under the overall command of Washington.[341] There also would be a modest-sized French naval squadron posted on a permanent basis with that army to give it mobility, not only for possible deployments up and down the coastline but also for an emergency evacuation to the West Indies, if that proved necessary. Versailles made this move in full appreciation that Spain would continue to press it to focus the bulk of their joint naval strength on the English homeland and other enemy territory in European waters, notably Gibraltar and Minorca; that there was little likelihood of gaining a decisive advantage in the war by virtue of military events on a distant North American continent; and that sending some 4,000 French Catholic soldiers (down from the originally planned level of 6,000 to 8,000) to live amid an Anglo-Saxon, Protestant population traditionally hostile to such men was in itself a risky proposition for the allied relationship, one made even riskier by their being dependent for success upon the fighting skills and spirit of a ragtag, dissension-ridden American Continental Army and its associated ephemeral state militias. Yet given the need for a bold, new military initiative, the French authorities, spurred on by a visiting Lafayette, felt there was no other choice. (Also motivating the French was that such a U.S.-based army and fleet could help divert the English from any plans to ship some of their forces from North America to the West Indies with a view to bolster Jamaican defenses and to conquer additional enemy territory there.)

Accordingly, by March 1780, specific assignments had been made for regular French military units, organized under the command of General Jean Rochambeau, to depart for a safe port in the U.S., transported and permanently accompanied by a squadron under Admiral Charles Ternay, whose task would include providing the only real naval presence the French and Americans would have at hand on that station to counter England's relatively large New York–based fleet.[342] As these French forces prepared to leave, Vergennes urged them to win battles that alone could "sharpen my quill" for the writing of a victorious peace treaty with the enemy—a metaphor that would remain in use for the rest of the war, as reflected in Lafayette's post-Yorktown message to him that that quill had now been sharpened beyond one's fondest hopes.[343]

Alongside this dramatic move to establish an important French military presence on U.S. soil, Versailles bolstered its naval and land forces in the West Indies, where, in cooperation with Spanish forces, they were to take the offensive against English shipping, west Florida, and enemy island bases—although few at Versailles believed the time was ripe for an assault on Jamaica, the largest of those islands and the one most coveted by the Spaniards, its former owner. Following a now well-established strategic pattern, the French naval commanders were instructed to detach what units they could prudently spare during the Caribbean's *hivernage*, or nonfighting hurricane season of midyear, to cooperate in any North American military campaign the Washington-Rochambeau team may be planning (the French expedition having safely landed at Rhode Island in July 1780 near the Washington-led northern U.S. army).[344] While that team undertook no major operations that entire year, this strategic naval pattern would be amply rewarded in 1781, when de Grasse, commendably taking full advantage of the flexibility given him, left the West Indies with the great bulk of his large fleet, and with thousands of troops, and arrived in the Chesapeake area in timely fashion to make his historic contribution to the great Franco-American victory of September–October at Yorktown, Virginia—a victory that was decisive but only insofar as the North American theater of operations was concerned.

Still, much anguish and many doubts in France, Spain and the U.S. would have to pass before that happy event could take place. For example, in the U.S., the enemy in early 1780 would finally succeed in its efforts to seize Charleston, South Carolina, the key southern port it needed to serve as a base for its army, under Cornwallis's command, to penetrate deeply into the Carolinas with a view to permanently truncating the U.S. This sequence created among the Americans a most dispiriting sense of the futility of their hopes for an early end to the war, especially when coupled with the deteriorating financial situation, the regional and personal squabbles among the leadership, the pay-related troop revolts in some of the American lines, the treason of Benedict Arnold and diminished expectations that Spain's entry into the war heralded the addition of a major ally for them. News of the impending arrival of a French expedition did, therefore, come at a most welcome period for the Americans, giving them an injection of fresh energy that they deeply needed as they entered the sixth year of their revolutionary struggle.

JOHN JAY'S MISSION TO SPAIN

The Congress was already in a rather gloomy mood as it elected a new set of diplomats in September 1779 to represent it abroad. This act provided a further occasion for the controversy regarding the Lee family to flare up, because it was Arthur Lee who was technically being replaced as America's designated representative to Spain. The pro-Lee camp sought to retain him by reviving a failed 1776 motion precluding members of Congress, such as Jay, the friend of Deane and Gerard, from accepting positions financed or sponsored by the government. While that motion unsurprisingly failed, especially given the checkered history of Lee's performance and the obvious need for the U.S. to make a fresh start with Spain, Jay's acceptance of that diplomatically and personally difficult assignment was, indeed, rather surprising. After all, he was well aware of Spain's standoffish policy toward the U.S. to date, a policy that was so firm that Jay knew, if he was to avoid the fiasco of Lee's abortive 1777 effort to get to Madrid, he would have to approach his task indirectly by landing initially in France, not in Spain, and only from Paris seeking Madrid's permission to reside in that capital.[345] On personal matters, Jay would have to leave behind a son not quite four years old, to be cared for by his wife's family in insecure New Jersey, and an aging father who was saddled, as noted above, with managing a complex household in an equally insecure New York. All this in order to make a most dangerous ocean crossing only to confront a possibly unreceptive host government.

Jay's profound patriotism and dedication to meet his country's needs alone explain his prompt acceptance of the post (Robert Livingston would negotiate with the Congress for two months over the terms and conditions of the office being offered him before agreeing in late September 1781 to leave his New York home to serve as Secretary for Foreign Affairs). If Jay had one personal consolation, it was that his wife, alone among all senior U.S. representatives who left America to serve in Europe, would be accompanying him. This was a decision that, given later events, might well subject him to criticism because it resulted in limiting his physical mobility, and in placing demands on his time and emotions, in ways perhaps detrimental to his European mission. In less than a month from his new appointment, Jay and entourage, expanded to include his wife's brother, Henry Brockholst Livingston, serving as his private secretary, and Peter Jay Munro, a preteen nephew whose Loyalist minister father had deserted the family, embarked from Chester, Pennsylvania, on 18 October aboard a U.S. frigate, the *Confederacy*, with a destination of Toulon, France. Also aboard were Carmichael and Gérard, who was anxious to return as soon as possible to his homeland.

The *Confederacy* had barely left U.S. waters when the first of a series of misadventures occurred. On 7 November, "off the banks of Newfoundland," it was severely damaged by rough seas, necessitating decisions as to whether to alter course. Gérard favored continuing toward Europe, while the consensus of captain and crew, ultimately endorsed by Jay, was to go southward to the French West Indies, where the ship could be repaired and resupplied before resuming its voyage to France.[346] As would be typical of almost all Jay's apparently narrow disputes abroad with colleagues and even members of his household, this one at sea would have diplomatic implications for the U.S. because it soured the Jay-Gérard relationship—and also produced an early sign of future friction between Jay and Carmichael, who had actively sided with Gerard against Jay's known preferences.

In the event, the ship limped into Martinique on 18 December, although not without one further dispute between Jay and Gérard as to which was the safest route to take in approaching that island through enemy-infested waters. The Jays next spent a revivifying ten days exploring the island and being well entertained by the French governor and the longtime congressional agent on the island (and business partner of Robert Morris), William Bingham. During this period, as noted earlier, Jay purchased a slave, Benoit, who would stay with the family through its Paris period, after which he was given his manumission, effective in three years. This episode is perhaps a good example of Jay's pragmatic nature, with its pattern of adjusting past positions to meet immediate practical needs. In the present case, he realized that his wife was pregnant and the family would be in need of additional assistance once in Europe. He also had, and used, the additional justification for his purchase, that he was thereby saving the boy from the horrors of sugar plantation slavery, a form of servitude that truly shocked him, never having witnessed it before.

One would like very much to give the benefit of the doubt to Jay regarding the purity of his motives and the consistency of his antislavery views, having by this period become a public advocate for the gradual, financially compensated abolition of that practice, a role he would maintain by correspondence from Europe and even more strenuously once back in America. And yet the behavior of the Jays at Paris, where the "servant" they had taken with them from the U.S., Abigail, had fled from the family, makes it hard fully to do so. (The only time the present author noticed Jay himself using the word "slaves" to describe his own holdings was in the form he filled out for the census of 1790.)[347] Sarah Jay, in John's absence on a trip in England in October–November 1783, but with his express written endorsement and the help and advice of the Franklins (Benjamin and William, his grandson), sought and obtained the assistance of the lieutenant general of the Paris Police, Jean-Charles Le Noir, to apprehend her. More than that, the Jays, as a disciplinary measure, had the police keep her in prison for weeks, barring her from returning to their home until she would promise not to run away again. By the time they relented, "Abbe" had become so ill that she died soon after her return to the Jays. The conclusion we must draw from this matter is that while the Jays certainly believed themselves to be, and indeed were, humane in their standard treatment of family slaves, they demanded obedience and performance in return; and they saw their holdings as a financial investment from which they expected commensurate remuneration.[348] (Lest we forget, even into the turn of the century, New Yorkers owned over 20,000 slaves, the institution only being gradually ended by 1827.)

With the *Confederacy* in need of extensive repairs, Jay and company resumed their trip on 28 December aboard a well-equipped and -maintained French frigate, the *Aurora*, which was made available by the governor. That improvement augured well for the group to reach its destination of Toulon without further mishap, but one more did arrive in the form of a near-skirmish just off the southwestern coast of Spain with a cruising enemy warship. That threat to the ship's safety had two important results for the start of Jay's diplomatic career in Europe: First, it led to the decision not to venture into the Mediterranean itself, where there reportedly was even greater danger of running into English patrols, and instead to remain in the safety of Cadiz, which the ship had entered in accordance with its standing orders "to touch at this port for intelligence;"[349] and second, it damaged Sarah's health, because during the alert she remained for hours relatively unprotected from the night weather on the exposed deck. Thus, Jay arrived unceremoniously in Spain on 22 January 1780.

His immediate problem was to decide whether to remain there or, as originally planned, to go directly to France, as Gérard was doing via Madrid. His decision was to remain in Cadiz, and to write the Spanish government for permission to reside near the court. Jay's rationale was that it would "have been indelicate and therefore imprudent, to have passed silently through this kingdom to that [of France], for the purpose of making a communication to His Most Christian Majesty, which could be fully conveyed by paper."[350] An unspoken, more personal reason for his decision was that his pregnant, ill wife was in no condition to continue the voyage, whether by a laborious and lengthy land route, Spain having the least developed road and transportation network in Western Europe, or by a hazardous sea route to a port on France's Atlantic or Mediterranean coast.

Jay's letter to the authorities in Madrid explained his situation. In a demonstration of his—and his government's—total lack of direct knowledge of the workings of the Spanish government, he took the rather surprisingly wrong advice of his ex-friend Gérard and addressed it to the Minister for the Indies, Galvez, and not to Floridablanca, the more appropriate official. Although it proved

From the French-Spanish Alliance

not to be a serious one, this opening error (along with his initial difficulties in correctly according titles to the kings of Spain and France, such as at times adding "Most" to the former's traditional designation as "His Catholic Majesty" and omitting "Most" from the latter's designation as "His Most Christian Majesty") is symbolic of the poor communication that would prevail between Jay and the Spanish throughout his two-year stay. The fact that he could not function without interpreters either in French (the lingua franca of all diplomacy) or Spanish did not help matters—in a word, as Jay himself would acknowledge, his stay in Spain was nothing less than a neophyte's education course in the ways and substance of his profession.

Carmichael, who did have the necessary linguistic qualifications, was sent ahead (in Gérard's most "personally kind" company, as he would later write to Jay) with the letter to Madrid, where he arrived on 11 February and, through Montmorin, established contact with both ministers. Floridablanca eventually wrote back to Jay, on 28 February, that he might come to reside there, although only as a private person and not as an accredited diplomat; nevertheless, Jay was assured that the government would be prepared to listen to any messages he may wish to deliver regarding the situation in America. To the relief of Versailles when informed of the situation, Jay took this invitation (as would Vergennes a few weeks later) as an encouraging sign and duly accepted it. With his entourage, he left Cadiz on 8 March, arriving only on 4 April after a difficult and financially expensive trip (not that long after Adams, having unexpectedly landed on the northern coast of Spain, was himself laboriously making his way across that rudimentary and price-gouging nation's road network to Paris).[351]

It has been commonplace for historians to dismiss Jay's Spanish mission as not warranting detailed study, its only noteworthy events, one wrote, being the date of his arrival and the date of his departure.[352] This approach might be acceptable had Jay been an ordinary diplomat whose Spanish assignment was unrelated to his ongoing one in Paris.[353] Of course, this was not the case, and

Jay's Madrid experience most definitely had a vital effect on his performance as peace commissioner and de facto lead negotiator with England. Therefore, it is important for our purposes to review at least the highlights of Jay's Spanish mission for the insight it provides into his work in France, where, in point of fact, he also continued to wear his hat as the (still unaccredited) minister plenipotentiary to Spain, whose ambassador, Count de Aranda, was now his unofficial interlocutor, vice Floridablanca.

Remarkably for a man of such deep personal pride and profound sense of his country's political independence, Jay in Madrid submitted to the humiliating role assigned to him by the Spaniards (readers will notice the near-parallel to Vergennes's also tolerating diplomatic treatment he would violently reject from any other court than Spain's—and for the same reason, the need to win it over to his national cause). Clearly, Jay did so entirely out of the conviction that the logic of the war would alter present Spanish policy and amply compensate any short-term cost to his U.S. pride. In his thinking, was there not a common enemy, whose every defeat in whatever theater of operations benefited all the co-belligerents? Did not the French, both formally in the secret article of their alliance treaty with the U.S., and in their subsequent advice rendered through Gérard in Philadelphia, encourage the hope, even the expectation, that Spain not only would enter the war, as it now indeed had done, but also would accede to that alliance, or in some other manner become an ally of the U.S.? Had not the Spaniards themselves, during the Grimaldi period, encouraged this expectation by providing the U.S. with a level of aid that fully matched that given by France? Even after that minister's replacement by Floridablanca, was not that official financial assistance continued, if at a greatly reduced level, and was not Miralles's mission to Congress an indication of Madrid's interest in establishing a cooperative relationship with the U.S.? Did not Floridablanca personally make clear to him on arrival at Madrid of his country's "friendship" for America?[354] Finally, was it not in Spain's long-term interest to develop that kind of relationship at the present, crucial time, when that would make the greatest positive impression on Americans and assure their future goodwill, rather than to do so only after the war, when a sense of resentment would prevail in the U.S., blocking truly friendly relations?

Jay's answer to all these questions was obvious, but he could never get Madrid to share his view. Only gradually would it become clear to him what his French counterpart, Montmorin, knew from the start and with personal regret worked to keep from him, that Spain had adopted a fundamentally hands-off policy regarding the rebellious colonies. That policy, aside from any ideological and political considerations, was based on Madrid's conviction that, especially with the end of its war against Portugal in 1777, it need not have any immediate, major security concerns in the American theater of operations—even as it embarked on war against England. In fact, that very war made the prospect of any Spanish material assistance to the U.S. even more unlikely, given the great strain it caused on the already overburdened Spanish treasury. Still, Jay valiantly would make his case to Floridablanca at every opportunity, which was not very frequent, because that minister, even as he teased Jay with hints of Spain's "one day becom[ing] America's ally," greatly limited his accessibility to the importuning American.[355]

Despite his unofficial standing, Jay's diplomatic activities ranged widely, from the elevated task of trying in one form or another to influence Spanish policy toward the quite separable American goals of recognizing U.S. independence, of cooperating militarily with it and of providing it with financial or other concrete aid, to more mundane, but hardly less frustrating and time-consuming tasks, such as these:

1. Staving off the endless flow of letters of exchange that were being drawn on him to finance European purchases for the American government pursuant to an authorization of the Congress issued "on the bank of hope" in such ill-timed and "singular" fashion shortly after he left Philadelphia. That unexpected and unilateral act by a desperate leadership in Philadelphia undermined his position in Spain because it exposed his country's need to beg for funds merely to stave off having to acknowledge inability to pay its debts by "protesting" those notes, which were being presented to Jay almost daily and had the

potential value of £100,000.[356] The premise—rather, the unfounded hope—underlying Congress' action was that surely the Spanish government would not want to see its de facto ally financially bankrupted and instead would agree to cover that relatively modest sum as it became due over a period of many months. The Congress acted in identical fashion regarding Henry Laurens in the Netherlands, thus burdening that minister's successor, John Adams, with the same problem confronting Jay and making the two competitors for whatever funds may be available outside their respective countries of assignment, notably those Franklin might be able to obtain from the government of France! Adams would prove to be more adept, and he avoided the "protest" that Jay, just weeks shy of his departure from Madrid for Paris, heartbreakingly was forced to make on a few thousand dollars' worth of paper, thereby at least temporarily damaging U.S. creditworthiness and diminishing its political stature in Europe. Although the protested bills were quickly covered by Franklin, Jay left Spain with a special bitterness over this matter, which further convinced him of the untrustworthiness of the Bourbon powers as dependable partners for the U.S.

2. Protecting the interests of American privateers arriving in Spanish ports, where complications inevitably set in regarding their acceptability, their disposal of prizes and their obtaining local services for refitting and replenishing.

3. Providing for the subsistence of American merchantmen and businessmen in difficulties for one reason or another in those ports; and also of American prisoners of war being held under poor conditions in England and in need of financial help to cover their subsistence costs. To Jay's constant regret, there were no U.S. consuls to assist him on the coast, the closest to one being a helpful American businessman at Cadiz, Richard Harrison. A special problem was that posed by American sailors escaping from English ships while in port and in long-term need of protection and financial help.

Far from being a comfort and an aid to Jay in his handling of these tasks, his official and personal household, always excepting his beloved and loving wife and his nephew Peter, proved to be a constant source of additional aggravation, with Carmichael at the head of the list. At first blush, that official would have seemed to be a good choice, which was made not by Jay but by Congress itself. He had a suitable professional background as a former staff assistant to the deputies in Paris, where he had a justifiable claim to having helped recruit Lafayette to the American cause, and as a member of Congress from Maryland until his diplomatic appointment. Moreover, from Jay's point of view, Carmichael by and large had taken the right side in the Deane-Lee controversy, at times actively working against the latter in the Congress by reporting on his personal knowledge of the Paris scene. However, he also was a habitual intriguer, malcontent and agitator (whose very loyalty was cast in doubt in the minds of some of his colleagues, including Jay himself); and he was in chronic poor health, not helped by a drinking problem. Furthermore, it soon became clear that there were important policy differences between the two, Carmichael being more flexible about giving up American claims to the left bank of the Mississippi, if that was what it took to obtain an alliance with Spain. Not surprisingly, and adding to the friction between the two, Jay began to look for opportunities to send a successfully resistant Carmichael out of the capital area on militia-type diplomatic problems, to Lisbon, for example. Jay found his secretarial work often slipshod, especially in the discharge of his duties as keeper of the delegation's financial accounts, whose accuracy and availability for eventual congressional scrutiny, as Deane's experience amply demonstrated, were fundamental to any U.S. diplomatic representative's defense of his personal integrity. We have seen how Carmichael's behavior during the sea voyage had already created a tense relationship with Jay, one that would not abate even after Jay's departure from Madrid (May 21, 1782), because Carmichael would procrastinate until nearly the eve of Jay's departure from Paris for America (May 16, 1784) before leaving Madrid (3 March), by express order of Congress itself, and arriving (27 March) with the financial accounts Jay had long been pleading for in order to have them reviewed by Congress' authorized agent in Europe for that purpose.[357]

It must also be said that Jay's own jealously guarded seniority over Carmichael contributed to the problems between the two. That aspect reached its peak when Jay refused to accord Carmi-

chael the title of chargé d'affaires upon his departure for France,
arguing, as he had from the very start of their mission in Spain,
and correctly so, that Carmichael's commission from Congress did
not provide for that title merely in the absence from post of the
minister but rather only in the event of "the death of the American
Minister here";[358] moreover, so Jay insisted, he would be retaining
his title and mission even during his stay at Paris, precluding
designating Carmichael as chargé. It took a congressional instruction for that issue to be resolved, for reasons of diplomatic policy
toward Spain, in favor of Carmichael; moreover, in August 1783,
partly because the Spanish authorities wished to preclude the return to Spain of Jay, whom they considered as prickly, he would
be formally received at court with that title by Charles III. (Carmichael, who married a Spanish woman, would remain in Madrid
as chargé until his death in 1792. This is almost inexplicable, Jay
as Secretary having left him at that post despite all the misgivings
he had about him, as documented in the present study;[359] its principal explanation traditionally has been that Carmichael was well
liked by the Spaniards, by most of his American colleagues in
Europe and in Philadelphia, not excluding Jefferson, and even by
key French officials at Versailles, notably the Gérard brothers.)

The undermining influence of Carmichael on Jay's sense of well-
being spilled over into his personal household, where Brockholst
Livingston, even in the presence of guests, began openly and
harshly to criticize members of Congress for unpatriotic and personally unethical behavior—documenting his case with information obtained during his own stay in Philadelphia and also with
details fed him by a sympathetic Carmichael. The two also began
to share information about Jay's official and personal correspondence, much to Jay's ire once he learned of it. Relations between
Jay and Brockholst, himself a future, Jefferson-appointed justice
on the U.S. Supreme Court, steadily worsened, and the younger
man on February 7, 1782, departed prematurely for America,
where Jay actually feared he would spread malicious reports
harmful to his reputation. Sarah shared this fear and wrote home
hoping her family would deter her brother from such behavior.
However, fortunately for the Jays, Brockholst was taken at sea on

25 April by an enemy ship and detained as a prisoner of war.[360] Also fortunately for Jay, who had been struggling as his own scribe since Brockholst's perceived defection to the distrusted Carmichael, nephew Peter by now was sufficiently mature to take on the role of personal secretary, a particularly useful development given Jay's health problems that, as he complained throughout his European stay, often made writing a "painful" task.

This litany of Jay's woes stemming from his own household would not nearly be complete without mentioning the ironic, even tragic, outcome of Jay's having agreed, as a favor to a friend prior to his departure from Philadelphia, to accept a total stranger as his ward in Europe. At the time, Lewis Littlepage was a teenager and studying on his own in France. After a brief correspondence with Jay, now in Spain, that young man accepted an invitation to join him in Madrid, where he arrived in October 1780. Problems soon developed that would lead to issues between the two lasting for many years and resulting in each of them sponsoring a number of self-justifying publications in connection with law suits back in the U.S. (It was in his correspondence with Littlepage that Jay recommended reading, as a way to further his "knowledge of mankind," the above-cited Duc de Noailles's memoirs, which, as presumably noticed by Jay, included the advice to anyone involved with the Spanish court "to take a dose of opium," a particularly pertinent suggestion that may have tempted anyone— other than a John Jay!—who had to deal with that court once Littlepage was added to the mix!) The origin of the problem was that Littlepage evolved, not into the studious prospective lawyer that Jay assumed he would be but into a world-class soldier of fortune and friend of royalty. He did so after having broken from Jay's tutelage, intrigued with Carmichael and Brockholst at Jay's expense, and, against Jay's advice, entered into the service of the Spanish military, starting June 1781, as an unpaid aide-de-camp to the Duc de Crillon, the general who commanded, first, the successful combined Spanish-French assault on Minorca in the winter of 1781–82, and then the failed one on Gibraltar in September 1782.

During the period leading to the break with Jay, Littlepage had become so well known to figures at the Spanish court and at the very pinnacle of the Spanish military that, by June 1781, he was able, and not without Carmichael's discreet assistance, to escalate his apparently private problem with Jay into a highly visible diplomatic one in which senior Spanish officials actually pressed an increasingly embarrassed Jay into acceding to his ward's desire to go to war. In doing so, Jay even agreed to pay for Littlepage's military uniform, equipment and upkeep notwithstanding that the latter's legal guardians back in America were not delivering—and never would—on their promise to defray Jay's outlays for the young man. As in Brockholst's case, this problem led to frantic letters from Jay in Madrid to friends in America transmitting the background papers for use to protect his reputation, if Littlepage were ever to raise the issue; and, as in Carmichael's case, Jay's going to Paris did not end this affair. Littlepage pursued him there and especially later in the U.S. for having protested the financial notes he had drawn on him, notes that Jay insisted exceeded the level of aid he had committed himself to in support of his ward. Despite the subsequent battles in the court of public opinion and in the legal forum, neither side would ever obtain the justice it sought, and Littlepage, after an illustrious career as a mercenary and a welcome figure in the courts of Europe, would die in his forties—and not on the field of battle.

Even before all these troublesome affairs with his official and personal household reached a peak, John and Sarah suffered the terrible blow, noted above, of the death on August 4, 1780, of their nearly one-month-old daughter. But their deep mutual love, and their equally profound religious faith, helped them to overcome the tragedy, eventually to be compensated by the birth in Europe of two more daughters (Madrid, February 20, 1782; Paris, August 13, 1783), both of whom would survive into their seventies.

A fateful measure of the strength of Jay's progressive dissatisfaction with his Spanish experience was that he began frankly and openly to say to the French ambassador in Spain, Montmorin, with whom he was maintaining a warm, if at times fragile, personal relationship, that he failed to detect any *concrete* evidence of

France's support for his mission.[361] This led him to question whether Versailles really was sincere in its proclaimed policy of promoting closer U.S.-Spanish ties. Jay, even as he recognized that France had its own problems with Spain, by now was charging that ally with always placing its priorities on its relationship with Madrid at American expense;[362] revealing to Spain reports from Luzerne giving details of his congressional instructions, thereby costing him negotiating leverage with a Floridablanca armed in advance with knowledge of just how much Congress was willing to forgo of its claims to the Mississippi as a boundary and as a trade route in exchange for Spanish aid and recognition;[363] barring Ambassador Montmorin from using whatever leverage *he* had to help budge Spain toward the more rational policy of giving the U.S. that political recognition and military support that could only redound to the benefit of Spain's own war effort; and having allowed the U.S. to suffer needless diplomatic and financial humiliation by standing by, along with the Spanish authorities, in March 1782, as he at last, just weeks before transferring to Paris, was forced to protest a mere £25,000 in temporarily uncovered bills.[364] While overstated, there was an element of truth in each of the above charges by Jay.

It was with this severe distrust of *both* Bourbon powers that Jay, not without serious reservations about its utility, and only after ascertaining from Floridablanca that his apparently still promising negotiations with Spain could just as well be conducted with Aranda, accepted Franklin's call in late April 1782 to come help him in his unexpectedly urgent situation of being alone in Paris to handle the slew of peace initiatives coming his way from the enemy in the aftermath of Yorktown and especially after the March change in government in London. Franklin wrote that appeal to Jay as the most available (and personally most compatible) of the five men designated by the Congress the previous June to serve as its negotiators in a conference that seemed likely, or so the then-desperate French were telling it, to be established in Europe, presumably at Vienna, under the mediation of Austria and Russia, who were looking toward a comprehensive settlement of the war.

Jay was not alone in his strong disagreement with one particular

element in Congress' instructions to the five negotiators, but, predictably, especially having already taken upon himself to alter a
congressional instruction regarding the terms he was to offer
Spain regarding the navigation of the Mississippi River, he clearly
was the most vocal one in protesting it to Philadelphia. That unacceptable element was its order for them to take their guidance
from Versailles and not reach any agreement without first having
express French approval. Jay, writing as early as September 20,
1781, made clear to the Congress, which remarkably would see
each and every one of its five negotiators at one time or another
seek to escape his assignment, that it should replace him as soon
as possible because, while he would go to the peace conference if
necessary in the absence of any replacement, *he there would not
abide by that order* but rather would act as his judgment as an
American patriot dictated, within the terms of the remainder of
his instructions. In this light, we see that Congress was advised
well in advance of the Paris peace negotiations that Jay would
never follow its policy toward France.[365] Jay considered that policy, which Congress would formally reaffirm in 1782, partly under
James Madison's influence, as going beyond treaty requirements
and making the U.S. subservient to a France that he, unlike the
Congress, now believed was an untrustworthy guardian of important American interests.[366] The key issue we will later address
is, Did Jay, in his turn, disregard that treaty of alliance and bring
the U.S. into a less-than-honorable separate peace agreement with
the common enemy?

CHAPTER 6

1781–82: An American Military Campaign Unexpectedly Changes the Shape of the War

Versailles was at its nadir in the winter of 1780–81. This was true regarding all aspects of its war effort: militarily, three fighting seasons without decisive developments; financially, a draining burden that undermined its every domestic reform program, much to the chagrin of Necker, who now undertook a surreptitious peace initiative through international banking circles at the expense of Vergennes's own diplomacy; politically, a frustration-caused dismissal of Vergennes's two most trusted, principal colleagues, Navy Minister Sartine (October 1780) and War Minister Montbarey (January 1781); and diplomatically, one ally, the U.S., militarily ineffective and financially importunate, while the other ally, Spain, stubborn in its insistence on implementing a doubtful military strategy in which an undue portion of the cost and risk fell on France, even as almost all the prospective, overly ambitious spoils of war belonged to Spain. The one major and possibly positive international development in this winter season was the Dutch decision to proceed with their plan to accede to the Russian-led Neutrality Association. They did so even in the absence of any assurances from the Association's members of military protection from the predictable English retaliatory attacks on their possessions, and even in the knowledge that their determination to join the Association would result in a precipitate English declaration of war in advance of its formally occurring so as to convert them from neutral to belligerent status prior to their membership. England duly made that declaration in December, rather bizarrely justifying it diplomatically, not by citing the real grounds relating to the planned Dutch accession to the Russian-led Armed Neutrality but by citing documents it had in hand as a consequence of the above-noted failure of Henry Laurens to sink them as he was captured at sea earlier in 1780—those documents imprudently included papers implicating local Amsterdam personalities in a three-year-old draft of a plan they had without authority signed with one of the U.S. deputies to have the Netherlands, at the right moment, recognize the independence of the U.S. That English declaration of war indeed preceded the Dutch accession to the Armed Neutrality on 5 January; but while it enabled England to consider Dutch shipping a legitimate target for seizures, and it afforded Catherine the Great an excuse not to become a belligerent alongside a no-longer neutral Netherlands, it added fresh military input on the allied side and a further straining of English naval resources due to the opening or widening of still other theaters of operation—the North Sea, South Africa, islands in the East and West Indies and so on.[367] But this development also cost the Bourbons the advantage of having access to the theoretically inviolate neutral trade of the Dutch merchant fleet, and it raised the possibility that France, too, would now be further strained by having to assure that this new, internally conflicted co-belligerent would not become a liability rather than an asset as a result of being unable to hold its own militarily, especially in protecting its far-flung colonies. For this and related, mainly diplomatic reasons, Versailles avoided giving them any hope, at least initially, that France itself would enter into a formal alliance with them: The French did not wish to take on still more formal treaty commitments that would further tie their hands militarily and diplomatically and that risked a conflict between France's commitment to its formal ally, Austria, and one to its de facto one, the Netherlands, whose land border with the Austrian Netherlands at least initially seemed to Vergennes to be a powder keg between those two powers.[368]

It was in this pessimistic setting that Vergennes, with the express authority of the king, began to orchestrate a diplomatic campaign to shorten the war—and, as that foreign minister put it, break the "Gordian Knot" of American independence—on terms that France itself could not be seen as endorsing, because they were not in keeping with the solemn engagements it had accepted in its alliance treaty with the U.S. of February 1778.[369] The minister's solution, as contained in his dispatch to embassy/St. Petersburg of October 12, 1780, was to seize upon a proposed potential mediation by Russia, conceived by Foreign Minister Panin with the subsequent endorsement of the empress, that would have as its core idea a long-term, worldwide truce, with all forces remaining in place (*uti posseditis*) and, with the exception of New York City, no provision for evacuation of English troops from U.S. territory, where, moreover, a state-by-state referendum would determine which of the thirteen wished to end its rebellion and return to English rule (presumed to be the three southernmost ones) and which preferred to continue the struggle.[370] The Russian premise, shared by Vergennes, was that only those states opting to remain in the U.S. would be accorded at least de facto recognition of independence during the truce period by all participating parties. Vergennes's involvement in this nascent mediation went so far as to include a policy of deception, not only toward the Americans, who were to be kept ignorant of France's active encouragement of the Russian initiative, but also toward Spain.[371] That was necessary because Versailles knew that Madrid was strongly opposed to any Russian—or Austrian—mediation, which it feared would lean toward English interests and certainly would preclude attainment of Spain's principal war aim, the restitution of Gibraltar, Minorca and the Floridas. Only a direct military defeat of England could produce that result, in the Spanish view. Vergennes, who incidentally wouldn't at all have disagreed with this Spanish assessment, took a page from Choiseul's 1762 diplomacy of deception and sought to get around this problem by developing an elaborate set of instructions to the relevant French ambassadors designed to give the Spanish authorities the false impression that France was doing all it could *to discourage* Russia from further developing its initiative. As with the Americans, he planned to plea *force majeure* whenever the mediation actually was formally proposed.[372]

Fortunately for Vergennes's—and France's—reputation, this scheme never got off the ground. It was blocked by (1) political obstacles within Russia itself, notably the waning of power of its proponent, Panin, who also had been the principal Russian organizer of the Neutrality Association, so inherently favorable to French and Prussian interests, (2) complications at the diplomatic level, notably England's unwillingness to have third parties intervene between it and its rebellious American subjects, as well as its having embarked on a futile bilateral negotiation directly with Spain, the Cumberland Mission, which both nations used as a dodge to hold off any and all Russian mediation proposals,[373] and (3) military developments, notably the decisive Franco-American victory at and off Yorktown. In the end, the would-be mediator (along with its unsolicited partner, Austria, which had been added at English initiative in early 1781 as a way to blunt the perceived Russian tilt toward France) had to be satisfied with only a ceremonial participation at the signing of the definitive peace treaties at Versailles between England and the Bourbon powers on September 3, 1783, the same date on which England and the U.S. signed their definitive treaty—at Paris.

Regarding military matters, as intent as Spain continued to be to concentrate Bourbon power on European targets during the upcoming 1781 campaign, it did, as noted, give some acknowledgment to the need for modification of the failed strategy of the previous two joint campaigns.[374] That modification would have great relevance to the outcome at Yorktown because it entailed a significantly greater allocation of French naval and land forces to the American theater, where Jamaica, at least theoretically, was now to be the principal target. Moreover, as already noted, it provided for enough flexibility to give the French the opportunity to exploit their major presence in those American waters by authorizing their fleet commander, de Grasse, to take to the U.S. coast as many of his ships as he prudently could during the Caribbean midyear hurricane season and conduct combined operations with the forces commanded by Washington and Rochambeau, including the Rhode Island–based French naval squadron, now being led by Admiral de Barras in succession to the deceased Ternay. As events would prove, Versailles' foresight in issuing these instructions, coupled with their energetic and bold implementation by de Grasse, who benefited from the tactical flexibility of the local Spanish commanders, provided the essential ingredients for that near-miraculous snapping of the military stalemate that, with the exception of events in Georgia and South Carolina, had prevailed in North America since the battle of Saratoga exactly four years earlier. (It should be kept in mind that, until the very end of the war in North America, England at sea kept the U.S. "totally shut up," notwithstanding the results of the battle of Yorktown.)[375]

But between the end of the 1780 campaign and that momentous Virginia event a year later, much diplomatic frustration would be the order of the day in all the world's major capitals. For example, London for nearly a year sponsored the above-mentioned Cumberland Mission, named after the senior official, Richard Cumberland, who managed to stretch out his stay with wife and daughters at the Spanish court from June 18, 1780, to March 24, 1781, by which time both sides had finally agreed to end what, if it hadn't been one from the start, had clearly become both a charade and a fiasco.[376] England's goal ostensibly was to reach a "separate treaty of peace" with Spain, per Hillsborough's instructions to Cumberland of 17 April, but implicitly also to create tensions within the Bourbon alliance; while Spain's goal ostensibly was to ascertain whether it could not obtain by this diplomatic route the restitution of Gibraltar but, also implicitly, once again to tweak the French and to keep the pressure on them to adhere fully to the terms of their April 1779 agreement on war aims and strategy. Although the ostensible goal of neither side proved compatible with that of the other, each of the two did enjoy some success in achieving its subsidiary, essentially unstated objectives. Certainly, the French were unnerved by the Cumberland Mission, despite the stream of assurances from Charles and Floridablanca that their allowing their enemy a presence on their soil, and in their very capital, was merely Spain's way of opening a door to a general peace and that, in any event, Cumberland did not have authority to make, in his king's name, any really interesting offers and surely would be going home empty-handed.[377]

Of course, Jay was at least generally aware of these European-specific diplomatic maneuvers during his Madrid mission.[378] Certainly, with Carmichael's help, he followed Cumberland's movements closely and consulted on them with his only real diplomatic associate, Montmorin, who, however, was severely circumscribed by instructions as to how much information he could share with the Americans.[379] Both men felt relieved when it became clear that Cumberland would end in complete failure.[380] Nevertheless, the experience did contribute to Jay's growing realization that Spain's war strategy and peace goals, despite periodic displays of a willingness to assist in America's war effort, were not fundamentally compatible with those of his own country, focused as the Spaniards strictly were on the restitution of territories previously lost to England, as well as on an obsession with the potential threat to Spanish America of an aggressive new neighbor, the U.S.[381] (England itself considered its war with Spain as different from its war with France, the former being unrelated to its struggle with the rebelling colonies.)[382]

It will be recalled that Jay also became progressively dissatisfied with the ineffectiveness of French efforts to help him sway Spanish policy toward a more positive and open relationship with the U.S. Had he been aware of the full range of Versailles' machinations, especially regarding the Panin idea of a referendum in the U.S., or even the "top secret" French policy of preventing the U.S. from taking and keeping Canada, he would have legitimately added to that dissatisfaction a deep suspicion of that ally's true loyalties and military staying power. As it was, by the time of Jay's departure for France, he had lost much of his confidence in, and "affection" for, France and now entertained a strong doubt that it was sincere in its protests that any negotiation it might undertake on behalf of the U.S. would be conducted as though it were France itself whose interests were involved and that its main, indeed only, postwar goal was to secure England's recognition of full American independence. Rather, the American was now convinced, and not without good cause, that France had become so enmeshed with its fellow Bourbon ally that it was prepared, reluctantly or not, to sacrifice U.S. interests in order to extract maximum gain for Spain during the remaining course of the war. It was with this conviction that Jay transferred his residence to Paris, where he was determined from the very first day to protect the U.S. from what he believed was a clear and present danger posed by the Bourbon powers to true American interests; moreover, he had no intention of allowing the U.S. to begin its international life by being perceived as a puppet of Versailles and unable to make its own sovereign decisions in the give and take of world diplomacy.

The most immediate of those endangered American interests was to withdraw as soon as possible from a war now all but won from the U.S. point of view but that France and Spain wished to see continued, not for the purposes stipulated in the treaty of alliance between France and the U.S. but for those totally alien ones contained in the still-secret Bourbon agreement of April 1779. Were the U.S. to fall into that Bourbon trap, so Jay feared, it would risk the great gains now all but assured it, that is, the secure establishment of the independence of all thirteen rebelling colonies and the unconditional recognition of that independence by the former mother country, whose defeatist attitude in the wake of the Yorktown capitulation must be promptly exploited by the Americans in order to reap the liberal terms coming their way from a new, perhaps transient, government leadership in London.

As Jay fully recognized, the only reason he was able to come to Paris with a strong negotiating hand was the Yorktown capitulation by Cornwallis, a remarkable second surrender of an entire enemy army in the same war.[383] That victory (which, as is evident from his letter to Franklin of August 20, 1781, he, as was true for almost everyone else, had so totally failed to foresee even as it was occurring) produced an overall improvement in his country's standing and vindicated the line of argument he had followed throughout his Spanish mission—that the U.S. was vital to Spain's own military cause and to its achieving its postwar goals in America, particularly the recovery of the Floridas with attendant mastery of the Gulf of Mexico, so strategically important to the welfare of Spanish America. Did not Spain's co-belligerents demonstrate the value of fighting together as close allies by capitalizing on the strategic errors of the common enemy and closing the trap on Cornwallis, who was initially cornered on the Chesapeake shore by grassroots American resistance and a Virginia-based, Lafayette-led relatively small contingency from the Continental Army? Did not the armies of the U.S. and France do so after a long march some 900 miles down the American coast? And, did not that maneuver on land nevertheless totally depend for its success on long-distance coordination with the major French fleet in the Western Hemisphere that appeared offshore early in the siege of Yorktown, in time to fight off on 5 September—seven long weeks before the English capitulation—an inferior enemy naval squadron coming from New York in a desperate effort to reinforce and save 8,000 overexposed troops ashore?

While Jay could well make these positive assertions in emphasizing the instrumental contribution of the Americans to the overall war effort by all four co-belligerents fighting England, he nevertheless seems to have unduly, and conveniently, lost sight of the importance to his country's success of the drain on the enemy's financial, military and naval resources resulting from having to do battle in other war theaters, most notably the one in Europe itself, just beyond the borders of his own country of assignment, Spain. Moreover, how definitive would Yorktown have been, either militarily or diplomatically, in the absence of England's continuing need beyond 1781 to fight simultaneously three European powers pressing it in home waters and attacking its key overseas possessions, whether the nearby ones of Minorca and Gibraltar or those in the far distant East and West Indies? After all, England still was the world's dominant maritime power, and despite its loss of Minorca in early 1782, events would prove that it was still capable of adding to its naval strength and inflicting defeats on the combined might of those three non-American enemies.

In a word, while Jay, along with most Americans, saw York-town and its political consequences in England's Parliament in February–March 1782 as marking the end of their war, that conflict in fact very much continued to be fought fiercely, even as the U.S. began to withdraw from it militarily and diplomatically. Basically, the Americans were leaving not only their co-belligerents, Spain and the Netherlands, to fend for themselves but also their *ally*, France, which now was having to face one of its worst nightmares, that of being militarily deserted by an ally fully capable of "a true treason" by reconciling with its fellow Anglo-Saxons to the detriment of Bourbon diplomatic, economic and perhaps even military interests.[384] We shall next see just how warranted was that French fear (which by policy was not to be revealed to the Americans) as the dramatic events of 1782 unfolded.

CHAPTER 7

Peace Negotiations, 1782–83

The defeat at Yorktown forced a major change in the English body politic. On the following 27 February, Parliament passed a resolution dictating the termination of offensive land operations against the U.S.; and on 1 March, the North government lost a confidence vote and was replaced later that month by one, although quite divided as to negotiating strategy, determined to enter into peace negotiations with both the French and the Americans. Only in distinct phases for the balance of 1782 would the peace process expand finally to comprehend all fronts worldwide and not just in North America. This was understandable, given the fundamentals of the situation:

1. England was far from a defeated power. Its navy's strength actually was on the increase, and the nation's fighting spirit, at least regarding its traditional Bourbon adversaries, was given a major boost by the satisfying victory over no less a person than de Grasse in a West Indies sea battle on 12 April that ended with the admiral being taken to England as a prisoner of war (and where, as we shall see, he would have the opportunity of playing still another key role in this war, that of initial message bearer to Versailles from an again-revised, but now more unified, English government, the post-March one having suffered the death on 1 July of its ineffective coalition leader, Rockingham).

2. If the war aims of the U.S. were now within reach, those of England's other enemies were not yet at this stage.[385] The French-backed Spaniards—although they now had captured Minorca and also Florida's

Pensacola—were still short of achieving their principal goal, the return of Gibraltar. In spring 1782, the diplomatic strategy of the Bourbon powers, unlike that of the U.S., was not to suspend military operations in favor of peace talks but the opposite—to keep adding to the military pressure on England. They intended to do so by intensifying the siege of Gibraltar with a view to undertaking a frontal attack using unique, battery-mounted fire boats that were being designed by a French military engineer especially for this operation; by focusing on strengthening their military presence in the West Indies (including the decision to combine their forces under the single command of d'Estaing) with a view to capturing Jamaica; and once again, by preparing for a possible invasion of the British Isles, one that this time would include the participation of Dutch forces.

3. Regarding the Netherlands, France was inextricably involved here as well, despite the absence of a formal alliance between the two—an absence Vergennes now was prepared to change. Thus, in 1782, they were coordinating naval strategy in the Channel–North Sea theater of operations, with France essentially providing the Dutch with a diversion of enemy attention to the southern sector of that theater in order to enable the otherwise outmatched Netherlands fleet to leave its northern port of Texel and undertake harassing cruises against England's maritime activity—the plan worked. Moreover, in a preemptive move, French land forces were successfully deployed around the globe to protect various Dutch colonial possessions, notably the Cape of Good Hope and key ports in the islands off the Indian subcontinent; in addition, those forces ejected the English from a Dutch island they had already occupied in the West Indies, St. Eustace (whose governor in November 1776, ignoring his government's policies, had been the very first foreign official—quickly disavowed and reprimanded by home authorities—to have recognized the U.S. flag, forecasting that island's illicit wartime role as a key base for European contraband trade with North America and with each other). Clearly, therefore, no English-Dutch peace could readily be negotiated without the close cooperation of a France very much disposed to use every means available to it, including the leverage offered it by having occupied some of the Netherlands' key overseas possessions, to keep that part of the war going until Bourbon demands were met.

4. France was facing a complex set of diplomatic considerations as its war with England entered its fifth year. If its major—really, its sole—

initial goal in entering the conflict was now, as a practical matter, fully met with England's post-Yorktown, post-North willingness to recognize the independence of the U.S., that achievement had necessarily come at the price of its having had to take on other commitments during the course of the war that now had to be honorably met before a peace settlement could be reached. (That Livingston well understood this fact of life is clear from Appendix B.)

Those French commitments were incurred as a direct consequence of their military judgment that France could not readily assure the victory of the American cause without the participation of Spain and later, more marginally, of the Netherlands. While Vergennes felt fully obligated to fight as hard to help Spain achieve its war goals as it had to help America achieve its, he— and crankily—suspected that the U.S. neither shared this sense of obligation nor understood how basic to its own military success was the participation of those two additional powers.[386] Accordingly, the foreign minister anticipated in spring 1782 that the Americans would be unwilling to continue in the war once England offered its recognition. More than that, he fully recognized that if the diplomatic manner in which the war was brought to an end was not handled properly, the very achievement of France's postwar goals in America would be jeopardized notwithstanding the great joint victory at Yorktown. If the U.S. was now to isolate itself from a France it perceived as being overly involved in European politics irrelevant to the treaties of February 1778, it could then very well "defect" and enter into a separate peace with England as a first step in that reconciliation with the former metropole that could blossom into a closed postwar system at the expense of Versailles' vision of a North America no longer tied to any one European power, whether commercially, politically or militarily. (Another, related French concern was the steadily increasing possibility that the U.S. would enter into commercial arrangements with the Dutch at French expense.)

In the French view, the way out of this dilemma, and also a way to meet the requirement of a prideful England so that no third party was directly involved in whatever understandings it might work out with its rebelling colonies, was to refresh an old idea and walk the tightrope of giving the American peace commissioners room to maneuver on their own in a separate negotiating track with the English, while also counting on being able gently to rein them in, if necessary, by virtue of the great authority given Versailles by the Congress to keep itself closely informed of the progress on that track and to exercise a veto power over the content and timing of any agreements that may come out of it.[387] Behind France's thoughts was that they and the Americans had committed themselves reciprocally by solemn, formal treaty not to enter into a separate peace with the enemy without the other's concurrence. The French also believed, and with good reason, that the American leadership, although not all of it, continued explicitly to recognize the importance to the U.S. national interest of maintaining its close alliance with France well into the postwar period as a way to protect it from vengeful attacks by an England unreconciled to its loss of the colonies.

It was with this set of concerns and hopes that Vergennes embarked in 1782 on what was becoming the endgame of France's now overly long, overly expensive, increasingly doubtful war with England, one that he was now determined to end that very year, whether diplomatically on victorious terms, or militarily on honorable ones, win or lose.

At the start of 1782, the outlook for a negotiated, comprehensive peace was far from bright, despite the news from Yorktown. Not only were there still many quite active military fronts around the globe involving England against its three European enemies, but also there clearly still were domestic political changes to be undergone within England itself before a consensus could be reached there on ending the war without first achieving major victories against those enemies. The successor government to North's that was led by the Marquess of Rockingham was but a loose coalition of opposition parties with attendant uncertainties and inconsistencies regarding issues of war and peace with the Europeans, as distinct from with the Americans, whose independence, if not the timing and negotiating context for according recognition of that independence, was now an accepted fact even by the king. A brief summary of the details of this new government's internal issues would be useful.

A major source of instability within the government was the irreconcilable conflict of ambitions and policies between Rockingham's two Secretaries of State, Charles Fox (foreign affairs) and Lord Shelburne (colonial affairs). The net effect of this bureaucratic conflict was a territorial competition that inevitably had its impact on England's foreign policy during the core three-month period of the government's existence, April–June. Basically, Fox and his formally empowered emissary to Versailles, Thomas Grenville, aimed at an immediate, unconditional recognition of the U.S. as the very first step in any peace negotiation. That would have the advantageous consequence for them of putting the now-independent U.S. under Fox's, and no longer Shelburne's, jurisdiction and also of freeing their country to intensify its fight against its European enemies without also having the burden of maintaining a major force in North America. For his part, Shelburne and his unofficial emissary to Franklin, Richard Oswald, were aiming at offering recognition only as part of a hoped-for general peace settlement among all the warring parties—the key point being that Shelburne did not want to give up the main issue at contest with France, American independence, without deriving some correspondent benefit from such an act in its negotiations with that Bourbon power. (As a close colleague of the hero of the American colonies, William Pitt [Lord Chatham], Shelburne also had a lingering hope, although admittedly not to be realized until a more amiable postwar period, that England, somehow, would be able to maintain some form of continuing legal relationship with the rebelling, but still beloved, American colonies.)

Of course, the supporters of each of these two Secretaries of State had solid substantive arguments to buttress their views. For Fox's camp, they were designed to counter Shelburne's above-stated position and, as put by Grenville with Fox's concurrence, went as follows:

France and Spain have the "expectation . . . of being supported by America" in their claims regarding Florida, Gibraltar, the Newfoundland fishery, and the West and East Indies; therefore, were England able to get
America, by way of a "separate and distinct treaty," to make clear that
it would not give that support, that would "put [the two Bourbon pow-
ers] more within our reach in the prosecution of a war"; but, if it is true
that America is now too close to France for England to succeed in getting
it to sign such a treaty, "we might . . . gain the effects, though not the
form of a separate treaty, [by] giving in *the first instance* independence
to America, *instead of making it a conditional article of general treaty* [em-
phasis supplied for reasons relating to Jay's own initial negotiating strategy, below]"; in that event, possibly more could be gained in that manner
"than would be lost in substance, [because] America, once actually possessed her great object," might well be "less likely to lend herself to other
claims than if that object should remain to be blended with every other
and stand part of a common interest."[388]

Grenville in May reported to Fox that, at times, Franklin, with
whom he was meeting in supplement to his official discussions
with Vergennes, "seems to me to glance towards these ideas" and
has hinted that America could "save the honor of her good faith
by supporting France in such articles as that of Dunkirk, than in
the more essential claims upon the East Indies."

Fox was able to override legal objections related to the limitations imposed by parliamentary acts and to obtain the endorsement of the cabinet, and a coerced, reluctant king, for his preferred
course of action. He then proceeded through Grenville to imple-
ment it in intensive discussions with the French and Franklin. The
offers regarding America consequently made in this period, even
though they lacked the clear legal authority from the Parliament
of direct negotiations with the Americans, would have a profound
negative effect on the negotiation process that followed Grenville's
leaving the scene in July in the wake of Fox's resignation from a
government now being led by Shelburne.

A major reason for this negative effect is that Jay, having arrived
on the scene during the final period of Grenville's mission, and
acting precipitately on an erroneous assumption about how far
Fox had actually gone in offering recognition, namely, that the

English commander in North America, General Carleton, had been authorized to acknowledge the independence of the U.S., would insist upon the very point the departing Fox-Grenville team had focused upon, English recognition "*in the first instance*" of U.S. independence—precisely the point that the new English government was now firmly rejecting in favor of making it, indeed, an "article of general treaty."[389] Not for the first time, London would soon find itself in a drawn-out contest with a solitary Jay, who was stubbornly insisting that it change its position to his—but whereas in that first confrontation back in 1773, when the young lawyer, as will be recalled, had successfully held back handing over to the government the official documents in his possession pending receipt of financial compensation due him, the results this time would be mixed at best for Jay. While England's formal, explicit recognition of U.S. independence would come only as part of a treaty, its implicit recognition already had been given months prior to that agreement, or so Jay would claim, when, to the stunned admiration of Vergennes, he managed to get London in September to make a major change in the language contained in its August commission to negotiator Oswald. That change, which carried the Great Seal, was no longer to describe the American body politic as "colonies" and "plantations" but rather as "The United States of America."

In the above light, it is understandable that the first half of 1782 was not a period of optimism and relief for anyone except the Americans, certainly not the French. However, there were some positive developments on the military side to compensate France for the April defeat of de Grasse: The joint Bourbon conquest of Minorca was a happy surprise to Versailles and specifically to Vergennes, who doubted that the 1756 precedent could be repeated given that place's strengthened defenses and leadership; and in a major new development, the East Indies, in a true "French and Indian War," was increasingly being put to the flame, mainly at English expense, by a French-supported local uprising led by Haidar Kahn and, even more impressively from a European point of view, by the brilliant operations of a French squadron under the command of a new naval hero and future admiral,

Pierre de Suffren, who was successfully fighting off English forces in waters ranging from the coast of India to the ports of Ceylon. Even with regard to de Grasse's defeat, the tangible French loss of five ships-of-the-line was, as Versailles quickly told itself and the French nation, easily replaceable, as it indeed soon would be by an accelerated naval construction program financed in important part by local and private donations; nor did that defeat in and of itself upset Bourbon campaign plans for the 1782 campaign, as those plans already were obsolete, given delays in their implementation. (Nevertheless, Vergennes would not hesitate to use the 12 April defeat as a debating point with Spain in an effort to encourage it to be more flexible in its peace demands.)

As for prospects of serious peace negotiations during these early months of 1782, France had reason to be pessimistic, not only due to the above-described policy debate within the English government but also by the lack of a firm foundation for a political consensus in that island nation as to whether to seek a negotiated settlement of the war against the European powers. Many there saw the English navy as only now achieving that level of fighting capability that surely, as in past conflicts, would bring its three enemies on the continent to heel. In this view, the victory over de Grasse was but a harbinger of a glorious end to the conflict along lines of 1763; moreover, win or lose against the colonies, England should not hesitate to take advantage of the great war machine it had now built up and go on (just as Vergennes had warned) to seize some of the colonies of its European enemies as compensation for the costs of the rebellion—*and* as punishment for the treacherous aggression these enemies had committed against it.

On the other hand, the bulk of the English body politic favored a negotiated settlement, the war already being long and financially costly, and the military situation far from as reassuring as the proponents of seeking a military victory would have it. The loss of Minorca, the boost in Dutch naval activity, the siege and blockade of Gibraltar, the problems in the East Indies, even the spirited French response to their defeat of 12 April, all these augured poorly for England, not to speak of the inability, by the situation on the ground and by parliamentary policy, to undertake any operation whatsoever against the U.S. Beyond these strictly military considerations, many in England, not excluding the king, recognized that they were on the cusp of an industrial and commercial development that could more than compensate economically for the loss even of the valuable American colonies. Fantastic progress in industrial techniques, coupled with the country's natural resources, maritime strength and remaining overseas possessions (of which India as a whole increasingly stood out as a priceless land within its reach), were opening up magnificent horizons for the economy, which now could best develop in circumstances of peace, not war. Finally, it is worth recalling that George III's political philosophy from the very start of his reign in 1760, made ever more practical by the great English victories of the Seven Years' War, attached a much greater priority to creating a peaceful, even hands-off, relationship with the European continent while exploiting England's commercial potential overseas (and enhancing his own prerogative). In this regard, it would be fair to say that, as suggested earlier, Versailles had consistently failed to take this monarchical policy adequately into account in maintaining its firm conviction that the England of George III would continue to be, as it had been under his two Hanoverian predecessors, the mortal enemy of France, always on the alert to attack and reduce it.

It was only when Shelburne, to the great relief of the king, won out over Fox and assumed the leadership of the government in London in July 1782 that this latter set of English policies, one totally devoted to negotiating an early end to the war on all fronts and not just in North America, came fully to the fore; and it blossomed so openly as to convince even the skeptical French authorities that peace on favorable terms was within reach. This came as a great and happy surprise to Vergennes, who naturally thought of Shelburne as still in the mold of his longtime senior political associate, the hated and feared William Pitt of Seven Years' War fame, and also as still the exceptionally slippery politician he was long reputed to be. (It would also come as a welcome surprise to the American leadership in Philadelphia, which naturally anticipated that the forthcoming American policies of the Fox-Grenville team, with its readiness immediately to set the colonies free, would now be upset by Shelburne, who had been known, like Pitt, as both a strong friend of the colonies and a staunch foe of England's giving them up entirely.) In still another irony, it was de Grasse, back in the spotlight once more, who, as noted, first bore that welcome message of friendship and peace to Vergennes, a message that not only could be read, in its profound consequences for the American War, as the diplomatic equivalent to the military events at Saratoga and Yorktown but also as the watershed event marking a permanent change for the better in relations between England and the Ancien Régime of France. De Grasse did so as Shelburne's main chosen channel for what the Englishman hoped would be but the opening phase of a revitalized direct dialogue between London and Versailles. And, indeed, that is what occurred: By early September, Vergennes had become sufficiently encouraged by Shelburne's signals, including a positive response of 3 September to his indirect message of 18 August through de Grasse, as to send his principal deputy, Joseph Gérard de Rayneval (the younger brother of Gérard, the former minister to the U.S.) to England on a closely held secret mission, concurred in by Aranda, to explore Shelburne's sincerity regarding peace and, if the answer was positive, to touch on specific terms of peace, the most difficult and prime issue being Spain's sine qua non demand for the retrocession of Gibraltar. Sadly, it was this very act of moving peace negotiations a giant step forward on the separate negotiating track between England and the Bourbons that would arouse the deepest suspicions on Jay's part of a French betrayal—Jay being overly focused on the U.S. aspects of that multitrack peace negotiation (and, in the present writer's view, also anxious to find plausible justification for his *predetermined* policy of showing the world that the U.S. was negotiating on its own and not under French direction).

By that time, Jay had been in Paris two months, having arrived on 23 June, but he was often out of action, in bed and fighting an illness that, in fact, would not leave him throughout his two-year stay in France. Before becoming incapacitated, he did manage immediately upon arrival and for the next four days to hold long, detailed conversations with Franklin, who introduced him to Vergennes and Rayneval on 24 June. These conversations with Jay were instrumental to Franklin's historically important drafting of an informal note given on 10 July to Oswald, England's still-unofficial negotiator with the Americans, containing a clear, if only broad summary statement distinguishing between the terms the U.S. considered as "necessary" to a peace agreement and those considered as "advisable" for such an agreement to have lasting effect (e.g., the cession of Canada to the U.S.). The points contained in that note were a product of the Jay-Franklin conversations, and in fact Franklin handed Oswald the note only after obtaining Jay's sickbed concurrence; moreover, the "necessary" terms were exactly the ones that England would agree to as early as 1 September and that, with refinements, such as making explicit the Mississippi boundary very much implied in the July American note, would serve as the basis for the treaty of 30 November as well as for the definitive peace treaty signed the following September.

Thus, the period from Jay's arrival in Paris to the signing of the separate, provisional peace agreement of 30 November between the U.S. and England was the critical time during which the North American war was brought to a formal, if still only tentative and de facto, conclusion. Remarkably, Vergennes and the French government as a whole were blocked out of those bilateral negotiations to such an extent that the signing of the November agreement would take them entirely by surprise, both as to its occurrence and its content.[390] That surprise, also due in important part to an American campaign of disinformation that totally misled Vergennes, as he himself confessed, was far from a pleasant one for Versailles, not so much regarding the contents of that agreement but rather regarding the unilateral way in which its American ally signed it even as France was still in the midst of a worldwide war with the common enemy. The important implications of that experience for America's reputation and for its relations with France warrant a more detailed and objective analysis than has been given to date in the historical literature.

Taking turns in sickbed, Franklin, whom Jay described as being in excellent mental and physical shape (Franklin would not miss a day attending the Constitutional Convention five years later), was himself, "the last week in August," suddenly stricken by an illness, kidney stones to go along with his near-constant case of the gout, that has some earmarks of having been as much one of convenience as real.[391] Claiming inability to leave his home, Franklin, from then until late September, made himself selectively inaccessible to his negotiating colleagues, especially Vergennes at Versailles. During this period, a recovering Jay had returned to work and was emphasizing to Franklin, and in his reporting to Philadelphia, the following points of view:

1. There was a need, even prior to the start of substantive negotiations, to change the language contained in Oswald's commission and full powers, which he had received in early August. The problem was the degrading way that document referred to the U.S. as "colonies" and "plantations"; moreover, it failed to serve, in and of itself, as the vehicle for England formally and explicitly to recognize America's independence in the first instance and not as a "conditional article" of the prospective peace treaty. Jay's opening demand was that this recognition be authorized by a new parliamentary act or by a Royal Proclamation, but he dropped these ideas upon learning of their impracticality for legal and other reasons.[392] Instead, he focused on obtaining his goals through a completely revised commission for Oswald under the Great Seal.

2. France was untrustworthy as America's senior negotiating partner, and therefore there was a need to exclude it totally from the bilateral American-English track, especially given that Versailles otherwise would have the "power" to "almost dictate the terms of peace for us."[393] (Gérard in Madrid in February 1780 had forecast to Montmorin that this is exactly the approach Jay would take in any peace negotiation.[394])

Franklin, of course, did not share Jay's views, labeling those regarding point (1) as the product of an overlegalistic mind and point (2) as based on unwarranted suspicions of America's proven and still-sole ally with whom he, Franklin, had built a relationship of confidence that was so profitable to the U.S. but that was now being destroyed day by day.[395] Still, Franklin, although he clearly was more anxious than was Jay to begin formal substantive negotiations so as "not be long about" reaching an understanding with England, well knew that he was no match for the youthful and energetic Jay—by circumstance and personality, the latter was a much more forceful and effective peace commissioner negotiating with the English than he had been as an unaccredited minister plenipotentiary to a government whose language and political outlook were beyond his ken. (Franklin would move from a posture of mere passivity in Jay's approach to one of active support of it, once Adams joined the two in late October, thereby giving him the justification of having no choice but to do so now that he was being outvoted 2:1 on these issues. However, this would not save him from having to combat, with solicitations of support from his negotiating colleagues, an undercurrent of postwar criticisms of his allegedly weak support for U.S. positions, according to the "anti-Gallican" camp fed with details by none other than John Adams; Franklin went so far as to send letters back to America criticizing Jay's own tactics, especially those based on the latter's suspicions of French machinations.)

In the English, Jay was negotiating from a position of strength against a power whose will to fight the U.S. had been broken and whose goal now was to strike as quick and amicable a bargain as possible so as to subtract the Americans from England's list of enemies as well as to lay the basis for a mutually profitable postwar relationship. This circumstance, along with the now quite clear fact that it was France who most needed the U.S. rather than vice versa, was tailor-made for Jay's long-demonstrated personal strong points: an iron will joined with a mastery of the terrain (of course, as he understood it), both of which would be used at every opportunity, but with an unfailing show of respect, to press the adversary seemingly to the point of obstructing an agreement unless there was a capitulation to his essential demands.

In the Spanish, Jay was negotiating with a power so opposed in principle to any rebellion against royal authority, and so certain of a permanent adversarial relationship with its new Anglo-Saxon neighbor in America, that it rigidly maintained a wary, stingy policy designed to grant as few diplomatic and territorial concessions to the U.S. as it could consistent with its diplomatic role as an ally of France and with its military role as a co-belligerent against England. At Madrid, Jay lacked that self-confidence, and that flexibility of style, that a different, more diplomatically experienced American negotiator might have utilized better to relate to the Spanish mind-set.[396] For example, instead of dismissing out of hand, as Jay had initially done, and in a rather didactic manner, an often expressed Spanish interest in obtaining U.S.-built warships as a quid pro quo for what additional financial and other material aids Spain might be able to render the fledgling nation, another personality might well have constructively offered to recommend that the Congress consider the request, whose financial feasibility was not as far-fetched as Jay so quickly had assumed. (The particular ship-of-the-line Spain had in mind was, in fact, given as a gift by the Congress in 1782 to a European power, but it was to France, not to Spain.) Another example worth citing is perhaps less substantive but nevertheless germane to an evaluation of Jay's effectiveness: his limited ability to work in spoken French. This clearly curbed the positive impact his outstanding human qualities might otherwise have had in a European setting where personal diplomacy traditionally played an important role. Instead, he had to rely in his rare meetings with Floridablanca and other Spanish officials on the interpreting skills of a Carmichael anxious to play a more visible role and with whom he had a strained relationship even regarding professional matters. At one point, Jay actually suggested to Floridablanca that Bernardo del Campo, a senior ministry official who had served in England, act as interpreter vice Carmichael, but the foreign minister declined on grounds that Carmichael was just fine.[397] This situation could not have made for the most effective of diplomatic relationships in Madrid between the Americans and the Spaniards—and it must have been to Jay's great relief that in Paris he could negotiate his country's independence in his own language!

The tense Jay-Spanish dialogue did not moderate significantly in Paris, where Jay, in a note of 25 June, warily initiated a not unfriendly, but still unofficial, relationship with Ambassador Aranda, who lacked the full powers Jay was demanding as a requirement for formal negotiations and whose own instructions left no room for movement from Floridablanca's unforthcoming policies. Adding to this bleak outlook for the future of U.S.-Spanish relations was Jay's having come to Paris with an understandably much more hardened attitude toward Spain. On this, he had the full support of the Congress and Secretary Livingston. The U.S. was unified in its determination now to hold to a rigid policy of its own, no longer willing to compromise its positions regarding boundaries and Mississippi navigation. As Luzerne reported on December 30, 1782: "It is impossible to change the ill-feelings of the Americans towards Spain. They daily become more deeply rooted."[398]

Unfortunately, Jay would be so carried away in his antipathy toward Spain that, partly for that reason and partly as an inducement for England to be liberal in agreeing to extend the U.S. boundary westward all the way to the Mississippi, he would negotiate with Oswald an unauthorized secret article in the 30 November treaty that provided for the English, if they were to reconquer west Florida, to have a northern boundary on the Mississippi three degrees latitude further to the north than the one they had inherited in 1763 from the Spaniards. Moreover, Jay also privately offered to recommend that Washington not interfere with, indeed that he facilitate the movements of, any English expedition that might be sent from bases in the U.S. to that region. Only the terms of the subsequent treaty between England and Spain giving the Floridas back to Spain saved that now-irrelevant secret article from a probable nullification by a Congress that, along with Secretary Livingston, was by and large appalled at the implications for U.S.-French relations of Versailles' never having been informed of that specific provision and also at its inappropriateness from the viewpoint of America's own long-term national interest, which was to have a weak Spain as its neighbor to the south rather than to see England in a position to contain it both there and in the north. It was the negotiation of this secret article that prompted Jay's friend and colleague Alexander Hamilton, now a member of Congress, to weigh in heavily in personal criticism of Jay, whom, as noted earlier, he openly labeled on the floor as tending always to undue suspicions of others. (Later in the year, Hamilton would write a congratulatory letter to Jay.)

Even prior to that episode, the Congress and Secretary Livingston would be upset at Jay's letters sent in September and October vividly deepening his confrontational approach vis-à-vis the two Bourbon powers. In those communications, and especially one to Livingston dated 18 September, which was extensively debated on the congressional floor at year's end, he set forth the reasons why, in effect he would ignore congressional instructions and keep the French entirely out of his negotiations with Oswald. What particularly concerned that body, as explicitly reflected in the counterarguments Livingston included in his letter to Jay of 4 January (several weeks before the news and text of the 30 November treaty would arrive at Philadelphia), was the consequence for the U.S. if it were to sign a treaty with the enemy that would amount to a separate peace in violation of its treaty obligations to France. Speaking for the large majority of the Congress, Livingston expressed a strong doubt as to the legitimacy of any such "separate peace," given the absence, from the perspective of Philadelphia, of any basis to justify such an action.

Jay sought to portray the issue as one mainly concerning whether he was justified in disobeying, as he explicitly acknowledged he was doing, the specific instructions of Congress regarding working with the French.[399] However, the heart and significance of that issue went far beyond that policy matter and posed the question, as Livingston and the majority in Congress well understood, of whether circumstances warranted America's commencing its independent life on the diplomatically unwise and morally doubtful note of even appearing to violate the terms of a treaty it had with another nation, as would be the case whatever legal fig leaf might be used to disguise a U.S. peace treaty with England, such as labeling it as merely a "provisional" one to take effect only when France itself signed its own treaty with that power. It is to this issue that we now turn.

We have seen that both the Congress and the French government knew well in advance of Jay's arrival at Paris that he was not likely to be cooperative with their respective policies. As for the Congress, the reader will recall that Jay wrote it quite bluntly in fall 1781 that he could never adhere to that part of his instructions requiring taking tutelage from Versailles. While Jay was not so explicit in expressing his sentiments on this point to Ambassador Montmorin, the latter could have no doubt that the American minister was entertaining progressively stronger misgivings about the limits of France's loyalty to its alliance with the U.S.— misgivings that could only have troubling implications for a France having to work closely with Jay, the peace commissioner. However, political and diplomatic realities precluded even considering cancellation of his appointment; for example, without Jay, only Franklin would have been available to conduct the negotiations, a clearly unacceptable situation for the Congress, if only for domestic political reasons. The two governments could only trust to controlling and tempering Jay's well-known capacity to stick stubbornly to his views, once they became fixed in his mind. In the way events actually unfolded, both would end up shocked at how far his strong will had carried him in his negotiating stance at Paris, where the vacuum in the American delegation, and the receptive policies of the Shelburne government, gave Jay practically free rein to act on his emotions as well as his policies.

The principal substantive issues between the U.S. and England were quite clear even as Jay held his first meetings at Paris with Franklin and then the French and the English. As we will be tracing the steps leading to their resolution during the course of the 1782 negotiations, it will be useful here briefly to describe them:

1. Recognition of U.S. *independence* and complete military *evacuation* of all its territory: Unqualified English acceptance of these American demands was a prerequisite to discussion of any other issues.

2. U.S. *boundaries*: the focus of this issue was on the western and northern limits of the thirteen states. The Congress was demanding (a) a return of Canada to its pre–Quebec Act of 1774 borders and (b) as a western boundary the Mississippi River above 31 degrees, and, in the

north, a line separating the U.S. from Canada at the St. John River
and then westward at the 45 degree line to the source of the Mississippi.

3. *Fishing rights*: the U.S. was insisting on England's granting Americans
   broad fishing "rights" in the waters off Canada and Newfoundland.

These issues formed the substantive core of the "necessaries"
that Franklin had listed in his 10 July informal note to Oswald,
and as stated above, they were at the heart of the final commitments that the Jay-led American team managed to obtain from
England—as early as 1 September—in negotiating the 30 November treaty.[400] It was the unexpected degree to which England
acceded to those "necessaries" that represents the most significant
achievement of Jay's diplomatic career and that helped lay the
foundation for his historical reputation as a Founding Father.
(However, we should note here that Franklin's "necessaries" had
been totally silent regarding *onshore drying rights* and that this
would be noticed and used as effective leverage by England during the negotiations later that year, especially when Adams arrived and focused his attention specifically on the fishing aspect
of the prospective treaty.)

Other troublesome matters arose during the negotiations, two
of which were tangential to the above three main issues but are
of particular relevance to our story. The first deals with the Mississippi River and its implications for U.S.-Spanish relations. The
Americans assumed that they, in effect, would be a third riparian
power, along with Spain and England, because the intended
northwestern boundary between the U.S. and Canada was being
purposely drawn so that it would touch the source of the river
(as subsequent explorations proved, the negotiators were wrong
in their geographical assumptions, and the agreed northwestern
border in fact would not extend to the Mississippi itself); one purpose the Americans had in mind in drawing up such a boundary
with England was that it would give legal credibility to England's
granting, as a continuing riparian power, the U.S., in turn, the
same navigational rights it had secured for itself on the Missis-

sippi under the peace treaty of 1763. As regards the Spanish presence on that river, the Americans throughout the war persistently
pressed Madrid (1) to acknowledge their right of free navigation
on a par with Spanish subjects all along that common waterway,
including down to the river's outlet into the Gulf of Mexico, even
though both shores south of the 31 degree line were to remain
under Spanish sovereignty, and (2) to allow the U.S. to establish
one or more free ports at that outlet in order to permit transship-
ments between ocean and river transports. As the war progressed,
the demand for unfettered navigational rights down to the Gulf
of Mexico was dropped by the Congress in the face of Spanish
(and French) resistance, but only if Madrid accepted the other
points; Jay in Madrid, as noted, had personally added another
condition, subsequently endorsed by Congress prior to his arrival
in Paris, that this offer to drop its claims down to the Gulf would
remain valid only during the war period and would be rescinded
if still not accepted by Spain by the time of the general peace.[401]

While this entire subject depended on U.S.-Spanish agreement,
the Americans from the war's start could not mistake the French
policy of actively promoting an understanding between the two
that favored Spanish interests over U.S. ones. It became increasingly clear to them that Versailles strongly preferred that the U.S.
make whatever concessions were necessary to induce Spain to
provide material assistance and diplomatic recognition to it as
soon as possible. By the time peace negotiations began in 1782,
many Americans, most certainly including Jay, perceived in the
French an additional purpose in their tilt toward Spain, that of
limiting the geographical reach of the U.S. to the extent possible
as part of an overall policy of keeping it weak and too divided to
pose a postwar threat to Bourbon power. (In this, the Americans
were remarkably close to Newcastle's complaint of 1755, that the
French were trying to restrict British America to a *lisière*, or edge
of land, between the Appalachians and the sea.)[402] This perception
was quite a reasonable one and points to an inherent, even at
times openly acknowledged, inconsistency in France's wartime
policy toward the U.S. On the one hand, it wanted it to fight the
English as a solid national unit under the direction of a strong

Continental Congress. However, on the other hand, it disparaged the potential of the U.S. as a unified, strong power, and it encouraged actions and policies there that tended to promote state over national authority (such as urging thirteen separate ratifications of the 1778 treaties between the two countries and secretly encouraging a Russian plan to convene a peace congress at which the U.S. would be represented by delegates from the assemblies of each state and not from the Congress); France, as we have just seen regarding the Mississippi as boundary and trade route to the sea, also worked to get Congress and its peace negotiators to establish overly modest postwar goals for the U.S.

Jay in Paris developed such a fixation regarding the untrustworthiness of the French and their inappropriateness as guardians of the American national interest that their every move was now seen as confirming the validity of his determination to exclude them totally from his negotiations with the English. More than that, Jay also saw the need to fend off those French moves by initiatives of his own, such as sending back to London in September 1782, and without informing Franklin, a trusted *Englishman* Benjamin Vaughan, with authority to make the *American* case to counter the advice he wrongly supposed Vergennes's secret emissary, Rayneval, was harmfully giving Shelburne and company about the timing and substance of peace terms it should offer the U.S.

The second troublesome matter for the U.S. tangential to its three main issues with England grew out of the American demand for broad fishing rights, because it generated the only direct, explicit diplomatic friction between the U.S. and France. Each perceived the other as seeking to impinge on its own rights. The Americans saw the French goal as obtaining *exclusive* rights, or rights to be shared only with England, to fishing and drying along and on much of the Newfoundland coast, as well as in the rich waters of the Newfoundland Banks. The French had a dual concern regarding the U.S., the first being that, by overreaching in its fishing demands on England, it would unnecessarily and unjustifiably force an extended war on France, whose alliance commitments of February 1778 did not include helping it obtain satisfaction regarding those demands; and the second being that the U.S., in doing so, would be seeking fishing privileges not only at English expense but also at the expense of France's own traditional and anticipated treaty-based rights in that region. (Spain in 1778 had made clear to France that it was uninterested in pursuing its own long-standing claims to fishing rights in Newfoundland waters.) Thanks to a provocative role artfully played by English agents in Paris in connection with a captured French diplomatic dispatch of March 1782 from Philadelphia to Versailles, a translated copy of which was opportunely passed on to Jay in September, it was specifically this second issue that would become a highly visible and emotional source of friction between Jay and the U.S. leadership in Philadelphia. Later, it also would create friction between Jay and Franklin, who, like Livingston and many members of Congress, was critical of what he believed was Jay's overreaction to that field dispatch's recommendations, which were for France, under the political cover of wartime military requirements, to occupy parts of Nova Scotia and some of the islands of the Gulf of St. Lawrence for the purpose of preempting the U.S. from securing a postwar share with France and England of the fishing grounds in those territorial waters.[403]

Finally to be mentioned here are the remaining, relatively minor, although at times sticky, issues that were strictly of a bilateral nature, or nearly so, between the U.S and England. They deal with the following matters:

1. England's demand for favorable postwar American treatment of Loyalists (or "Tories," as Americans tended to call those in their ranks who showed by their actions that they favored England over the U.S.), including those who became refugees in English territory. England wished to see this group protected, if residing in the postwar U.S., and financially compensated for confiscations carried out at the hands of U.S. or state authorities.

2. England's demand for American guarantee of payment to British mer-

chants of the prewar commercial debt incurred by those who were now U.S. citizens.

3. The U.S. counterdemand for reimbursement by England for damages the latter's troops had caused to American property by brutally and gratuitously ransacking towns and property and for the losses incurred by American owners of slaves who were permanently lost to English blandishments, which had included promises of emancipation and possibly transportation abroad in exchange for military service.

But before any of the above issues could even be discussed by Oswald with the American team, Jay in August insisted upon obtaining the change in language of his commission that has been described above. In demanding this change, Jay was acting in keeping with congressional policy, which, from the war's start, had been never to negotiate on the basis of America's prewar colonial status. While the situation in 1782 may well have caused the Congress, if given the opportunity, to be more flexible in view of the clear political reality that the mother country was now reconciled to recognizing U.S. independence, it is true that, had Jay agreed with Franklin to treat formally with Oswald on the basis of his original "powers" document, the two might well have exposed themselves to the risk of censure, at least in some American quarters.

This incident of the wording of Oswald's powers provided the first of three major occasions for convincing Jay of the validity of his suspicion that France was not truly willing to help the U.S. negotiate a peace on terms that were essential to assure the kind of complete independence envisaged in the 1778 treaty of alliance. The circumstances were as follows:

With Jay in tow, Franklin met with Vergennes on 10 August to review the state of play regarding the U.S.-English negotiating track. At that meeting, the Americans explained why they had suspended the talks pending a linguistic revision of Oswald's powers, an advance copy of which had been sent by Franklin to the minister on 8 August and which occasioned the meeting. Vergennes, playing the avuncular role he thought the Congress had assigned him, advised his visitors to put less emphasis on wording and more on the political reality that London, including the Parliament, was clearly committed to granting recognition of U.S. independence. Therefore, he continued, they should not now stand on ceremony and instead should proceed expeditiously to accept Oswald's commission and exchange their respective powers—a procedure that in and of itself, would be a way to win England's "tacit admittance" of U.S. independence and allow the start of substantive negotiations looking toward a preliminary understanding on a peace agreement.

The minister would repeat this advice at their next meeting on 19 August, by which time Oswald had his official commission and also his negotiating instructions, including the now-famous paragraph four confirming England's intention to recognize American independence. Oswald, on his own initiative, and in the hope of dissuading Jay from forcing him to seek the language change in his commission, showed that paragraph to the Americans and even gave them a certified copy of it. (London on 1 September would approve his action.) As noted earlier, at that second meeting, Vergennes hoped to cement his argument by rather jocularly, but relevantly, observing that France had been negotiating for centuries with the English, even though their kings, in treaties signed with France, regularly proclaimed themselves kings of France as well as England. However, Jay, the overly careful "lawyer," as Franklin apologetically described him to Oswald at this time, adhered to his insistence on the need to change Oswald's document, not only on the grounds that U.S. dignity required it but also that England's doing so would achieve the most basic of America's goals, that is, irrevocable evidence of England's acknowledgment of U.S. independence separate from, and not conditioned on, any provisions of a general treaty.

By interpreting Vergennes's advice as "singular reasoning" and evidence of lack of French trustworthiness, Jay was giving unwarranted vent to his natural proclivity toward excessive suspiciousness. After all, the minister here was not being the obstructionist to America's obtaining English recognition of its independence, as Jay was now arguing, but rather the opposite, because his advice was fully consistent with the provisions of the

alliance treaty's minimum requirement only of "tacit" English recognition of American independence; moreover, Vergennes's obvious goal was to see the U.S.-English negotiation move forward
toward the attainment of the ultimate U.S. objective of definitive,
explicit recognition in the only way realistically feasible: by treaty
and not by a unilateral, rescindable document, such as Oswald's
commission. (As the parliamentary debate of February 1783
would show, even the 30 November "provisional" treaty's recognition of the U.S. was not universally accepted by London as
necessarily irrevocable, so long as the definitive treaty had not yet
been signed and ratified![404])

In fact, we might well wonder at that Frenchman's goal, given
his overall scheme of playing for time while also reaching a simultaneous conclusion to *all* the negotiating tracks. Even in that
period, there was scant reason for Vergennes to be optimistic: He
was still to have that level of confidence in Shelburne's sincerity
that would be reached only a few weeks later with Rayneval's trip
report on his mission to England; the Spanish-English track
seemed blocked by the Gibraltar issue, which not only was a diplomatic one but a looming military one, as well; the Netherlands
had not as yet even designated anyone to participate in the prospective Versailles negotiations; France was still reeling from the
news of de Grasse's 12 April defeat by an England obviously still
full of fight versus its European enemies; the Russian-Austrian
mediation offer was still a diplomatic football between England
and France; and so on.

In summary, Vergennes's advice, if anything, should have
added to mutual confidence, rather than subtracted from it. Furthermore, as Jay was aware, Vergennes on 6 August had informed
Franklin that he, Vergennes, "could do nothing with Mr. [Alleyne]
Fitzherbert," Grenville's successor, because both sets of negotiations "must go on together, hand in hand."[405] The deeper irony is
that, from the American perspective, the foreign minister's position was more in keeping with the objective needs of the situation
than was Jay's own. Consider: Shelburne was proving to be the
English political leader most able and willing to reach an honorable, even a most liberal, peace agreement with the U.S. and its
ally, France; Oswald, convinced that the U.S. was already playing

the major diplomatic role that its predictable greatness would assure it, was so easy a negotiator that he risked being reprimanded
by London, as indeed he would be in September, for appearing
more as an American than an Englishman in his Paris role; the
present English government was manifestly a weak one and likely
to be replaced sooner than later by one with a tougher set of positions, just as the businessman Oswald, if not entirely supplanted,
was likely to be given the professional colleague he obviously
needed once the full extent of that negotiator's deference to American positions became clearer; and last but far from least, England,
facing an uncertain military fate at Gibraltar and around the globe,
was more amenable to American pressure at this stage in the negotiations than it was likely to be at a later one. An additional,
political consideration was that Parliament was scheduled to return in November and could well unravel all progress to date,
unless some preliminary agreement was reached.[406] (Worth noting
in this regard is that the September change in Oswald's "full powers" language would, as noted, be made by the government and
the king with much legal trepidation, because that change lacked
the authority of Parliament, whose resolution of 27 June giving
authority to open negotiations with the rebels had prescribed the
language used in Oswald's original commission that Jay had
found so offensive.)

If ever was the time for the Americans to extract concessions
from England it was now. However, by suspending substantive
talks for weeks over an easily discardable, unilateral, purely
executive-level document, Jay was risking his immediate leverage
and facing the prospect that an improvement in England's military fortunes, or a change in its domestic political situation (Jay
in March 1783 would express "astonishment" that Shelburne
would lose power merely when he "loses a question"), would
complicate his negotiations.[407] And, indeed, that is what occurred
once they dragged on past the major English success in defending
Gibraltar against the long-anticipated Bourbon assault that took
place in September.

The second major occasion for convincing Jay of the correctness
of his suspicions regarding the French as trustworthy negotiating

partners grew out of his meeting on 5 September at Versailles with Rayneval, at the latter's request, specifically on U.S.-Spanish matters.[408] This meeting, and a subsequent fateful memorandum from Rayneval that grew out of it, came literally on the eve of Rayneval's top-secret departure on 7 September for England, described above. That memorandum—despite its having been written specifically at the request of Jay during that 5 September meeting, its unlikely claim to be merely an informal way for Rayneval to pass on some "personal ideas," and its disclaimer that "it is up to you if I am wrong, because only you know of the title the U.S. may have" to the disputed territory—reflected the unfortunate tendency of the French to be overconfident of their superior diplomatic wisdom and of their guaranteed supervisory role over the American negotiators. The memorandum was long and didactic— and studded with unworkable, uninformed suggestions regarding how to establish a mutually agreeable western boundary between the U.S. and Spain's Louisiana. Moreover, the history it offered regarding the negotiations a generation earlier between France and England over this same territory was inaccurate in important respects.[409]

The essence of Rayneval's memorandum and accompanying map, like that of Aranda's proposals to Jay of 10 August, was to have the U.S. cut back on all of its demands, whether for a western boundary up to the Mississippi itself, or for free navigation rights all along that river down to its mouth or, finally, for a free port at that entrance into the Gulf of Mexico. Rayneval rehearsed all the tired past debating devices the Europeans used in support of their respective claims west of the Appalachians, notably: that most of that territory belonged to the Indians and sovereignty should rest with them under protectorates, in the present case by Spain and the U.S.; and that Spain should have direct sovereignty over the land immediately to the east of the Mississippi, while the U.S. should have it over the western slopes of the Appalachians extending into the Ohio valley but not as far west as England's Illinois territory, southern portions of which Spain itself was legitimately claiming by right of conquest.

The tactlessness of that paper and Jay's learning third hand on

9 September that the reason for Rayneval's sudden disappearance was his mysterious trip to England (only on 26 September would he be told by Vergennes of that mission and its purpose) combined to convince him that the primary purpose of the French was to block England's giving in to American insistence that Oswald's commission be altered to give recognition to the "United States" and also to discourage England from granting it a western boundary up to the Mississippi. This was also the very period when Jay was given the translated copy of the French diplomatic dispatch from Philadelphia urging action that would have the effect of curbing American fishing interests in the Gulf of St. Lawrence, another presumed Rayneval goal in London. Now more certain than ever that the U.S. had to be totally free of French tutelage, Jay took that extraordinary step of empowering the Englishman Vaughan to go for him to London on a special mission. While Vaughan had "no public character," he had been in Paris for some time and in close touch with the American commissioners, who knew that he had direct access to Shelburne; moreover, Vaughan was a member of a family that had American roots. He himself had worked with Franklin while in England, where he helped arrange for the publication of some of Franklin's writings, and Jay, on Franklin's recommendation, had become a friend of the family when Benjamin's younger brother, John, came to Spain in May 1781 for travel and study en route to the U.S. (When he left for America in February 1782, Jay entrusted him with confidential dispatches "to be sunk if England threatened his capture." Interestingly, Brockholst Livingston was not given any such confidential material to carry back to the U.S. at that time; and both men would be caught at sea by England en route to America.)

In written instructions from Jay, Benjamin Vaughan was told to reassure the English authorities that the Americans would proceed with the negotiations immediately upon obtaining the change in the language of Oswald's commission that they were demanding. Jay, who had already given that self-same assurance to Oswald, would later claim to the Congress and Secretary Livingston that the Vaughan mission had been a brilliant "success" because, first, the English soon thereafter did deliver to Oswald

(23 September) a revised commission acceptable to the Americans, who thereby were put "on an equal footing" as a first step toward an "unconditional acknowledgment" of independence; and second, Rayneval (who ironically would himself take credit for this English revision!) had clearly failed to block England's agreeing either to that accommodation of the Americans or to the great bulk of America's substantive demands—London, at the time it advised Oswald that his commission would be changed along lines demanded by the Americans, also stated that in order to streamline the negotiations it would accept all the "necessaries" contained in Franklin's 10 July note but would not go beyond them.[410]

Yet an examination of the record, and of France's long-established policies toward the U.S. and its relations with Spain, does not nearly justify Jay's suspicions regarding the purposes of Rayneval's mission or his claims regarding the role of Vaughan. First of all, from the war's start, French policy had been made exquisitely clear to the Americans that they should limit their territorial and related demands on Spain; therefore, Rayneval's memorandum, which not so incidentally had its origins, as noted, in a request from Jay at his 5 September meeting with the Frenchman for just such a precise exposition, represented no substantive departure from that established policy—its only error being an unprecedentedly direct, written intrusion into that issue. Rayneval's initiative was both predictably unsuccessful and, most important, completely unnecessary and irrelevant to the achievement of France's main goal at the time, which was to assure that the U.S.-English negotiating track would not trail that of France and England. After all, U.S.-Spanish issues were not, and would not be, an obstacle to the peace agreements that were reached in 1783. What is clear is that Rayneval, with Vergennes's concurrence, thought he could facilitate an understanding between Jay and Aranda as an informed and acceptable third party, never imagining that Jay would take his rather offhanded intervention as an interference in his negotiations with *England*.

The primary purpose of Rayneval's mission to England was to confirm directly with Shelburne de Grasse's message that there indeed was a political will to negotiate a peace on mutually honorable terms. If Rayneval, who arrived incognito in London on 10 September, before Vaughan even set out from Paris, found that to be so, he was to explore possible solutions to the most difficult problem that would have to be resolved before there could be any peace in Europe, that is, the Spanish demand for the retrocession of Gibraltar. While the American situation did come up in Rayneval's talks with Shelburne and his foreign minister, Grantham, that was done so lightly and perfunctorily, so much merely as a passing formality, and so lacking in substantive weight, if only because the French were largely ignorant of the details of the American negotiation with Oswald, as completely to undermine Jay's grounds for having sent the Vaughan mission.

Second, the cabinet in London, prior to the arrival of Vaughan, had already made the policy decision to change the language of Oswald's commission, if legally possible without parliamentary endorsement, and it had already made their basic, favorable decisions regarding Franklin's "necessaries." All this was based largely on the reporting and recommendations of Oswald sent in the first week of September and under cabinet consideration as early as 14 September. Moreover, Vaughan as a person, despite the general impression in Paris, was far from a respected figure either on Shelburne's part or that of the king. Finally, while Rayneval, in his few passing comments on the demands of the U.S., did show a dislike, a "jealousy," of some of the more ambitious of them, as Shelburne informed the king, he never pressed the English to reject them, and he certainly never tried to block England's changing the language of Oswald's commission, a central suspicion of Jay as he sent Vaughan on his mission.[411] Furthermore, it could not have come as a surprise to London that Rayneval had not come over in order to give enthusiastic support to the American demands, each of the parties involved in the Paris negotiations knowing well that it was established French policy to urge all the others to moderate their demands so as not to obstruct the earliest possible agreement on a general peace.

That Jay was self-conscious about the Vaughan mission is evident from his having deceived Franklin by purposefully not informing him of it until it was an accomplished fact. (This was not

Jay's only deception of Franklin that month, having fed Oswald on 10 September a paper he had drafted containing ideas as to how to revise that Englishman's commission but that he had promised Franklin—who feared it would be a tactical error so formally to put down rigid prerequisites for commencing negotiations—he wouldn't give to Oswald.) Astonishingly, Jay also excluded any reference to the Vaughan mission in his above-mentioned, detailed letter of 18 September to Livingston that had created such a bombshell in the Congress, whose policy toward France it had so contradicted. The timing of that letter had been prompted in part by his having learned (10 September) the contents of the above-mentioned French diplomatic dispatch of March having a bearing on fishing issues between France and the U.S. That dispatch was written and sent by Luzerne's deputy, Barbé-Marbois (an irony, given that diplomat's consistently warm and supportive posture regarding nearly all things American, and given his future role as finance minister under Napoleon when, in 1803, he would negotiate the sale of Louisiana with now-minister to France Livingston and President Jefferson's special envoy James Monroe). Fully consistent with previous dispatches sent to Versailles by Luzerne himself, Marbois's letter contained recommendations, as earlier described, that, if acted upon, would have greatly harmed the alliance with the U.S. Here was the third major occasion cementing Jay's suspicions regarding France as a loyal negotiating partner for the U.S. in the peace negotiations, suspicions that led him to attribute England's post-Gibraltar tightening of reins over Oswald to Rayneval's trip to England having succeeded in getting that government to put "a spoke in our wheel."[412]

The highly significant response of 4 January by Secretary Livingston to Jay's letters, especially that of 18 September, was expressly based on the unanimously approved resolution of Congress of October 4, 1782, confirming its established policy "that they will not enter into the discussion of any overtures for pacification but in confidence and in concert with His Most Christian Majesty," and on the consensus of opinion he detected in the just-concluded congressional debate of 24 and 30 December on

Jay's communications.[413] For that reason, as well as for its value as a pure expression of the views of the U.S. government while the outcome of the peace negotiations was still uncertain, and because it has been both unwarrantedly derided and neglected in the writing of the diplomatic history of the American Revolution, its essential parts will be summarized below.[414] The exchange of letters documents in a dramatic way the true stakes of a U.S. negotiating strategy in Paris that indeed paid off in a most rewarding treaty assuring that the fledgling American nation would have the territorial and legal and commercial attributes fundamental to its future, domestically and internationally but that also was carried out at a still inadequately acknowledged cost to the moral and diplomatic standing of the United States. Furthermore, in the opinion of many at the time and since, that strategy was not even a necessary one for the achievement of that desirable treaty—an issue that can never be resolved.

Here is the text of that Livingston letter (except where otherwise noted, emphasis is supplied as in the original):

It is of much importance that both you and we should judge rightly of the designs of the Court, to whom we have intrusted such extensive powers, that I most earnestly wish you had enlarged on the reasons which have induced you to form the opinion you intimate; an opinion, which, if well founded, must render your negotiations extremely painful, and the issue of them uncertain. If on the other hand, it should have been taken up too hastily, it is to be feared, that in defiance of all that prudence and self-possession for which you are happily distinguished, it will discover itself in a reserve and want of confidence, which may afford hopes to our artful antagonist of exciting jealousies between us and our friends. I so sincerely wish that your conjectures on this head may not be well founded, that I am led to hope you carry your suspicions too far, and the more so as Dr. Franklin, to whom I dare say you have communicated them freely, does not (as you say) agree in sentiment with you. But I pretend not to judge, since I have not the advantage of seeing from the same ground. Perhaps some light may be thrown upon the subject by such facts as I have been able to collect here, and with which it is impossible you should be acquainted.

The policy you suppose to influence the measures of France, can only be founded in a distrust, which I persuade myself she can hardly entertain of those who have put their dearest interest into her hands. She is too well informed of the state of this country, to believe there is the least reason to suppose, that we could have the most distant idea of a *separate peace* [emphasis supplied]. If such a distrust really exists, it would, in my opinion, dictate to them, to let Great Britain acknowledge our independence at once, rather than make it the subject of subsequent negotiation. When satisfied on that point, we can with more advantage contend for those our allies have at heart. Whereas by withholding it, and making it the price of concessions on the part of France, which she may not choose to make, an opportunity would be afforded to embroil and incline us to listen to separate proposals. Upon this principle, France seems to have acted in all the answers, which she has hitherto given, as well to the direct proposals of Great Britain as to those made by the Imperial Courts. When Mr. Grenville proposed to treat of the independence of the United States with His Most Christian Majesty, an opportunity was afforded to take the lead in the negotiation, and to suspend that part of it; yet we find the reply of the Court of Versailles led to a direct negotiation between Great Britain and us, and ended in the offer of unconditional independence. The reply of the Court of France to that of London, communicated to Mr. Grenville on the 21st of June, speaks the same language.

From these and the following facts you will, when you have compared them with those within your own knowledge, draw your inferences with more judgment than I can pretend to do without those you possess. . . .

In Vergennes' letter to Luzerne of the 14th of October, he mentions with great apparent satisfaction, the alterations in Mr. Oswald's commission. From the general tenor of this and his preceding letters, I can discover nothing but an anxious desire for peace, which might very naturally lead him to wish that objections, which he did not conceive as essential in the first instance, after having declared to Great Britain that no peace could be made till our independence was acknowledged, should not break off a negotiation which must end in the attainment of an object, which they have as much at heart as we.

Whatever the sentiments of Vergennes may be, as to the claims of Spain, in a letter which I have seen, he treats them as well as ours, as chimerical and extravagant, and declares, that he does not mean to interfere in them. You can best judge of the sincerity of this declaration. If insincere, I cannot conceive for what purpose it was made, or the subject treated so lightly, or why this should be confided to me. For my own part, I believe their situation with respect to Spain is very delicate, and that they are embarrassed by her demands. . . .

As to the letter of Marbois, I am by no means surprised at it, since he always endeavored to persuade us that our claim to the fisheries was not well founded. Yet one thing is very remarkable, and I hope evinces the determination of France to serve us on this point. The advice given to discourage the hope is certainly judicious, and yet we find no steps taken in consequence of it. On the contrary, we have been repeatedly told in formal communications since that period, "that the King would do every thing for us that circumstances will admit, and that nothing but dire necessity shall induce him to relinquish any of the objects we have at heart, and that he does not imagine that such necessity will exist." This communication was made on the 21st of last November, from letters of the 7th of September, *previous to our* success at Yorktown, and has been renewed at different periods since. You will undoubtedly avail yourself of this engagement if necessary. Congress, relying upon it, have made no alteration in their instructions since the change in their affairs, by the blow the enemy received at Yorktown.

This letter of Marbois, and the conduct of the Court of France, evince the difference between a great politician and a little one. France can, by prohibiting the importation of fish, supply herself; she cannot do more. Our exclusion from the fishery, would only be beneficial to England. The enmity it would excite, the disputes it would give rise to, would, in the course of a few years, obliterate the memory of the favors we have received. England, by sacrificing a part of her fisheries, and protecting us in the enjoyment of them, would render herself necessary to us, our friendship would be transferred to her, and France in the end be considered as a natural enemy. I am persuaded, she has wisdom enough to see it in its true light. . . .

You see, Sir, I have purposely leaned to the opposite side from that which you appear in some measure to have taken; not because I think you *are* wrong in the opinion you have adopted, but because you *may possibly* be so. Such essential injuries may flow from the slightest jealousies, that I wish you to examine yours with all the coolness you are master of. I am persuaded, the last hope of Britain is founded on the distrusts they may sow among their enemies. . . .

Vergennes' letters dated a day later than yours give no account of your propositions. I should conclude from the circumstance, that they had not been communicated. If I were not convinced, that acting under the instructions you do, you would not withhold them, except for the most weighty reasons, and that if such reasons existed you would have assigned them ['fully'] your letters, and presuming, therefore, that you had communicated them, I have made no secret of them to Luzerne. . . .

We are far from regretting that Aranda has no powers to treat. We think, with you, that it is time to adopt the Spanish system. We may treat at any time with more advantage than at present. . . .

I must again entreat you to write more fully to us. I have received *from the Count de Vergennes' letters*, the whole progress of the negotiation. Information of this kind it would give me more pleasure to receive through another channel.

Of course, Livingston's letter was written well after the deed he sought to prevent was done with the signature on 30 November of the peace treaty between the U.S. and England without any American consultations with Vergennes—except for disinformation purposes. Perhaps for legitimate reasons of confusion between Livingston and Jay regarding the code used in that letter, Jay never substantively responded to it, although he did join with Adams and Franklin in July 1783 to rebut the criticism contained in Livingston's more historically treated letter of 25 March. This second letter was written after receipt on 12 March of the text of the 30 November treaty and also after learning of the signing, but not of the contents, of the preliminary peace treaties of 20 January between England and the Bourbon powers. Those January treaties, especially once all the details became known, rendered moot for all immediate practical purposes the heated exchanges generated by this long-distance correspondence.

Worth noting is that, contrary to normal practice for such a major diplomatic step, no provision was made at the time of the signing of the 30 November treaty between the U.S. and England for the establishment of a formal armistice. There can be little doubt that this omission, coupled with making the activation of the treaty's "provisional articles" technically dependent upon the reaching by France and England of a corresponding settlement of their own, was part of a conscious American effort, totally unsuccessful from the French point of view, to avoid blatantly violating the expressly stated terms of their 1778 alliance treaty with France by entering into an openly declared, separate and formal end to the fighting. That bilateral armistice would only be signed on January 20, 1783, when all the co-belligerents of the U.S. would also enter into one on the day of their own signing (except for the Netherlands, temporarily) of preliminary peace treaties with England. This sequence was fully in keeping with Jay's long-expressed awareness that the manner in which the U.S. reached a peace agreement with England would have a profound bearing on the standing of that newly independent nation in the world community. As he told Oswald in August: The U.S. was too young "to forfeit their character at the first outset," by not fulfilling their treaty with France, because then "they would never be trusted again and should become a proverb amongst mankind."[415] (We, today, must wonder whether, more than the legal technicalities and diplomatic fictions that Jay and Adams installed with England's cooperation in the 30 November treaty, it was not actually the purely fortuitous circumstance of a Bourbon-English agreement, reached so unexpectedly soon after that date, that best accounts for the comparatively cost-free way in which the Americans escaped from their now burdensome commitments to the French—and from the moral burdens that Jay in that month of August had feared his country might have to bear if it was perceived by the rest of the world to have brazenly violated those same commitments.)[416]

There is one more point to be made on this exchange of letters between Jay and Livingston: The 18 September letter, in effect, was Jay's swan song as sole negotiator of the peace. By early October, Franklin would be more actively involved, and Adams, as noted, would appear later that month (26 October), after a most dilatory trip from the Netherlands and presumably having run out of reasons for not joining as but one member of a team negotiating what originally was assigned solely to him—a team, moreover, that included his hated rival for fame, Franklin, and that had virtually been instructed to take its direction from a man,

Vergennes, with whom he had exchanged harsh words during past stays in France. It should also be recalled that this October trio of Americans would add a fourth member, Henry Laurens, who arrived just in time to add a provision to the draft treaty protecting U.S. slavery interests.

Therefore, after September, and especially after Adams's arrival, Jay, with a sigh of relief mainly for reasons of poor health, would reduce his role as lead correspondent with the Congress through Livingston and now only sporadically would write in his own name, usually in justification and explanation of the decisions and actions of the entire U.S. team, such as his lengthy retrospective of 17 November—which one admiring historian correctly described as the most important document in the archives "detailing the steps leading up to the preliminary treaty with England and emphasizing the success of the American Commissioners."[417] He might also have added that the document should be handled with care because it is slanted to make the strongest case possible for the record in support of the commissioners' tactics and strategy;[418] for one example, its subject matter dropped September's focus on the difficult issue of the suspicion-arousing behavior of the French and was now concentrated on the more comfortable subject of how advantageous the prospective treaty was for the United States. Still another vivid example of Jay's late 1782 effort to make his best case for the way the 30 November treaty was negotiated is that of his 12 December letter to Livingston, in which he directly contradicts himself by now asserting that "perfect harmony has hitherto prevailed among your commissioners here, and I do not recollect that since we began to negotiate with Mr. Oswald there has been the least division or opposition between us."

Not surprisingly, Adams in Paris continued to give Jay the full backing, as regards holding a firm line with both the English and the French, that he had provided by his rather sporadic correspondence from the Netherlands.[419] Jay had used that correspondence to forward his negotiations with Oswald, as when, in early September, he read out to that Englishman two letters from Adams backing his demand for English recognition of U.S. independence prior to the signing of a treaty. By the time of his arrival on the scene, the issue of Oswald's commission had been settled (although on terms, as we have seen, far from Jay's original demands for an explicit parliamentary or royal statement of that recognition). Moreover, with that change in language, the two sides had indeed moved quickly, as Jay had promised they would, and completed a draft text of "a final treaty," prepared by Jay and Franklin as early as 15 October. Nearly simultaneously with Adams's arrival, a second English negotiator, Henry Strachey, came on 28 October from London to stiffen Oswald's negotiating stance: The decisive military confrontation at Gibraltar had now taken place, and the English, as the winners, predictably became less liberal in their positions both with the Bourbons and the Americans, threatening to undo the deal just reached with Oswald on all the articles for a treaty.

A reflection of this change in English attitude is seen in Fitzherbert's dispatch of 3 October to Grantham:[420]

I see a possibility of soon reaching an understanding, "as Vergennes begins . . . to manifest an unequivocal desire" to end the war due to: (a) "the state of this country, . . . the miserable conditions" of its "inhabitants," who can't even pay for normal taxes, let alone wartime ones, and who have long "universally reprobated" France for being the "dupe" of the U.S. and Spain; (b) the declining state of the navy, "considered both absolutely and comparatively with that of Great Britain"; (c) "the evident relaxation which have hitherto united them so firmly to America"; and, (d) the failure of the Jamaica expedition undertaken "for Spain," as it is seen as "the greatest loss and disgrace that had ever attended the arms of France," and as having occurred even as its entire European force was used "in an idle and ill-concerted attempt to subdue Gibraltar for the same crown," with consequent exposure of the French West Indies "to no small share of danger."

In one sense, the defeat at Gibraltar should have eased France's negotiating problems because, despite George III's unchanged preference to exchange it for Minorca, it was now generally recognized as unlikely that he could carry the government and Parliament in that view. However, Spain refused to give up on the matter and continued to insist both on the return of Gibraltar and on permanent retention of recaptured Minorca (not to speak of west Florida). Consequently, there continued to be diplomatic discussions, including a lengthy second Rayneval mission to London starting in late November at the urging of Spain, regarding possible alternative equivalents for England's return of that fortress to Spain. The latter buttressed its demands by threatening to continue the war for still another campaign and by ostentatiously welcoming d'Estaing to Madrid as the unprecedented commander of a planned unified French-Spanish expedition focused on what Vergennes called a "risky" Jamaica operation, especially given de Grasse's defeat of 12 April.[421] (As if to underline that risk factor, Indies Minister Galvez was so disappointed that his nephew was not to be the commander of that expedition that he had now become unenthusiastic about it and a proponent of a quick peace.)[422] In pressing for this continuation into 1783 of major military operations as a buttress to its peace demands, Spain created still one more round of diplomatic misery for Versailles, because the alternative equivalents to be offered England, once Spain adamantly refused for strategic reasons even to consider Puerto Rico, whose possession by England would pose an intolerable threat to the Greater Antilles, inevitably boiled down to *France's* economically and militarily valuable West Indies islands, ending with Martinique and Guadeloupe, which, like dominoes, would be "indefensible" once St. Lucie was to be given up to England.[423] In pressuring France to make this sacrifice, Spain argued that France must keep its commitment under their agreement of April 12, 1779, not to end the war without the retrocession of Gibraltar. As compensation, Spain rather derisively offered Versailles Santo Domingo, its part of the island of Hispaniola shared with France's St. Domingue (Haiti). On top of all this, Spain also was insisting that the two allies must again prepare for another military attack on Gibraltar, "a sterile and onerous rock," according to Vergennes (probably unknowingly echoing the similar sentiments of George III noted earlier).[424]

It was in the midst of this diplomatic and military crisis that the Americans, at the very end of November, sprung the news on

Vergennes that they and the English were signing an agreement containing "provisional articles" for a peace treaty—in effect, a "defection," in Vergennes's retrospective words, from the French-U.S. alliance.[425] That minister's concerns over the details of that agreement were but incidental and minor as compared to his realization that the English could now direct against their three European enemies the full attention of their navy, which was experiencing a rejuvenation in fighting spirit and an increase in firing power. Vergennes also feared what he saw as a possibility that England might well have at its side as fighting allies the Americans, whose post-Yorktown military inactivity, popular-based form of government and, now, their unilateral diplomatic action in Paris demonstrated both their antipathy toward the Bourbons and their long-anticipated, natural inclination to reconcile with their fellow Anglo-Saxons. (Considering that Jay, in an overly enthusiastic and optimistic assessment, described the agreement with England as having removed "all causes of future variance" between the two nations, Vergennes's fear was not necessarily misplaced.)[426] Moreover, Versailles at this moment was concerned over a looming war between Russia and the Ottoman Empire, a situation adding to the imperatives for an early peace with England, achievement of which was now made more difficult by the English success in drawing the Americans out of the war.[427]

In sum, France, at this self-described "critical moment," was facing its long-standing worst scenario, one that stemmed from, and was made likely by, the now obvious incompatibilities between its commitments of 1778 to the U.S. and those of 1779 to Spain.[428] If there was one basis for hope, it was that, just as France in December 1777 had counted on in signing an alliance with the Americans, the sheer duration of that alliance during the course of a long and apparently successful war in North America, in and of itself, must have diminished the prospects, clearly not of an eventual American defection in favor of a separate peace but at least of an outright American switch of alliances in which they would actually turn their arms against France on the side of England.[429] In this hope, France was not to be disappointed.

Still, had the European powers continued their war into 1783, the American defection would have had profoundly damaging consequences not only for the French military outlook but also for the U.S., both domestically and internationally. That is because, as reflected in Livingston's letters to Jay and colleagues during the first few months of 1783, the congressional debate in December demonstrated that a majority opinion held strongly to its resolution of October 4, 1782, regarding the need for the nation, in all honor and self-interest, to live up to its treaty commitments— commitments that, in that majority's view, were not at all invalidated by the French actions Jay had found so "suspicious." Therefore, the very fabric of the highly fragile continental union in North America, if the war had continued, would have been stretched to a danger point. Of course, the U.S. internationally would have found itself isolated, not being in a position to reconcile with its recent bitter enemy, England, whose leadership likely would have passed from Shelburne into more hardened hands ready to retrieve previous losses in the war (in fact, North returned to government leadership in a bizarre association with Fox in March 1783, when Shelburne lost the confidence of Parliament); nor would the Americans have had the benefit of any allies well disposed toward them and in a position to render them significant aid.

Happily, this potential crisis for all the negotiating powers (again, temporarily excepting the politically slow-moving Dutch) was suddenly and peacefully ended with a sharp, unexpected moderation in Spain's demands on England. Due credit for this change remains mysteriously buried in Spain's diplomatic archives, if there. (As Montmorin would say, "I myself am confused by all this.")[430] The known facts are that Aranda took the initiative, probably based on royal authority only implicitly granted him starting in late August and extending to an instruction of 23 November, to advise Vergennes on 16 December that he could live with the terms developed with Grantham by Rayneval during his current, second mission to England and, therefore, that he would request Madrid's authority to initial a preliminary treaty without the retrocession of Gibraltar.[431] This announcement burst the bubble and, to Vergennes's "personal relief," which led him to "thank

God for Charles' giving up Gibraltar without France ever asking him to do so," allowed the parties in days to reach an informal agreement on all outstanding issues.[432] (It must be said, however, that, while Vergennes was openly assuring Montmorin of his confidence that the war was over, even a week later, in a 25 December dispatch to Luzerne, he would be keeping Congress on edge by writing: "All is as yet uncertain."[433] Presumably, the minister's motive was to avoid a premature letdown that might endanger Bourbon possessions in the West Indies by the ever untrustworthy Anglo-Saxons.) Despite some negative posturing by Madrid, documents were promptly drawn up and signed at Versailles on 20 January containing the preliminary terms of the peace and also, as noted, providing for a comprehensive military armistice on all fronts. (Definitive treaties were signed in separate ceremonies on September 3, 1783, between the U.S. and England, at Paris, and between the Bourbons and England, at Versailles.)

One factor on the U.S.-English side of the negotiations that helped assure this rapid and successful conclusion to the peace negotiations was that the American negotiating team in October had been able to finesse England's post-Gibraltar stiffening of its peace terms. In those final weeks, London most strongly insisted on protection and financial compensation for those of its American Loyalists whose property had been confiscated and on effective payment by America of its bona fide prewar commercial debts to English merchants. While the U.S. declined accepting any responsibility for the Loyalists who had become refugees in English territory, it did give its assurance in the treaties of 30 November and the following 3 September that, as also regarding payment of the commercial debts, it would do its best to have the individual states, who alone had the authority to act under the Articles of Confederation, to meet all legitimate claims by the affected parties. The Americans also now dropped their demand for compensation for damages caused by ransacking enemy troops, a demand that had always been more a bargaining chip to counter English compensation demands than anything else.

Far more important, of course, was that the treaties substantially met all of Franklin's "necessaries." This was the major policy breakthrough, and it came, per above, as early as 1 September, when London advised Oswald of its acceptance of them. Thus, England, whose domestically driven pressures focused mainly on the fate of the Loyalists and payment of the commercial debts, agreed to boundaries that, in the West, extended U.S. territory to the very shores of the Mississippi River and the waters of the Great Lakes and upper St. Lawrence River. Only in the Northeast were the two sides unable fully to agree on a boundary, and they accordingly, upon the suggestion of Franklin on 8 October, provided for a future commission to settle the relatively minor issue of which neighboring river should be used to form the line between Maine (then under the jurisdiction of Massachusetts) and Canada—a line that was finally established only in the 1840s.

The 30 November agreement also provided for the total evacuation of all English troops in the U.S.—an act that took place only at the end of 1783, despite Jay's hopes and expectations that it would occur even before the signing of the definitive peace treaty. It is interesting that Jay, aside from urging that the U.S. not disband the army while a foreign one remains in the country, soon was ascribing the delay in the English evacuation of their troops to a hope of using that issue as "a rod over our heads" to pressure Philadelphia to help the Tories "more than they otherwise expect."[434]

In any event, the overall result of the peace treaty between the U.S. and England was in keeping with Shelburne's opening position of April 1782, when he instructed Oswald that, regarding Franklin's already known advice that it would be "advisable" for England to cede Canada to the U.S., "it is to be hoped that some more friendly method will be found . . . to prevent future wars" than making that cession.[435] However, in that same message, Shelburne would overextend himself by saying that "Penobscot [is] to be always kept"—in fact, the final outcome would be a boundary drawn at the St. Croix River, a bit further to the northeast of the Penobscot.

As earlier noted, fishing was the one major matter that created a direct and explicit issue between France and the U.S. Much of the heat generated by that issue was unnecessary because there really had been no basis for American fears, such as Jay's, that the French goal was to exclude them entirely from the rich fishing grounds off Newfoundland and elsewhere in that part of the globe. France never had such an intention, only one of extracting from the English a more iron-clad, clearer agreement as to which parts of those fishing grounds *falling in English territorial waters, but where France had certain treaty rights,* were for France's *exclusive use.* As its note to England of 6 October put it:

Regarding "Newfoundland fishing," the best way to end our quarrels "is to separate our respective fisheries." Therefore, France will give up its rights under Utrecht's Article 13 "from the Cape of Bona Vista to the Cape St. Jean ['whose true latitude we'll have to determine'], on condition that it would have exclusive rights from the said Cape St. Jean, passing northward" and then down the western coast to "the Pointe a La Lune, which forms the western end of the Bay of Despair." France will also need an *abri* [shelter] on solid land, and England, therefore, "should cede to it one or several islands, regarding which France would have full and total ownership and sovereignty without any restrictions whatever." Furthermore, in accordance with Utrecht, France should also have a "right" to shelters on its above-allocated portion of the Newfoundland's shore, "but without the right to winter there." Finally, French fishermen should also continue to have the use of "the island of Bellisle located between Newfoundland and Labrador."[436]

It is clear that none of the above positions undermined, or even related to, the claims of the U.S. or any other third party to a right to fish in international waters, such as the Newfoundland Banks. Nor did they impinge upon U.S. demands that England allow its citizens to fish in those territorial waters where England itself was unencumbered by any treaty-based restrictions in favor of third parties. It was Vergennes's policy to assure Congress that France would always be ready to lend its good offices in support of its legitimate fishing demands and that France would never press it to "renounce explicitly" those demands, which could always be renewed at the right time, that is, in negotiating a commercial treaty with England. And, in fact, the outcome of U.S.-English negotiations, as reflected in their peace treaty, was that the Americans were given certain privileges of sharing in the unencumbered portions of England's territorial waters, including in the Gulf of St. Lawrence itself—although not within variously stipulated limits close to shore, where only English subjects might fish. England also accorded Americans the privilege of drying their fish ashore, but only on specified islands in the Gulf of St. Lawrence and only as a "liberty" conditionally granted them, rather than as an unqualified "right." These artful distinctions in treaty language would lead to endless postwar controversies as to the duration and extent of the fishing and drying privileges the Americans won at Paris.

As for any French fears that the U.S., in turn, would block *them* out of their long-established, treaty-guaranteed access to Newfoundland's fishing grounds, those, too, were unwarranted, as more level-headed officials than Luzerne and Marbois fully recognized. Even before Marbois's letter became a political football in the peace negotiations, Vergennes on 12 August had written Luzerne that he rejected the suggestions contained in that letter because France was not involved in those fishing issues, and in any event, it would be premature to act under current circumstances.[437] Only a few of the most determined New Englanders, at least at the governmental level, envisaged having a monopoly shared only with England over the Newfoundland Banks and related drying facilities ashore. Certainly, both Jay and Franklin, prior to Adams's arrival, were far from such thoughts. For example, when Oswald, on 11 October, typically seeking to accommodate the Americans, wrote to London urging it to reconsider his present instructions to oppose granting them, he used the following arguments: "[W]hen Dr. Franklin stated the privilege of fishing" in his July note, "I suspected drying was included, though not mentioned, otherwise I should have wondered at his asking our leave for Americans catching fish in the open seas, so near their own coasts." Oswald added that, as regards Jay, he "seems not positively to say that the [drying] privilege is indispensable."[438] However, by 24 October, Oswald changed his tune when he realized that his government felt strongly about barring American fishermen from any shoreline where English subjects were active; thus, his dispatch of that date stated, regarding "the drying of fish," that he apparently made "a great mistake in thinking of it of less importance than it really is," and so, afterward, he took a much firmer line with the Americans on this issue. (The English government's policy standard meant that, regarding specified shores in the Gulf of St. Lawrence where Americans *would* be allowed, but not as a "right," to set up drying facilities, those places, too, were liable to be withdrawn if and when English subjects began to use them.)

If there ever was a bona fide French-American fishing issue, it was earlier in the war, over whether the French would, or should, continue their participation in the war in a situation where the only remaining goal was to secure for the U.S., more precisely for New England, the same fishing rights that had belonged to the Americans as colonials. And here, too, as noted earlier, not even the Congress was prepared to endorse presenting New England's maximum, legally dubious demand as an "ultimatum" that would have to be satisfied by England before there could be a peace. If that was so, how much less basis in reality could there have been for the fear at Versailles that the U.S. would insist that France keep fighting with it until the English capitulated on this point? Still, that fear, coupled with the frankly open opposition by the French to any American pressure in this direction, *did* create tensions within the alliance—and, in fact, within the U.S. leadership itself. For example, Vergennes felt it necessary to write Luzerne on March 23, 1782, the same day as Marbois's famous letter, that France won't keep fighting for the purpose of winning for the U.S. a greater extent of its fishing rights. That this issue remained muddy even after the peace with England is evident from Secretary Livingston's confused report of March 12, 1783, to General Washington that the agreement of 30 November (received that very day) puts U.S. fisheries "on the same footing that they were before the war."

The U.S.-Spanish negotiating track produced the controversy but not the concrete result that the U.S.-English track had. Jay, we will recall, was still wearing his hat as minister to Spain in warily conducting his negotiations with Aranda, doing so on the basis of a policy and an attitude that were largely shared by the Congress. The policy was no longer one of offering significant concessions regarding the Mississippi as a shipping channel in exchange for Spanish recognition and/or financial aid but rather one of demanding guaranteed, unmolested navigational rights down to the river's mouth, where, moreover, one or more free ports were to be made available to the U.S.; and the attitude was one of sternness—that is, no formal talks without Aranda's showing and exchanging proper full powers. Underlying both policy and attitude was a determination to make Spain feel the full weight of U.S. power and give it cause to regret its standoffish policies during the war and, by doing so, to have it steer clear of any plans it might have to ally with England in North America with a view to curbing U.S. commercial and territorial growth. Inasmuch as Aranda lacked the powers demanded by the Americans, Jay and he never got beyond informal contacts, and a U.S.-Spanish agreement on the navigation of the Mississippi would not be reached until the Pinckney negotiations of the mid-1790s.

(It should be recalled, as an example of how strongly regional issues still divided the U.S. body politic at war's end, that there was an undercurrent of suspicion on the part of some states that Jay had an incentive, as a New Yorker, to fail in his attempt at winning Spanish agreement on giving the U.S. navigational rights down to the Gulf of Mexico—that incentive being, were the Mississippi to be closed to Americans in the western territories, they would have to use other trade outlets, notably the water routes flowing through New York. It was this suspicion, which Jay detected, that had added to his conviction, while still at Madrid, that his having put his own time limit on the congressional offer to Spain to relinquish its navigation claim, thereby conceivably diluting the effect of that offer, made him that much more controversial in Congress and therefore that much less acceptable as a possible successor to Franklin as minister plenipotentiary to France.)

But Jay, spurred on in part by Aranda's clear statement to him that even if the U.S. obtained the left bank of the Mississippi north of 31°, only Spain would control the navigation south of that line, did negotiate in the 30 November treaty with England a provision according the U.S. the same navigational rights on the Mississippi that England enjoyed after 1763.[439] More than that, the agreement, as previously noted, also included a secret article (one that was kept secret from Versailles even as it was given the text of the rest of the treaty) whose purpose was to accede to Oswald's proposal that the U.S. reward the English, if they were to reconquer west Florida, with recognition of a northern boundary further up the Mississippi River than the 31° line. In this, and in his accompanying private offer to Oswald to urge Washington to facilitate English troop movements to west Florida from New York and Charleston, Jay contradicted congressional intentions on both substantive and procedural grounds. Jay acted with a view to cutting Spain out of its present blocking role regarding opening up the Gulf of Mexico to American trade. He did so on the following premises (all quotations are taken from Oswald's above-cited early October reporting to London):

1. Were the English in fact to reoccupy west Florida, then "it was a matter of little consequence whether that upper part [i.e., the land between 31° and the prospective 34° proposed by Oswald] . . . was under British Government or theirs," because, in either case, that country would be "in a manner dependent on Great Britain as having the command of the navigation into the Gulf of Mexico, through which the bulk of that trade must pass," and regarding which the U.S. would enjoy free navigation rights on a par with England's.

2. Future U.S. commercial development was necessarily heavily dependent upon good relations with England, he told Oswald a few days later, and, therefore, "as an encouragement to the undertaking" by England of a military reconquest of west Florida using troops from New York and Charleston, he "has agreed to give us, in the treaty, a full freedom of navigation on the Mississippi," as set forth in the 1763 treaty with Spain, and "without duties of any kind, the same as for their own people."

3. England's having moved the Florida boundary line up the Mississippi to 34° after 1763 did not "interfere with the English Charter of Geor-

gia," and therefore the article would not mean the "dismemberment" of that part of the U.S.

4. It was for the "common good" of both the U.S. and England that west Florida "not be left in the hands of the Spaniards," and therefore England should "prepare immediately for the expedition to execute [its reconquest] this winter." Accordingly, he asked Oswald, "What are you doing with 20,000 men lying idle, spending of money in New York and Charleston, and keeping up a jealousy and animosity between you and us, at a time when we are here endeavoring to bring about a restoration of friendship and good will? Why not employ some of the troops to recover that colony?"

As for keeping the west Florida article secret from the French, Jay consulted Franklin and then told Oswald, in the words of his report to London on 5 October, that "for the sake of the connection of Spain with their ally, they might still wish to keep their part [of the plan] as much out of sight as possible." However, Franklin did balk at Jay's idea of writing directly to Washington to facilitate English troop movements and not permit their harassment by Rochambeau's army (which, in any event, soon picked up and left the U.S. unilaterally in December 1782 to go and protect the West Indies), telling Jay that such a letter would not be "proper" because once the treaty between the U.S. and England was signed, Washington and General Carleton would as a matter of course "settle a convention" on evacuation.[440]

When the text of the 30 November treaty arrived in Philadelphia on 12 March, a mere eleven days prior to news of the general peace between England and all its enemies, it was above all this secret article kept from Versailles that caused the most anguish, especially on the part of Secretary Livingston. The personal pathos with which he communicated the problem to Congress and then back to the commissioners in Paris is nothing less than startling and went beyond the difficult policy issue of whether and how to inform the French of that provision. For Livingston, it was even more painful than the delicate exercise of writing his 4 January rebuttal to Jay's message of 18 September; it also was a crisis of friendship because he concluded, with substantial congressional support, that he had no choice but directly and immediately to reveal the article to Luzerne—otherwise, the French would surely learn about it from the English, making matters even worse. In the words of one historian, he proceeded to do so, giving explanations regarding the "deplored" secret article that were "designed to prevent a sense of injury on the part of France."[441] (News of the signing on 20 January of the preliminary peace treaties between England and the Bourbons greatly eased the substantive problem, although it would still be some time before the *contents* of those treaties, such as England's cession of the Floridas back to Spain, became known in the U.S.)

Livingston's communication of March 18, 1783, to Elias Boudinot, president of Congress, openly describes the writer's emotional difficulty in dealing with the diplomatic problem posed by the secret article:

The important matter contained in the dispatches lately received render me unwilling to reply to them without being well satisfied of the sentiments of Congress thereon . . . Previous to this, it will be necessary that Congress come to some express determination upon a point of great importance and which, if they see in the same light that I do, they will consider as one of the most embarrassing that ever came before them [since it involves in it either a disavowal of an act of ministers to whom they are in debt for a treaty which at least equals our highest expectations, and in part disqualifies them for further negotiations with the Court of France]. . . . The ministers unfortunately have thought they had sufficient reason to suspect the sincerity of the Court of France—and have not only found it prudent to agree upon and sign the treaty without any communication with the ministers of His Most Christian Majesty, but have inserted a separate article which they still conceal from them. . . . I feel the more pain on this subject, because as well from the manner in which this treaty is drawn, as from the article itself, I am inclined to believe that England had no other view in the insertion than to be enabled to produce it as a mark of confidence we had in them and to detach us from our ally, if they should find the nation inclined to continue the war.

Congress will easily believe that . . . I feel extreme pain in hurting the feelings of the gentlemen now in Europe to whom we are indebted for their zeal and assiduity, and with one of whom I have had the closest and most intimate friendship from my earliest youth. But, Sir, it is a duty which my office requires.

And so it was on this note that Jay's three-year quest to extract substantial direct advantage for his country from Spain's co-belligerency ended—not full circle but in a cul-de-sac, both diplomatically and personally.

CHAPTER 8

Concluding Assessments

Typical of victorious powers in a major war, the U.S. fought for its independence in unusually favorable international circumstances:

1. England, following its great victory in the Seven Years' War a generation earlier, was now a feared, militarily isolated power in Europe, where the intangible balance-of-power was working to diminish that island nation's influence on continental and maritime affairs. Moreover, its domestic leadership was in a trough between the two Pitts, and George III, neither constitutionally nor in his personal qualities, was in a position to fill the gap. This political situation would have a negative effect on England's military, naval and diplomatic performances as well.

2. France was being given a burst of energetic new leadership with the replacement of Louis XV's sixty-year-old regime by that of his young grandson, Louis XVI. A major policy goal of that new leadership was, yes, to take "revenge" on England for forcing France into the shameful 1763 peace treaty but also, and more meaningfully, to restore the kingdom to its rightful and traditional place as the major power in continental affairs following the debacle of 1763 and the humiliation of having been ignored by Russia, Prussia and Austria as they divided up parts of Poland, France's historical ally.

3. The rest of the European continent was in a period of relative diplomatic and military calm. Recovering from the costs of the Seven Years' War was still a preoccupation in all the kingdoms financially and

emotionally; the spoils of Poland's partition and Russia's border war with the Turks were being digested; and the alliance system was helping, if barely, to keep dangerous rivalries in check, notably between Austria and Prussia.

The upshot of all this was that France was able to focus its military energies on its maritime war against England, unlike the disastrous previous war, when it unexpectedly was *drawn* into a draining land conflict on the European continent even as it contested England on the high seas and in distant continents. Vergennes spent much of his time during the American War keeping the European continent peaceful (much to the misconceived regret of John Adams, who, like Secretary Livingston, failed to understand the importance for victory of a calm Europe) and at arm's length diplomatically from an England always on the lookout for military and political allies to counter the Bourbon powers.[442] That he was brilliantly successful in doing so was a key element in the victory of the American cause, as was his having brought into military play—although not without harm to his own relations with the U.S.—the Spanish navy, which, at a key period, so damagingly distracted English attention from the North American theater.

At war's end, the U.S. leadership, broadly speaking, well understood that fact and the importance of the French contribution to their finally achieving English recognition of their independence. After all, Shelburne only put into words for Oswald what all the world well understood was the critical English negotiating position that fall of 1782: "[Y]our whole endeavor should be pointed to [our retaining] every means possible to gratify America at a future, I hope not very distant day, when the negotiation will not be carried out at a foreign capital, not under the eye, if not control of, inveterate enemies, nor under the reputed impulse of absolute necessity." Similarly, Shelburne, on that same day, 21 October, wrote his other negotiator in France, Fitzherbert, that "it is our determination that it shall be either war or peace, before we meet the Parliament"—and since Shelburne's clear preference was strongly for a "peace" with all England's opponents, this "determination" could only have meant additional incentive for him to adopt the most forthcoming of attitudes in his negotiating strategy, not only with the Americans but also with Vergennes and his Spanish allies.

In the above light, it is no surprise that America's two diplomatic heroes at war's end were Franklin and Jay, nor that the crowning achievement of each of these two took place in the same foreign country, France, bracketing the successful American effort to win Europe to their cause—militarily at the start and diplomatically at the end. In the dominant American perspective, Jay's achievement was a logical consequence of Franklin's four years earlier, because English recognition of the U.S. was precisely the fulfillment of the Franco-American alliance treaty, which is widely, if exaggeratedly, attributed to Franklin's skill.

But this was not the French perspective. Versailles considered the 1782 treaty between the U.S. and England as contrary to the terms of the 1778 alliance treaty. Those terms, reinforced by the personal assurances given Vergennes at that time by the American negotiators in France, included a ban on any separate peace with England by either signatory. As Shelburne's above-quoted October message makes clear, the French were still very much England's "inveterate enemies" and still in the midst of a bitter war, whose final results remained quite uncertain. Many Americans in the Congress shared this French view, and Franklin himself, in Paris, had tried but failed to temper Jay's policy of entirely cutting the French out of the American negotiations with England in the months prior to the signing of the 30 November accord. Franklin, on that date, and with Laurens alone accompanying him, could only apologetically present that treaty to an unhappy Vergennes as an accomplished fact, even as he simultaneously pleaded for fresh financial aid from France to help the Congress meet its budgetary requirements. When that treaty was carried to Philadelphia, many members of Congress reflected the ambiguities of that American action by both joyously welcoming it (as did Washington, who "cried upon learning of the peace") and also regretting that their negotiators had ignored congressional instructions and, worse, violated U.S. treaty commitments to France banning such a unilateral move.[443]

France decided to take the high road and not press the Congress in any formal way to rescind the U.S.-England treaty in part or whole, or to "reprimand its plenipotentiaries," although Vergennes, Luzerne and Marbois did make French unhappiness amply clear in their private communications to the U.S. leadership.[444] Of course, their not making a major issue out of the matter was dictated by diplomatic and political realities—most especially, that it was in France's immediate and also long-term interest to avoid a useless confrontation with the Americans, one that, while the war lasted, could well drive them actively to side with the enemy and attack Bourbon possessions in America, and, in the postwar period, could only set back prospects for France's harvesting the anticipated benefits of its having joined in a military alliance with them at a crucial moment. Reflecting this soft French approach was Vergennes's belated decision—even though he already knew that peace was close at hand, and even after having angrily written to Luzerne on 19 December that France would no longer give financial aid to the U.S.—to go ahead and provide the Americans with additional aid, as Franklin had desperately hoped.

Fortunately for all the belligerents, the Spanish diplomatic capitulation regarding Gibraltar broke the remaining logjams and allowed all the powers quickly to settle the armed conflict. Still, there remains the historical implications of the separate peace negotiated by the U.S. with England that November 1782. Naturally, most Americans, then and since, more comfortably couched the issue in terms of whether Jay was justified in his decision, freely acknowledged, to violate his instructions *from the Congress* to take his guidance from the French. But the more significant and difficult issue was not about that primarily internal matter but about whether, in doing so, he led the U.S. into violating its *treaty commitments* to France with attendant practical and moral implications for the fragile new nation and for the longer-term relationship between it and the French.

Jay's position was objectively and politically more defensible regarding the issue of whether he was justified in not following instructions than whether he had a basis to lead his country into a separate peace. Many informed Americans, after Yorktown, felt at least some regret at those congressional instructions, which were established months prior to that battle and reflected a deep sense of military, financial and also diplomatic dependence on the one ally the U.S. had in what still promised to be a long war of doubtful outcome. Even prior to Yorktown, many shared Jay's visceral reaction, that those instructions went so beyond the necessary in curtailing the negotiating room of America's peace commissioners as to be unworthy of an independent nation. Nevertheless, as Madison summarized the situation in that emotional period when Congress debated the problem as it understood it in the few days between its receiving the text of the 30 November agreement and its hearing the news on 23 March of the signing on 20 January of the preliminary peace treaties between England and the Bourbons (emphasis supplied):

At the time Congress decided on its instructions of June 15, 1781, to the peace commissioners, France was seen as needed to "extort" concessions from Great Britain by "managing the mediators." The "intention" was for its ministers not to "oppose a peace recommended by them [the mediators] and approved by France," and "it was thought good policy to make the declaration to France, and by such a mark of confidence to render her friendship the more responsible for the issue. *At the worst, it could only be considered as a sacrifice of our pride to our interest.*" Those members who are still here from that decision of 15 June still feel that way. "All the new members . . . disapproved it. *In general, however, the latter joined with the former in opposing*" proposals to change that decision, on the following grounds: we shouldn't show "instability"; France in any event "could not prevent" us from obtaining what England is willing to give us; only France could win our demands, if England is recalcitrant; to change would lead to a loss of French confidence and aid; the change for the better in our situation since that decision is due to the "friendly succors of our ally" and, therefore, to alter our decision would be seen as "ingratitude" and an end of French willingness to assist us; we are more in danger of English seduction than of France's making a sacrifice of us; the French national interest "in the main" coincides with ours; and, the Marbois letter, "even if genuine," was "communicated for insidious purposes" and seems not to be Versailles' policy.[445]

While, given all the above considerations, it is not surprising that the subsequent controversy over the negotiators having ignored their instructions was short-lived and overwhelmed by the joy of their having wrung such liberal concessions from the English, the issue of whether the U.S., by virtue of that separate peace, had taken its place in the family of nations on a false, even shameful, note is the more long-lasting and significant one, casting a permanent shadow on French attitudes toward the Americans and giving the U.S. a solid reason to curb its pronounced tendency to rank its moral stature above that of all other nations.

A balance sheet on that issue may be drawn, as follows:

IN DEFENSE OF THE U.S. ACTION

France's own wartime policies violated its 1778 treaty with the U.S. and justified Jay's suspicions and actions. Vergennes, in negotiating that alliance treaty, as noted above, purposefully left the Americans "in the mistaken belief that Spain was receptive to signing with us." Moreover, the provisions of the 1779 Franco-Spanish agreement were kept secret from the Americans, even though they intrinsically altered and expanded U.S. war goals, tied as these obviously were to those of France by virtue of the Franco-American alliance. Furthermore, France's true Canadian policy was carefully kept as an "impenetrable" secret from the Americans to war's end.[446] Finally, although the U.S. was largely unaware of it at the time, France, in 1780–81, was secretly encouraging a Russian mediation that would have ended the war on terms that fell well short of the goals established by its 1778 alliance treaty, because it contemplated independence for fewer than all thirteen states, and in less-than-complete circumstances, given that the English would be allowed to keep a military presence in at least some parts of those thirteen states (although not New York).

Had Jay and colleagues not acted as and when they did, the narrow window of opportunity to obtain independence on such liberal terms would have been lost, leaving the U.S. without a satisfactory peace and also possibly saddled with having to continue in a war now being fought for objectives alien to its national interests. As Jay put it in his major *apologia* for the record of November 17, 1782: The French policy during the U.S. negotiations with the English was "to postpone, if possible, the acknowledgment of our independence to the very conclusion of a general peace," and to keep it "suspended until after the war," and thus "to oblige us by the terms of our treaty and by regard to our safety, to continue in it to the end." In this situation, Jay continued: (a) England should "cut the cords which tied us to France, for that, though we were determined faithfully to fulfill our treaty and engagements with this Court, it was a different thing to be guided by their or our construction of it"; (b) thus, in accordance with the U.S. engagement not to enter into a "separate peace, or truce, we must remain in the war," although perhaps the greatest obstacle to a peace arose neither from the demands of France or America [i.e., from Spain]; and, (c) therefore, were the British to recognize the U.S., "we should be at liberty to make the peace, the moment that Great Britain should be ready to accede to the terms of France and America, *without our being restrained by the demands of Spain*, with whose views we had no concerns [emphasis supplied]."

IN CRITICISM OF THE U.S. ACTION

The bottom line of the 1782 Anglo-American treaty was that it violated America's 1778 alliance treaty with France—indeed, that it was a repudiation of that treaty. Omission of an accompanying armistice agreement was but a legal fiction that could not hide the fact that, notwithstanding Jay's disclaimers, the two former enemies had signed a separate peace prohibited by congressional policy and U.S. treaty obligations. Thus, Jay, in his private correspondence, would drop the pretense that the agreement of 30 November merely consisted of "provisional articles" and would call it what it truly was, "preliminaries" to a definitive peace treaty.[447] In fact, Fox in early 1783 argued in Parliament that the agreement with the Americans lacked any reference to a definitive treaty between the two parties and, therefore, could simply be finalized, as is, by a "mutual ratification." Henry Laurens, too, would note that the Franco-American treaty of alliance did not require a definitive peace treaty.[448]

Not one of Jay's stated grounds for acting as he did proved valid, as revealed by the evidence of internal French and English documents, such as Rayneval's trip report and the memoranda of involved English officials, and as well explained in Livingston's 1783 letters to Jay and his colleagues. Nor was Jay's subsequent claim valid, that the September change in the language of Oswald's commission gave Britain's explicit, formal, irrevocable recognition of the independence of the U.S.[449]

Jay's tactic of delaying the start of negotiations over the issue of an immediate English recognition of U.S. independence likely cost the Americans easier terms in the peace treaty regarding (1) the northern boundary with Canada, Oswald having agreed to a line giving the U.S. all of the first four Great Lakes and (2) U.S. responsibility for the prewar commercial debt and for compensating the Loyalists.

Perhaps the fairest conclusion to be drawn from these conflicting points of view is to grant that (1) Vergennes, in part, deserved what he got from Jay and company in 1782 and that Jay, in part, deserved the criticisms he got from the French, from his superiors in Philadelphia and (mostly after the fact) from Franklin; and (2) both Vergennes and Jay, on balance, deserve mostly only acclaim from their respective compatriots, because each had been instrumental in the attainment of the most basic of the shared goals of their two countries—an independent U.S. of all thirteen states with a boundary up to the Mississippi River, recognized as such by England, and achieved with the active, *visible* support of French power. Fittingly, Jefferson wrote Jay on April 11, 1783, congratulating him "on the singular happiness of having borne so distinguished a part *both in the earliest and latest* transactions of this revolution. The terms obtained for us are indeed great, and are so deemed by your country" (emphasis supplied).

APPENDIX A

A Contemporary View of Pre-Independence Military Events and Their Consequences

The following is a summary of what the contemporary History cited in the Preface has to say about military and attendant events prior to the Declaration of Independence:

The Parliamentary resolution for shutting up the port of Boston was no sooner taken than it was determined to order a military force to that quarter in accordance with the King's "prerogative" to station his troops where in his opinion the public service requires. In a combined assignment irritating to the Americans, General Gage in 1774 was assigned to Boston as both commander-in-chief and governor of Massachusetts, arriving there on the very day that the inhabitants thereof passed their vote for recommending the measures of non-importation and non-exportation to be adopted by all the colonies. Nevertheless, they received him with all the usual honors for royal governors. Then came the troops and artillery. Gage's subsequent effort to obtain recognition of Parliamentary superiority was like that of those who sail against the wind, tide and current. The Bostonians were uncommonly ingenious in evading disagreeable acts of Parliament. For example, town meetings were held even after the ban of August 1, 1774; and, in the absence of troops in the rural areas, the population there was able to arm itself.

The courts of justice expired one after the other or were unable to proceed on business. The troops, who were seen as instruments of tyranny, and the population, considered by the government as seditious rioters, greatly irritated each other. The troops were placed at Boston neck ostensibly to block desertions, but this move was seen as a step toward isolating the city. Gage's proclamation for the encouragement of piety and virtue, and for preventing and punishing vice, profanity and immorality, was seen as sheer hypocrisy and a studied insult. This added considerably to the increasing exasperation of their inflamed minds, which then so deepened by the probably defensive moves of Gage, regarding gunpowder and the fortification of the neck (perceived by the people as its prospective enemy quietly getting ready), as to excite a fomentation more violent and universal than any that had yet taken place.

All this occurred just at the time the Continental Congress was trying to keep matters under control, restrain the population's tendency toward impetuosity, and issuing advice to avoid extremism. It was fortunate for the colonies that the royal army was posted in cool-headed New England and not in southern latitudes, where inhabitants show, under a warmer sun, a greater degree of irritability in contrast to the New England population's having their passions much more under the command of reason and interests. A premature flare-up at this early period, though successful, might have done infinite mischief to the cause of America. In civil wars and revolutions, it is a matter of much consequence who strikes the first blow. Had the New England colonists done so, it would have cost all the Americans their European friends, whose compassion would have been with England; and, it would have weakened the disposition of the rest of the thirteen colonies to befriend them.

Therefore, the nine months of Bostonians' conduct following Gage's arrival is well worthy of imitation by those who wish to overturn established governments. During all this period, though one of self-restraint in the face of provocation, they were steadily preparing for the last extremity. The novel distinction of minute men was adopted. It was these men who discovered, by the firing of guns and the ringing of bells, the English troops heading toward Concord, 22 miles from Boston. At the battles there and Lexington, the British suffered 273 casualties and prisoners, and the militia 69 killed or wounded. The Massachusetts provincial congress was in session at this time and sent an account of it to England with many affidavits to prove that the British troops were the aggressors. It also, in an address to the people of Great Britain, protested its continuing loyalty to the King, but that it would not tamely submit to the persecution and tyranny of his evil ministry: "We determine to die or be free."

Now, in all thirteen colonies, martial rage took possession of the breasts of thousands. Hitherto, the Americans had no regular army. From principles of policy, they cautiously avoided that measure lest they might subject themselves to the charge of being the aggressors. Militia and other military activities were still all under the old established laws of the land. Those laws, while they had always authorized military training from youth with a view to defend against the French and Indians, until now were never closely executed; but, for some months previous to the battle of Lexington, they were never better observed. After that battle, the militias took possession of forts, magazines, and arsenals in the King's hands; Ticonderoga was taken by adventurers from different States.

Even moderates, whose goal had been to avoid extremities, or at least not lead in bringing them on, and who had been keeping under control fiery spirits whose courage exceeded their prudence, now approved all this, including the raising of an army, which, prior to Lexington, would have led to disunity. The Lexington battle gave the Americans not only an army but inspired them with ideas of their own prowess. However: old sages saw America as bound to lose; European philosophers had published theories setting forth that, not only vegetables and beasts, but even men degenerated in the western hemisphere; and, even American folklore had it, that no people on Earth were equal to those with whom they were about to contend. Perhaps in no subsequent battle did the Americans appear to greater advantage than in their first essay at Lexington; it was rare that yeomen put to flight troops equal in discipline to any in the world.

The Americans now embodied the strange combination of religious fervor with military enthusiasm. The first gun fired against the royal forces was prefaced with a fervent prayer by militia Captain Smith in the following words: "Oh Lord of hosts, who directed the stone in the sling of David, give success to our exertions in defense of our rights."

Distant provinces heard of Lexington at the same time as news of London's determination to enforce submission to the Parliamentary acts. They also assumed British troops would now proceed immediately to a military coercion of the refractory colonists in their provinces, as well. Thus ended, in early 1775, hopes of a repeat of England's reversal of policy of the 1760's concerning the Stamp Act. New England had an army of country farmers even as the Continental Congress was contemplating one, and that army cooped up an irritated Gage, who was confidently assumed by England to be able to force submission of the whole country. He followed standard procedures and issued a proclamation on June 12, 1775, offering a pardon to all except Samuel Adams, John Hancock, and all their other associates and correspondents; he also instituted martial law, given the shutting of all normal courts. It was supposed that this proclamation was a prelude to hostilities.

Few actions in the last French war were so destructive to the British officers and troops as the affair of slight works thrown up at Bunker Hill in a few hours. Its important results included teaching the British so much respect for Americans entrenched behind works that their subsequent operations were retarded with a caution that wasted away whole campaigns to very little purpose. For the Americans, it added to the confidence they began to have in their own abilities from the success that attended them at Lexington. But it also led to over-confidence by some at the Continental Congress regarding militia or troops engaged for short terms of enlistment and, therefore, delayed the establishment of a permanent army. They conceived that the country might be defended by the occasional exertions of her sons without the expense and danger of a standing army. Later, the militia would lose much of their first ardor just as the Continental Congress and other bodies were neglecting the proper time for recruiting permanent regular troops. Consequently, the American cause was more than once brought to the brink of destruction.

New England had to act, because Lexington occurred at a time when the Continental Congress was not in session, having ended on October 26, 1774, with a view to learning what would be the English policy before it next met on May 10, 1775. Therefore, that date, at first, was only a tentative, conditional one; it became a fixed one once it was clear that London was unreceptive to the Congress' appeals. Therefore, new deputies were elected by the provinces, despite circular letters to the governors from London. Also, Massachusetts now very respectfully transferred to it the direction of that army which by their own authority had assembled. After April 19, the sword succeeded the pen, commercial pressure and legislation.

While Americans are used to arms from early in life, Europeans, on other accounts, are more susceptible of military habits. Moreover, the proportion of necessitous men in the New World is small compared to that in the Old. Also, America has that extreme sense of liberty and equality which indisposes to that implicit obedience which is the soul of an army. The same causes which nurtured a spirit of independence in the colonies were hostile to their military arrangements. In addition, past wars, with the colonies only serving as appendages to British troops, and only assigned to services which, although laborious, were not honorable, were not ones where the military spirit had opportunity of expanding itself.

In 1775, military ardor, unabated by calculations about the extent, duration, or probable issue of the war, overcame a sense of military inferiority. Moreover, the feeling was that, even if she lost a particular battle, America would eventually win and drive the invaders out; furthermore, because the general view failed to consider that, in modern war, the longest purse decides oftener than the longest sword, America feared not the wealth of Britain. Also noteworthy is that there was not a single armed vessel of any kind in America's service in 1775. Nevertheless, the fact that the English navy had at its mercy all her seaport towns was disregarded even as it was believed.

The sober discretion of the present [i.e., postwar] age will therefore more easily admire than imitate the fervent zeal of the patriots of 1775 who, in idea, sacrificed property in the cause of liberty with the same ease that they now sacrifice almost every other consideration for the acquisition of property.

Unlike Britain, America's colonies possessed neither money nor funds, nor were their people accustomed to taxes equal to the exigencies of war. To tax for war would have been impolitic, since the war was over taxation.

Also unlike Britain, the colonies' dependent form of government precluded their citizens from gaining that practical knowledge which is acquired from being at the head of public departments. Therefore, no wise statesmen and experienced officers abounded in America as in Britain; America also lacked experts in financial management as well as military fortifications and engineers.

On the other hand, the colonies' advantages were: (a) geography—though the Americans could not conquer, yet they might save themselves from being conquered; (b) the Parliamentary acts regarding trade and commerce forced many to become soldiers; (c) paper money for upwards of two years produced to them more solid advantages than Spain would derive from her super-abounding precious metals; and, (d) the Americans believed their cause to be just and that heaven approved their exertions in defense of their rights.

Coeval with the resolutions of the Second Continental Congress for organizing an army was one appointing July 20, 1775, as a day of public humiliation, fasting and prayer in the hope: to bless their rightful sovereign, King George, to give him wisdom, and to have him act in the true interest of his subjects. The Congress, despite now having added military to other weapons, in other respects followed in the same line of firmness and moderation as in the previous Congress. In answer to New York, it advised it to act on the defensive, and to permit the anticipated British troops to remain in the barracks, but not to suffer fortifications to be erected, or any steps to be taken for the cutting of communication between the town and country.

The Congress now: (a) cut off exports to all parts of British America which had not adopted its Association; and, (b) ordered that no supplies be provided to British fishermen. These and other congressional acts against Britain and its military may be considered as the counterpart of the Parliament's Restraining Acts. Among those other acts was a cut off of the way in which England had largely been financing the war. It had been supplying its troops, not by shipping money out of the Kingdom, but by using government bills in America. This had made the colonial war subservient to commerce by including the sources of remittances, i.e., because the colonists were in general so much in debt to Great Britain, government bills had almost always commanded a premium. Ending this practice meant ending a system so helpful to Britain; now, supplying the British army was rendered both precarious and expensive.

The Continental Congress' actions were not so much the effect of resentment as of policy. Thus, it also now made a second trial of the power of eloquence in its cause. Its address of May 20, 1775, to the inhabitants of Quebec was followed by one to the inhabitants of Great Britain and Ireland, and also by a letter of thanks to the City of London. But the performance which, of all others, contributed most to the success of its cause was a second decent but firm petition to King George III. It was carried through the Congress in September [sic: 5 July] 1775 largely by its drafter, Dickinson of Pennsylvania, who was devoted to a reconciliation on constitutional principles as a worthy citizen and friend to both countries. The members of Congress unanimously approved it out of regard for him, although they generally conceived it to be labor lost.

The British government's neglect, or rather contempt, of the petition contributed not a little to the union of the colonists. It would be used during the war to steady doubters, men of serious reflection, as to whether non-military means could have and could still be used to reconcile England and America constitutionally. By the King's speech of October 26, 1775, America was charged with preparing for a general revolt in a rebellious war looking toward having independence. Yet, at that time and for months after, a redress of grievances was America's ultimate aim. Now, it felt that the King had accused it of studied duplicity.

Nothing contributes more to the success of revolutions than moderation. Intemperate zealots overshoot themselves and soon spend their force, while the calm and dispassionate persevere to the end. The bulk of the people are attracted to the latter types.

Those in England who backed the King and government's rejection of the petition noted that it contained no offers of submission and, therefore, was unavailing as a ground work of negotiations. Nothing was further from the thoughts of Congress than those concessions which were expected in Great Britain, where the wish was for absolute submission to its authority.

None by rank, birth, title, military background has special claim to head the American army. In elevating one man by the free voice of an invaded country to the command of thousands of his fellow citizens, no considerations were regarded but the extended self-interest of the community. A southerner was seen by the Congress as necessary to attach the uninvaded colonies more closely to the common interest; Virginians, by all criteria, were the most prominent. George Washington's military genius led to a unanimous vote on June 15, 1775, in answer to New England's application. It is a fortunate circumstance that his election was accompanied by no competition and followed by no envy.

General Washington was born on ____ in ____ county, Virginia. Posterity will do him justice; here we will only give those details in his life that are shared with all men and, therefore, won't offend his delicate sensibility and modesty. [There follows a long description of his early life and education.] This background was the foundation for his solid mind and vigorous body. Washington began his career of fame in opposing that power along side of whose troops in a change of circumstance he acquired his last and most distinguished honors. He saved Braddock's army lost due to that general's excess of bravery which induced him to sacrifice it rather than retreat from an unseen foe.[450]

Postwar, Washington remained on his private estate until 1774, when he served as a member of the Continental Congress starting in September. He also was captain of a private company of militia. Washington was possessed of a large proportion of common sense directed by a sound judgment—happily, he lacked what others who, to a greater brilliancy of parts, frequently add the eccentricity of original genius.

[There next follows a brief analysis of the background and personal qualities of each of the four major generals, one adjutant general, and eight brigadier generals elected by the Congress to serve under Washington. Some of the points made there include:] Major Generals: Artemis Ward, Massachusetts, a professional colonel; Charles Lee, native, and professional soldier, of Britain, and whose pre-war writings in favor of the American cause had greatly increased his popularity in the Congress; Philip Schuyler, New York, a colonel in the Seven Years War; and, Israel Putnam, Connecticut, a major in that war. Adjutant General (with rank of brigadier general): Horatio Gates, native, and professional soldier, of England. Brigadier Generals: Warner Seth of Vermont; Richard Montgomery, native of Ireland and ex-captain in the British service during the previous war, after which he married one of the Livingstons of New York [Robert's sister, Janet, per text, above] and became a New York resident; David Wraster, captain in the British service during the previous war and commander of a provincial regiment; William Heath, Massachusetts; Joseph Spencer, Connecticut, a provincial regimental commander in the previous war; John Thomas, Massachusetts, in the provincial service during the previous war; John Sullivan, New Hampshire; and, Nathaniel Greene, Rhode Island, a Quaker without prior military service.

[Next comes a long description of Washington's command at Boston from July 3, 1775, including the following points:] of Washington's 17,000 troops, 2,000 lacked guns and powder; Washington, in January 1776, sent an advance party under Charles Lee to New York to prepare it for the arrival he already was anticipating there of British troops, once they evacuated Boston; and, Washington was visited by a Congressional committee of three, including Franklin, to consult as to how to maintain and recruit a continental army after the expiration of the enlistments of 1775.

It is certain that the abandonment of their friends and the withdrawing their forces from their position in Boston, whatever the truth of its being a voluntary one in order to establish their troops in a more central position at New York, was the first act of a tragedy in which evacuations and retreats were the scenes which most frequently recurred and the concluding one of which was a total evacuation of the United States.

Governor Carleton's June 9, 1775, declaration of martial law in Canada, and his raising there of a militia (Britain having sent 20,000 stand of arms and other materiel for it), clearly had the goal of cooperating with Gage in Boston. The effect of martial law was the abolition of the Quebec Act, putting that province on its former footing and upsetting the French Canadians, who united with the British settlers there to repudiate it as tyrannical and oppressive. But the Americans in the thirteen colonies were suspicious of British intentions and uncertain of popular attitudes in Quebec—they therefore feared the worst. Experience in the late French war had taught the British colonists that the proper line to attack them was by the lakes which stretch from the sources of the Hudson to the river St. Lawrence. The great principle of self-defense which had impelled to the taking of arms pointed out the propriety of securing the passes which connect New York with Canada. Therefore, spontaneous, uncoordinated actions by several detached parties naturally occurred after Lexington, of which one headed by Ethan Allen, of the district called Vermont, as well as another under John Stevens of Connecticut, thought of taking Ticonderoga, the key to all connection between New York and Canada. It was taken by them in May 1775 along with Crown Point.

The posts on the lakes between New York and Canada, for the securing of which the British and the Americans had in the war between 1756 and 1763 mingled their kindred blood, became once more the objects of contention, but now between those whose joint exertions had only lately reduced them under the British Crown. France and England fought for one hundred years in that sector, and the Continental Congress, once decided on military resistance, had it in mind, as well. Hence, its appointments of Schuyler and Montgomery, whose principal task, at first, would be to strengthen Ticonderoga, the thoroughfare to Canada, but also Britain's to New York from Canada, especially with the help of its Indian friends.

At the time Schuyler arrived at the American-captured Ticonderoga, it was in a state of anarchy given the competing provincial troops there. His arrival immediately ended the squabbles of rank, and he was received as the commander-in-chief on the basis of the Congress' appointment. By now, the Congress well knew (a) of the discontents in the Canadian population, and of the pro-American views of the British settlers there; (b) an early attack was necessary on Canada itself before Britain's troops there would be able to offer strong resistance, especially given the Ticonderoga–Crown Point effect on Canadian morale and on having paved the way into Canada; (c) an American attack on Canada would also change at once the whole nature of the war, from defensive to offensive, and, therefore, would make them liable to the charge that they were the aggressors, with consequent loss of support in Great Britain; (d) nevertheless, past efforts there by the British Opposition and merchants had anyway been unable to change the policy of the King and government—therefore, the only relief for the Americans would be from the smiles of heaven on their own endeavors; (e) America had to block an attack on its rear, and, having in its hands Carleton's orders from London authorizing extraordinary powers for him to send troops anywhere in America to put the rebels to death, it had to try to forestall him; and, (f) since it already had adopted a war policy, excepting Canada would be an unavailing plea for indulgence from an irritated British leadership. It also seemed probable to the Congress that the French Canadians, other than the nobility and clergy, were as much discontented with the present system of government as even the British settlers, and that they would consider the provincials rather as friends than as invaders.

Therefore, the invasion was determined upon by June 27, 1775, but only if Schuyler found it practicable and that it would not be disagreeable to the Canadians. If these conditions were met, as indeed they soon would be, he was to go to Fort St. John, and then Montreal, or any other major points. Accordingly, the American troops reached St. John on 6 September—115 miles north of Ticonderoga and the first British post in Canada. Schuyler's illness then resulted in Montgomery's becoming the commander-in-chief. Before that event, Schuyler had withdrawn his army twelve miles south of St. John to Fort Ile-aux-Noix, but Montgomery returned it to St. John and initiated a weak siege, during which he sent Major Brown to take the inconsiderable Fort Chambly, five miles away—it surrendered on 20 October, yielding five tons of powder for the Americans. That enabled the siege of St. John to become more vigorous. Meanwhile, Carleton at Montreal was being blocked from coming with reinforcements, helping convince St. John's commander, Major Preston, finally to request a capitulation agreement, which resulted in Montgomery's taking as prisoners over five hundred British regulars and two hundred Canadians, including some of the principal members of the Canadian nobility fighting with the British. He also captured thirty nine canon, seven mortars, and a howitzer, which were immensely valuable items.

All this greatly enhanced Montgomery's reputation. Meanwhile, Ethan Allen took a small party to Montreal, but he was defeated outside the city and became a prisoner along with forty of his men, all of whom were taken in irons to England aboard a warship. Subsequently, Montgomery established a post at Sorel on the St. Lawrence River in order to block ships at Montreal from reaching Quebec. He moved from there to Montreal, where there was but a small garrison. Declining an appeal from the civilian population of Montreal for a capitulation agreement, Montgomery did offer them the fullest protection of their lives and property. Meanwhile, Carleton had managed to reach Quebec by way of a rowboat in the dark of night with muffled paddles, even though the Americans had guards and batteries on both sides of the river at Sorel, and also had sundry vessels stationed in the river itself. With Carleton's escape, Montreal quickly surrendered, to the personal benefit of Montgomery's army, which was greatly short of supplies. The surrender resulted in the capture of eleven armed vessels and 120 regulars, among other troops. Montgomery subsequently set off to capture the capital, Quebec, by way of a difficult land route, the river now being too frozen for easy transportation.

Much to be pitied is the officer who, having been bred to arms in the strict discipline of the British army, is afterwards called to command men who carry with them the spirit of freedom into the field. The continental army was continental in name and pay, but in no other respect: divisions between colonies and between regiments within a colonial unit, plus problems with periods of enlistment and desertions and pretended illness—all this characterized the army under Montgomery's command, not to mention its being in a strange, harsh land. The ideas of liberty and independence which roused the colonists to oppose the claims of Great Britain operated against that implicit obedience which is necessary to a well-regulated army. This added to Montgomery's difficulties in his assignment to secure the affection of the Canadians, because, in order to achieve that goal, he had to restrain the appetites and control the licentiousness of the soldiery at the same time that any appearance of military harshness on his part was dangerous lest the good will of the army might be forfeited. But his military genius overcame obstacles, and he deserves admiration for his goodness of the man as well as for the address of the general.

Meanwhile, away from the usual route, Benedict Arnold's considerable detachment from the American army at Cambridge left in September by a new and unexpected passage to Canada with the hope that a force at Quebec would direct General Carleton, still at Montreal, from the relief of Fort St. John. Arnold's successful operation in reaching Quebec thereby acquired for him the name of the American Hannibal. In an earlier operation, he had gone to Ticonderoga with a commission dated May 3, 1775, from the Massachusetts Council of Safety to take that fort and also the British vessels on the adjacent lakes. From Crown Point, he wrote the Continental Congress on 18 June that he could take Quebec and all of Canada with only 2,000 troops. This was even before the Congress, still striving hard to effect a reconciliation between Great Britain and her colonies, had organized an army or appointed a single military officer. It took three more months, but Arnold's impetuosity of temper paid off by the Congress' approving his importunity on this subject.

Such was the increasing fervor of the public mind in 1775 that what was deemed insolent and dangerous in the early part of the year was, before its close, pronounced not only moderate but expedient. Arnold left Cambridge for Canada with 1,000 troops by ascending the Kennebec River against an impetuous current, cataracts, etc. He then crossed the ridge of mountains which separate New England from Canada and descended the Chandiere to the St. Lawrence River at a point just above Quebec: three hundred miles of uninhabited country, many portages, thick woods, difficult mountains, and craggy precipices. His party sometimes made only four or five miles a day. Some men were so hungry they ate their dogs; one-third returned to Cambridge for want of necessities. After thirty one days of not seeing another human being, Arnold and his men arrived at the inhabited parts of Canada, where they were well-received and supplied liberally. The Canadians were amazed at this force emerging from the wilderness. While moving toward Quebec, Arnold disseminated George Washington's Proclamation to the Canadians assuring that the American troops were there not to plunder but to protect them. He arrived at Point Levi, on the St. Lawrence shore opposite to Quebec, on 8 November.

Only the river now blocked him from then and there taking that fortress capital, whose garrison was unprepared for this unexpected threat. Arnold's instructions included that he be especially tender with the son of Lord Chatham, if he was captured, in return for the great exertions of his father in behalf of American liberty. Carleton, that gallant officer who had tried to oppose Montgomery in the extremes of the Province and therefore not at Quebec, where he now was in command, was taken totally by surprise at Arnold's presence. That American now rounded up canoes from the Canadians, enabling him to cross the river to Quebec without confronting the British ships protecting the city.

[Here ends the History. On Christmas day, Montgomery would be killed, and Arnold wounded, in their joint, unsuccessful assault on the city.]

APPENDIX B

Secretary Livingston's Unsent Analysis of "The Present State of Europe" (December 1781)

Sir,

Presuming as well from the preamble of the resolutions for organizing the department of foreign affairs as from the nature of my appointment that I am not to consider myself as a mere executive officer through whom dispatches are to be forwarded, but that I am to digest such plans with respect to foreign negotiations as I conceive the United States interested in promoting, to submit them to the examination of Congress, to attend their debates, to collect their sentiments and make them the thematic rule of my conduct.

I take the liberty to submit to their examination what I conceive to be the present politics of the leading powers of Europe so far as they may be interested in our affairs, and from them I shall endeavor to draw such deductions as I conceive applicable to our present situation. As I feel the importance of the station in which Congress have done me the honor to place me, I shall not diminish its dignity by a language less free [than] I thought myself entitled to hold while I was honored with a seat in Congress. . . .

As a peace [i.e., a negotiation for peace] will probably be made under the mediation of the Empire and Russia, it must necessarily take its completion from the views and interests of the mediators. The Emperor, not being a maritime power, can have no direct interest in our freedom or dependence except so far as it will alter the balance of power in Europe, and so far unfortunately he is directly engaged against us. The House of

Austria, fallen from the grandeur which made her for a long time the successful rival of France by the mutilation of the low countries and the translation of the crown of Spain to the House of Bourbon, has gradually lost its power and, changing places with England, has permitted her to become a power of the first order and of course to be her principal barrier against France, convinced by experience previous to the treaty of [1756 with France] that she [Austria] was unable to cope alone with the power of France. England, then, may be considered as the natural ally of the Emperor. The justice of our cause and the improbability of bringing about a peace upon other terms will induce him to decree in favor of our independence. Yet, we ought to persuade ourselves that he will make that decree as favorable to England as possible and leave her as large a share of this continent as she can show any color to claim to.

Russia, as a commercial nation, can hardly be said to be much interested in our favor. Commerce is not yet so well understood by her as to be a great spring of her politics, nor, if it were, would the similarity between the products of both countries permit her to hope for much trade with us, or free her from the apprehension that we might in some circumstances be considered as rivals. As a naval power, she is . . . engaged against us. Her true interest is to let France and England balance each other, in which case her fleets, although inconsiderable in themselves, . . . could not fail to command respect. That this is not an imaginary idea, I conceive, may fairly be deduced from the part that Russia has taken during the war. England, having in the last two wars and the beginning of this shown an avowed superiority to France at sea, it was the interest of Russia to lessen it without risking her own navy. On this plan, she probably projected the armed neutrality. Upon the same principle, when, by the junction of the fleets of Spain to those of France, and the union of Holland with both, the weight was in the other scale, she offers her mediation to England and Holland and forgoes the honor she might acquire by enforcing her first project of an armed neutrality, it becomes a dead letter, France and Holland complain that it is infringed and England enjoys the benefit of its infraction. But this reasoning still does not go so far as make Russia absolutely indifferent about our independence. She sees the efforts of which England is capable, she knows that in case of a reunion with America and a continental war which would in part divert the resources of France from the support of her navy, Great Britain would resume her ancient superiority and the balance which Russia wishes to hold be snatched from her hands. This will influence her in detaching America from Great Britain but not wholly so. She will leave her [Great Britain] such footing here as will enable her to dispute command of the seas with France. Her concurrence with the Emperor on this point will incline them both to favor every colorable claim Great Britain may lay to territory on this continent.

The United Netherlands have several jarring and delicate interests to manage. As a commercial people, they wish our independence. As possessing colonies, they have an interest in the division of this continent among different powers whose vicinity will make them enemies and keep up a kind of violence in America which will contribute to the security of their colonies. In Europe, they must dread the increasing power of France and labor to prevent the ruin of England. The present state of the United Netherlands, the reluctance with which they entered into the war, the character of those who now (in the words of their reply to the British manifesto) "sight for a peace with their old allies," all mark that the reasoning they hint at has its weight in the United Provinces. This, together with their desire to procure the restoration of their own islands and to indemnify Britain out of lands in America, will induce them to fall in with what I suppose to be the views of the mediators—to wit, to make the States properly so called independent, but to admit every claim of Britain that will lessen their extent and leave the British so much territory as to maintain a degree of rivalry with us on this continent.

The only barrier that Congress have hitherto endeavored to oppose to this . . . is the affection and power of France, to engage which the more firmly, they have thought it wise to repose confidence in her, and rendered the Court of Versailles absolute master of the treaty, so far at least as relates to the . . . territory not within the express limits of the United States. But although we have every reason to rely upon the attachment of France to our cause, of which it has given the most convincing proofs, still I believe Congress will agree with me, that Court favor is too slender a foundation for a great people to build its dearest interest upon. Man and measures may change. Courts have their factions and that France is not without them the removal of Mr. Necker evinces.[451] We ~~are not with-~~ ~~out our enemies at Court~~ have—but the subject is delicate and I waive it. It is upon the interests of nations and not upon adventitious circumstances that we should judge of their measures. The interest and honor of France conspire to render us independent, and we have every assurance which the wisdom and virtue of a great people can afford that they will never lose sight of this important subject. But this last does not perhaps carry her guarantee so far as our claims extend. It may be worthy of consideration to ascertain how far her interest would lead her in supporting them. Upon this, I would venture a few conjectures which I confess to be crude and imperfect as indeed I feel the case with all I have urged. To keep up our aversion for England, to strengthen the connection between this country and France, England must have possessions on the continent; disputed boundaries conspiring with other causes which always operate between neighboring nations will excite enemies and render the protection of France important.[452] The Court of Versailles have discovered their wisdom in slighting possessions on the continent and even refusing to make themselves masters of Canada. The same principle justifies their enlarging the power of Britain; they [the British] should be in some degree formidable to us. France, too, having colonies, is in part, although not wholly, engaged to pursue the same policy as the United Provinces to render their possessions more secure. Interest and ambition both direct her to divide the power of America and to hold the balance. Although this reasoning should be inconclusive, there are, notwithstanding, a variety of others to conduce us to fear that France will not think herself justified in continuing the war for the extension of our western boundary. We are not her only ally, she must recover for the Dutch what the English have taken from them. She had brought the Court of Spain into the war; she must find some equivalent for their expectations. It is not unreasonable to suppose she has engagements of this nature with both. If England loses these States, gives up her possession of them together with the conquests she has made from the Dutch, not only the mediators, but all the belligerent powers will conceive that at least her claims to Louisiana [i.e., east of the Mississippi] should be established, for how just are those we espouse may appear to us, I am fearful that they will not have the same weight with an interested tribunal. I forbear going into an investigation of our right and the plausible argument that may be urged against it. It has frequently been a subject of discussion on the floor of Congress and they have I presume satisfied the members of the reality of their right. But if, as I presume, the greatest possible western extent is an object of some importance to the United States, if the mediating powers are interested in abridging it, if Holland is interested against the extension of our claim, if France is not bound to support it and may even have reasons for rejecting it, if England had every motive for opposing our extension, we, surely, must, if we hope to succeed, oppose them by something more stable than the arguments drawn merely from the justice of our demand. Did Spain hold a part of this territory by our title [here abruptly ends the memorandum].[453]

Notes

ABBREVIATIONS

The following abbreviations are used in the notes to designate frequently cited unpublished collections, libraries and individuals:

BC/NYPL Bancroft Collection at New York Public Library

BF   Benjamin Franklin

B-M   Luzerne's secretary, Barbé-Marbois

FB   Spanish Foreign Minister Floridablanca

G   First French minister to U.S., Gérard

JA   John Adams

JJ/CU   Jay Papers at Columbia University

JJ/NYHS Jay Papers at New York Historical Society

L   Second French minister to U.S., Luzerne

M   France's ambassador to Spain, Montmorin

NYHS   New York Historical Society

O   British negotiator at Paris, Richard Oswald

RL   U.S. Secretary, Foreign Affairs, Robert Livingston

RL/NYHS Livingston Papers at New York Historical Society

V   French Foreign Minister Vergennes

1. Introduction to *Chronicles of the American Revolution*; ed. Alden T. Vaughan; Grosset and Dunlap; New York, 1965.

2. JJ/NYHS. Its use is courtesy of the New-York Historical Society, as is the material contained in Appendix B, which is from RL/NYHS.

3. The 1779 letters of newly arrived B-M give a charming and sympathetic account of the American lifestyle: *Our Revolutionary Forefathers; The Letters of François, Marquis de Barbé-Marbois*; tr. and ed. Eugene P. Chase; Duffield; New York, 1929. B-M's 1829 book on the Louisiana Purchase continues his praise of the U.S. and its people (*Histoire de la Louisiane . . .*, Firmin Didot, Paris).

4. Corberon (St. Petersburg)-V, September 10, 1779 (BC/NYPL, vol. 201): Potemkin said English policy and war strategy only made sense if one sees King George III as trying "to extend his power over his nation."

5. In an exchange with O, his English counterpart, as recorded in the latter's minutes of August 7, 1782 (ibid., vol. 253), Jay charged England with having "taken great advantage of the French" in the Peace of 1763; O retorted that England had acted "entirely on account of America," while France had violated its prior treaty commitments to England, and that the 1763 treaty put the colonies "out of the reach of all farther danger" from the French in Canada and from French-promoted "cruelties by the savages"; Jay answered, "At that time, North America, being considered as part of the British Empire, . . . had an equal title to the protection of government and, therefore, England can't now plead any one merit by way of distinction, so as to have any particular claims on America"; O's private comment was that here he felt Jay fell short of his hope he was a man of "candor and impartiality, regarding objects not strictly American, and so we passed to other subjects."

6. In January 1766, the French embassy at London reported that Chatham (William Pitt) and Shelburne tried, but unsuccessfully, to get Parliament to agree that it only had authority in Great Britain; instead, the government's position won out (ibid., vol. 179).

7. Doniol's *Vergennes . . .*, pp. 26 and 94.

8. V-Beaumarchais, May 2, 1776 (BC/NYPL, vol. 185).

9. BC/NYPL, vol. 183, December 1774. (Also in Doniol's *Histoire*, vol. 1, pp. 2ff. As a general rule, much of the Vergennes correspondence to be cited here in manuscript or transcribed form may also be found in Doniol's work, although, as Bemis's *Rayneval*, p. 82, correctly warns, the reader should use that work with "caution" in view of its tendency to selectivity, including within dispatches.)

10. Per Doniol's *Vergennes* . . . , p. 97, V was de facto prime minister for nearly all his years in Louis XVI's government, "because even though M. de Maurepas had the authority, it was Vergennes who acted."

11. In his debate notes for December 1782 (Library of Congress' *Journals* . . . , vol. 23, pp. 872–75), Madison explains these 1781 appointments as follows: JA, until that time and since 1779, had been the sole U.S. peace negotiator, and "he was personally at variance with the French ministry; his judgment had not the confidence of some, and his impartiality in case of an interference of claims espoused by different quarters of the U.S., the confidence of others; a motion to associate with him two colleagues, to wit, Mr. Franklin and Mr. Jay, had been disagreed to by Congress"; BF having interest in land company claims in territories that would benefit by "repossession" by England, and Jay, "belonging to a state interested in such arrangements as would deprive the U.S. of the navigation of the Mississippi and turn the western trade through New York; and neither of them being connected with the southern states"; therefore came the "idea of having five ministers taken from the whole union"; [Madison added:] "*It was supposed*" that Laurens wouldn't get out of the Tower and Jefferson "would not go" and that "the greater number of ministers, the greater the danger of discords and indiscretions" [emphasis supplied].

12. Aside from the question of BF's physical health, there were other limitations in the discharge of his responsibilities. These were well recognized and reported on by no less a person than his staunch supporter, V, who, in a February 19, 1781, dispatch to L (BC/NYPL, vol. 209), described them as follows: age, love of tranquility and an apathy that at times was "incompatible with his duties." V's purpose, of course, was not to have him replaced but to solicit from Congress the appointment of an energetic senior assistant for him—one was so appointed but was lost at sea en route to France, and BF never did get such a person during the war, opening himself to the charge of nepotism for the hiring of his competent, but young and untrained, grandson for much of that professional role. (Note that BF was not simply older than any of his principal colleagues and counterparts but a *full generation* older than even those who came closest to him in age—only Chatham approximated him, and he was nearly two years younger and would be gone by May 1778, along, incidentally, with Voltaire and Rousseau that same year.)

13. Townshend-O, September 1, 1782 (ibid., vol. 254).

14. Richard Morris, in his *Witness* . . . , pp. 84–85, strongly faults BF

for his poor drafting of this note, saying that it (a) "lacked precision," for example, regarding drying rights and the western boundary to the Mississippi; (b) showed undue deference to the French by relegating the American demand for Canada to the "advisable" category; and (c) needed a "tough-minded lawyer" to plead and "define" the U.S. position more precisely—"Jay was clearly the right man at the right place." This is a difficult argument to sustain. After all, it was by design an informal communication given, with Jay's concurrence, to a still-unaccredited English negotiator, who would receive his commission only the following month. Moreover, the note, in fact, did provide the conceptual framework for the entire negotiation, leading to its successful culmination in the signature of the U.S.-British agreement of November 30, 1782. I will return to this important issue with Morris, because it is illustrative of several that will arise deriving from that historian's perspective on the peace negotiations, a perspective and corresponding analysis akin to those of Bemis before him and driven by a near-uncritical enthusiasm for Jay's (and JA's) performance and a corresponding denigration of the performances of those who often disagreed with Jay, notably BF, RL and, of course, V. Accordingly, it is one of the purposes of the present study to offer explanations of key events that are alternatives to those contained in that standard work on the subject. For example, Morris's *Peacemakers* . . . , p. 290, in claiming that a French-dominated RL flip-flopped within three days in order to water down Congress' claims of a boundary to the Mississippi River, mistakenly attributes an RL message to his friend Gouverneur Morris, of January 10, *1781*, prior to his appointment as secretary, as having been written three days *after* his official letter to BF one year later, on January 7, *1782*. (All Jay correspondence cited here in manuscript form, unless stated otherwise, will be found in JJ/CU; most also are in Morris's two volumes on Jay's papers, *Winning* . . . and the preceding volume *Making* . . . , or in Johnston's *Correspondence*. . . .)

15. Jay's instructions of February 21, 1780, to Carmichael, his secretary while in Spain, were that, in his discussions with the French ambassador at Madrid, he was to be candid and polite, but was not to show "unbounded confidence, which is seldom necessary," and, in his conversations with Spanish officials, was to show "our strong attachment to France, yet so as to avoid permitting [the "people about the Court"] to imbibe an opinion of our being under the direction of any counsels but our own. The former will induce them to think well of our constancy and good faith, the latter our independence and self-respect."

16. By this period, according to some historians, Jay had become a victim of "xenophobia," for example, Hudson's *Minister* . . . , pp. 178–79.

17. Autobiographical Notes: "Committee for Address to the King, appointed 1 October 1774 . . . Committee for Memorial to Colonies and Address to Great Britain, 11 October 1774 . . . Committee for Address to Quebec, 21 October 1774"; "17 October 1777: appointed Chief Justice of the State of New York" [note: this was the same day as Burgoyne's surrender at Saratoga; RL, too, was commissioned on this day as the state's Chancellor]; "December 10, 1778, elected President of Congress." Also, per Jay-President Boudinot, July 25, 1784: Jay left Paris 16 May and Dover 1 June, arriving at New York 24 July. A metaphor may be detected in Jay's having left the U.S. for Europe in October 1779 aboard an American frigate but requiring a French frigate to arrive there, while returning to the U.S. aboard an English packboat.

18. V-L, December 24, 1783 (BC/NYPL, vol. 213). As pointed out by Robert Darnton (*New York Review of Books*, February 28, 2002), in that period, "cosmopolitan" was a pejorative term, which was defined (a) by the Academie Française as "someone who does not adopt any fatherland. A cosmopolitan is not a good citizen"; and (b) by Rousseau's *Social Contract* as someone who "pretends to love the world in order to have the right to love no one."

19. Autobiographical Notes: Jay's grandfather, Auguste Jay (1665–1751), arrived in America in his thirties and, in 1697, married Anne Marie Bayard (1670–1756), a daughter of the son of a sister of Peter Stuyvesant, making John a great great nephew of that former New York Governor. Auguste's younger brother, Pierre, was killed at the Boyne, in 1690, fighting with William III against James II. Jay's father, Peter (1704–82), was an only son; he married Mary Van Cortlandt in 1728.

20. Morris's *Seven* . . . frequently observes in one way or another that all of the Founding Fathers were revolutionary elitists. That work lists the following as Founding Fathers: BF, Washington, JA, Jefferson, Jay, Madison, and Hamilton; while Ellis's *Founding Brothers* lists six of the above—all but Jay—and adds Abigail Adams and Aaron Burr.

21. Autobiographical Notes: "1786: Elected President of New York Society for Promoting the Manumission of Slaves."

22. Doniol's *Vergennes* . . . , pp. 86–87: Although a "faithful Christian," V's diplomatic work was "absolutely free in all its extent to meet the needs of the moment or to achieve the stated objective." Thus, he opposed any Spanish tendency to return to the Inquisition; and he suc-

ceeded in convincing Louis XVI to return the Protestants to civil status. Per Hennin, he was a *philosophe*, who "never wavered in his view of the necessity to remedy the disastrous decision by Louis XIV to revoke the Edict of Nantes by giving civil status to non-Catholics. . . . He couldn't conceive of being a Christian and a Frenchman without also desiring to see that considerable portion of his compatriots, subjects of the same monarch, no longer having to choose between living under humiliating conditions or becoming expatriates." V's efforts, Doniol concludes, helped these 3 million Frenchmen get their liberty "twenty years earlier than otherwise would have been the case." In still another parallel with Jay, it was V's interest in orderly record-keeping that led him in 1779 to establish a filing system that, for the first time, made the ministry a real "department." Jay did the same as postwar secretary. Furthermore, (a) what the *Dictionary of American Biography* (Scribner; New York, 1928–) says of John Jay might also apply to Vergennes: "Jay was a very able man but not a genius"; and (b) each of the two readily confessed a lack of expertise in military matters.

23. O'Callaghan's *Documents . . .* , vol. 8, pp. 349ff: Governor Tryon–Secretary of State, Dartmouth, February 7, 1773: re: "partition line" between New York and New Jersey: "Mr. Jay, clerk to the Commission, [is] refusing to deliver up the Commission and papers unless authorized by an express order of the Crown under the great Seal, or act of the [New York] Legislature," because of moneys he feels are due him. Dartmouth-Tryon, April 10, 1773: "I do not well see on what ground it was, that Mr. Jay had his doubts as to the delivery of the Commission and the proceeding thereupon. . . . I am to presume, however, from the step taken by the Legislature [to meet his demands], that there was some foundation in law for those doubts; . . . *I hope that the final confirmation by the Crown will not meet with any further obstruction from Mr. Jay"* [emphasis supplied].

24. Actually, Jay's opening demand at Paris was for a parliamentary act acknowledging U.S. independence or, failing that, a Royal Proclamation.

25. For orders of magnitude, note that the £5 million equated to over 110 million French livres, or at least half of the annual value of France's international trade, including with its own colonies. That amount also represented about half of total British foreign trade. By 1772, America's overall commercial debt to British suppliers amounted to as much as £41 million (*The Transformation of Early American History*; ed. J.A. Henretta; Knopf; New York, 1991).

26. BC/NYPL, vol. 180.

27. Ibid.

28. BC/NYPL, vol. 182.

29. BC/NYPL, vol. 181; Doniol's *Vergennes* . . . , p. 26.

30. BC/NYPL, vol. 181.

31. V-M, October 6, 1782 (BC/NYPL, vol. 199).

32. Brecher's *Losing* . . . , pp. 8, 32, 129.

33. V-M, October 6, 1782.

34. Also called by his own people "Frederic the Unique."

35. B-M to RL, May 17, 1781: "Maria-Theresa's death [1780] had given France reason to fear a land war, even though its earlier fears about the European situation had dissipated; but now the French again have 'our hands free, and this country will enjoy our attention' " (RL/NYHS—all future citations of RL's correspondence will relate to this source unless specified otherwise).

36. Brecher's *Losing* . . . , pp. 174–76 and 179.

37. Ibid., p. 88.

38. BC/NYPL, vol. 180.

39. Dull's *French Navy* . . . makes a series of factual errors regarding events prior to the American War of Independence. Illustratively (pp. 8, 9, 16, 18, 78, 143): that Prussia was a "great" state alongside Austria at the signing of Westphalia (Prussia only became so in the next century); that the 1761 Family Pact between France and Spain obliged each reciprocally to provide the other, if attacked, twenty ships-of-the-line (the actual number was twelve, plus six frigates); that England "captured Belle-Ile off Brittany" in 1759 (it was actually in 1761); that England's 1755 naval actions against France in a time of peace targeted "the Newfoundland fishing fleet" (in fact, they were much broader than that, having included attacks on French warships and, under Admiral Hawke operating in European waters, having swept up the French trade); and that English treaty rights to prevent fortification of Dunkirk only dated from 1763 (copying the error on this point by Bemis's *Hussey* . . . , p. 6, which perhaps also accounts for Meng's similar error in his error-prone *The Comte de Vergennes; European Phases of His American Diplomacy*; Catholic University; Washington D.C., 1932; p. 24—in fact, French restrictions at Dunkirk stem from the Utrecht Treaty, while the treaty of 1763 merely confirms its provisions regarding that port).

40. Garniér (London)-V, November 30, 1774 (BC/NYPL, vol. 183).

41. Choiseul-Chatelet, October 12, 1768 (ibid., vol. 181). Compare

these French statements (a) with the more candid one made by V, in his message of November 12, 1782, to M, that the only reason France had occupied and retained Corsica was to deprive England of it (ibid., vol. 199); and (b) with Jay's use at Paris of the French seizure of Corsica and their 1782 military intervention in Geneva to help put down a popular uprising as examples of why the U.S. should not put its negotiating interests into French hands.

42. July 18, 1769 (ibid., vol. 182).

43. July 15, 1768 (ibid., vol. 181).

44. As reported by Choiseul to Chatelet on December 20, 1768, and February 6, 1769 (ibid., vol. 181).

45. Choiseul-Chatelet, October 12, 1768; Guines-d'Aiguillon, June 24, 1772 (ibid., vol. 183). V's future nemesis as England's ambassador to France, Stormont, also was described, soon after his arrival at post in 1773, as following a "friendly policy which all the more merits our confidence" in England (D'Aiguillon-Guines, April 4, 1773—ibid.).

46. Guines-d'Aiguillon, December 27, 1772 (ibid., vol. 183).

47. Garniér-V, January 8, 1775: England's "biggest fear" is the colonial desire "to be free of the laws restraining their freedom of commerce" (ibid., vol. 183).

48. For example, a royal instruction to Conway, Secretary of State, Northern Department, on August 11, 1765 (ibid., vol. 82), included: (a) England's having taken a French fishing boat off Newfoundland is likely to lead to a French complaint; there is no way England has troops enough to block French settlers on Newfoundland, as it has "more places to garrison than we have troops to supply"; (b) therefore, "make France observe ["this and every other article of our treaties"] strictly, but don't hurt its honor, which is more important to the French than their interest"; and (c) note "how very unable we are at this hour to make war." Fully consistent with this propensity to downplay the military factor in his relations with other nations, George, in 1782 (*Letters . . .* , p. 150), would almost alone strongly prefer that England, notwithstanding its recent success in warding off a major Bourbon attack on Gibraltar, cede that "accursed fortress" back to Spain in favor of having a purely commercial port at Minorca from which to facilitate and protect English trade in the Mediterranean.

49. Also note that Guines reported to V, August 20, 1775, that George had degarrisoned Hanover, and he "doesn't any longer have the same

feeling" of hatred for Frederic II as did his predecessor (BC/NYPL, vol. 184).

50. D'Aiguillon-Garniér, March 27, 1774 (ibid., vol. 183).

51. Per Guines-D'Aiguillon, March 23, 1773 (ibid., vol. 183). Choiseul, while sharing the French concern over that Englishman's domestic leadership skills in the service of his anti-Bourbon policies, nevertheless, as regards his diplomatic skills, said that "he was the worst major statesman in Europe" and that "I would rather go row on the King's galley ships" than once again to have to negotiate a peace with him (Brecher's *Losing* . . . , p. 171; also see pp. 106–7 and 146).

52. BC/NYPL, vol. 185. Garniér-V, March 20, 1775: Chatham was using the excuse of the gout to stay away from the House of Lords; his real reason was that "he's awaiting developments in America. He has undoubtedly given his instructions to the ablest man the Americans have here, Dr. Franklin, who has left today for . . . Philadelphia" but has "promised to return in October" (ibid., vol. 184).

53. Noailles-V, ibid., vol. 187; and V-Noailles: The Bavaria problem [see below] is "secondary" and "England is our primary . . . " (ibid.).

54. Doniol's *Vergennes* . . . , p. 10: V "seems to have been affiliated with this veiled service from the start of his career, probably starting prior to his 1750 appointment as Minister to the Elector of Treves." (He had begun his diplomatic career around 1741, spending some ten years in Portugal.)

55. Per ibid., p. 32: It was the count de Broglio who reportedly was the one to suggest to Louis XVI's court V as foreign minister.

56. For examples of de Kalb's reporting to Broglio in 1776 and 1777: BC/NYPL, vol. 203. For Washington as "murderer," see Brecher's *Losing* . . . , pp. 47ff.

57. Doniol's *Vergennes* . . . , pp. 34–36: Hennin vice Gerard, May 14, 1778, but with Gerard's younger brother, Rayneval, taking over American affairs in the Political Department. Hennin was a former secretary of Broglio. V in 1775 had obtained the court's approval for Hennin to marry a Protestant in Geneva. Hennin's appointment was made permanent when Gerard, back in France, left the ministry; he kept it until 1787. Re: d'Eon: V-Garniér, June 23, 1775 (BC/NYPL, vol. 184).

58. For an account of the political importance of the "parliaments," see Brecher's *Losing* . . . , pp. 36–43.

59. BC/NYPL, vol. 192.

60. Garniér-V, January 23, 1775 (ibid., vol. 183).

61. Ibid., vol. 184.

62. Ellis's *Founding Brothers*, pp. 136–38, which described the Franco-American alliance as having "been so instrumental in gaining French military assistance for the winning of the American Revolution." Predictably, Jefferson (an "infamous act, which is really nothing more than a treaty of alliance between England and the Anglomen of this country") and Madison (it was due to "the exertions of Aristocracy, Anglicism, and Mercantilism") were in the forefront of critics of Jay's treaty.

63. Jay to Charles Thomson, April 23, 1781.

64. Monaghan's *Jay* . . . , pp. 60–61. Even as he wrote that appeal, Jay was ambivalent enough to have been dickering with London over a possible appointment as a judge (Morris's *Seven* . . . , pp. 166 and 260–61). On the other hand, Jay's son, William, proudly points out in his biography (vol. 1, p. 30) that Jay was the youngest of the members of the first Continental Congress (and the one who survived all the rest).

65. As discussed in a Jay-drafted message of July 10, 1776, from the New York Convention to Congress, there was a related religious issue: How, with "propriety," to expunge from the *Book of Common Prayer* those parts that "interfere with the interest of the American cause. . . . It is a subject we are afraid to meddle with—the enemies of America having taken great pains to insinuate into the minds of the Episcopalians that the Church was in danger. We could wish the Congress would pass some resolve to quell their fears." In 1777, Jay made an unsuccessful effort to install a political loyalty test for all those of the Roman Catholic faith seeking public office. Finally, of incidental interest, is his letter of July 14, 1780, to New York Governor George Clinton: "A late resolution of Congress recommends the naturalization of French subjects agreeable to the articles of Treaty [of February 6, 1778]—this strikes me as a measure which requires some caution. I would have every article of the treaty fully complied with, but I am not clear that American Protestants are intended to be naturalized in France, except as to certain purposes. This I think should be precisely known and be made the standard of immunities to be granted by us to them."

66. Letter to Timothy Matlack of September 17, 1780, thanking the American Philosophical Society for having made him a member.

67. Jay elaborated on his elitist, but increasingly merit-oriented, social views in the following letter of March 24, 1784, to Benjamin Vaughan:

They who know the nature of man expect perfection nowhere. There are certain degrees in refinement and art which are more favorable than others to those principles and manners which wise men prefer. In this as well as some other circumstances, we [Americans] have the advantage of other countries. Various causes conspire to give every man his weight, and I believe the old maxim of *quisque sera labor est fortune* has fewer exceptions in America than elsewhere. They who bring with them ideas borrowed from the regions of fancy and romance will be disappointed. The golden age will not cease to be a fable until the millennium. Until that period for separating life from death, pleasure from pain, virtue from vice, and wisdom from folly, every society and country will continue to partake more or less of the heterogeneous and discordant principles which seem to be the seeds both of moral and natural evil. Were I in your situation, I would see for myself and then determine.

68. Guines (London)-V, July 28, 1775 (BC/NYPL, vol. 184).

69. A good illustration of Jay's concern for his father, and its intimate connection with his religious stoicism, was his reaction to an "offer" from General Schuyler, soon after the victory at Saratoga of October 1777, to move the Jay family to a farm on his property near that battle site. Jay's 11 December letter to Schuyler thanked him for the offer and said he would consider it: "This place, at which all the family now reside [the New York highlands along the Hudson River at Fishkill], is by no means agreeable or convenient, if secure, which is also doubtful." Jay next wrote Schuyler on 26 February declining the opportunity to be his "Saratoga neighbor," because he thought it ill-advised to move his ill father (that same month, he would write to Sarah regarding his father: "It gives me pain to be so long and so often absent from him"). Later, while he was serving in Spain, the family home indeed would be briefly occupied and ransacked by a gang of marauders, who fortunately refrained from harming the Jays. The same lack of security would apply to the New Jersey home at Elizabethtown of his wife's family; it was partly burned by enemy troops in February 1779, at which time Jay consolingly wrote his sister-in-law, Catharine Livingston, perhaps in a less than candid way, that "my family as well as myself have met with so many similar losses. ... They never have and I hope never will cost me an hour's sleep. Perseverance in doing what we think right, and resignation to the dispensations of the Governor of the world, offer a shield against the darts of this sort of affliction to everybody that will use it."

70. In Jay-RL, February 25, 1776, Elizabethtown, NJ, he says he's been with Sarah ever since leaving Congress—childbirth (24 January) and

"rheumatism" have damaged her health; and May 29, 1776, Fishkill: Sarah is now well enough "to leave her room. . . . I have been so disturbed by the ill health of my wife and parents." That Sarah would begin to have a lifelong struggle with depression is illustrated by Jay's letter to her sister, Catharine, on February 27, 1779, from Philadelphia, where he still had not been able to make arrangements for Sarah to join him (she would the next month): Sarah's "want of spirits is an unfortunate circumstance, and it gives me the more pain as it results from a cause [Jay's absence] in which I am so nearly concerned."

71. A medical doctor by training (Edinburgh University), Sir James also was inventor of a process for corresponding in invisible ink that was used in 1776 by Silas Deane in reporting from France to the Continental Congress through John Jay in New York. One reason he was suspected of being a Loyalist was his having "imprudently" gone to Elizabethtown, New Jersey, where he was taken prisoner by the English (RL-Jay, April 20, 1782). In that status, he made his way to England, where Secretary of State Townshend, in a letter of 11 October to O, complained that he had been in London "for some months" and "treated by us with common civility," but, as an "indifferent man," he was "in great disgust with us all, . . . having been kept here at a considerable expense, to which I am at a loss to know how he is entitled." Townshend went on to warn O that Sir James was now planning a trip to the continent, where he may have "ill designs" at England's expense (Stevens's *Facsimiles . . .* , vol. 24, document 2105). Sir James did go on to Versailles trying to sell to the government his "proposal and plans of maritime warfare." In a letter of January 18, 1783, to Vergennes, signed as "Le Chevalier Jay," he wrote (in French): "It is certain that the measures I proposed would be highly injurious" to any target and "could be executed by England as well as by France. [Therefore,] I hastened to France" to warn it. Sir James then pleaded with V to have L tell that to the Congress. Exactly one week later, Sir James would write V once again to urge him to instruct L to write the Congress and also the governor of New York to attest that he, Sir James, was attached "to his country" and that the French government has had "great and decided proofs of his zeal for the interest of America and the common cause. . . ." (Stevens, who wrongly gives 1782 as the year of these two letters, notes that there is no record of V having written to L on Sir James's request.) One cannot but observe that John Jay, too, would act sternly in defense of his personal financial interests, as in the above-cited instance of his contest of wills with the government in 1773

regarding money due him as clerk to the New York–New Jersey boundary commission.

72. A letter Jay wrote on September 17, 1782, to an old friend, Peter Van Schaack, reveals the intensity of his feelings regarding Sir James: "You mention my brother—if after having made so much bustle in and for America, he has (as is surmised) improperly made his peace with Britain, I shall endeavor to forget that my father had such a son." Earlier in that letter, and further to his views on Loyalists as outlined to FB in 1780 (noted above), Jay drew a distinction between two types of Loyalists, a distinction that would guide him throughout the war and the peace negotiations—that is, those who sided with England due to "principles" of reason and those who did so "not from any such principles," but "from the most dishonorable of human motives, taking up arms against us," and thus betraying a "conduct of a piece with their inducements, for they have outstripped savages in perfidy and cruelty." As for the estrangement between Jay and Sir James, John in Paris wrote his younger brother, Frederick, on April 6, 1783: "James is here but has not visited us." On 17 July, he would write G. Morris that "Sir James is here, yet why I don't know." In early 1784, Sir James would object, in writing, to the way Jay was taking the lead for the family in settling a modest inheritance of £1,000 due to the brothers from a distant relative who had lived and died in England, which Jay was visiting in part to settle the affair, which turned out to be thornier and more time-consuming than he had expected or wished. (Notwithstanding the above mention, Sir James was in sufficiently good standing with the family to have helped medically attend Governor Livingston at his death in 1791.)

73. As he wrote from France in 1784 to his son in America: "The Bible is the best of all books . . . regulate your life by its precepts." On the death of his daughter in 1780, he wrote RL (6 October): "You see I have not left my philosophy or rather my Christianity behind me" (JJ/CU). Morris's *Seven . . .* , pp. 269–70, describes Jay as the most religiously orthodox of the Founding Fathers.

74. As Montgomery's "only surviving executor," RL's duties included obtaining a signed receipt from Mary Almar of Quebec, dated December 26, 1776, for a payment from him of £2-2-6 for "one month's washing" in Montgomery's service. Earlier that year, on 15 August, RL's mother wrote to urge him, as a "civil," to let others "be exposed to the fire" of our enemies: "I hear you are to be with General Washington. . . . Oh, my dear child, consider your situation with respect to myself and

my other children [Henry was a colonel in the continental army and John, too, was in the service, although he soon would leave it to make his way in business at Boston, from which place he would frequently plead for Livingston's political influence in obtaining contracts and appointments]. . . . Do not expose yourself needlessly," as your country and your family have "need of your counsel." Henry, too, would press his brother to use his influence with Washington and the Congress to obtain choice military assignments for him.

75. For extracted examples: (a) to RL on February 25, 1776: "Amusement and exercise ought to be your objects . . . go to the camp, [or] to Philadelphia, in short anywhere, so that you are but moving"; (b) to his wife, still in New Jersey, the next month: "Go riding, play shuttlecock—don't be negligent of exercise"; and (c) again to RL, in March 1776: "My parents' impending death and your distress have occasioned more gloomy ideas in my mind than it has ever before been the subject of—despondency ill-becomes a man—it gives me consolation to reflect that . . . our great and benevolent creator will (if I please) be my guide through this vale of tears to our eternal and blessed habitation."

76. Autobiographical Notes: October 23, 1768: "Admitted to the Bar."

77. Ibid.: "1770: Partnership with RRLivingston dissolved." Re RL per RL/NYHS: King's College Diploma, 1768, "B.A"; "Marriage Contract, Mary Stevens, April 24, 1770." While the cause of the law partnership's dissolution is not made clear in either the Jay Papers or the RL Papers, or in their biographies, one cannot but conjecture that it is related in some way to the change in circumstances created by RL's marriage that same year.

78. Of a piece with this sentiment of friendship is Jay's letter of November 19, 1780, to Robert Morris (JJ/CU): "There are some hearts which, like feathers, stick to everyone they touch and quit each with equal ease. Mine is not of this kind. It adheres to ['but'] few, but it takes strong hold."

79. RL wrote B-M, August 24, 1781, that he wished he "could think so favorably of [his election] as you appear to do. The subject is new to me . . . and foreign to the line in which my studies have lain." Bemis's *Rayneval* . . . , p. 85, goes so far as to say that (1) "we now know that the Secretary of Foreign Affairs in the continental congress owed his office to the French Minister at Philadelphia, La Luzerne"; and (2) because the congressional instructions of June 15, 1781, to Jay et al. as peace commissioners "were insinuated by" L "at Vergennes' orders, . . . I say, we

can only applaud the action taken by the American Commissioners in violating their instructions and in signing, without consulting France, the preliminary and conditional [actually, the more accurate and significant word is "provisional"] articles of November 30, 1782."

80. That Jay, particularly during the early phase of the Revolutionary War, was as much a "New Yorker" as an "American," and caught up as much as anyone in regional jealousies, is clear from the strength of his views regarding the Vermont issue and also regarding other matters, such as the following letter (JJ/CU) he drafted for the New York Convention, which sent it to the Congress on July 10, 1776 stating: (1) New York was upset at the Congress' usurping its right to nominate military officers; and (2) Congress' use of "the necessity of the case" was an ancient argument that was both a fruitful and a dangerous "source of power" because it destroys the "fruits of patriotism and public spirit. . . . We shall ever be ready (however calumniated by individuals [read, New Englanders] whose censure we consider as praise) to risk our lives and fortunes in supporting the common cause."

81. However, under the pressure of war-related issues, Jay's relations even with his closest friends would become tense, as when RL on September 10, 1778 (RL/NYHS), wrote to G. Morris: "[Y]ou mistake me wildly, if you think there is any coolness between us, though I have found myself sometimes a little hurt by his dogmatic manner and incommunicableness," to which Morris responded on 22 September: "Your tempers are so very different that you will make the best friends in the world. You are too lazy, he is too proud. He is too hasty, you too inattentive to the public offices. Shall I go on? No. With all the faults both of you have, I have as many as both of you together. You both pardon me. Therefore you must pardon each other"; and, as when Hamilton, who had first met Jay as a teenager staying briefly in William Livingston's home during the period of Jay's courtship of Sarah, would, according to Madison's Notes, say of him openly on the floor of the Congress on March 19, 1783: "[A]lthough he was a man of profound sagacity and pure integrity, yet he was of a suspicious temper, and . . . this trait might explain the extraordinary jealousies which he professed [the subject matter was the French role in the peace negotiations and Jay's having kept from them a secret paragraph concerning the boundary of northern Florida in the 30 November Anglo-American agreement—to be discussed below]" (United States' *Journals . . .*, vol. 25, pp. 932–33). This episode and its aftermath, including a congratulatory Hamilton-

Jay letter, prompted Richard Morris to describe Hamilton as "Janus-faced" (*Seven* . . . , p. 253).

82. Letter to Henry Brockholst Livingston, Sarah's brother, February 21, 1781 (JJ/CU). Incidentally, Jay, while in Spain, bought "two pistols." (He did not fight a duel there, but Brockholst did!)

83. Brecher's *Losing* . . . , pp. 59–60.

84. Weymouth-Grantham (Madrid), January 17, 1777: The government will ask Parliament "for leave to grant letters of marque," because without that authority, there was no incentive for private "vessels of force" to capture ships attacking their ships, in that those prizes "become a droit of Admiralty, and they would not be benefited by the prize. . . . The government of France has been told of this plan and do not object" (BC/NYPL, vol. 240).

85. Ibid., vol. 191.

86. V-Noailles, July 19 and August 2, 1777 (ibid., vol. 186).

87. V's dispatch to Des Noyens (The Hague), April 25, 1776, concisely summarizes the basic French policy: (1) "Our ports are open to all nations without distinction; we won't block access to any so long as they conform to the laws and to common practices; we won't issue any special proclamations restricting American ships' entrance. All who show up flying the English flag is given a good welcome and is well treated"; (2) France will not allow any "recruitment or collecting of arms or munitions of war"; (3) France was perfectly neutral and will not "at all contribute to the oppression of the Americans"; and (4) France would not permit anything that could justly be criticized by the English, nor will France offer its good offices without a request from both sides (ibid., vol. 201).

88. England's argument would be: American privateers are "pirates" because, by international law, "only a sovereign state" can issue by its "supreme authority" a "commission" to a "captor," who otherwise is a "pirate," and whose prizes must be freed and returned to owners by countries into whose ports those prizes are brought. England defined a "sovereign state" as one "whose political existence is admitted and acknowledged by other sovereigns." As early as June 21, 1776, in a dispatch to the embassy in London, V wrote: (1) England was assuming that France was doing what it would do and, therefore, that France was selling to America; accordingly, it was taking it for granted that all French ships were carrying English-defined contraband, whereas "our policy" is that anyone could come and trade with France; and (2) as regards the congressional resolution of April 16 opening all American ports, that

would be too risky for France's traders; what was more interesting was the Congress' having authorized privateers to attack English ships worldwide—France was certain to have a difficult problem once the Americans brought English prizes into its ports (ibid., vol. 185).

89. Ibid., vol. 183. The embassy's chargé d'affaires, Garniér, buttressed his analysis of England's policy of avoiding warfare with France by asserting, in a dispatch of March 3, 1775: England was "genuinely" friendly toward France; otherwise it would have informed France that the American situation was worse than it is, forcing it to send in large number of forces; and that would have given it cover for having on hand there a sufficiently powerful military presence to enable it to conquer French possessions in the Americas; in fact, the only error the English were trying to induce France into was that of believing the American situation is not really serious—"they fear that, otherwise, France's envy would lead it into a policy of taking advantage of England."

90. Ibid., vol. 239.

91. V-Garniér, February 16, 1775 (ibid., vol. 183).

92. Ibid., vol. 184. That V sincerely feared an eventual English attack is suggested by his correspondence with Louis XVI (Hardman and Price's *Louis XVI* . . . , p. 57).

93. Garniér-V, April 12, 1776 (ibid., vol. 185).

94. V-Guines, August 7, 1775, reported that: the King approved his suggestion regarding Bonvouloir; although Versailles had no record of his alleged military service in the navy, it trusted Guines's judgment; it was especially important that Bonvouloir receive only oral instructions, which should include his telling the Americans that, contrary to what the English were insinuating to them, there was no need to fear France; and that, as "Canada is the focal point of the concern they have regarding us," France "has no ambitions at all there [except to leave it in *English* hands!]" (ibid., vol. 184).

95. Bonvouloir's reporting on these meetings, starting December 28, 1775, provides the first appearance of Jay's name in French diplomatic correspondence; also, on March 11, 1776, the French embassy in London described Jay, along with BF, as among "the most accredited" of the fifty-plus members of Congress, "all of whom are of superior quality" (ibid., vol. 185). Morris's *Witness* . . . , p. 76, erroneously already places Silas Deane in Paris while Bonvouloir was in Philadelphia in 1775.

96. V-Garniér, March 17 and 24, 1776 (BC/NYPL, ibid., vol. 185).

97. Ibid., vol. 240.

98. Ibid., vol. 184.

99. Ibid., vol. 191. St. Domingue would, indeed, prove to be a "cemetary" in 1802 for a Napoleon army tragically commanded by his brother-in-law, General Leclerc.

100. Ibid., vol. 192.

101. Ossun-V, March 31, 1777 (ibid., vol. 192).

102. V-Garniér, June 15, 1776 (ibid., vol. 185). For Ferdinand VI's inertia, see Brecher's *Losing* . . . , pp. 76, 147, 162 and 166. Also note Jay's letter of September 28, 1781, to G. Morris: "The King means well but knows nothing."

103. Summary by V's ministry of recent correspondence with Spain regarding the American War, dated August 17, 1778 (BC/NYPL, vol. 194).

104. Bourgoing (Madrid)-Rayneval, May 25, 1778 (ibid., vol. 192). For a possible additional motive for Bourbon aid in 1776, one relating to Spain's conflict with Portugal, see Hardman and Price's *Louis XVI* . . . , p. 54.

105. V-Ossun, January 4, 1777 (ibid., vol. 192).

106. Ibid.

107. Approximate population figures available to V were (in millions): British America, 3; Great Britain, 11 (England/Wales, 7; Scotland, 1.5; Ireland, 2.5). The French in 1776 estimated that, in the Seven Years' War, "20,000 American sailors were incorporated in the royal navy," and, therefore, England, in its current war against America had lost one-fourth of its naval manpower pool; moreover, if England were to fight and defeat France and Spain, it would not only have to make up that one-fourth, but also find an additional one-fourth, that is, one-half of its Seven Years' War total. As for the quality of the German mercenaries being recruited by England, the French embassy at The Hague reported in February 1776 that "the methods were harsh and resembled the chasing of animals trying to escape into the forest" (ibid., vol. 201).

108. Ibid., vol. 184.

109. V-Guines, August 7 and December 3, 1775 (ibid., vols. 184–85).

110. V-Garniér (ibid., vol. 185).

111. Memorandum to the king, July 23, 1777 ("January or February," 1778, "is the period beyond which France and Spain would only regret having neglected not taking the opportunity"); and V-Noailles, August 9, 1777 (ibid., vols. 192 and 186).

112. Ibid., vol. 193. This is still another example of the remarkable, as

well as politically useful, similarity in thinking between V and Choiseul about English intentions. Choiseul was still very actively pressing from provincial exile for a return to the political arena as a replacement for V; Marie-Antoinette, whose marriage he had arranged, was his main hope for achieving this.

113. For examples: Garniér (London)-V, July 26, 1776 (ibid., vol. 185); *Considerations* memorandum of August 1776 (ibid., vol. 186); Vauguyon (The Hague)-V, March 10, 1777 (ibid., vol. 201); memorandum to the king, July 23, 1777 (ibid., vol. 192); V-M, December 27, 1777 (ibid., vol. 192); and V-FB, January 20, 1778 (ibid., vol. 193).

114. Vauguyon-V, March 10, 1777 (ibid., vol. 201). That this threat was at least a plausible one in the contemporary view and not an artificial creation of V's is clear from comments made during the widely reported debates in both houses of the Parliament and from various English documents as well. For example, the French Foreign Ministry obtained a copy of a letter from a New York–based British military officer, dated May 24, 1777, and addressed to an official in London, urging that if the rebels held out that upcoming campaign, England should make them its allies and turn on the French for having caused them, by their support (such as the recently arrived French ships in U.S.-controlled ports "notoriously laden by an agent of the French Court"—read Beaumarchais), to reject all of England's peace proposals (ibid.).

115. See Appendix A.

116. Garniér (London) on May 17 and 24, 1776 (BC/NYPL, vol. 185), was reporting that as many as five of the thirteen colonies were "against independence" (citing only Georgia, North Carolina, Maryland, New Jersey, and Pennsylvania—with Virginia "still debating" the issue).

117. Jay-N.Y. congressional delegation, May 29, 1776. Jay would write FB on April 28, 1780 (JJ/CU) that, prior to the Declaration of Independence, the American goal was "redress of grievances;" but that, after July 4, the Americans were more united than ever before.

118. JA-BF, August 25, 1781 (BC/NYPL, vol. 211). If anyone met Jacques Barzun's definition of a person suffering from "the Octopus Complex" it was JA, who cheerfully spread ink at random whenever attacked (e.g., by Secretary RL).

119. Guines's dispatch of September 8, 1775 (ibid., vol. 184), regarding the congressional petition to the king of 5 July, "proposes nothing and could only have the goal of having itself rejected." (This Petition was drafted by John Dickinson and endorsed by Jay, who had written his

own, even more conciliatory draft, which Congress rejected in favor of Dickinson's.) Also see Appendix A.

120. Garniér, on May 31, 1776 (ibid.), sent a copy of *Common Sense* to Versailles along with his opinion that it was written by BF, and not Sam Adams, as others were saying. On October 25, 1778, G would write V that the "famous pamphlet," *Common Sense*, which had heavily contributed to the passage of the Declaration of Independence, was written by Paine, who had been brought to America by BF (ibid., vol. 204).

121. Jay also was absent from Philadelphia from 7 January to 2 March, mainly to be at Elizabethtown with his wife and firstborn child.

122. For example, see Morris's *Making . . .* , pp. 12–13.

123. BC/NYPL, vol. 186.

124. For the memorandum of January 5, 1777: ibid., vol. 203.

125. An early and important reflection of this new Spanish posture was contained in FB's major policy statement to V of August 8, 1777 (ibid., vol. 192), which was a response to the latter's own proposals of the previous month (based on a memorandum to the king of 23 July— ibid.) urging the setting of a "firm" date (i.e., January or February 1778) for a Bourbon entrance into the American War. FB's position was a flat-out rejection with attendant arguments as to why Spain will basically go its own way vis-à-vis the English and the rebelling colonies. In the face of this statement, V nevertheless continued to encourage the Americans into thinking that a Spanish accession to the looming Franco-American alliance was within the realm of possibilities; indeed, that it was a likelihood.

126. Beaumarchais's meeting with the king was on September 22, 1775, per his letter of that date to V (ibid., vol. 185). That letter advised that he gave the king a report on the "exact situation of men and things in England," and that he offered to fill in the gap pending the government's completion of its preparations for war.

127. In another of that remarkable series of overlapping American policies between Choiseul and his otherwise antagonistic successor, V, a near-identical proposal (minus the arms element) had come to Choiseul in the late 1760s from a private French businessman. It was long and seriously considered before being dropped on grounds that its main, if not sole, beneficiary would be the businessman himself. Beaumarchais, too, would not be immune from the profit motive and would press the U.S. Congress for alleged debts to his company (eventually partly paid to Beaumarchais's descendants decades later).

128. For example, in London, to Arthur Lee in spring 1776, in explanation of why he could not agree with Lee's request for military engineers as well as supplies (ibid., vol. 185).

129. This note of 2 May (ibid.) was in response to Beaumarchais's plaintive letter from London of 12 April complaining that it was almost a year since their plan of aid to America had first been elaborated and urging V to press the king for a positive decision, given that the proposal would have a great return for France without risking a war and, moreover, would end up with France getting its money back, one way or another, after the American conflict. V's 2 May added: The lack of French actions should not be taken by Beaumarchais as a rejection. Beaumarchais's relieved reply of 11 May: "You have given me renewed hope," and consequently he was returning quickly to France. (He left London only in mid-June.)

130. Beaumarchais-V, July 25, 1776 (ibid., vol. 186) observed that he had "two theaters in Paris, two credits at the Court; one is to raise the spirits of men of letters, the other to create the means for useful activities." (As put by Jean Meyer in his *La France Moderne: The Barber of Seville* and *The Marriage of Figaro* [1784] "announce . . . the end of a world" in their "ferocious" and informed criticism of contemporary French society.)

131. RL, writing Washington's aide-de-camp, Alexander Hamilton, from the militarily beleaguered Kingston, New York, on April 2, 1777 (RL/NYHS): "We are happy to hear of the arrival of the vessel with arms from France, as no supply can be more necessary." Per Beaumarchais's letter to V of July 25, 1776, he that day met Deane, and "the two of us are working well together. . . . Have you arranged for the cannons I want? . . . I'll also be needing the cooperation of the Spanish ambassador." For his part, Deane had already written to V's senior assistant, G, on 22 July (BC/NYPL, vol. 203) informing that, as he had asked, "I shall apply to [Beaumarchais] in preference to any other person."

132. As early as April 1774, while in England on military leave under the name of "Chevalier de Moustier," Lafayette showed a strong interest in American events. He wrote Versailles on the fifth of that month (ibid., vol. 183) asking for an extension of leave until the end of the parliamentary session he was observing, because English-American problems were offering an important opportunity for France to weaken England. Lafayette continued: his regiment was at quarters and divided, and England was in danger of being wiped out as a major power by the loss of North America—this was not a civil war, but one in which "a nation is arising

and is exercising nascent power" against a nation "approaching its de-
cadence."

133. After the battle of Brandywine, in which Lafayette was wounded,
G wrote V on October 20, 1778 (ibid., vol. 203), that he had become
"without exception . . . the idol of the Congress, the Army, and the people of America." In fact, of course, there was much dislike and jealousy
of Lafayette among the senior ranks of Americans in the Continental
Army, and they ridiculed Lafayette's performance in what, after all, had
been a military defeat for the U.S. Later, Lafayette aroused jealousy by
his close association with Washington and his appointment to head the
eventually aborted Canadian expedition: (a) Anthony Wayne wrote Horatio Gates (commander of the nothern department), January 26, 1778
(ibid., vol. 81), that he or Thomas Mifflin should have that assignment,
not a "foreigner"; (b) Robert Troup wrote Gates, February 6, 1778 (ibid.):
(1) Lafayette was a "Fabian," like Washington, and only tardily arrived
at Albany; (2) when Lafayette praised Benedict Arnold, who had criticized Gates for having ordered the Canadian expedition without giving
it adequate support, he, Troup, fought a duel with him and gave him
a "wound" like "the scar on his leg" from Brandywine; and (3) Gates
should return him to the southern army, where he had displayed "the
blunders of his youth and inexperience." (On the basis of these American
attitudes, one can only be grateful for the sake of the victory at Yorktown
that Rochambeau and his army—see the following—were *not* integrated
into the Continental army!) For evidence of Washington's love of Lafayette, see the following correspondence (RL/NYHS): Lafayette (Cadiz)-
Washington, February 5, 1783, asking for the honor of bringing to
England the U.S.-ratified treaty of 30 November; Washington-RL, March
19 and 29, 1783; RL-Washington, April 9, 1783; and Washington-RL,
April 16, 1783. The upshot of all this correspondence between the two
Americans was a recognition that Congress would only authorize a "native" to have that honor, if only for diplomatic reasons. Thus, Washington's final observations to RL were: (1) "There is no man upon Earth I
have a greater inclination to serve than the Marquis Lafayette," but not
if it's a matter hurtful to "our national character, dignity, or interest"
and (2) Lafayette would understand that—[signed:] "with much truth,
regard and affection."

134. BC/NYPL, vol. 192.

135. The Americans, of course, continued to recognize that Lafayette
had direct influence in Versailles, and this led to a recommendation of

November 25, 1780, from Jay to a New York member of Congress (Schuyler) that, given Lafayette's "great weight in France, . . . perhaps a grant of eight or ten thousand acres of land conceived in [high] sounding and honorary terms would not be unacceptable" to him. Similarly, V, a year later, upon receiving Lafayette's report of the Yorktown victory, wrote back on December 1, 1781 (ibid., vol. 210): "You can be sure your name is venerated by the French nation."

136. Ibid., vol. 180. Even prior to the French embassy's dispatch of August 12, 1768, it praised BF in 1767 as an effective defender of the interests of British America and for his commercial analyses. Also, on November 18, 1768 (ibid., vol. 181), it wrote Versailles: "Benjamin Franklin is one of the most fair-minded of men and the most enlightened of those who have come out of America." (The dispatch added that the embassy consulted with him regularly.)

137. On February 11, 1774, the embassy reported (ibid., vol. 183) that "Franklin was turned out" of his deputy postmaster-general for the colonies post, which "pays £2,000 and had been created by this celebrated academician, and the pay provided the major part of his income." The government in 1774 in open parliamentary session accused BF to his face in the most personally humiliating of terms of having illicitly obtained and leaked confidential reporting by its Massachusetts-based officials and of having done so in order to show up the allegedly anticolonial policies of those officials. Partly out of fear of a possible arrest order, Franklin some months later quietly left for America. In sweet revenge, so goes an apocryphal story (Becker's Benjamin Franklin . . . , p. 29—debunked by John Ferling's Setting the World Ablaze [Oxford U. Pr.; New York, 2000]), BF, at the signing ceremony for the peace agreement with England of November 30, 1782, put on the same distinctive suit he had worn at that humiliating episode of 1774 but not since.

138. BC/NYPL, vol. 184.

139. Stevens's Facsimiles . . . , vol. 14.

140. Sarah Jay-Susannah French Livingston, her mother, on board the Confederacy, December 26, 1779 (JJ/CU).

141. Even several years after his return from France to the U.S., BF would have sufficient health not to miss a single day at the Constitutional Convention. Of course, there were patches during his Paris service when he was too ill to fulfill his duties. Also: Jay wrote BF, August 20, 1781 (JJ/CU), to advise that he had sent a "private letter" to the President of the Congress, regarding Franklin's request for permission to retire, to

say that, while Franklin remained mentally acute, he was "an ancient patriot going in the evening of a long life early devoted to the public, to enjoy repose in the bosom of philosophic retirement." (BF had alerted Jay to his intention to retire in the hope that Jay would be the one to succeed him as minister plenipotentiary to France, but, in this letter to Franklin, Jay explained his reluctance to apply for that post, because his candidacy would provoke "debates on a subject which could only affect my personal concerns, especially as the policy of the measure did not, upon the whole, appear to me unquestionable." Jay was referring to his having added his own condition to an offer of Congress to Spain to forgo U.S. claims to free navigation on the Mississippi in exchange for Spanish military cooperation and financial aid—Jay put a time limit on that offer, which, he told FB, would remain valid only so long as the war contin-ued—despite Jay's doubts, Congress did subsequently give its retroac-tive endorsement to Jay's condition.)

142. Beaumarchais was so well informed by Deane that, as early as September 25, 1776 (BC/NYPL, vol. 186), he was able to report to V that two other "Deputies" were coming with new instructions. Typically, Beaumarchais used the news of the Declaration of Independence to argue that "the time is arriving for you to say yes or no" to openly supporting the U.S.; and a few days later, he would needle V that BF is a "coura-geous old man . . . and we, the French, we should have fear!" However, this is not the line V would take throughout 1777 with regard to relations with the American deputies. For example, on 22 February (ibid., vol. 186), he would have the French embassy in London rebut any criticisms of France by telling the English government "to go back to examine its own conduct regarding Corsica"; even now, Pasquale Paoli, the exiled Corsican leader, was "sending emissaries" there; and the French govern-ment does "not know what Benjamin Franklin's purpose is here"—he's only meeting *philosophes* and, far from any governmental ministers, only those opposed to them. In fact, of course, as V informed Ossun in dis-patches of 4 and 12 January, he had met with BF and Deane and a "third" deputy on 28 December, when they presented him with what he labeled as "limited proposals" for a commercial treaty, although, on 12 January, they had followed that up with new, "less enticing" overtures, which would turn France into mere "mercenaries." V went on to say that the deputies, to counteract France's major fear that a reconciliation between the two parties would leave England fully armed and ready to indemnify itself at Bourbon expense, offered, "and I don't doubt their sincerity, *to*

commit the U.S. not to make peace without the mutual agreement [emphasis supplied]" of France.

143. V-Ossun, January 4, 1777: the U.S. already has MFN privileges in French ports (ibid., vol. 192).

144. V-M, December 3, 1777 (ibid., vol. 192).

145. Maurepas-Sartine, April 23, 1777 (ibid., vol. 203).

146. Ibid., vol. 192. Of course, a month later news would arrive of the American victory at Saratoga, changing France's timetable back to its original schedule of July 1777.

147. V-Ossun, October 3, 1777 (ibid.).

148. V's November 7, 1777, to Ossun (one of his very last before his replacement by M) reported that the king had decided to give the Americans not 6 but 3 million livres for 1778 (ibid.). That same message reported that the deputies were upset at his report to them of Spanish "indignation" at the seizure by an American privateer of a French merchant ship carrying Spanish-owned goods and taking it to America; and at Spain's consequently suspending all aid to the Americans over this action by, as they put it, "one individual only." V's message added that he was urging them, nevertheless, to comply with Spanish policy. On 3 December, V, in his dispatch to M for use in conversations with the Spanish, would try to assuage Charles's known aggravation at this American seizure by characterizing it as an "act of piracy" at Spanish commercial expense.

149. Ferguson's *Power* . . . attributes the modesty of French financial aid to the U.S., 1778–80, to "lethargy" on BF's part (see Dull's *Franklin* . . . for an opposite, positive view of Franklin's efforts). In doing so, Ferguson makes several erroneous statements, such as that John Laurens was Henry's brother, rather than (very young) son; that a 1781 Dutch loan of 10 million livres was due to John's having been sent in February 1781 on a special aid mission to France, whereas JA and BF had been working on it well prior to his arrival in Europe; and that this loan had been obtained by the U.S. with a French guarantee, whereas in fact that formula proved insufficient to satisfy the Amsterdam bankers, and in the end it was France itself that had to assume the sole role of borrower, with the U.S. figuring only in side Franco-American understandings. There are other weaknesses in Ferguson's presentation of the international aspects of the financing of America's war, such as his failing to note Spain's cash contribution of 1 million livres to Beaumarchais's initial capital, or the negative consequences for the diplomatic and financial

credibility of the U.S. in Europe of Congress' having unilaterally drawn substantial funds on Jay and Henry Laurens—Ferguson does not even report that Jay in March 1782 was forced to "protest" some of the bills of exchange thus drawn on him (pp. 40–42, 46, 56, 126–28). On the other hand, that writer's detailed account of the congressional approach to obtaining domestic sources of financing for the war effort is rightly accepted as authoritative. (He considers Robert Morris a "genius.")

150. In a sense, Spanish policy seemed to be a step *ahead* of the still-cautious France: Per V-Ossun, November 7, 1777, Versailles sought to share the reporting from Philadelphia of the unofficial Spanish agent being sent from Havana (i.e., Juan Miralles) to report on the American situation; the French would have liked to do the same, but "we don't as yet have anyone there," because it is hard to find someone with a good sense of "discretion" (BC/NYPL, vol. 192).

151. Noailles-V, January 24, 1777 (ibid., vol. 186).

152. V-M, December 3, 1777 (ibid., vol. 192).

153. Hillsborough-Cumberland, August 3 and 4, 1780 (ibid., vol. 243). Also: Cumberland-FB, June 28, 1780: Toward the end of the Seven Years' War, "France was in engagement with Austria and other allies; yet, she determined upon distinguishing the differences in America from those in Europe. . . . It is hoped Spain will regard her quarrel with England to be distinct from that of France" (ibid.).

154. Memoranda to the King, January 7 and July 23, 1777 (ibid., vols. 203 and 192); M-V, December 18, 1777 (ibid., vol. 192); and V-FB, January 20, 1778 (ibid., vol. 193).

155. The emperor was at the French capital as "Count Falkenstein" between April 18 and May 31, 1777. V's report to Ossun of 9 May (ibid., vol. 192) commented that the visit was nonpolitical, Joseph not yet having raised a single issue of substance between the two countries (nor would he during this entire visit); and that he hoped Joseph's two-hour meeting with Stormont had been equally without political substance, Vienna having long had a soft policy toward England.

156. Emphasis is supplied here and also in the final Spanish point below it, because these viewpoints seem to the present writer to touch on the true core of the realities facing Jay as he sought both to change Spanish policy toward America and to obtain major aid from them during his mission to Madrid; moreover, they proved in the main to be valid, such as FB's forecast that America would betray an inadequate appreciation of the important diversionary role played by the Bourbon

threat to Gibraltar and Minorca (documenting the Spaniard's point was a principal purpose of Dull's fine study of the War) and, regarding the final Spanish point, such as Jay's precisely becoming dogged by the fear of America's having to keep fighting despite its already having achieved its objectives.

157. Ibid., vol. 192.

158. As reported by Ossun to V, September 22, 1777 (ibid.). The proximate cause of this confrontation was the entrance into "La Corogne," not for the first time, of a privateer commissioned by the U.S. deputies. The ship was the *Revenge*, under the fabled captain Justas Conyngham (or Cunningham), who was active up and down the coast of Europe during 1777 and 1778 conducting "daring raids on British shipping in the North and Irish seas, as well as the Azores and the Atlantic" (per Morris's *Making . . .* , p. 615). The only American ship captain operating in European waters to compare to Conyngham in fame was, of course, John Paul Jones, whose French-assisted activities came in the two years following the former's exploits and the signing of the Franco-American alliance.

159. FB-Aranda, December 18, 1777 (BC/NYPL, vol. 192).

160. Brecher's *Losing . . .* , pp. 25–26, 29, 89, 170–71, 175–76 and 181.

161. BC/NYPL, vol. 192.

162. Even a year after entering the American War as France's ally, FB would continue to berate France by, as M reported on September 11, 1780, still harking back to how "we forced Spain into ending the Seven Years' War, having entered it only for France's sake" (ibid., vol. 197).

163. For example: V-Ossun, January 4 and 12, 1777 (ibid., vol. 192); and V-G, October 26, 1778 (ibid., vol. 204).

164. Ibid. and V-M, December 17, 1782 (ibid., vol. 199).

165. Ibid., vol. 194.

166. V's 2 November response to M (ibid.) spelled out in a bit more detail his strategic vision for a postwar North America: there was no way France could leave England in New York or Rhode Island, as these were "citadels" that England could use to lay down the law to the U.S.; but England's retaining Canada and Nova Scotia would be acceptable and, if coupled with a return of the Floridas to Spain, would assure that the ability of the Americans to trouble their "neighbors" would be "contained." In this same message, V wrote that the more he saw of the Americans, the less impressed he was by their "talents, their views, their firmness, and their patriotism." (As regards Canada, V later in the war, would come to see the desirability of either the French or the Americans

retaining Nova Scotia's Halifax so as to deny England that strategically located port.)

167. That the deputies' colleagues in America were cheering them on in this effort at entanglement is illustrated by Hamilton's correspondence with Jay and company in May 1777, in which he expressed the hope that English seizures of French ships in the West Indies will lead to "a more general hostility" (RL/NYHS).

168. V-Ossun, August 26, October 3 and 31, 1777 (BC/NYPL, vol. 192).

169. FB-Ossun, October 17, 1777 (ibid.).

170. V-Ossun, October 31, 1777 (ibid.); and V-M, May 1, 1778 (ibid., vol. 193).

171. V to M, October 23, 1778 (ibid., vol. 194). This comment seems to be a conscious play on Pitt's famous statement toward the end of the Seven Years' War that "America was conquered in Germany" (see Brecher's *Losing . . .* , p. 145).

172. Madariaga's *Britain*, pp. ix, 9, and 21.

173. Ibid., p. 167.

174. As pointed out by Bemis's *American Secretaries . . .* , vol. 1, p. 155, England "preferred having the weak Dutch navy as belligerents than the numerous Dutch merchant marine as neutrals under the principles of the League of Armed Neutrality." Madariaga agrees with that analysis.

175. JA-Jay, May 15, 1780 (JJ/CU): France, Spain, and the U.S. should try to get Portugal to close its ports to all "belligerents' armed vessels" instead of following its present "neutrality"; the same applied to Denmark, which had restored to English owners the prizes brought into its ports by John Paul Jones and Pierre Landais. Also: V-M, June 26, 1782 (BC/NYPL, vol. 199): Portugal's accession to the Neutrality League showed that it, under the Queen, was "cured of [its] hereditary fear of Great Britain"; therefore, France should try to get authorization from the signatories to accede to the Portuguese-Spanish Treaty of May 1778.

176. Turgot's note to V, November 23, 1777 (ibid., vol. 186) reported that word had arrived at Bordeaux of "miraculous news" that Burgoyne has been defeated, and Howe and Clinton, as well; and that, "As Benjamin Franklin is dining at my home today, I'll learn if there is any truth to this, and I'll pass it on to you tomorrow morning." Also: Instructions to G, March 29, 1778 (ibid., vol. 203), stated that Saratoga had made the king feel the necessity of finally taking a "definitive" decision, and that England's reconciliation proposals to the Americans "quite clearly show

its hostile goals versus France," which therefore had to act quickly "to prevent" its achieving them.

177. Ibid., vol. 187. This note was followed by a major internal memorandum prepared by V on 7 December under the title *Overtures Regarding the Possibility of Our Union with the Americans*. (This action-oriented wording is in marked contrast with all previous titles given by Vergennes to his major policy memoranda regarding the American War: *Considerations, Reflections*, etc.) In this latest policy paper (ibid., vol. 203), the foreign minister argued that only now can France be certain of the "solidity" of the rebelling colonies and of their "solidarity" and that "[r]ecent military victories seem to offer a new perspective."

178. Noailles on 21 November reported that the king's parliamentary speech used, for the first time, the word "peace" regarding the colonies. On January 24, 1778, V informed Noailles, "We are at a moment of solution for this important problem" of the American War, and Versailles would like to know whether Parliament was planning, as reported, to offer the Americans an "absolute cancellation" of the Navigation Acts. V continued: Stormont barged in on him and then on Maurepas (who for the previous three weeks had declined to see him on grounds that he was suffering from the gout), and this rudeness could only have been on government orders—therefore, if this was indeed the case, France could only envisage this action as an "indirect, contingent declaration of war." On 3 February, Noailles reported that, in the House of Lords, Chatham was urging an English-American alliance against the Bourbons, whose continuing failure to provide substantial aid to the colonies, so Chatham argued, made the latter more susceptible to accepting proposals from England—especially given that their victory at Saratoga allowed the Americans to negotiate with the mother country with honor. On 27 February, Noailles reported that England was sending a peace commission to America under Lord Carlisle and that this meant there was a real threat of a reconciliation between the two parties. Accordingly, the royal Council at Versailles discussed this threat on 18 March and concluded that *all* English political elements were now seeking a "prompt reconciliation" in view of the evidence of "insuperable obstacles" to a defeat of the Americans and that their ultimate goal was to establish an alliance with the Americans in a common war against the Bourbon powers. All this, coupled with Lord North's known plan to open up a negotiation with the deputies in Paris prior to the return of Parliament on 28 January,

vindicated, according to the Council, its own action in December of assuring the Continental Congress of France's "protection and support" as
an ally of the U.S., because the alternative would have been a war against
the combination of England and America.

179. V-M, December 13, 1777 (ibid., vol. 192).

180. Ibid. and Stevens's *Facsimiles* . . . , vol. 20. Beaumarchais's 11 December: "[T]he race was on between France and England as to who
would reap the rewards as the first to recognize the U.S."

181. V in December was advising that the combined power of England
and the Americans would be "too superior for us to counter-balance"—
for example, his dispatch of 13 December to M, which continued: As
even the present havoc at sea being caused by American corsairs showed,
imagine the situation if they also had the help of English fleets versus
Bourbon maritime trade; like England, the French were "on the precipice
but still have a slight means of support to prevent our falling from it";
let France beat England's offers to America; even if this only forced the
English to extend their reconciliation talks into the next campaign, the
French would have "earned our salaries." On that same day, he wrote
Noailles (ibid., vol. 187): The "masterly stroke" by George and North to
counter the Opposition's peace motion gave them "latitude in proposing
peace coupled with independence [*sic*], and in forming a confraternity
which would establish a family compact between Old and New England
similar to that which exists between France and Spain"; North's great
military buildup, including "60,000 sailors," even while planning to
make a deal with the Americans, showed that it was "not difficult to
forsee what use he would propose to make of them if he were untram-
meled by America." Elsewhere around this time, the foreign minister
elaborated: Howe was likely to be isolated at Philadelphia, while
Washington's forces daily grew stronger and capable of defeating him
in a repeat of Burgoyne's surrender at Saratoga; therefore, English policy,
once they "see the light," could soon change to one of seeking reconciliation; France must act faster than England before there was a "reamal-
gamation"; whatever France decided, it would be "difficult for us to
avoid war with England," therefore, it was better to have the Americans
with France than against it in the inevitable war; even a later American
defection would be better for France than losing them now, because at
least then they would not actually turn their arms against France; although France had already made its decision in favor of recognition by

then, Franklin, unaware of this fact, showed him, Vergennes, a letter he had received from the Congress proving France had no time to lose given that body's impatience with the "inertia and lack of firm reporting" from the deputies regarding the prospects for solid Bourbon assistance. (Regarding V's optimism about the chances of forcing Howe into a surrender, note that the deputies' message to him of 4 December reported that they had "just received" reports of Burgoyne's defeat; and, that Howe at Philadelphia lacked naval backing and, therefore, might repeat Burgoyne's surrender. The deputies enclosed the text of the latter's capitulation agreement.)

182. V-M, December 13, 1777 (ibid., vol. 192): "George and Chatham were already meeting"; once in power, Chatham would try to "humiliate" France and Spain; France may have to act unilaterally; would Spain be understanding? France would still give Spain time to consider the matter, so it should have "no reason to complain to us"; M should show FB this and related personal letters in their originals, and prepare the ground for French actions. (Even Chargé Escarano, as late as March 27, 1778, was reporting to Madrid that Chatham was being rumored as certain to return to power "sooner or later"!)

183. V-M, December 27, 1777 (ibid., vol. 192). To justify V's concerns regarding a possible English-American reconciliation, but also to turn his own argument against him and add to the paradoxical post-Saratoga situation, note that RL, upon learning that the French-U.S. alliance was signed, wrote on June 13, 1778, to G. Morris: "John Bull's hatred of his old enemy will induce him to close with us on our own terms in order to go to loggerheads with Lewis—they love the sport, let them go at it, and God send us a good deliverance, for I do not find that this war has produced the effect I expected from it" upon the bulk of the people, who were unworthy of the "blessings of a free government" as a consequence of "virtuous" behavior in a war for independence. As will be shown later in the present study, there would be a period of a few weeks, in December 1782, when the war situation became one quite like that envisaged and even wished for by RL, much (again, "paradoxically") to his personal chagrin as Secretary for Foreign Affairs.

184. Versailles' above-cited message of January 20, 1778, to FB reported that "[A] French frigate was on the way to alert the Continental Congress, by a dispatch from its deputies in France, not to entertain England's propositions in view of the promising Bourbon role"; and,

France's course was the "least dangerous" of the two troublesome choices before it, because it "could not risk having the Americans against it or even indifferent towards it."

185. It also was designed, at a minimum, to force still one more military campaign between England and America, as per the above-cited V-M, December 13, 1777.

186. V-M, December 13, 1777: "England's Parliament was making moves towards reconciliation with America while also authorizing increased naval recruitment; 2 February was the date scheduled for its next debate on the American War; England had a twenty-day head start on France in letting its reconciliation policy out."

187. For purposefully misleading the Americans regarding prospects for an alliance with Spain, see V-M, January 8, 1778 (ibid., vol. 193).

188. V-G, October 26, 1778 (ibid., vol. 204). Madariaga's *Britain . . . ,* p. 21, accepts the military treaty's self-description as one establishing a "defensive" alliance, but this seems not to be a satisfactory way to refer to an accord whose very signature, when coupled with the simultaneous and unavoidably more public commercial one, was known—*and desired*—by the parties to be a *casus belli* in the eyes of England—hence, the present writer prefers such alternate terms as "contingency" or "prospective" alliance; moreover, the goals of that alliance, as well as its intrinsically aggressive origin, were far from purely defensive ones but rather envisaged certain territorial and commercial gains by each party, and implicitly by Spain as well, that went beyond mere maintenance of the status quo. In support of this view of the aggressive intentions of the French, note V's message to M of 13 December, in which he reported that the deputies on the previous day had only requested a commercial treaty, saying that this would let the Bourbons avoid a war with England and that he easily rebutted this overly narrow view of the purpose of their negotiation ("This sophistry was too easy to destroy to let stand.").

189. In its message of 8 December, addressed explicitly now to "Vergennes," in answer to his of 6 December, the deputies wrote that they have been proposing both a commercial treaty and "engagements for uniting our forces" with those of France and Spain and that any such engagements would provide for the barring of any "peace but in conjunction with those courts," should the two join in the war on England. At the subsequent meeting between the two on 12 December, the deputies, according to V's above-cited report to M of 13 December, also stated that the U.S. would never "raise difficulties regarding the respec-

tive boundary limits" between the U.S. and Spanish territory. On June 26, 1778, V would report to G that the frigate that took the 6 February treaties to the U.S. had returned with a report that they were greeted with joy by the Americans.

190. As V would underline to the U.S. in no uncertain terms on October 26, 1778 (BC/NYPL, vol. 204), in strong reaction to a query from members of the Continental Congress as to whether war with England had been formally declared: (1) "[D]espite the lack of a formal declaration of war, France and England were now in such a conflict," and therefore the contingency military alliance treaty of 6 February had already been activated "as had been foreseen in its drafting"; and, in May, even prior to the first exchange of fire weeks later, he had informed Congress that, given England's diplomatic steps rupturing relations with France, "we have to regard the peace as broken" and (2) France's "contingency" commitments with the U.S. as "activated" (ibid., vol. 203). (Consistent with that position, France had already dispatched a naval squadron from Toulon to North America under d'Estaing, as will be discussed below. It was during this period that V instructed G to correct newspaper reports in the U.S. quoting that newly arrived diplomat as having said that America could make its peace with England immediately upon the latter's giving its recognition to U.S. independence; V-G, June 26, 1778; ibid., vol. 204.)

191. It is with regard to the secret article that we see France, right at the start of its alliance with the U.S., taking the first of what would be a series of important policy steps that were expressly designed, not merely to be kept secret from its American ally, as we might normally expect any country to do even as part of an alliance, but actually to mislead that ally (including Jay throughout his period of service in Spain). As V wrote to M on January 8, 1778: "France has discarded its earlier idea of signing the treaty for a contingency military alliance with the condition that its validity depended on Spain's also signing it. Instead, it will include in the treaty a secret paragraph keeping it open for Spanish accession. This will meet Spain's concerns over maintaining strict secrecy regarding its involvement with the Americans, and also its related concerns over the security of the exposed Spanish fleet and forces still in American waters. *This new approach, moreover, will have the advantage of leaving the American deputies 'in the mistaken belief' that Spain was receptive to signing along with France.* If England learns of the secret paragraph, that might usefully mislead it to perceive a split between France

Notes

and Spain, thereby giving it one more reason not to attack those Spanish naval and military units. Also note that France will try to keep its treaties with the Americans secret at least until the return to Spain of those units and of the Spanish treasury ships." (A year later, in another revealing V message, that of March 19, 1779, to M [ibid., vol. 195], he would describe the secret article regarding Spain in the Franco-American treaty of 6 February in somewhat different terms, namely, as having implicitly neglected U.S. interests, because it provided the way for Spain to enter the war without being required to negotiate directly with the Americans, or to recognize them, or to guarantee their independence. In a word, V acknowledged that the article played into Spanish hands by allowing them to get help from both France and the U.S. without their first having to offer much of a commitment from their own side and that Madrid might well take advantage of this opening, because "nothing is gratis on Spain's part"—a trait to which, so the minister confessed, the secret article had deferred. One particular fear V expressed here was that, were the European powers now to learn of that secret article and its neglect of the U.S., the reputation of France would be damaged. His instructions to M accordingly included that he ask Spain to use that article *only in direct negotiations* with the Americans and not reveal it to other powers.) Among V's arguments to Spain were that the French-U.S. treaties protected Spanish interests (e.g., the Floridas and Newfoundland fishing rights) and that Spain would have a harder time negotiating with the U.S. during the war as compared to right then. As to Newfoundland fishing rights, FB would soon make quite clear that Spain had no real interest in pursuing them (ironically, Spanish fishing vessels toward the end of the twentieth century would suffer armed attacks off Newfoundland at the hands of the Canadian navy in a continuing dispute over access rights to those waters); and as to the best timing for Spain to negotiate with the Americans, Jay would, in Spain, extend V's point by arguing that if Madrid were to wait until the postwar period to enter into a treaty relationship with the U.S., it would not get the relatively liberal terms, nor the intangible but important long-term benefits of an appreciative American warmth, that it would were it to recognize and aid the U.S. during its period of great wartime peril.

192. V-Vauguyon, March 18, 1778, and V-M, June 20, 1778 (ibid., vols. 201 and 194).

193. Ministry memorandum of January 27, 1778 (ibid., vol. 187).

194. Ibid., vol. 187.

195. Ibid., vol. 204.

196. Ibid., vol. 193.

197. V-G (ibid., vol. 204).

198. G-V, May 14, 1779 (ibid., vol. 205).

199. Ibid.

200. Ibid., vol. 206.

201. M-V, December 23, 1777, and January 5 and April 10, 1778 (ibid., vols. 192–93).

202. On January 19, 1778, FB wrote Aranda that given recent developments between France and America, he was suspending his offer to the Americans of 23 December, which, in his message of that date to Aranda, he had conditioned in the following terms: "provided they behave towards us with fidelity and secrecy" and sought Spanish "protection," on which basis Spain then would negotiate a suitable deal with England for them (ibid., vol. 192).

203. December 24, 1778 (ibid., vol. 194).

204. Ibid., vols. 192–93. In this regard, it is interesting to learn what the Spanish in Madrid were telling Grantham with respect to their reaction to the February treaties signed at Versailles: (a) On 24 March, Grantham reported that, according to FB, France and the Americans already had a "treaty" and that had been done to Spain's "great surprise," although it "neither condemns nor justifies the steps taken by France"; Spain felt "perfectly free from all engagement" concerning the French, and its "conduct . . . shall be exactly guided by Great Britain's towards Spain"; M "is to be carefully precluded from all knowledge of what passes between" the two of them (FB and Grantham), except, it pressed, to acknowledge that he, Grantham, was told by FB of his awareness that there was a Franco-American treaty; and (b) on 31 March, Grantham, reporting that FB told him of a "total want of concert with France," and that M "seems much disappointed indeed," opined that Spain would act toward England "in the most friendly but reciprocal manner." He also reported that the Treasury fleet had been in Havana in February and was now heading to Spain; and that the Cadiz fleet would undoubtedly in part go out to "meet it" in view of Madrid's wariness of the military situation (ibid., vol. 241). (Grantham, like M and Jay, would end up emotionally worn out in dealing with the difficult FB; he left Spain at the break in relations in 1779 with the observation that Spain had betrayed both its word to him and its own national interest.)

205. V wrote Ossun, May 14, 1776 (ibid., vol. 191) that he needed the

cooperation of the Controller General to do the things he would like with Spain for their mutual defense against England; "we don't have it for the moment," but Turgot's successor was the *Intendant* [senior administrative official] of St. Domingue and will "better understand the needs of our defense."

206. After that evacuation, Boston would be known for the rest of the war for its enjoyment of an unmolested, even prosperous and to some (such as RL's brother, John, who would write him from that city on February 2, 1777, in that vein) also a "dissipated" lifestyle, although New England as a whole would continue to provide a more than proportional share of the soldiers for the Continental Army either through direct enlistments or in the form of supporting state militia. Edmund S. Morgan clearly errs in writing, "When the British abandoned Boston in March 1777 . . . Washington hastily departed in pursuit of Howe" (review of Elizabeth Fenn's *Pox Americana*, in *New York Review of Books*, February 14, 2002).

207. That New York would stay as the focus of the war in North America down to Yorktown is evidenced by an exchange of letters in January 1781 between RL, then serving at Albany as chancellor of that state, and General Washington (RL/NYHS). On 9 January, RL wrote of the "discontent" among New Yorkers, who felt that, because their state was carrying much of the war's burdens, its economic situation was too tight to meet its congressionally allotted contributions in support of the national effort; RL accordingly urged the general to write the Congress that it was "relying . . . too much upon the exertions of this State," and he gave as an example the claim that Pennsylvania "had greater resources to contribute to your army" than it was providing at that time. On 31 January, Washington replied that he had written to the Congress urging it to ease up on the resources of both New York and New Jersey, the area where the Continental Army was based in this period (and where it would remain until its march jointly with the French army down to Yorktown, Virginia—worth noting is that, during that march, a financially desperate R. Morris successfully appealed to Rochambeau to advance him $20,000 in specie needed to pay Washington's troops, who otherwise were threatening not to proceed to Yorktown).

208. It will be recalled that in October 1776 Jay removed the entire Jay family from its Rye home on the shores of Long Island Sound, which was too exposed to enemy attack, to a temporary residence at Fishkill, in the Hudson Highlands, and that, in the meanwhile, his wife was with

the Livingston family at Elizabethtown, New Jersey, which, too, was exposed to enemy attack, as indeed it was in the summer of 1776. Jay wrote Sarah on 12 July (JJ/CU), saying, "I much commend the coolness and presence of mind with which you received the alarm" caused by English troops from New York having seized "the barracks" at Elizabethtown. (In this period, Jay's son was being weaned and staying with his father's family and not with Sarah.) Jay wrote Egbert Benson, July 10, 1783 (ibid.), that the next year he would be a private citizen, and that he should tell his Poughkeepsie family this good news, but also should warn it not to move to Rye until England evacuated New York (that would occur only in late December of that year).

209. That Jay would soon become restless as chief justice is clear from an April 1778 letter to G. Morris: "I am now engaged in the most disagreeable part of my duty—trying criminals. They multiply exceedingly." That duty also involved too much travel away from his family to suit him.

210. In that December message, Jay said: "We do not fight for a few acres of land, but for freedom"—a perhaps not-so-coincidental similarity to Voltaire's famous, and quite erroneous, phrase, in his *Candide* of the Seven Years' War period, belittling that contest as being over "a few acres of snow around Canada" (Brecher's *Losing* . . . , p. 11).

211. Before Burgoyne's expedition southward, there were 14,300 troops stationed in Canada; after Saratoga, only 3,500 to 4,000 would be there.

212. The consequences of Burgoyne's move southward from Ticonderoga perhaps vindicated Montcalm's decision, following *his* victories on the New York lakes during the French and Indian War, *not* to proceed from there to the Hudson—a cautious decision heavily criticized by Vaudreuil, the governor general of Canada (Brecher's *Losing* . . . , pp. 123–26): Burgoyne took weeks to get from Lake George to the Hudson, having to laboriously cut an artillery road through the wilderness separating the two waters, especially between Skenesborough and Fort Edward (G. Morris-RL, July 20, 1777). This cost him valuable time and gave his American enemy the opportunity to regroup, helping to account for the eventual surrender of Burgoyne's army in October.

213. General de Kalb, ever skeptical and critical of the American military leadership, wrote Count Broglio in September that Ticonderoga had been lost due to "cowardliness or treason by the commanding general." A close friend of Schuyler, John Carter, in letters written to Walter Liv-

ingston at the very moment of the loss of Ticonderoga (RL/NYHS), vividly captures the emotions of the period: (a) 7 July: while accompanying Schuyler part of the way on his trip from Albany to Saratoga, the two learned of the American garrison's evacuation of Ticonderoga and Mount Independence, and of the enemy's having pursued those troops to Skenesborough; (b) 9 July: The U.S. troops had left Ticonderoga "with tears in their eyes. . . . What could be the motives of the general officers for this precipitate retreat I cannot conceive, their reasons ought to be very good to preserve them from the resentment of their country." A similarly critical B-M, in his August 1781 "Portraits of American Generals," would write of Schuyler, that he "never was in any battle" (ibid.). General Arthur St. Clair was in command at Ticonderoga upon its evacuation, not Schuyler, and he, too, was court-martialed and acquitted. The nub of the charge was that the American garrison had failed to install defenses on a mountain top that dominated the fort and that its precipitate flight, once Burgoyne controlled that site, was so hasty that it failed to destroy the valuable artillery that then fell into enemy hands. That, as noted, Jay, too, had his regional biases is clear also from a comment in a letter to a friend, Leonard Gansevoort, on June, 5, 1777 (JJ/CU), that the state's constitution was universally approved even in New England, "where few New York productions have credit."

214. Philip Schuyler attended the New Rochelle French Protestant Church School in 1748, four years before Jay. (In this close-knit society, Hamilton soon would marry Schuyler's daughter.)

215. For example, per L-V, January 28, 1781 (BC/NYPL, vol. 209): Sam Adams was spreading the alarm that Washington was under foreign [read: French] influence and had the goal of being head of state based on his increasing fame, and Adams was a leading example of an American favoring sectional party interests and overruling those citizens "who are resolved to sacrifice for the public good."

216. John Carter–Walter Livingston, August 10, 1777 (RL/NYHS): American troops "retreated successively" from Fort Edward to Moses Creek to Saratoga, and "are now at Stillwater"; all depended on the timely arrival of a "large body militia" or Albany would be lost; the Indians were "hanging" on the American troops' "rear . . . and scalps are daily taking"; at nine the previous night, Fort Schuyler was "invested," but General Herkimer, on his march with 900 militia to the relief of the fort, had been attacked by the enemy, "the greatest part of the militia left him on the first onset; however, with the remainder he beat the

enemy and kept the field, . . . fifty dead Indians on the ground" (Battle of Oriskany); but he would need reinforcements or would lose "the country"; Burgoyne's army was "greatly superior" to that of the U.S., which was "out of order, wants discipline," but it would "ruin" Burgoyne if he kept "coming on" and if the U.S. army got input from all available troops. After the victory in October at Saratoga, Jay would write Schuyler on 11 December (JJ/CU) that he was glad "your attachment to your country is unabated by its ingratitude," and that he believed the future would prove "that the foundation of our success in the northern department was lain by the present commander's predecessor." Also at this time, Jay wrote his friend, R. Morris, in Philadelphia (ibid.): "Military matters with us are strangely mattered. Gates is playing with his laurels at Albany," and Putnam was "catching oysters on the shores of the Sound. . . . In my opinion, the resolutions of the Congress respecting the forts and navigation of the Hudson River will not be properly executed, if at all, unless under direction." This denigration of Gates was fairly typical of New Yorkers in the period (postwar, he'd move to New York and marry RL's sister!) and brought them even closer to an appreciative Washington as he confronted opposition to his continuing as commander in chief. For example, G. Morris's letter of March 1778 from Valley Forge to RL (RL/NYHS) reported that Gates was a "scoundrel" who was at the head of an anti-Washington clique. Moreover, the New Yorker's low opinion of Gates as a military man would be largely justified by his subsequent, unsatisfactory performance elsewhere during the war, notably in the southern department, from which he would be peremptorily removed after Cornwallis's successes in the Carolinas. Following that event, Jay would write BF on October 30, 1780 (JJ/CU), that Europe was exaggerating America's problems with Henry Laurens "in the Tower" and Cornwallis having "cropt some of Gates' laurels." (RL once observed during the war that laurels were the most expensive plants to grow; he would personally learn the bitter truth of that view when he sought to minimize Monroe's role, and magnify his own, in the negotiation of the 1803 Louisiana Purchase.) Nevertheless, it would only be well after Yorktown before Gates would completely disassociate himself from efforts to undermine, or have him replace, Washington. It must be said, however, that, in 1777, and notwithstanding Richard Morris's contrary view in his *Seven . . .* , p. 240, even an Alexander Hamilton would confess frustration with Washington's so-called Fabian tactics of avoiding major battles with the enemy, always drawing further back into the hinterland in line with his priority—and ultimately winning—strategy of assuring the continuing existence of a Continental Army capable of capitalizing on enemy errors and finally of outlasting it in an endurance contest that the home forces were bound to win. For example, Hamilton wrote Jay and company from Wilmington, Delaware, on September 1, 1777: Unless the army fought a pretty general action, "which I personally favor," it would lose Philadelphia. "I would not only fight them, I'd attack them, as it is always three to one in favor of the party attacking." (In the event, the upcoming confrontation took place at Brandywine, just north of Wilmington, and it was lost by the Americans, who soon evacuated Philadelphia.)

217. For a balanced analysis of General Howe's moves, see Willcox's *Portrait* . . . , pp. 102ff and 142ff.

218. Jay-Schuyler, July 28, 1777.

219. Washington-RL, July 18, 1777. Typically, Arnold during the Saratoga battle would find himself so unduly restrained by Gates from exercising his talents that, at a key point, he could not resist taking an unauthorized initiative against the enemy and thereby earned both historical credit for being instrumental in turning the battle in favor of the Americans and also Gates's deep personal enmity. According to a letter of early October to RL from his soldier brother, Henry, serving with Arnold, Gates's jealousy of that general explains why he was unreceptive to constructive advice and proposed initiatives by him that would have forced Burgoyne's defeat. (After the battle, when Henry failed to get the promotion recommendation to the Congress that he felt he deserved from Gates, even though the latter in September, as Henry wrote Robert on 1 October, had taken the trouble to assure him of his "friendship for all New Yorkers, particularly our family, among which you are distinguished," RL on 8 December wrote Washington at Valley Forge urging his support for that promotion. The general answered in a noncommittal fashion on 27 December, by which time RL had also written a newspaper piece under a pseudonym defending Henry's performance as a colonel in Arnold's unit at Saratoga, including Arnold's "declaration" praising it.)

220. RL/NYHS and Morris's *Seven* . . . , p. 239. What makes Hamilton's correspondence with the New Yorkers so much more remarkable is that, alongside his insightful military analyses, we find him, as a kind of warm-up for his (and Jay's!) subsequent role in the writing of the Federalist Papers, paying close attention to constitutional issues then being worked out for the new State of New York. For example, (a) on 7

May, he thanked them for the document on New York's new form of government; it was the best in the world, but he saw a few "defects," although he was refraining from giving them "my modest opinions"; and (b) on 19 May he wrote that what their constitution lacked "is a want of vigor in your executive"; the chief executive should be elected by "a select assembly, and cannot be safely lodged with the people at large"; while "popular governments" were not necessarily unstable, "when the deliberative or judicial powers are vested wholly or partly in the collective body of the people, you must expect error, confusion and instability"; the best solution was to have a real election "by the people" of the "legislative, executive and judiciary authorities," but only by establishing "the right of election [on a basis that was] well secured and regulated"; and the proposed senate was a problem, because, "from the very name, and from the mere circumstances of its being a separate member of the legislature, [it] will be liable to degenerate into a body purely aristocratical."

221. By 1 September, Hamilton would be writing from Wilmington, Delaware, Washington having learned of Howe's sailing up Chesapeake Bay and landing near Elkton, Maryland, with Philadelphia as his target. This solid news had come only after weeks of doubt regarding Howe's intentions. For example, even before the start of August, Washington knew that seventy English ships had sailed—possibly for Philadelphia or possibly, as we have seen, Charleston. To be certain of their destination before making his own move, he then decided to await their arrival at the "capes of Philadelphia," that is, Delaware Bay, and only then to send his army past the Delaware River: "We shall act the most cautious possible in our circumstances," so Hamilton wrote Jay and company on 29 July. However, by 10 August, it was obvious that Washington was confused by the fact that the English ships did not enter that Bay but rather went further southward. This confusion was soon clarified by the news of Howe's sailing up *Chesapeake Bay*.

222. On Bennington's lessons for future events in this war, note B-M to V, October 24, 1780 (BC/NYPL, vol. 208), which, in reporting the good news that a 1,600-man militia fighting in the Carolinas against 1,400 English regulars had led to the death of the famous English devestator, Ferguson, and the surrender of 800 troops, presciently went on to remind V that "the Saratoga capitulation was heralded by a similar event between militia and English regulars."

223. Per the above-cited John Carter to Walter Livingston, August 10,

1777. Herkimer was severely wounded at the battle and died soon after it.

224. BC/NYPL, vol. 204.

225. Deputies-Ministry of Foreign Affairs, April 10, 1778 (ibid.). The relatively benign treatment and ultimate fate of these prisoners of war, a high proportion of whom would choose to remain in the U.S. after the war, compares with the cruelty with which the English treated their American captives, mainly on prison ships, which were death traps in which more Americans died—over 11,000—than were killed in action—6,800 (*New York Times*, October 15, 2000, and November 4, 2001).

226. Ambassador Noailles reported from London on December 5, 1777 (ibid., vol. 187), that General Howe was being blamed for going "south, when he might have cooperated with Burgoyne." As early as the following 13 February, that ambassador reported Clinton's appointment to succeed Howe.

227. Stormont, according to V's dispatch to the French embassy in London on November 12, 1777 (ibid.), claimed that Howe's landing in Maryland, and Washington's subsequent retreat, meant that Philadelphia was taken and "all America returned to obedience."

228. For part of the basis of this assessment, see Chargé Garniér's report of February 20, 1775, from London to V (ibid., vol. 183) on the circumstances of General Howe's hesitant acceptance of his appointment in replacement of Gage. Perhaps negatively influencing the Howe's motivation against the Americans was their family's past close association with the colonists: Their eldest brother, George, had fallen in 1758 as a universally beloved leader under General James Abercromby in a failed Anglo-American assault on Montcalm's Ticonderoga (see Brecher's *Losing . . .*, pp. 137–38). Also worth noting is that Admiral Howe was a close political associate of Chatham (Garniér's dispatch of April 12, 1776—ibid., vol. 185) and went in spring 1776 to fight the Americans (and hopefully to negotiate with them as a co-peace commissioner along with his brother) only out of loyalty to the king; remarkably, that sailor also, in 1755, was the ship captain who, during a period of ostensible peace and full diplomatic relations with France, fired on, and captured, two French warships off Newfoundland, an act that, as the above text shows, was constantly referred to by French officials as the true start of the Seven Years' War and an example of the "treacherous" English habit of resorting to surprise attacks, giving their country no choice but to be on the alert and prepared for war at all times. Thus, when Garniér, upon

news of Howe's appointment as a plenipotentiary with his brother, and as commander of the fleet in North America, reminded Secretary of State Suffolk of this past, the latter rebutted that the hostilities started before 1755, when George Washington attacked Jumonville's party in the Ohio in May 1754. (Interestingly, the English by this were dropping their original line, that the Seven Years' War began with the *French* attack on Washington's Fort Necessity a month after the Jumonville incident and were now more conveniently charging Washington with responsibility for that war—see Brecher's *Losing* . . . , pp. 51–58.) For completeness regarding Admiral Howe's unenthusiastic attitude toward his American appointment, it should also be noted that he had been promised by North appointment as lieutenant general of the navy, but Sandwich gave that senior post to a more politically acceptable officer. As regards the Jumonville incident, L wrote V on August 25, 1783 (BC/NYPL, vol. 213) that the congressional resolution authorizing a statue of Washington to be created by French artists offered a good opportunity to paint that general's character on the basis of frequent meetings with him: "I don't believe he merits the great glory and praise heaped on him. . . . He is neither impetuous nor given to violence, and the murder of M. de Jumonville committed at his orders about thirty years ago shows how little he then was in control of himself. . . . The public is unaware of his outbursts. . . . He doesn't possess the great qualities of a warrior [but] his great qualities erase these blots."

229. L-V, August 1, 1781 (ibid., vol. 210): "[F]or the past two years, only the south had experienced war, while most of the U.S. lived peacefully, including commercially and agriculturally, even as France and Spain were fighting hard with England all over the rest of the world."

230. In his typically lighthearted, humorous way, Morris ended this letter: "From the bottom of my paper, Adieu Adieu!" Similarly, in his letter of 5 February, while on an official congressional visit to Valley Forge he complained, "There are no fine women at York Town. Judge then of my situation." (In a tragic road accident around Philadelphia, Morris, as noted, lost a leg during the time of Jay's service in Spain.)

231. The Delaware River could be navigated by ships-of-the-line up to Philadelphia itself and by smaller ships up to Trenton.

232. The numerical strength of the U.S. was detailed by Jay as part of his April 1780 response to FB's battery of opening questions. The precision, down to fractions, and the blatantly artificial matching of some

states' populations with those of others show that Jay's figures, which
he had carried with him from his post as president of Congress, were
really the result of political negotiations rather than actual field investi-
gations, although they undoubtedly do offer us a ballpark estimate of
the size and distribution of the U.S. population during the Revolutionary
War. They are as follows: total: three million (estimated; includes "Ne-
groes and mulattos"): New York, Connecticut, North Carolina and South
Carolina—248,139 each; Rhode Island—71,959½; New Hampshire—
124,069½; Massachusetts Bay—434,244; Virginia—496,278; New Jersey—
161,290; Pennsylvania—372,208; Maryland—310,174; Delaware—37,219;
and Georgia—missing. (It has been estimated that of the 3 million some
700,000 were slaves, 10 percent of whom residing in the northern states;
since some 22,000 resided in New York State, according to the 1790 census, approximately one-third of the slaves in the North were in that
state.)

   233. Jay-R. Morris, December 26, 1777, includes: "[I]s there any probability of a French war?" (Morris was a member of the Committee of
Secret Correspondence, which the next year became the Committee for
Foreign Affairs. It was to him that Jay forwarded the letters written by
Deane from France in invisible ink.) That Americans, much to the con-
sternation of V and FB, as we have seen, had long been led by the deputies in Paris to expect a Bourbon participation in the war is illustrated
by Hamilton's letters to Jay and company on April 20 and May 7, 1777:
"In a private letter from Philadelphia, I am informed that a treaty of a
very particular nature is on the point of being concluded" between
France and the U.S.; and "Dr. [Arthur] Lee indeed writes that from the
face of affairs there a war cannot be postponed longer than three
months." On the other hand, RL, while fully recognizing the value to the
American cause of a French war against England, was astute enough to
realize by July 3, 1778, that a "foreign war"—that is, a major land war
in Europe—was a doubtful prospect and that the Americans would have
to "work out our own solutions" (letter from New York to William Duer,
member of Congress) (RL/NYHS).

   234. BC/NYPL, vol. 195.

   235. Ibid., vol. 209.

   236. London felt so overtaxed at sea that it actually at this time was
fruitlessly proposing a defensive and offensive alliance to Russia with a
view to adding that country's "fairly powerful navy" (as described by
Madariaga's Britain . . . , pp. ix, 9, and 21) to its own naval strength.

237. Noailles-V, March 15, 1778 (BC/NYPL, vol. 187). The message reported that, upon receiving the French Declaration, Weymouth seemed surprised at it and nearly had tears in his eyes, either from tenderness or anger.

238. V-M (ibid., vol. 194).

239. Ibid., vol. 201.

240. Ibid., vols. 192 and 195.

241. Ministry note (ibid., vol. 193).

242. V-M, April 3, 1778 (ibid., vol. 193).

243. V-FB, December 24, 1778 (ibid., vol. 194).

244. Military Plan of Operations, January 27, 1778 (ibid., vol. 193). A factor surely helping to explain France's only limited willingness to allocate directly to the North American theater of operations a major portion of its military and naval assets was, as George Bancroft put it informally in his papers, that "not one in the French Cabinet truly friendly to America. Majority adverse to America." Throughout the war, Vergennes had to buck this trend in shaping France's military strategy.

245. D'Estaing, while in Boston harbor in September 1778, on instructions from Versailles, did release a public appeal to "all his countrymen in North America . . . to depend upon" King Louis XVI's "protection and support" and not to fight against the "nephews" of the "brave Montcalm." For reasons why such an appeal was totally misconceived, and could only land on deaf ears, see Brecher's Losing . . . , p. 217. D'Estaing left Boston for the West Indies on November 4, 1778 (Dr. Samuel Cooper-BF, January 4, 1779, Boston)—just as the French army under Rochambeau would precipitately, and unilaterally, do in December 1782.

246. D'Estaing returned with part of his straggling squadron to Brest on December 7, 1779 (Stevens's Facsimiles . . . , vol. 23).

247. V-G, November 18, 1778 (BC/NYPL, vol. 204).

248. V-M, November 2, 1778 (ibid., vol. 194). Among contemporary and historical criticisms of d'Estaing was that he personally was ill-equipped for the American assignment because his strength and experience were not those of a naval commander but of a soldier. (Even during the 1760s, d'Estaing was advising Versailles on policy toward British America.)

249. G-V, January 17, 1779 (ibid., vol. 205). Ironically, Sullivan, as a member of Congress for New Hampshire in 1781, was paid by the French minister for working against the "Eastern League" effort to curb French

influence in that body. L, in a 13 May dispatch (ibid., vol. 209), cited him as having been the key man in that successful effort. Sullivan was reputed to have acted in part out of personal financial need.

250. Schuyler-RL, August 29, 1778 (RL/NYHS).

251. Colonel Henry Livingston-RL, August 31 and September 5, 1778 (ibid.). Sullivan was particularly appreciative of the key role played in that evacuation by Henry, whom he personally "thanked" in private in early December.

252. G-V, January 17 and May 7, 1779 (BC/NYPL, vol. 205): Sullivan was the general who "had excited all the East against this vice-admiral and the French"; and his 7 May: "[T]he Boston papers were blaming France for alone being responsible for the U.S. not having 'conquered all North America.' "

253. Before the end of that year's campaign, d'Estaing would conquer Grenada from the English. St. Lucie was returned to France by England at war's end.

254. V-M, December 17, 1779 (ibid., vol. 195). At the time of his injuries, that courageous Frenchman was riding alongside the Polish volunteer on the American side, Count Pulaski, who, two days later, aboard the U.S.S. *Wasp* heading toward Charleston, died of wounds received during that same attack on enemy lines. As regards General Benjamin Lincoln, B-M, in his above-cited August 1781 "Portraits of American Generals," would: (a) attribute to his "weakness of character" the decision in 1780 to capitulate at Charleston, South Carolina, rather than to attempt an admittedly dangerous evacuation (see below); and (b) on the other hand, say of him that, although a novice, he has become a fine officer, after having been nearly caught by the English at Lexington, where he was at the head of 2,500 militia troops. (Lincoln in 1781 would be appointed by Congress as its first Secretary for War, alongside RL and Superintendent of Finance R. Morris. Lincoln's appointment would provoke the following comment by RL, in a letter of 2 November to James Duane [RL/NYHS]: It was a surprise, because, for "all his virtues as a man and an officer, I fear, from the little knowledge I have of him, [he] will want sufficient activity of genius for so embarrassing a Department.") As for Morris, note Jay-G. Morris, who was the superintendent's deputy, October 13, 1782 (JJ/CU): "our friend, Morris, whom I consider as the pillar of American credit."

255. The French, in connection with the attempt on Savannah, also lost sixty men taken as prisoners by the English when, per L-M, August 7,

1781 (RL/NYPL, vol. 198), they were "separated from d'Estaing's squadron and thrown on the Georgia coast."

256. Ibid., vol. 205. That G message included: "I only dared share this secret [plan for taking Halifax and Newfoundland] with the President of the Congress [Jay]" and selected members of key committees, and they authorized him (G) to work out the plan with General Washington; the latter agreed that attacking New York, as some in Congress were urging, would not be "practicable"; Washington would only agree with d'Estaing's proposal, that American troops participate in the Halifax operation and garrison it after the conquest, if France could guarantee French naval supremacy—otherwise, he felt he'd be leaving "the center of the United States to the mercy of the enemy"; Washington did recognize, however, that, if France could give that guarantee, that would possibly make the upcoming campaign the "decisive" one in the war.

257. L-V, September 26, 1779 (ibid., vol. 206): General Washington advised that, with Spain now in the war, future operations would include orders to General Lincoln to work with it with a view to evict the enemy from Georgia; and that the U.S. would support a permanent return of the Floridas to Spain as a necessary condition for the Americans to have a solid peace on the continent. (Compare this with the secret article on Florida negotiated by Jay in the peace treaty of November 30, 1782!)

258. V-M, October 15, 1779 (ibid., vol. 195): (1) Spain must authorize Miralles to offer the U.S. more naval and military cooperation than it had in mind so far, if the planned U.S.-Spanish expedition was to have any success of ousting the enemy from Pensacola, because there was no way for American troops to get there except by sea, unless the English were first forced out of Georgia; (2) in this last regard, had Spain alerted d'Estaing to its Florida plans, he could have attacked Savannah—where the English commander in the area, General Prevost, "had retired to"— en route to Halifax and Newfoundland.

259. That V was concerned over the negative fallout in the U.S. from d'Estaing's operations, even prior to learning of the Savannah attack, is clear from his October 26, 1778, message to G (ibid., vol. 204) advising that Versailles was greatly perplexed at the lack of reporting from d'Estaing, especially given "his upsetting run of bad luck with winds, slow Boston repairs," and so on; and that the government also was concerned at the news that Admiral Byron had arrived to fortify the English fleet at New York. V added: *"Nor do we have reports of how all this has affected the Americans"* (emphasis supplied).

260. That Carmichael got along well with the French in general (as he would with the Spanish, as well, much to Jay's discomfort) is suggested by L-M, October 10, 1779 (ibid., vol. 206): "Carmichael's enthusiasm for the alliance was without limits"; he was a true Francophile, "practically a romantic about us." (Considering that, according to Dull's *Franklin* . . . , p. 40, Carmichael in Paris had an opposite reputation, Luzerne's attitude, shared by many others, is truly remarkable. Typically, Carmichael's overly gentle biographer, Samuel Coe, takes a most positive view of Carmichael's activities and relationships in Paris as well as in Madrid. The historical consensus is that Carmichael was loyal to the U.S.)

261. V-M, May 1, 1778 (ibid., vol. 193): The Brest fleet was "practically complete and all our troops will be at the coast before 10 May." (It is important to note that Brest is not a Channel port but rather opens into the Atlantic Ocean via the Gulf of Gascony. In August 1778, France responded to an "informal" Spanish proposal, that London itself be an invasion target, with a list of obstacles, including that France lacked a port in the Channel.)

262. V-G, June 26, 1778 (ibid., vol. 204): On 17 June, France's watching frigate, *La Belle Poule*, was attacked off Ouessant "by an English frigate." (This skirmish was a standoff which the French, ever-defeatist in outlook when it came to fighting the English navy, greeted as a morale-builder on the grounds that the English frigate, H.M.S. *Arethusa*, not only had failed to defeat the closest of two French frigates it had encountered, *The Belle Poule*, but also had allegedly been the first one to leave the scene of battle in order to rejoin its nearby squadron, which was under Keppel's command.) As for d'Orvilliers's orders not to fight inside the Channel itself, this was known to the English: On 6 August, Grantham reported to London (ibid., vol. 241) that the French ambassador had informed his port consuls of this restriction on that admiral's orders, which, in the words of that Englishman, were "to commit hostilities and to seek and engage Admiral Keppel."

263. V-G, June 26, 1778 (ibid., vol. 204): France is stationing a large number of troops along its coast under Marshal de Broglio, and they "will be used depending upon circumstances."

264. Ibid., vol. 241. Keppel also felt his fleet was inadequately manned, among other qualitative problems.

265. FB-M, August 11, 1778 (ibid., vol. 194). M-V, June 22, 1778, which also contained the ambassador's comments that Charles would like to see England's "humiliation"; FB preferred to use mediation as the best

method to win Spanish goals; and, if Spain did enter the war as a full-scale belligerent, its "ambitions" would be so great as to make Spain "a burden more than a help" to France. Another, more cynical motivation for Floridablanca's advice that occurred to some of the French officials (internal paper dated August 17, 1778—ibid.) was the possibility that Spain believed a France lacking a major victory would then have to agree to give in to its major demands in order to get it into the war (in the event, this does seem to have helped drive France to accede to those demands in negotiating the agreement of April 12, 1779). On 17 August, M reported that, to get Spain into the war, France would have to offer it, as prerequisites for a peace agreement with England, Gibraltar, at least part of Florida, and Jamaica (possibly first to France and then to Spain in exchange for St. Domingue). The latter island, indeed, would figure in a possible peace deal in late 1782, much to Versailles' discomfort; also note that, at this stage, Minorca seems not to have come up in Montmorin's talk with the Spaniards.

266. Ibid.

267. As the English consul at Cadiz was reporting to London in May 1779 (ibid., vol. 241), Spain had there 36 ships-of-the-line and ten frigates, all armed and ready to leave in a few days' time.

268. Note that this French push did not go so far as to urge the American *cause* on Spain. Rather, the French regularly denigrated the U.S. to Spain, both as regards that nation's near-term prospects as a military power and as regards its political stability and values. Illustrative of this last point is V's above-cited message to FB of January 20, 1778, on the very eve of signing the alliance treaty with the U.S.: France shouldn't bring the U.S. into its secrets, which would then become public worldwide, because of the widespread sharing of secrets within republican governments as opposed to monarchies; therefore, France only tells the Americans "that which is indispensable for us to inform them about, and only at the moment when their cooperation is absolutely necessary."

269. Some American-Spanish trade would be continued, mainly through a channel at Bilbao controlled by Joseph Gardoqui and Sons, one of whom, Diego, would become Jay's interpreter and unofficial contact point at Madrid with the Spanish government and would go on to become Spain's first official diplomatic representative to the U.S., where Jay was then serving as the country's second Secretary for Foreign Affairs under the Articles of Confederation. Note that Havana, too, at times

served as a base for exchanging essential supplies and for financial transactions.

270. M-V (ibid., vol. 193).

271. V-M, March 27, 1778 (ibid.): France is keeping its promise to hold
its 29 ships-of-the-line at Brest in order to divert England from attacking
the returning Spanish fleets and troops; if Spain wished, France would
help it conquer Jamaica, Pensacola, and so on; as France's only goal was
to decrease English power, it would do anything Spain desired against
England. Also see V-M, June 20, 1778 (ibid., vol. 194).

272. V wrote M, February 12, 1779 (ibid., vol. 195), giving him the
authority to sign whatever changes Spain might want to make in the
enclosed draft convention between their two countries. (This came on
the heels of a lengthy evolution in French attitude and policy toward the
negotiation with Spain. For example, in June 1778, Vergennes candidly
recognized that Spain's war aims were likely to be so much more ambitious than France's that it "was doubtful we could support them." In
the event, Versailles, by this message of 1779, was evidently desperate
enough for it, in fact, to support them!)

273. George Bancroft's papers contain the following informal charac-
terization of V's stance: "impatient but submissive" (ibid., vol. 194). V-
M, private letter, March 10, 1778 (ibid., vol. 193).

274. M-V, January 28, February 26 and March 20, 1778 (ibid., vol. 193).
This attitude had a long tradition among the French, as is clear from the
advice given by a Royal Council member, the Duc de Noailles, in the
early 1750s, to a colleague departing Versailles to serve as ambassador
at Madrid, where he himself had once spent time on a special mission:
He was to go slow at the start and listen for the first six months, and
"then become phlegmatic; if possible, take a dose of opium so as to be
in unison with more than one great person at the Court to which you
are going—and all will be well." Jay surely must have been struck by
this and perhaps himself "trembled" upon reading Noailles's published
Memoires during his voyage of 1779 from Philadelphia to Europe, and
which, as noted below, he recommended to Lewis Littlepage, in a letter
of June 16, 1780, advising how to earn a "knowledge of mankind."

275. M-V, April 10, 1778 (ibid.): FB "exploded" at France's point that
a defeated France would be followed by England's then turning on
Spain; he said Charles is not a "vice-roy or provincial governor" of
France, and his "sacrifices" in the Seven Years' War entitled him to
greater respect, as did his age, experience and wisdom.

276. V-M, May 1, 1778 (ibid.).

277. V-M, March 19, 1779 (ibid., vol. 195).

278. M-V, August 31 and November 4, 1778 (ibid., vol. 194).

279. M-V, August 17, 1778 (ibid.).

280. M-V, March 29, 1779 (ibid., vol. 195): In view of England's un-satisfactory responses, Charles instructed FB to send it an ultimatum [which M enclosed] regarding which M was given the assurances of FB that, notwithstanding its lacking any provisions for an English evacuation of New York or Rhode Island, Spain would never propose anything contrary to France's treaty commitments to the Americans. (M would soon berate himself for not having taken the opportunity, when he was shown the text of the ultimatum prior to Spain's sending it off to London, to object to it, or at least to insist that Versailles be given the opportunity to review it before the English received it. Once the Americans got wind of the terms being suggested by the Spaniards, that mediation effort would also generate political problems for the French at the Continental Congress, which naturally associated Versailles with it.) V-M, December 24, 1778 (ibid., vol. 194); G-V, May 4, 1779 (ibid., vol. 205); and V-L, July 18, 1779 (ibid., vol. 206).

281. M-V, November 4, 1778: If France did what Spain wanted, that would "change French war goals" and make the war's "duration uncertain."

282. V-M, June 1 and October 9, 1778 (ibid., vol. 194); and M-V, February 26, March 20 and November 4, 1778 (ibid., vols. 193–94).

283. V-M, February 23, 1778 (ibid., vol. 193) reported that the Council had been occupied, aside from the American War, "with less important but unavoidable matters, especially those of Germany, regarding which we are necessarily involved given our Westphalia role as guarantor of the peace." For the Westphalia Treaty, see Brecher's Losing . . . , pp. 107–8 and 161.

284. Noailles-V, January 9, 1778 (ibid., vol. 187) reported that England saw the death of the Elector of Bavaria as opening a possibility for France to be distracted by that area's problems. V's response of 17 January: The Bavarian problem could only be a "secondary" one for France; England was "our" principal enemy.

285. V-M, October 9, 1778 reported that the Prussian armies had withdrawn to Silesia and Saxony.

286. V-M, December 24, 1778 (ibid., vol. 194) reported that Prussia and Austria had accepted the mediation of France and Russia regarding Ba-

varia, which was a major new problem for him and was taking time away from the government's working out a joint strategy with Spain for 1779.

287. V-M, June 12, 1780 (ibid., vol. 197).

288. However, as will be discussed further, the successful mediation of the Bavarian crisis immediately opened the flood gates for additional mediation offers, unwelcome at Versailles and Madrid, regarding the English-Bourbon conflict: Maria-Theresa, the same month as the Teschen Treaty, enthusiastically wrote Charles (15 May) with an "offer" to help Spain mediate the conflict between France and England (ibid., vol. 195). Charles's 7 June answer was that England's "hostile acts have reached the point of already having compromised my honor." France's answer to a similar Austrian *demarche* to it was along the same lines. As Russia, too, now was trying to get into the mediating act, an exasperated M would write V on 11 June: "I wouldn't be surprised if now the King of Sardinia doesn't soon join the ranks and offer his services."

289. A reference to the previously cited treaty between Russia and the Ottomans of 1774 at Kuchuk Kalnarji. That agreement was under great strain, however, by the time of Jay's letter, due to continuing competition over the Crimean peninsula.

290. V-M, January 28, 1778 (ibid., vol. 194). Madariaga probably would fault V here for overstating the extent of Prussian influence over Russian policies (*Britain . . .*, p. 167).

291. Regarding Spain, Versailles' above-cited internal paper of August 17, 1778, would rue that Charles unfortunately is holding to the line that the alliance treaty with the Americans of 6 February effectively canceled out the commitments of Spain under the Family Compact of 1761, because the present war between France and England was directly caused by that new, unilaterally enacted French alliance with a third party. In a message to Aranda that same month (BC/NYPL, vol. 194), FB expanded on Charles's position by drawing an analogy between Spain's unwillingness to accept the Family Pact as binding on it under present circumstances and France's asserting to Austria that it is not bound by its commitments to Austria under their alliance treaty of May 1756, given the circumstances of how the Bavarian conflict began.

292. Gates-Washington, June 25, 1778 (ibid., vol. 81). Also see Willcox's *Portrait . . .*, pp. 233–37.

293. L-V, September 26, 1779 (ibid., vol. 206), reported that Washington would like to take Canada, but not with the same impatience or

ambition as the "Eastern provinces." (In this regard, note Washington's March 12, 1778, letter from Valley Forge to RL [RL/NYHS]: "I wish all the men on the upper part of the [Hudson] River had been drawn down to the Highlands, instead of being kept to carry on an expedition in which I never believed . . . [and] could never succeed.")

294. G-V, May 14, 1779 (ibid., vol. 205), reported that Washington saw through the French policy not to help the U.S. conquer Canada but would not act on this insight against France.

295. G-V, February 15, 1779 (ibid.).

296. G-V, December 6, 1778 (ibid.), advised that there was no "metallic money" in the American economy, and the inflation rate, based on the price of flour, which served as "the common measure for establishing proportionate values of all goods and services," was five times the pre-war price; the Congress up to then had issued $88 million, of which $50 million was that year alone; the total debt of the U.S. was about $140 million. On June 17, 1779, G added: "[U]nhappily, I have never sensed there was in the Congress the least spark of financial genius" (ibid., vol. 206).

297. G-V, September 20, 1778; V-G, December 25, 1778, and February 19, 1779 (ibid., vols. 204–5).

298. Aranda-FB, April 13, 1778 (ibid., vol. 193), reported that: JA told him Lafayette was the commanding officer of, "or at least is involved in, a detachment" to enter Canada; he (Aranda) knew Lafayette well—he was very bright and decided to go and fight "in a war so singular instead of spending his youthful years among the delights of Paris"; and the Americans had given him this assignment in the hopes of winning over the Canadians.

299. Ibid., vol. 206.

300. G's dispatch of October 20, 1778 (ibid., vol. 204), reported that R. Morris was arguing that it was in France's interest to see Canada, including Halifax, as part of the U.S.; otherwise, England would be able to upset French fishing in Newfoundland waters at will; the U.S. would fully back a permanent French retention of Newfoundland; and Spain may well be pressuring France to assure that Canada remain in English hands, a development that, in fact, would actually promote, not deter, a friendship between England and the U.S. and, by doing so, would be harmful to Spain, because then England would be more prone to cooperating with the U.S. in any conflict with the Spaniards over the control of the west. G went on to report that he answered Morris, as follows:

Spain believed that England's having populated the Natchez region with 5,000 settlers in recent years, coupled with current American threats to St. Augustine and Pensacola, were reasons to distrust Anglo-Saxon intentions towards its American possessions; therefore, Congress would do well (a) to give Spain "assurances," (b) to "establish, on its own initiative, limits beyond which it will forbid Americans to settle," and (c) to forgo claims to the Floridas and to navigation rights on the Mississippi.

301. Per V-L, October 22, 1780 (ibid., vol. 208). The main French goal was to block English access to those ports, which could be used as bases for their fighting navy against Bourbon possessions and trade in the Americas.

302. M's dispatch of June 1, 1778 (ibid., vol. 193). The governor of Louisiana, Bernardo de Galvez, reported that a U.S. expedition covering some 2,000 miles along the Mississippi River was taking English forts along the left bank "by courage alone, without strict military discipline, and with only *sans culottes*" [literally, those without knee breeches; politically, those from the lower classes without uniforms or the leadership of trained officers—a term that would become more universally known during the French Revolution].

303. Still as chancellor, never having resigned that post even while serving as Secretary for Foreign Affairs, RL had the privilege of swearing in Washington at his inaugural in New York City as president in 1789. In March–April 1782, RL took a leave of absence, during which he obtained the agreement of the legislature that he could retain both of his positions. That, in turn, this dual incumbency did not sit well with some in Congress is clear from G. Morris's letter from Philadelphia of 2 April (RL/NYHS): "I observe you are not to quit your office in the state; probably you are not aware that when this is known in the great council [the Congress] it will give some uneasiness there, at least I have heard sentiments since you left us [he would be back in Philadelphia by at least 17 April] from some members to that effect. . . . This hint I think myself bound to drop for I should expect the same from your friendship had I been in your place." However, the issue would not disappear throughout his tenure as secretary; for example, in November 1782 (ibid.), friends in Albany informed him that "very vigorous exertions are making to deprive you of the Chancery." This helped decide him to write President Boudinot, 2 December asking that he obtain Congress' acceptance of his resignation so that he might serve as New York Chancellor.

304. Morris's *Making* . . . , p. 11. Duane-RL, July 6, 1777 (RL/NYHS), re-

Notes 299

fers to the Vermonters as "revolters." Vermont in 1777 declared itself a republic; it would be accepted as the fourteenth state in 1791.

305. BC/NYPL, vol. 210.

306. Jay-Clinton, June 3, 1779: Henry Laurens had proposed that Vermont be invited "to send deputies to represent their case" directly to the Congress, but nobody seconded him.

307. At the peak of the Saratoga battle, per Jay's Autobiographical Notes, he "carried Mrs. Jay to Kent in Connecticut—took lodging"— October 11, 1777. Jay was on a military supply mission.

308. Jay-V, January 27, 1780, Cadiz: "Sir, it is with very sensible pleasure that I commence a correspondence with a minister."

309. Per Jay's Autobiographical Note: "Appointed President of Congress," December 10, 1778. That Jay's being a New Yorker was a key to his appointment is clear from the fact that, in the months prior to his acceptance of the appointment as a New York delegate, it was Schuyler who was rumored to be the one to join the New York delegation at Philadelphia; in that period, the correspondence between RL and the then-members of that delegation (RL/NYHS) assumed Schuyler would succeed Laurens (e.g., RL's: "Is it your opinion that General Schuyler ought to continue in the army, or to accept of the Presidency of Congress?"; and Morris's: If Schuyler came, "I believe he would be made President and certainly the best President Congress has had. His [wealthy] wife would be worth the gold of her heir.").

310. As president, Jay's policy was to "prevent the flames of civil war to rage" (letter of September 25, 1779, to Clinton); therefore, he prevented the presentation of strong pro–New York resolutions as "imprudent," despite pressure on him—his goal was congressional "unanimity" (JJ/CU). In that letter, Jay, increasingly the nationalist as opposed to the New Yorker, explained (1) that Congress' debates and resolutions had helped show the Confederacy as going beyond mere "security against foreign invasions," and that the "union" must include assuring peace "and established boundaries," even though this approach had put New Hampshire and Massachusetts "on a footing with New York"; and (2) that congressional resolutions on this issue had established the policy that any "violation" of the "principles laid down" in them "to be a breach of the peace of the Confederacy," thereby making clear that the Congress had declared its resolve "to maintain" the union.

311. B-M's dispatch of September 25, 1780, reported that Congress was awaiting Maryland's ratification of the Articles before making reforms,

including appointing nonmembers to run executive departments. L's of August 11, 1781: RL was "a close relative of John Jay, and his friend"; therefore, he (L) would have to adopt a policy of "great circumspection towards him" (BC/NYPL, vols. 208 and 210).

312. FB-Aranda, September 1777 (ibid., vol. 192). V-M, October 9, 1778 (ibid., vol. 194): "Gérard found in Philadelphia a M. Mirales, who is there for Spain but without official status." Per Ozanam's *Diplomates Espagnoles* . . . , Madrid had sent Miralles on a "secret mission from Cuba to George Washington"; and when he died on April 28, 1780, he was succeeded "in his commission," effective 20 October of that year, by his secretary, Francisco Rendón, a career official who had been appointed to the American post in January 1779.

313. V-M, December 24, 1778; V-G, December 25, 1778 (BC/NYPL, vols. 194 and 204).

314. G-V, July 14, 1779 (ibid., vol. 206).

315. This pattern was made explicit in V's message of September 25, 1779, to L (ibid., vol. 206): If war failed to bring France a "definitive treaty" for all the belligerents, it might have to go back to the idea of a truce, which, as the history of European republics showed, needn't upset the U.S., especially given that France was willing to guarantee it. Similarly, see L-V, June 8, 1781 (ibid., vol. 209).

316. G-V, July 20, 1779 (ibid., vol. 206).

317. G freely and revealingly admitted to members of Congress in July 1779 that if the U.S. forced France to choose between it and Spain, it would always choose Spain (G to V, July 14, 1779); he did so in the expectation that this warning would pressure the Congress to be flexible and moderate in its policy toward Spain for fear that, otherwise, it risked losing the cooperation of France. Two months earlier, in a message of 5 May to V, that Frenchman strongly criticized the Lee family for basically saying the same thing that he himself was now acknowledging; that is, France would always give a higher priority to the Family Compact than to its treaty with the U.S. G did not like the logical conclusion that the Lees were drawing—that the U.S. will only end up being sacrificed to that Bourbon connection—and he therefore advised the minister that Arthur Lee should not be entrusted to carry out congressional resolutions. This, of course, was redundant advice in view of V's own long-standing distrust of Lee.

318. For example, B-M wrote RL on May 9, 1780: It seemed that the late Miralles "had no positive ["instructions"]: but his Court shows a

disposition so favorable that I have much reason to have hopes of a successful Jay mission" to Spain.

319. Morris's *Seven* ... , p. 209 (and his *Making* ... , p. 642) credits Jay with having drafted this circular—all the evidence suggests it was drafted by a committee established for that purpose, per United States' *Journal* ... , vol. 15, pp. 1019–20 and 1051–62.

320. G-V, September 25, 1779; L-V, October 10, 1779 (BC/NYPL, vol. 206).

321. Jay-Washington, April 26, 1779 (JJ/CU); L-M, October 10, 1779 (BC/NYPL, vol. 206); Aranda-V, December 11, 1777 (ibid., vol. 192); G-V, May 4 and July 14, 1779 (ibid., vol. 205); V-L, July 18, 1779 (ibid.); G-V, January 28, 1779 (ibid.). Also see Hardman's *Louis XVI* ... , pp. 65–66, for the king's reported 1792 regret over the "shameless" secrecy of the pre-1778 aid, but not over that aid, per se.

322. G-V, March 1 and July 14, 18 and 20, 1779 (BC/NYPL, vols. 205–6); G. Morris-RL, July 22, 1779 (RL/NYHS); V-L, June 28, 1782 (BC/NYPL, vol. 211).

323. Jay-Clinton, September 25, 1779 (JJ/CU).

324. L-V, October 8, 1779 (BC/NYPL, vol. 206) reported that JA left France "without having received orders to do so"; L spent two months with him crossing the Atlantic; L knew that V did not get to see JA much, so he was enclosing his biographical data; if negotiations were to go badly, JA was capable of misleading Congress by casting doubt on the purity of French views and by trying "to cool the ardor of the friends of the alliance"; JA said he'd left France without orders, because "I couldn't deal with the total oblivion where I'd been placed by the appointment of M. Franklin as Minister Plenipotentiary"; JA also resented BF's popularity, while he remained largely unknown; L feared all this had "inspired him with some kind of bias against us," although not V personally—JA appreciated the testimonial certificate V had given him and which would be, he said during the crossing, "a great help to him here" [this is probably the basis for G's saying Congress assumed JA was acceptable to France]; Adams's new post predictably would likely lead to friction between him and Franklin, who hadn't played up to his amour proper—but Franklin would be uninvolved in peace negotiations so the "rivalry" should not be so damaging for French interests. V-L, February 5, 1780 (ibid.), noted that he met with Adams and had the impression that he had absolutely no knowledge of "the nature or the objective of his commission." (A modern reader is struck by the willingness of an

American diplomat, JA, to so-criticize a fellow American colleague to L, an official of that colleague's host government.)

325. V-L, September 7, 1781 (ibid., vol. 210); BF-Jay, January 19, 1782; B-M to Rayneval, April 12, 1782 (ibid., vol. 211). (Adams left France for Amsterdam in July 1780, that is, prior to Laurens's capture at sea in September.)

326. JA-Jay, July 8, 1782 (JJ/CU); B-M to Montmorin, July 13, 1781 (BC/NYPL, vol. 198): "John Adams' loan negotiations in Holland lacked any success." Jay-Schuyler, November 25, 1780 (JJ/CU): "The Dutch, I believe, will remain pacific—they have too much in the funds to risk—and some of them seem surprised that Congress should be at a loss for money, while the produce of the country continues to exceed the consumption of its inhabitants." RL-Jay, October 20, 1781, and May 9, 1782 (ibid.); V-Vauguyon, May 17, 1781 (BC/NYPL, vol. 201).

327. V-M, May 29, 1779, and January 13, 1780 (ibid., vols. 195–96).

328. V-M, October 15, 1779; M-V, January 9, 1780 (ibid.).

329. V-M, September 21, 1778. FB's idea of warring on England as Rome did Carthage "does honor to his elevated soul"; V-M, February 12, 1779 (ibid., vols. 194–95).

330. V-Ossun, March 22, 1777; V-M, January 13, 1780 (ibid., vols. 192 and 196).

331. V-M, May 29 and September 21, 1779, January 13, 1780, and October 2, 1782 (ibid., vols. 195–96 and 200).

332. M-V, September 27, 1779, and December 21, 1780 (ibid., vols. 195 and 197).

333. V-M, April 29, 1779 (ibid., vol. 195).

334. V-M, July 23, 1779 (ibid.).

335. M-V, November 26, 1779 (ibid.).

336. V-M, July 23, 1779 (ibid.): V was not writing directly to FB "lest my dark mood due to the mishaps we've experienced" be passed on to him.

337. V-M, August 18, 1780 (ibid., vol. 197): France had to maintain the state of neutrality in which Europe had found itself these past three years: "a true political phenomenon."

338. JA-BF, August 25, 1781 (Wharton's *The Revolutionary Diplomatic Correspondence . . .*, vol. IV, pp. 336–37).

339. M-V, February 22, 1780; V-M, March 13, 1780 (BC/NYPL, vol. 196).

340. Corberon (St. Petersburg)-V, March 10, 1780 (ibid., vol. 202); Madariaga's *Britain . . .*, p. 158.

341. V-L, February 5, 1780; V-M, January 7 and 29, 1780; M-V, May 13, 1780 (BC/NYPL, vols. 196 and 206).

342. Ternay died on December 16, 1780, in Rhode Island and would be replaced by Admiral de Barras.

343. Lafayette-Maurepas, October 20, 1781: "The play is over, M. le Comte, and the fifth act has just ended." Lafayette-V, same date: "[H]ere is the fine quill we have at last just politically sharpened." V-Lafayette, December 1, 1781: Maurepas received Lauzun's report prior to dying; "Don't tire of sending me good quills: it's not with one only that one can write a work so voluminous as that as the next peace" (ibid., vol. 210). Jay, too, noted the connection between military and diplomatic success, as when he wrote Washington on March 3, 1779 (JJ/CU): "[W]e certainly should remember that to be formidable in the field is necessary to be successful in negotiation."

344. Bemis's *Hussey* . . . , pp. 115–16, confuses the West Indies *hivernage* with "winter."

345. United States' *Journals* . . . , vol. 15, pp. 1182–83: President of Congress Huntington-BF, October 16, 1779: "Mr. Jay and Mr. Carmichael will embark on board the *Confederacy*, Continental ship of war, now in Delaware ready to sail *for France* [emphasis supplied]." Jay wrote BF, January 26, 1780 (JJ/CU), that the *Confederacy* left Chester on 18 October "bound for France." Jay wrote V, January 27, 1780 (ibid.), that he sailed "for France" on "the 26th of October last." (Unfavorable winds had kept Jay's ship from leaving Delaware Bay for a full week after he had boarded it.) Jay-Galvez, January 27, 1780 (ibid.): "Providence having thus been pleased to bring me directly to Spain." M-V, February 22, 1780 (BC/NYPL, vol. 196). Jay-RL, February 28, 1782 (RL/NYHS).

346. Jay-Captain Seth Harding, on board the *Confederacy*, November 26, 1779; Jay-BF, January 26, 1780; Jay-Clinton, February 1, 1780; Jay-RL, February 19, 1780.

347. The three Jay brothers in that census year owned nineteen slaves.

348. Morris's *Winning* . . . , p. 13, generously labels Abigail's fate as "tragic." Benoit was very upset by these events.

349. Jay-BF, January 26, 1780 (JJ/CU).

350. Jay-President, January 27 and March 3, 1780 (ibid.).

351. JA wrote Jay, February 22, 1780 (ibid.), that "I, too, have had my hair-breadth escapes"; and that it took him two months to get to Paris from his landing on the northern coast of Spain.

352. Bemis's *American Secretaries* . . . , vol. 1, p. 197.

353. Even under that circumstance, it still would have been worthwhile to study Jay's mission to Spain in detail for the insight it afforded into the true strength, nature and extent of the French commitment to the American cause and also into the all-important military and diplomatic role Spain played during the war.

354. Jay-Carmichael, August 17, 1780.

355. FB-Jay and Carmichael, March 9, 1780.

356. Jay-Lovell, October 27, 1780; Jay-President, November 6, 1780 (JJ/CU). Per Ferguson's *Power* . . . , pp. 46 and 56, the nominal dollar value of the £100,000 in specie in 1780 was $10 million, and that ratio would greatly increase from then on, as the continental currency rapidly lost almost all its value due to depreciation. (Bemis's *Pinckney* . . . , pp. 371–72, errs in attributing to, then-private citizen, Robert Morris the "notorious and desperate device of writing drafts on American diplomatic agents in France and Spain.")

357. Jay-Deane, October 26, 1780 (JJ/CU): "You were blamed not for omitting finally to settle your accounts in France, but for not being in a capacity to show what those accounts were."

358. United States' *Journals* . . . , vol. 15, pp. 1116–17 and 1160.

359. Among Jay's papers at his Homestead family home, Katonah, New York: [Archivist: "JJ note accompanying William Carmichael Correspondence, 2/95," London:] "Care should be taken of these papers—They include letters to and from William Carmichael—a man who mistook cunning for wisdom; and who in pursuing his purposes, preferred the guidance of artifice and simulation to that of truth and rectitude. He finally yielded to intemperance, and died a bankrupt."

360. RL-Jay, May 9, 1782 (JJ/CU).

361. Jay-President, November 6, 1780; Jay-BF, August 20, 1781.

362. G wrote V, July 14, 1779 (BC/NYPL, vol. 206), that he told Jay and other members of Congress that the apparent determination of the Adams-Lee party was "to break ties between the U.S. and the Bourbon powers," and that, "if so, it will see that France, if it must choose between its two allies, won't choose the U.S. over Spain." V-M, January 29, 1780 (ibid., vol. 196): "[S]ince the U.S. knows from France's own declarations to it that, having to choose, France would stay with Spain and not the U.S., it could very well then also consider France as being potentially indifferent to its achieving independence."

363. B-M wrote M, October 21, 1780 (BC/NYPL, vol. 197), that he had been "given Jay's instructions—contained in a 'secret letter'—for M's

use; and, that this was a great compliment to France as America's ally." Jay-Clinton, April 25, 1781 (JJ/CU): "I am as ignorant" of developments in the U.S. "as if I resided among the ten tribes whose habitation no travelers have hitherto found." V-L, September 7, 1781 (BC/NYPL, vol. 210): "As for Mr. Jay's conduct in his negotiation, I'm still led to believe that he hasn't made use of his powers in all their extent, and that, for too long a time, he has obstinately refused to offer the concession the Congress had decided to make to Spain." (The fact that V—and therefore Spain—had Jay's instructions understandably greatly upset that American negotiator.)

364. In all fairness, Jay could just as, or even more, reasonably have faulted his *American* colleagues for ignoring his need to cover his bills. After all, 1781 witnessed the largest flow of funds coming to the Americans from French sources, especially as a consequence of the French loan in Holland of 10 million livres. Those funds were bitterly fought over by R. Morris (for Congress), by John Laurens (in Europe that spring on a special mission for the Continental Army) and by each of the U.S. ministers in Europe to cover their own bills—BF, JA and Jay, with the latter coming in last. V—not to speak of BF's own bitter exchanges with John Laurens over the latter's unilateral purchases—was caught in the middle of all this, much to his vocal disgruntlement, especially as he sought to ward off young Laurens's excessive, bluntly presented demands as well as Morris's pressure to obtain the bulk of the funds in the name of Congress.

365. RL wrote Jay, December 13, 1781 (JJ/CU), that Congress' silence meant that it wanted Jay to "execute the commission"; and B-M wrote Montmorin, (BC/NYPL, vol. 199), that "Congress has put its interests entirely in the hands of the King at the future peace negotiations," because it was the only way out of its impasse over what to instruct the plenipotentiaries. For JA's conscientious acquiescence in those instructions (as well as his expressed relief at having four colleagues now with him as peace commissioners), see his August 25, 1781, to BF (JJ/CU).

366. Recall the earlier instructions Jay gave to Carmichael (January 27, 1780, JJ/CU) regarding how to protect the "independence and self-respect" of the United States.

367. Madariaga's *Britain . . .*, p. 158.

368. V-Vauguyon, March 13, 1782; V-L, September 7, 1783 (BC/NYPL, vols. 201 and 213).

369. V-M, January 13 and 22, 1781; Vergennes-Verac (St. Petersburg), February 16, 1781 (ibid., vols. 198 and 202).

370. Ibid., vol. 202.

371. V instructed M, September 28, 1780 (ibid., vol. 197), not to tell Spain that France's real hope was in Russian mediation.

372. V-Verac, February 16, 1781 (ibid., vol. 202).

373. FB informed Aranda, March 23, 1781 (ibid., vol. 197), that, "[W]ith Cumberland gone, Spain could no longer delay the Russian-Austrian mediation."

374. V-M, October 3, 1781: "[L]ast year, we made Jamaica the basis and the object of all our plans, at Spanish initiative"; M-V, November 4, 1780 (ibid., vols. 197–98).

375. RL-Jay, May 9, 1782 (JJ/CU).

376. Dull, in his *Diplomatic History*, p. 179, regrets that Bemis "treats with far more seriousness than they are worth the supposedly secret British-Spanish negotiations of 1780."

377. V wrote M, March 31, 1780 (BC/NYPL, vol. 196), that, "I'd believe anything of Spain except your report it opened a negotiation with England," and that he concurred that any such negotiation "without our knowledge would be at the expense of America's interests."

378. Jay-Carmichael, August 17, 1780; Jay-BF, September 8, 1780.

379. V-M, April 26, 1780 (BC/NYPL, vol. 196): "[L]eave it up to us here to decide what to tell the U.S. of Cumberland."

380. Jay wrote the President, April 25, 1781 (JJ/CU), that Cumberland had left Spain, that the Englishman's mission had been based on mutual efforts at deception, and that "Whatever we may get from this court is clear gain."

381. For example, FB was not above shamelessly using even Jay's unexpected arrival in Spain for his own purposes, as in his March 2, 1780, to an intermediary, Hussey, whose 16 February had said England was ready to name a negotiator and to give its assurance that the cession and exchange of Gibraltar along with terms of a peace may be treated: "[F]rom day to day is expected Mr. Jay . . . *and I shall not be able to retard long his negotiation*" (emphasis supplied) (BC/NYPL, vol. 243).

382. Hillsborough-Cumberland, August 3 and 4, 1780 (ibid.).

383. BF-Jay, January 19, 1782 (JJ/CU): "The infant Hercules has now strangled his second serpent that attacked him in his cradle." Duane wrote RL, September 11, 1781 (RL/NYHS), that Cornwallis would probably "make desperate efforts to save his reputation. I remember he was very free of his censures against Burgoyne for capitulating instead of fighting."

384. V-L, December 24, 1781, and March 23, 1782 (BC/NYPL, vols. 210–11).

385. RL-Jay, November 28, 1781 (JJ/CU): "These conquerors of America hold about 20 square miles of this continent [RL obviously was only thinking of coastal areas!], and even that they hold by a very precarious tenure. . . . [Congress] feel themselves satisfied with everything both at home and abroad."

386. V-L, December 24, 1781, and March 23, 1782 (BC/NYPL, vols. 210–11).

387. V-M, July 6 and December 20, 1781. Actually, as early as 1779, V, in his internal paper, "Overview of Objectives to Achieve during the Upcoming Pacification," wrote that England "could negotiate directly with the Americans, it being understood that the two negotiations would proceed at the same pace; and that the two treaties would be signed at the same time, and the one wouldn't be valid without the other" (ibid., vols. 198 and 187).

388. Grenville-Fox, May 14 and June 4, 1782; Fox-Grenville, May 21 and 26, 1782 (ibid., vol. 252).

389. Shelburne-O, July 27, 1782; Oswald's notes for August 1782 (ibid., vol. 254; and for O's notes, also in Morris's *Winning* . . . , pp. 303ff). It was on the basis of this error that Jay, credibly in American historiography, charged V with having purposely thrown a monkey wrench into his negotiations by getting Grenville's successor, Alleyne Fitzherbert, in August to alert London to reverse its alleged policy of recognition of U.S. independence in the first instance; in fact, of course, not only was Carleton never given the authority that Jay initially believed he had, but also the Shelburne-led government, both for policy and legal reasons, never had any intention of so quickly recognizing the U.S.

390. As late as 23 November V was writing Luzerne of how far the Americans and English were from reaching an accord (BC/NYPL, vol. 212)—in fact, so far that he didn't yet feel the need to step in and use the "authority" Congress had given him to intervene.

391. Regarding the dates for Franklin's "illness," see O's notes (BC/NYPL, vol. 254) and Morris's *Winning* . . . , pp. 303ff.

392. O-Townshend, September 10, 1782 (ibid.); and Jay-RL, November 17, 1782 (JJ/CU).

393. Ibid.

394. M-V, February 22, 1780 (BC/NYPL, vol. 196).

395. O-Shelburne, July 10, 1782 (ibid., vol. 253); Jay-RL, November 17, 1782.

396. M wrote V, July 17, 1780 (ibid., vol. 197), that he had urged Jay "to show a bit more self-confidence at his meetings with Floridablanca, and, since then, they get along better."

397. Jay-President, November 6, 1780 (JJ/CU). "According to Aranda, Jay spoke Spanish and French very imperfectly" (Bemis's *Rayneval* . . . , p. 30).

398. BC/NYPL, vol. 212; also see RL-Rendon, March 6, 1782 (RL/NYHS), and RL-Jay, January 4, 1783 (text below).

399. Jay-G. Morris, October 13, 1782 (JJ/CU)—"Had I not violated the instructions of Congress"; Jay-RL, November 17, 1782.

400. Townshend-O, September 1, 1782 (BC/NYPL, vol. 254).

401. That this move was a politically awkward one for Jay, the New Yorker, see Madison's Notes on the congressional debates of December 1782 (United States' *Journals* . . . , vol. 23, pp. 872–75).

402. V-L, September 25, 1779, and V-M, April 21 and December 4, 1780 (BC/NYPL, vols. 206 and 197); and Brecher's *Losing* . . . , p. 159.

403. BF-Samuel Cooper, December 26, 1782 (*The Writings of Benjamin Franklin*; ed. Albert H. Smyth; Macmillan; New York, 1906).

404. Also note that the "King's Orders and Instructions" of April 12, 1778, to the Carlisle Commission stated: "You are hereby directed to address them by any style or title . . . and we authorize you to admit of any claim or title to independency in any description of men, *during the time of treaty, and for the purpose of treaty* [emphasis supplied; 'treaty' here means the period of negotiations]. . . . You are not authorized finally to conclude any treaty or agreement. . . . [A]s such ['claim or title to independency'], not being legal acts, will be in effect rescinded by the conclusion of the treaty. . . . [If a treaty seems possible, don't break off negotiations over any] point . . . short of open and avowed independence (except such independence as relates only to the purpose of treaty)" (Stevens's *Facsimiles* . . . , vol. 4, document 440; also see Bemis's *Hussey* . . . , p. 3, and *Diplomacy* . . . , pp. 82–83). Of course, Jay's requirements were at a more significant diplomatic level in that he was demanding English acknowledgment of the "U.S." in O's full powers and under the authority of the Great Seal.

405. V-M, August 10 and September 14, 1782 (BC/NYPL, vol. 199).

406. V-L, September 7 ("It takes a man of politics to know to cede on a matter of form when one has reason to feel satisfied on its substance") and October 14, 1782 ("American representatives do not shine by their sensible views adapted to the European political situation") (ibid., vol.

212). Oswald went so far as to have agreed with Jay on 5 October on a northern line that would have given the U.S. all of the first four Great Lakes.

407. Jay-Benjamin Vaughan, March 28, 1783 (JJ/CU).

408. Per Jay-RL, November 17, 1782, Rayneval wrote Jay on 4 September requesting a meeting specifically on western limits and Spain; and Rayneval-Jay, September 6 and 7, 1782 (JJ/NYHS).

409. The most notable error was Rayneval's claim that England in 1755 gave "almost the whole course of the Ohio" to France, which, in 1761, offered it to England—in fact, England's final peace offer of March 7, 1755, accepted too late by Versailles to prevent the outbreak of war, most certainly pushed French sovereignty back from the Allegheny to the Wabash River (Brecher's *Losing . . .*, pp. 86–87, 167 and map 1).

410. Jay-RL, September 28 and November 17, 1782; O's Notes for August–September (BC/NYPL, vol. 254); Jay-John Vaughan, February 15, 1783 (JJ/CU); V-L, October 14, 1782 (BC/NYPL, vol. 212); Benjamin Vaughan-James Monroe, September 18, 1795 (Morris's *Winning . . .*, pp. 340–45).

411. George III's *Letters . . .*, pp. 123–25, where Shelburne on 13 September reports on his talks with Rayneval—only in the middle of the tenth paragraph does the subject of the U.S. come up: "He appears rather jealous than partial to America" upon points other than independence, "as well as that of the fishery"; Shelburne added: *"He desired to be governed by my advice"* (emphasis added).

412. Jay's Diary, entry for October 24, 1782.

413. See Appendix B for a fuller understanding of RL's view of the French alliance and its role in the negotiations of 1782. That document lends support to the view of his biographer that RL could never be bought by the French or anyone else and that his cooperation with France derived from his own prior convictions (Dangerfield's *Chancellor . . .*, pp. 10–11—a position quite justifiably contradictory of Bemis's, cited above).

414. For example, Morris's *Winning . . .*, p. 439, where Livingston's "laboriously drafted" message is harshly dismissed, perhaps in part due to that historian's misconception of how Jay was to conduct his negotiations: *Seven . . .*, p. 272, states that Jay rightly "defended" himself for conducting "direct negotiations" with England—of course, there was no such prohibition in his instructions, but rather the opposite, given Vergennes's own strategy of a two-track negotiation. Also note that Morris's

earlier *Peacemakers* . . . similarly denigrates this "rebuke" (as he rightly labels it in *Winning* . . . , p. 443); in that earlier work (p. 549), he not only relegates it to an endnote but also misdescribes it (limiting it to the issue of B-M's letter), misdates it (30 December) and assigns it the wrong location in Wharton's *Revolutionary* . . . (it is actually in volume 6, not 5). (As in Bemis's case, it might have been better had Morris reversed the order of his studies and first edited Jay's papers before taking on his *Peacemakers*.)

415. O's Notes, BC/NYPL, vol. 254. JA went even further, telling the French ambassador in the Netherlands in April 1782 that a separate peace with England made by the U.S. "could become disastrous for its solidity and tranquility" (Vauguyon-V, April 18 and 19, 1782—ibid., vol. 201).

416. That moral issues, indeed, were involved here is explicitly made clear by RL-Jay, May 1, 1783 (RL/NYHS).

417. Jay Letterbook #2 (JJ/CU); Johnston's *Correspondence* . . . , vol. 2, p. 366.

418. Jay-Carmichael, October 2, 1780: "*I believe there are few instances of persons conducting business with the same minute attention that I do* . . . being in a responsible situation—the servant of a republic in which the spirit of . . . *ostracism* [emphasis supplied here and elsewhere in this message— note that at this very period Jay was inviting his 'friend,' the 'ostracized' Deane, to come visit him; also note that Jay rather strangely and unfortunately for the U.S. national interest spent almost as much time negotiating and pleading with his subordinate, Carmichael, as he did with FB] always exists—exposed to attacks from men I have never seen, on points I never dreamt of, and perhaps *to be called upon, as others have been, to answer to one generation for transactions in the day of another. . . . I had determined to walk with the utmost circumspection and be always ready and able to render a reason for every part of my conduct in public life. . . .* ['It would give me pain to attack any man—all I aim at is to be able to defend myself if attacked']" (emphasis supplied).

419. A vivid linguistic reflection of the contrast in relations between JA and Jay and JA and BF was the frequent use of "your excellency" in the correspondence between the latter two and the total absence of that phrase from the more relaxed correspondence between JA and Jay.

420. BC/NYPL, vol. 255.

421. V-M, November 29, 1782 (ibid., vol. 199).

422. M-V, December 18, 1782 (ibid.).

423. V-M, December 9, 1782 (ibid.).

424. V-M, November 26, 1782 (ibid.). Also note M's accurate prediction to V of May 5, 1782 (ibid., vol. 198), that if the Spanish "do not succeed in seizing that accursed rock, I greatly fear that Gibraltar will become as disastrous an obstacle in our negotiations for peace as it has been in developing our war plans."

425. V-L, July 21, 1783 (ibid., vol. 213).

426. Jay-Benjamin Vaughan, March 28, 1783 (JJ/CU).

427. V-M, October 2, 1782 ("Peace is necessary in order to prevent the success of Catherine II's policies and her designs against Turkey") (BC/NYPL, vol. 199).

428. V-M, December 1, 1778, January 29, 1780, and November 12, 1782 (ibid., vols. 194, 196, and 199).

429. V-Ossun, January 12, 1777; V-M, December 29, 1781 (ibid., vols. 192 and 199). Some writers assert that Vergennes actually welcomed the 30 November agreement, because it gave him added leverage over Spain in his effort to reach an accommodation with England; this assertion lacks documentary support and would seem to take on validity only in a retrospective sense.

430. M-V, December 28, 1782 (ibid., vol. 199).

431. In this context, it is worth recalling Aranda's admonition of 26 August to Jay, who was pleading lack of authority to modify his instructions regarding U.S. boundary demands, that any minister plenipotentiary should be willing to exercise "discretionary authority" (Jay-RL, November 17, 1782).

432. V-M, December 17, 1782 (BC/NYPL, vol. 199).

433. Per RL-Washington, March 12, 1783 (RL/NYHS).

434. Jay-Benjamin Vaughan, March 28, 1783; Jay-Governor Clinton, June 12, 1783 (JJ/CU).

435. Shelburne-O, April 28, 1782 (BC/NYPL, vol. 252).

436. In answer to England's "note" of 4 August (ibid., vol. 253).

437. The relevant documents include V-L, October 7, 1781, and, in 1782: 23 March, 28 June, 12 August, and 23 November; and V-M, August 22, 1782 (ibid., vols. 210, 211, 212, and 199). Also note that Jay's account (Jay-RL, November 17, 1782) of a conversation with Rayneval on October 24, 1782, at BF's home states: (1) When Rayneval asked about fishing issues, "We insisted on enjoying a right in common to them with Great Britain. He intimated that our views should not extend further than a coast fishery"; (2) Jay's reply was that there could be no peace without

granting the U.S. its rights; (3) BF underlined the Eastern states' particular needs; and (4) Rayneval then softened his position (JJ/CU).

438. BC/NYPL, vol. 254. (Note that Jay and Franklin concurred that
no claim should be made for drying rights on Newfoundland's shores.
Also: Franklin's omission of a demand for drying rights on Canadian
shores in his 10 July summary of U.S. peace requirements has been criticized by Richard Morris and others, but to have done so would have
undermined Franklin's claim to all of Canada in that same note.)

439. The negotiators placed the northwestern boundary at the Lake of
the Woods on the assumption that the source of the Mississippi River
was there, thus retaining England's role as a riparian power on that river
and giving further credibility to the above-cited provision of the 30 November agreement. As reported above, the "gap" between that Lake and
the Mississippi was "not discovered until Washington's Administration"
(Bemis's *American Secretaries* . . . , vol. 1, p. 322).

440. BC/NYPL, vol. 254. Also: RL-Washington, March 12, 1783 (RL/
NYHS): A Paris proposal is that British troops "might be permitted to
embark without molestation and endeavor to recover West Florida from
the Spaniards."

441. *Dictionary of American Biography*, article on RL.

442. For example, RL-James Duane, November 2, 1781 (RL/NYHS):
"The more general the war, the more necessary we become to the belligerent powers."

443. RL-G. Morris, June 13, 1783 (RL/NYHS).

444. L-V, March 29, 1783, and V-L, July 21, 1783 (BC/NYPL, vol. 213).

445. United States' *Journals* . . . , vol. 23, pp. 873–75.

446. V-L, October 14, 1782 (BC/NYPL, vol. 212).

447. Private letter to Livingston, December 7, 1782 (JJ/CU).

448. Correspondence of August 1783 between Laurens in England and
the American commissioners in Paris (JJ/NYHS).

449. For example: Jay's Diary entry, October 18, 1782, conversation
with Aranda.

450. Typical of historians of the Revolutionary War, Morris makes a
series of substantive errors regarding the French and Indian War of a
type that he would never make regarding the Revolutionary War, such
as giving the wrong date for Braddock's defeat of July 9, 1755 (*Seven* . . . ,
p. 21: December 1755); and as confusing the boundary lines of the Proclamation of 1763 with those of the Treaty of 1763 (*Peacemakers* . . . ,
p. 346).

451. It is likely that this section's sensitivity is what most decided Livingston not to circulate the memorandum among the members of Congress.

452. This makes clear that Vergennes's emphasis on the need for secrecy regarding France's policy of assuring that Canada remain English was for naught. It also helps corroborate Dangerfield's above-cited rejection of charges that Livingston was a dupe, or worse, of the French—although Livingston clearly did give undue credence to most of the diplomatic advice he received from them, such as regarding the prospects of a U.S. deal with Spain (e.g., Livingston's December 13, 1781, to Jay [JJ/CU]. "I congratulate you upon the determination of Spain at length to open a way to a treaty.").

453. As noted, this Appendix is courtesy of the NYHS and is taken from RL/NYHS.

Bibliography

Anderson, Fred. *Crucible of War*; Knopf; New York, 2000.

Anonymous. *Politique de Tous les Cabinets de l'Europe Pendant les Règnes de Louis XV et Louis XVI*; Chez Buisson; Paris, 1794.

Bancroft, George. *History of the United States*; Little, Brown; Boston, 1854.

———. *Histoire de l'Action Commune de la France et de l'Amérique pour l'independance des États-Unis*; tr. Adolphe de Circourt; vol. 3—documents inédites; F. Vieweg; Paris, 1876.

Becker, Carl L. *Benjamin Franklin: A Biographical Sketch*; Cornell U. Pr.; Ithaca, 1946.

———. *The History of Political Parties in the Province of New York, 1760–1776*; U. of Wisconsin Pr.; Madison, 1960.

Bemis, Samuel F. *Jay's Treaty: A Study in Commerce and Diplomacy*; Macmillan; New York, 1923.

———. *Pinckney Treaty; A Study of America's Advantage from Europe's Distress, 1783–1800*; Johns Hopkins Pr.; Baltimore, 1926.

———. *The Hussey-Cumberland Mission and American Independence: An Essay in the Diplomacy of the American Revolution*; Princeton U. Pr.; Princeton, 1931.

———. The Rayneval Memoranda; in *American Antiquarian Society Proceedings*; New Series 47, 1937.

———. *The Diplomacy of the American Revolution*; Indiana U. Pr.; Bloomington, 1957 (c. 1935).

———, ed. *The American Secretaries of State and Their Diplomacy*; Cooper Square; New York, 1963 (c. 1928–).

Bosher, J.F. *French Finances, 1770–1795: From Business to Bureaucracy*; Cambridge U. Pr.; Cambridge, 1970.

Brecher, Frank W. *Losing a Continent; France's North American Policy, 1753–1763*; Greenwood Pr.; Westport, CT, 1998.

Burnett, Edmund, C., ed. *Letters of Members of the Continental Congress*; Carnegie Institution of Washington; Washington, DC, 1921.

Chartrand, René, and Back, Francis. *The French Army in the American War of Independence*; Osprey; London, 1991.

Conkling, Howard. *Le Chevalier de la Luzerne*; New York, 1908.

Corwin, Edward S. *French Policy and the American Alliance of 1778*; Archon Books; Hamden, CT, 1962.

Coxe, William. *L'Espagne Sous les Rois de la Maison de Bourbon; Ou Memoires Relatifs a l'Histoire de Cette Nation*; tr. Don Andres Muriel; de Bure Freres; Paris, 1827.

Dangerfield, George. *Chancellor Robert R. Livingston of New York, 1746–1813*; Harcourt, Brace; New York, 1960.

Doniol, Henri. *Histoire de la Participation de la France a l'Établissement des États-Unis d'Amérique*; Imprimerie Nationale; Paris, 1886–.

———. La Premiere Negotiation de la Paix de 1783 entre la France et la Grande Bretagne; in *Revue d'Histoire Diplomatique*; vol. 5, 1892.

———. *Le Comte de Vergennes et P.M. Hennin, 1749–1787*; Armand Colin; Paris, 1898.

D'Ormeson, Wladimir. *La Première Mission Officielle de la France aux États-Unis*; Librarie Ancienne Edouard Champion; Paris, 1924.

Dull, Jonathan R. *The French Navy and American Independence; A Study of Arms and Diplomacy, 1774–1787*; Princeton U. Pr.; Princeton, 1975.

———. Franklin the Diplomat: The French Mission; in *The American Philosophical Society*; vol. 72, Part 1, 1982.

———. *A Diplomatic History of the American Revolution*; Yale U. Pr.; New Haven, CT, 1985.

Egret, Jean. *Necker, Ministre de Louis XVI, 1776–1790*; Honoré Champion; Paris, 1975.

Ellis, Joseph J. *Founding Brothers; The Revolutionary Generation*; Knopf; New York, 2000.

Ferguson, E. James. *The Power of the Purse; A History of American Public Finance, 1776–1790*; U. of North Carolina Pr.; Chapel Hill, 1961.

Fitzmaurice, Lord [Edmund]. *Life of William, Earl of Shelburne*; Macmillan; London, 1912.

France. *Recueil des Instructions Données aux Ambassadeurs . . .* ; Commission des Archives Diplomatiques au Ministere des Affaires Étrangeres; Paris, 1960.

George III. *The Correspondence of King George the Third from 1760 to December 1783*; ed. John Fortescue; Macmillan; London, 1928.

———. *The Letters of King George III*; ed. Bonamy Dobree; Cassell; London, 1935.

Gipson, Lawrence. *The British Empire before the American Revolution*; Knopf; New York, 1958–.

Hardman, John. *French Politics, 1774–1789*; Longman; London, 1995.

———. *Louis XVI: The Silent King*; Arnold; London, 2000.

Hardman, John, and Price, Munro, eds. *Louis XVI and the Comte de Vergennes: Correspondence, 1774–1787*; Voltaire Foundation; Oxford, 1998.

Hoffman, Ronald, and Albert, Peter J., eds. *Diplomacy and Revolution: The Franco-American Alliance of 1778*; U. Pr. of Virginia; Charlottesville, 1981.

Hudson, Ruth S. *The Minister from France: Conrad-Alexandre Gérard, 1729–1790*; Lutz; Euclid, OH, 1994.

Hutson, James H. *John Adams and the Diplomacy of the American Revolution*; U. Pr. of Kentucky; Lexington, 1980.

Israel, Fred L., ed. *Major Peace Treaties of Modern History*; Chelsea House; New York, 1967.

Jay, William. *The Life of John Jay*; Harper; New York, 1833.

Johnston, Henry P., ed. *The Correspondence and Public Papers of John Jay*; Putnam's Sons; New York, 1890–.

Labourdette, Jean-Francois. *Vergennes: Ministre Principal de Louis XVI*; Desjonqueres; Paris, 1990.

Legg, L.G. Wickham, ed. *British Diplomatic Instructions, 1689–1789*; Camden Society Publications; London, 1903.

Library of Congress. *The Development of a Revolutionary Mentality*; Library of Congress; Washington, DC, 1972.

Louis XVI. *Louis XVI a la Parole; Autoportrait du Roi Trés Chrétien: Lettres, Discours, Écrits Politiques*; O.E.I.L.; Paris, 1989.

Lyon, E. Wilson. *The Man Who Sold Louisiana: The Career of Francois Barbé-Marbois*; U. of Oklahoma Pr.; Norman, 1942.

———. *Louisiana in French Diplomacy, 1759–1804*; U. of Oklahoma Pr.; Norman, 1974 (c. 1934).

Mackesy, Piers. *The War for America, 1775–1783*; Harvard U. Pr.; Cambridge, MA, 1964.

Madariaga, Isabel de. *Britain, Russia, and the Armed Neutrality of 1780*; Yale U. Pr.; New Haven, 1962.

Marion, Marcel. *Histoire Financière de la France depuis 1715*; Arthur Rousseau; Paris, 1914.

Marsangy, Louis Bonneville de. *Le Chevalier de Vergennes; Son Ambassade a Constantinople*; Plon; Paris, 1894.

———. *Le Comte de Vergennes; Son Ambassade en Suède, 1771–1774*; Plon; Paris, 1898.

Meng, John J. *Dispatches and Instructions of Conrad Alexandre Gerard, 1778–1780*; Johns Hopkins Pr.; Baltimore, 1939.

Meyer, Jean. *La France Moderne de 1515 a 1789*; Fayard; Paris, 1985.

Monaghan, Frank. *John Jay: Defender of Liberty*; AMS Pr.; New York, 1972.

Morris, Richard B. *The Peacemakers: The Great Powers and American Independence*; Harper and Row; New York, 1965.

———. *Seven Who Shaped Our Destiny: The Founding Fathers as Revolutionaries*; Harper and Row; New York, 1973.

———. *Witness at the Creation; Hamilton, Madison, Jay and the Constitution*; Holt, Reinhart and Winston; New York, 1985.

———, ed. *John Jay: The Making of a Revolutionary; Unpublished Papers, 1745–1780*; Harper and Row; New York, 1975.

———, ed. *John Jay: The Winning of the Peace*; Harper and Row; New York, 1980.

Murphy, Orville. *Charles Gravier, Comte de Vergennes: French Diplomacy in the Age of Revolution: 1719–1787*; SUNY Pr.; Albany, 1982.

Namier, Lewis. *England in the Age of the American Revolution*; St. Martin's Pr.; New York, 1966.

O'Callaghan, E.B., ed. *Documents Relative to the Colonial History of the State of New York*; AMS; New York, 1969.

Ozanam, Didier. *Les Diplomates Espagnoles du XVIIIe Siècle*; Case de Velazuez; Madrid/Bordeaux, 1998.

Parry, Clive, ed. *The Consolidated Treaty Series*; Oceana Publications; Dobbs Ferry, NY, 1969.

Pellew, George. *John Jay*; Houghton Mifflin; Boston, 1894.

Perrault, Gilles. *Le Secret du Roi; La Revanche Américaine*; Fayard; Paris, 1996.

Petrie, Charles. *King Charles III of Spain*; Constable; London, 1971.

Philips, Paul C. *The West in the Diplomacy of the American Revolution*; Russell & Russell; New York, 1967.

Price, Munro. *Preserving the Monarchy; The Comte de Vergennes, 1774–1787*; Cambridge U. Pr.; Cambridge, 1995.

Sabine, Lorenzo. *A Historical Essay on the Loyalists of the American Revolution*; Walden Pr.; Springfield, 1957.

Scott, H.M. *British Foreign Policy in the Age of the American Revolution*; Clarendon Pr.; Oxford U. Pr., 1990.

Sorel, Albert. *L'Europe et la Revolution Française*; Plon; Paris, 1897.

———. *The Eastern Question in the Eighteenth Century*; Methuen; London, 1898.

———, ed. *Recueil des Instructions Données aux Ambassadeous*; vol. 1, *Autriche*, with introduction and notes; Felix Alcan; Paris, 1889.

Soulavie, Jean-Louis. *Memoires Historiques et Politiques du Règne de Louis XVI*; Treuttel et Wurtz; Paris, 1801.

Stevens, Benjamin F., ed. *Facsimiles of Manuscripts in European Archives Relating to America, 1773–1783*; Mellifont Pr.; Wilmington, DE, 1970.

Stinchcombe, William C. *The American Revolution and the French Alliance*; Syracuse U. Pr.; Syracuse, 1969.

Stockley, Andrew. *Britain and France at the Birth of America: The European Powers and the Peace Negotiations of 1782–1783*; University of Exeter Press; Exeter, UK, 2001.

Thomson, Buchanan P. *Spain: Forgotten Ally of the American Revolution*; Christopher Publishing House; North Quincy, MA, 1976.

Tocqueville, Alexis de. *L'Ancien Régime*; Clarendon Pr.; Oxford, 1933.

United States. *Journals of the Continental Congress*; Library of Congress; Washington, DC, 1909.

Véri, Abbé de. *Journal de L'Abbé de Véri*; Jules Tallandier; Paris, 1928.

Wharton, Francis, ed. *The Revolutionary Diplomatic Correspondence of the United States*; Government Printing Office; Washington, DC, 1889.

Willcox, William B. *Portrait of a General; Sir Henry Clinton in the War of Independence*; Knopf; New York, 1964.

Index

Abigail (Jays' "servant"), 147
Adams, John, 14, 36, 58, 116, 140, 220; in Netherlands (1780–82), 14, 130–31, 152, 220; peace commissioner (1779–81), 128–29, 149; peace commissioner (1781–83), 131, 181, 186, 202–3, 212; representative in France (1778–79), 121
Adams, Samuel, 85
Aiguillon, Emmanuel-Armand de Richelieu, duc d', 22–23, 53
Aranda, Pedro, Conde de, 50, 53, 73, 116, 150, 157, 178, 182–83, 194, 196, 202, 208, 213–14
Armistice (1783), 202–3, 209, 225
Arnold, Benedict, 89, 91, 94, 144
Austria, 70, 140–41

Barbé-Marbois, François, marquis de, 198, 201, 213, 222–23
Barras, Melchior Saint-Laurent, comte de, 163
Bavarian crisis of 1778–79, 70, 77–78, 112–14

Beaumarchais, Pierre-Augustine Caron de, 3, 62–66, 80
Bennington, battle of, 93–94
Benoit (Jays' "servant"), 146–47
Bingham, William, 146
Bonvouloir, Achard de, 47–48
Broglie, Charles-François, comte de, 25–26
Broglie, Victor-François, duc de, 25, 107–8
Burgoyne, John, 67, 90–95

Campo, Bernardo del, 182
Canada: French war aims in, 53, 75–76, 83–85, 103, 115–17, 164; U.S. invasions of, 57, 115–16, 227–39; U.S. war aims in, 179, 185–86, 210
Carleton, Guy, 175, 216
Carlisle Peace Commission (1778). *See* North, Frederick, Lord
Carmichael, William, 107, 146, 149, 152–56, 164, 182
Catherine II, 2, 78, 140. *See also* Neutrality Association

About the Author

FRANK W. BRECHER is a former career member of the United States Senior Foreign Service. Among his earlier publications are *Reluctant Ally: United States Foreign Policy Toward the Jews from Wilson to Roosevelt* (Greenwood Press, 1991) and *Losing a Continent: France's North American Policy, 1753–1763* (Greenwood Press, 1998). He is presently completing the final volume in his trilogy on early Franco-American relations, *Negotiating the Louisiana Purchase: Robert Livingston's Mission to Paris, 1801–1804.*